Getting the Message

The work of the Glasgow University Media Group has long established their place at the forefront of Media Studies, and *Getting the Message* provides an introduction to recent work by the group.

Contributors discuss themes such as the relationship between the media and public opinion, the emergence of TV news formats and styles, and the relations between theory and method in media research. Recent work undertaken by the group on the media's role in reporting on AIDS, Vietnam, Northern Ireland, Ethiopia, and the Gulf War is also represented.

In its fresh approach to the relationship between journalists and their sources and reception analysis, the collection also illuminates how the earlier work of the group has been extended, and the ways in which its research has developed both individually and collectively.

Getting the Message offers an invaluable and far-reaching exploration of the interrelations between the production of media messages and their reception – an invaluable guide for any study of the development of media theory.

John Eldridge is Professor of Sociology at the University of Glasgow and a founder member of the Glasgow University Media Group.

Communication and Society
General Editor: James Curran

Getting the Message

p 25
156 - 138

News, truth and power

Glasgow University Media Group
Edited by John Eldridge

London and New York

First published 1993
by Routledge
11 New Fetter Lane, London EC4P 4EE

Simultaneously published in the USA and Canada
by Routledge Inc.
29 West 35th Street, New York, NY 10001

Collection as a whole © 1993 Glasgow University Media Group;
individual contributions © 1993 the contributors

Set in 10/12 pt Times by Florencetype Ltd, Kewstoke
Printed and bound in Great Britain by T J Press (Padstow) Ltd, Cornwall

British Library Cataloguing in Publication Data
Glasgow University Media Group
  Getting the Message: News, Truth and Power. – (Communication & Society
  Series)
  I. Title   II. Eldridge, J. E. T.   III. Series
  302.23

Library of Congress Cataloging in Publication Data
Glasgow University Media Group.
   Getting the message : news, truth and power / Glasgow University Media
   Group ; edited by John Eldridge.
      p.   cm. — (Communication and society)
   1. Mass media.   2. Journalism.   I. Eldridge, J. E. T. (John Eric
   Thomas)   II. Title.   III. Series: Communication and society
   (Routledge (Firm))
   P91.25.G57   1993
   302.23 — dc20   92-26616

ISBN 0-415-07983-7
ISBN 0-415-07984-5 (pbk)

Contents

Figures and tables

Acknowledgements

Rebecca Barden, Sue Bilton and Sarah Conibear of Routledge have given good guidance and help in getting this volume ready for publication and we thank them. The editor of the series in which this book appears, Professor James Curran, has been supportive throughout and we thank him for his encouragement.

We have been greatly helped in the preparation of some of this text by the secretarial skills of Pip Townsend and Kathleen Davidson and we thank them. Lesley Henderson has prepared the index with skill and competence and we appreciate her help in this respect. Other, more specific, acknowledgements are noted at the end of some of the chapters.

Help and encouragement is one thing, responsibility is another. For what follows, we, the authors, are responsible.

Notes on contributors

Peter Beharrell is Honorary Research Fellow, Department of Sociology, University of Glasgow.

Lucinda Broadbent is an independent film producer.

Howard H. Davis is Reader in Sociology, Department of Sociology, University of Kent at Canterbury.

John Eldridge is Professor of Sociology, Department of Sociology, University of Glasgow.

Jenny Kitzinger is Research Fellow, Department of Sociology, University of Glasgow.

Brian McNair is Lecturer in Media Studies, Department of Media Studies, University of Stirling.

David Miller is Research Fellow, Department of Sociology, University of Glasgow.

Greg Philo is Senior Lecturer, Department of Sociology, University of Glasgow and Director of the Media Research Unit, University of Glasgow.

Kevin Williams is Lecturer in Media Studies, Centre for Journalism Studies, University of Wales College of Cardiff.

Brian Winston is Professor of Media Studies, Centre for Journalism Studies, University of Wales College of Cardiff.

Part I

Introduction

Chapter 1

News, truth and power

John Eldridge

The essays in this collection have all been written by people who, at one time or another, have contributed to the work of the Glasgow University Media Group. The diversity of topic and substantive areas of interest is evident from the list of contents. However, in their various ways and with differing emphasis, the essays explore the relations between theory and method in media research. Specifically, they contribute to our understanding of the processes of encoding and decoding media messages. Much of our work has focused on the analysis of message content, using both quantitative and qualitative methods. However, it was never exclusively that. The concern to place such work in the overall process of message production and message reception was early stated and then amplified in practice in later studies. We saw the analysis of content not as an exclusive or superior form of communications research but as a bridge that could facilitate our understanding of the communications process. Without it we cannot comment effectively on what producers produce (as distinct from their beliefs or intentions) nor what it is that audiences are responding to. Parts 2, 3 and 4 of this book reflect in sequence this interrelated concern with message production, content and output.

One of the questions pursued in the Glasgow research has been to ask what it is that takes place in British television news under the banner of objectivity, impartiality and neutrality. The BBC's licence requires it to refrain from editorializing on its news programmes and the Independent Broadcasting Act of 1973 laid down the ruling that due impartiality must be preserved on the part of persons providing programmes as regards to matters of political or industrial controversy or relating to current public policy. This, at least in a formal sense, sets television journalism apart from print journalism where editorial viewpoints and distinctive political perspectives are intrinsic to the activity. — To T.V.

Television news has become a major source of information about the world we live in for millions of people, in the UK as elsewhere. In the course of its coverage it will deal with many controversial matters. There are on-going disagreements between the political parties, about industrial disputes, matters concerning defence, war and foreign policy and the continuing conflict in Northern Ireland. Dr Colin Morris, formerly head of the BBC's Religious Broadcasting and later Controller of BBC Northern Ireland, devoted the 1986 Hibbert Lecture to the subject of broadcast news. He is sympathetic to the journalists:

> In the book of Genesis, it is God who brings order out of chaos; in the modern world, television journalists have to make a stab at doing it. They subdue into harmony a mountain of telex printouts, miles of video tape and a pandemonium of ringing telephones. They organise into a coherent picture a riot of impressions, a chaos, a bedlam of attitudes and opinions that would otherwise send us scurrying to the hills in panic. And they have to construct this world at lightning speed, in a welter of instant judgments.
>
> (Morris 1986)

Morris goes on to state that to do this work means putting a context round experience and that journalists knit together verbal or visual symbols into some semblance of reality. Now, to bring order out of chaos and coherence out of bedlam is clearly a formidable task and might forestall the fiercest criticism. Still, we are reminded that however natural, actual and immediate it all looks, television is a massive feat of social construction. Yet it is not reality that is constructed but a semblance of it. And how could it be otherwise? Apart from the constraints of time, budgets and resources there is, necessarily, selection, compression and simplification in the construction of news stories. In a formulation that is more sceptical than Morris, Tom Burns has written:

> because television news and current affairs programmes convey action, movement, facial expression and demeanour, scenes and actors, as well as verbal messages, they seem *more* complete, *more* satisfactory than any account provided by newspapers. 'Viewability' is easily construed as reliability because any intervention by broadcasters is largely invisible, and because the dramatic intensity of film and video recording carries conviction and guarantees authenticity in ways in which words cannot. And the constant striving for 'viewability' sets its own traps.
>
> (Burns 1977: 206)

The issue for us, as researchers, was this: if television puts 'reality' together what is the nature of the product? The naturalistic quality of news presentation with its stress on immediacy and accessibility to world events, grounded in professional claims to objectivity and impartiality, led us to ask what kind of cultural artefact it is. One way of breaking into this, and it was the way we chose, is to look at matters that are controversial in a society, or more generally on the international scene, and examine how they are treated on television news. We can proceed to look at the news story as narrative: at the verbal and visual grammar in which it is expressed; at the use of graphics and other symbolic expressions; at the use of headlines; at who is interviewed and the form and content of those encounters; in short, at the way information is organized and at the implicit and explicit explanations that are put before us.

In an amused comment on the debates surrounding the work of the Glasgow University Media Group, Schlesinger (1987: xxxviii) suggests that it has something of the character of a soap opera. I take his point. At the very least it has been a long-running story. As one of the original group members this itself has been one of the most surprising things. When we began in 1974 the Annan Committee on the Future of Broadcasting was beginning its work. It reported in 1977. Channel 4 was still a gleam in the eye of Anthony Smith, although the commercial version set up post-Annan was in contrast to the publicly-owned trust that he had advocated. The twin peaks of the BBC and the IBA represented what some of its critics called 'the comfortable duopoly'. Now in the early 1990s we are in the post-Peacock, post-Broadcasting Act world of deregulation and satellite television. It is also, of course, the period of post-Thatcherism. In 1991 we witnessed the spectacle of the chairman of TV-AM receiving a letter from Mrs Thatcher saying how sorry and mystified she was that they had not been successful in their bid for the franchise to run the commercial breakfast television station. They lost out in the very bidding system she had promoted. So the everyday story of media folk also continues in changing times and with a changing cast.

What also continues from politicians are accusations of political bias against broadcasters, more particularly in relation to television news programmes. So, in late 1991, the then Conservative Party Chairman, Chris Patten, complained to the BBC about its coverage of the health debate at the party's annual conference. John Birt, the director-general designate of the BBC became involved in correspondence on the matter with the Conservative Party Central Office. In the 1970s, Birt, with Peter Jay, now the BBC's Economics Editor for television news, had written a series of articles on the 'bias against understanding' which they believed to characterize television news and current affairs. So there is some piquancy in the situation in which these advocates of television's 'mission to explain' are finding that such an answer does not turn away the wrath of the angry politician.

In my view, so long as television news seeks to establish its professional credibility on the basis of claims to impartiality, neutrality and objectivity, those involved will be constantly immersed in challenges and attacks they will find difficult to defend. They can resort to various stratagems of defence: we know our own business and we should be left to get on with it; or since we are attacked from all sides we have got it just about right. Yet as Anthony Smith pointed out in *The Shadow in the Cave* (1976), while broadcasters are under instructions to be 'objective' in many societies, what this means in practice varies enormously. The very concept of objectivity is continuously contested in practice.

Yet none of this detracts from the importance of the concern for accuracy in reporting. At the simplest level, when the football results are given we expect them to be accurate and have good reason to think that they are. Any mistake will be quickly corrected. Verification of such events is straightforward. It is helpful to take a simple example because it reminds us that issues of truth are also involved. The alternative to objectivity in this sense is not undisciplined subjectivity where anything goes and one account is as good or as bad as another. Respect for the nature of evidence remains crucial and that is a proper basis for establishing credibility. Often, however, this is intrinsically much more difficult than in the case of football results. Even in this case we can recognize that once an account of a particular game is given then we are into a narrative with its own selection of facts, judgements, interpretations and sometimes speculation.

If, as the adage has it, journalism is the first draft of history, then we can appreciate that, as with history, selection and interpretation will take place and that we are dealing not with a world of unassailable facts but with provisional accounts. Moreover, to put it formally, the epistemological status on which these accounts are based can vary. We, as audience, will not necessarily be aware of this.

What I am touching on here is the difficult issue of the relationship between truth and power. It is always salutary to go back to Orwell. I do not mean primarily his Appendix on the Principles of Newspeak in *1984* (Orwell 1954) chilling though it is in its perception of the ideological use of language. There, it will be recalled, in his fictional anti-utopia, 'the purpose of Newspeak was not only to provide a medium of expression for the world-view and mental habits proper to the devotees of Ingsoc, but to make all other modes of thought impossible' (Orwell 1954: 257). It is the extreme example of the powerful becoming the mind managers of the powerless, the ultimate conspiracy of control from above of the many by the few. But if we turn to the comments on the press and propaganda recorded in *Homage to Catalonia* (1962) we see that this is grounded in his own experience. He argues that nearly all the newspaper accounts of the fighting in Barcelona during the Spanish Civil War were manufactured by journalists at a distance. On the basis of what he had actually seen and heard at first hand he claimed that much of what appeared in the press was untrue and intentionally misleading. In the course of responding to this he writes:

> In the English press, in particular, you would have to search for a long time before finding any favourable reference, at any period of the war, to the Spanish Anarchists. They have been systematically denigrated,

and, as I got to know from my own experience, it is almost impossible to get anyone to print anything in their defence.

I have tried to write objectively about the Barcelona fighting, though obviously no one can be completely objective on a question of this kind. One is practically obliged to take sides, and it must be clear enough whose side I am on. Again, I must have inevitably made mistakes of fact, not only here but in other parts of this narrative. It is very difficult to write accurately about the Spanish war, because of the lack of non-propagandist documents. I warn everyone against my bias, and I warn everyone against my mistakes. Still I have done my best to be honest. But it will be seen that the account I have given is completely different from that which appeared in the foreign and especially the Communist press.

(Orwell 1962: 153)

In a characteristically clear way Orwell draws to our attention the propaganda war which surrounds and impinges on the world of the journalist when controversial events or politically significant issues are in focus. The comment that truth becomes the first casualty in time of war has now reached cliché status, yet any discussion of the relationship between truth and power has to come to terms with what this implies. It is the burden of Philip Knightley's *The First Casualty* (1982) which provides extended illustration of the argument from the Crimean to the Vietnam Wars.

Among the many examples that could be cited we may recall the experiences of journalists like James Cameron, Rene Cutforth and Ed Murrow in the Korean War (1950–3). Cameron and his photographer, Bert Hardy, witnessed and photographed the brutal treatment given by the South Koreans to political prisoners. The account was prepared for publication by *Picture Post*, with the support of the editor, Tom Hopkinson. But its proprietor, Edward Hulton, insisted that the article be withdrawn on the grounds that it gave aid and comfort to the enemy. Hopkinson was sacked. Yet the activities depicted were taking place close to the UN headquarters in Seoul and it was on behalf of President Syngham Rhee's government that the UN had intervened. Rene Cutforth's account of the effects of American napalm bombing on the population was not broadcast by the BBC, which Cutforth was to describe as a moment of some disillusionment.

The American Ed Murrow of CBS, who became famous for his Second World War reporting, found that CBS did not want his reports about some of the unpleasant facts concerning the conduct of the Korean War. Knightley himself judged:

the prospect of the Korean War's being reported fully and truthfully receded rapidly, under a variety of pressures, foremost among which was the political atmosphere in the United States at the time. Not one major daily newspaper opposed the war, and even among left-wing journals the *National Guardian* was almost alone in its anti-war policy. The *New York Daily Mirror* demanded: '*Isn't it time to do something about our native communists?*' Alger Hiss had been convicted, the Rosenbergs had been arrested, and Senator Joe McCarthy was becoming a decisive, dominating Cold War force. Censorship by an army sensitive to its early failures in the field had reached ridiculous heights.

(1982: 331–2)

Since the Vietnam War the role of television in news reporting has been much debated. But there is a conventional wisdom that attributes to television a decisive part in bringing that war to an end. By showing the horror of war and bringing the brutal reality of it into the home the American government was forced by public opinion to end it. This argument is critically reviewed in this volume by Kevin Williams (Chapter 12). We can readily see that for different reasons the conventional wisdom can be acceptable to hawks and doves: the one can blame the media for an inglorious defeat by a Third World country; the other can celebrate the power of democratic forces from below. For the media, it is a mark of their independence of government. Williams's reassessment puts a strong question mark against this. He argues that media coverage, for the most part, was characterized by control from above. Dependence on élite sources and informants and a willingness to impose self-censorship strongly impinged on the agenda-setting process. Indeed, some parts of the press were more successful in detaching themselves from the official line than television and, within television, the news was most closely tied to official élite sources. In Williams's view, it is only when there were differences within the élite about the conduct of the war that the Vietnam War was the subject of more critical reporting. So, to think of that period as an example of the media challenging government policy and thereby discharging a democratic function of questioning the powerful is wide of the mark. Yet the pervasive belief in that myth has fed into subsequent discussions and policy concerning the role of the media, especially television, in war reporting.

In their different ways the Falklands/Malvinas conflict, the American invasion of Grenada and the Gulf War presented governments with the problems of what to do about the media, especially television. Nowhere have questions of news' management been raised more sharply in the British media than during the Falklands crisis. Even so, the British journalist Robert Harris who has worked in press and broadcasting, including during that period BBC's *Newsnight* programme, came to the following conclusion:

The episodes which caused most disquiet, and which have been described in this book, were not necessarily unique to the Falklands crisis.

The instinctive secrecy of the military and the Civil Service; the prostitution and hysteria of sections of the press; the lies, the misinformation,
the manipulation of public opinion by the authorities; the political
intimidation of broadcasters; the ready connivance of the media at their
own distortion . . . all these occur as much in peace-time Britain as in
war.

(1983: 151)

When the Argentinian invasion of the Falklands took place the future of
the British government was in jeopardy. The Islands had been left unprotected and the British Foreign Secretary, Lord Carrington, resigned over
the affair. However, the decision to send a task force following the
emergency parliamentary debate did receive extensive cross-party support.
As battle was joined in the South Atlantic a parallel conflict broke out – a
media war (Glasgow University Media Group 1985, Harris 1983; Mercer,
Mungham and Williams 1987).

In particular the BBC came under attack from the government and
sections of the popular press, notably the *Sun* and the *Daily Mail*. *The
Times*, which like the *Sun* is owned by Rupert Murdoch, was also critical of
the BBC. Referring to Peter Snow, one of the *Newsnight* presenters, John
Page wrote of his 'superior tone of super-neutrality which so many of us
find objectionable and unacceptable' (*The Times*, May 1982).

The BBC's *Panorama* current affairs programme, which examined the
Falklands conflict on 10 May and included some dissenting views on
government policy alongside those of Cecil Parkinson, a member of the
war cabinet, brought the political storm to a head. Conservative MPs
complained that some programmes on the BBC appeared to give the
impression of being pro-Argentinian and anti-British, while others
appeared to suggest that this was an issue over which the BBC could
remain loftily neutral. A senior conservative, Sally Oppenheimer, referred
next day at Prime Minister's Question Time, to the *Panorama* programme
as 'an odious, subversive travesty in which Michael Cockrell and other
BBC reporters dishonoured the right to freedom of speech in this country'
(cited in Cockrell, Hennessy and Walker 1984: 157–8). In her reply the
prime minister indicated that she shared the concern which had been
expressed. She continued:

I know how strongly many people feel that the case for our country is
not being put with sufficient vigour on certain – I do not say all – BBC
programmes. The Chairman of the BBC has assured us, and has said in
vigorous terms, that the BBC is not neutral on this point, and I hope his
words will be heeded by the many who have responsibilities for standing
up for our task force, our boys, our people and the cause of democracy.

(cited in ibid.: 157–8)

In subsequent exchanges between members of the House reference was made to 'treachery' and 'treason' and the Speaker advised members that such language did not advance the argument and was better avoided. The dissenting voices on *Panorama* were, it should be remembered, Members of Parliament.

The *Panorama* programme was itself renamed 'Traitorama' by the *Sun* and the chairman and director-general of the BBC were summoned to the House of Commons to meet the back-bench media committee of the Conservative Party. The meeting was by all accounts a stormy one. The director-general, then Alasdair Milne, said in an interview in the London *Standard* on 12 May:

> The notion that we are traitors is outrageous. There is no one in the BBC who does not agree that the Argentines committed aggression. But this is not total war. One day we will be negotiating with the enemy so we must try to understand them. We at the BBC have re-examined our broad policy and will not change it. We have no sense of guilt or failure.

What I want to emphasize is both the strength of feeling that was generated and how government hostility was specifically directed at the BBC. Mercer, Mungham and Williams cite a member of the war cabinet as follows:

> At a war cabinet meeting there was a general hate of the BBC whom we reckoned to be biased and pro-ITN whom we reckoned were doing much better. One minister said; 'well, you know we give all this information to the bloody BBC and what do they do with it? We don't help ITN enough and we ought to help ITN more'.
>
> (1987: 134)

What emerged from our analysis in *War and Peace News* (GUMG 1985) was not a conspiracy theory of the media, but a set of professional practices, which while valuing the principle of independence, relies heavily on official sources for its news. In some ways this is the very mark of its professionalism that it has access to these sources. But by the same token it does result in tight limits on the amount of dissent that can take place outside those parameters especially in a time of crisis, which the Falklands undoubtedly was for the government.

This point was illustrated more recently in the case of the Gulf War. Here, however, we were involved in an international conflict with many participants, where the United States co-ordinated a United Nations' sponsored military force against Iraq, following the Iraqi invasion of Kuwait. Unlike the Falklands, where only British correspondents were with the Task Force and where there were delays in getting pictures back, the Gulf War was reported by the international press and broadcasters from all over the world. So what we received on television was a mixture of 'instant news' plus comment from a range of 'experts', politicians and correspondents.

But what was this instant news? Here we should recall the pervasive role of Cable News Network (CNN), the American 24-hour news network with its headquarters in Atlanta, Georgia. Even before the Allied attacks began CNN had the reputation of being the channel which the whole world watched, including the protagonists President Bush and President Hussein. Indeed, some of their policy decisions, as well as polemical exchanges, were delivered to the world and to each other through this medium. To some extent, this seemed to take the place of more diplomatic exchanges. When the Allied offensive began, it was to CNN that British TV channels frequently turned. So when the first Iraqi Scud missiles attacked Israel we had film of Larry Register and his CNN colleagues in their Jerusalem newsroom struggling to put their gas masks on, wondering whether to open the window to see if they could hear anything and being told by their colleague in Atlanta not to do so. They did not know what was going on. They became their own story as we witnessed their confusion and uncertainty. 'There's a bit of a panic here right now, as you might well imagine', said Register (*Channel 4, News*, 17 January 1991).

These CNN reports had a raw quality about them. They were unfiltered happenings. We see one reporter knock another over as the sirens wail out in Dhahran and they instinctively duck to avoid the anticipated missile. At times, because of the noise or because their voices are muffled by gas masks we can scarcely hear what they say. But what kind of knowledge is this? It was fairly described by one critic on BBC 2's *Late Show* as 'immediacy without understanding, drama without information' (22 January 1991). And Jonathon Alter, media critic for *Newsweek* said this has come to be regarded as 'good television' in that it has the quality of *cinéma-vérité* – something real that's going on.

But what was going on? The executive producer of NBC *Nightly News*, Steve Friedman, criticized CNN by saying that they did not discriminate in their coverage because they were a 24-hour news service. NBC, by contrast, did not have to trouble the world with false alarms and the like. Yet it was not such a clear distinction. On Day Two of the war NBC reporter Martin Fletcher, wearing a gas mask, reported from Israel that they had been hit with a chemical weapon. This was relayed on BBC news, where the source for this story was claimed to be NBC monitoring of police radios in Tel Aviv. However, the BBC's veteran reporter Charles Wheeler, in Washington, urged caution: 'Everybody here's getting in a dreadful panic.' As the programme went on, more uncertainty about the missile attack on Israel seeped through. Towards the end of the bulletin we hear this exchange:

Martyn Lewis: So that report from NBC could well be wrong?

Charles Wheeler: A lot of reports could well be wrong.

That kind of scepticism was very important, but it could easily be forgotten in the bombardment of messages coming in by satellite, some of which were uninformative and some of which untrue, as when BBC 1 reported that 'Israel is retaliating' to the Scud missiles and their supposed chemical warheads. This is why, I think, that there was widespread comment on the feeling of euphoria surrounding the first night of the war, concentrating on the allied bombing of Baghdad, compared to the panic of the second night when the Scuds were fired.

But there was another kind of 'on the spot report' which was not what it appeared. After the war we learned more about this. This was well described by an ITN reporter, Alex Thomson:

> One of the standard devices is the live two-way . . . you go to your man on the spot . . . Bill, what's the latest? That's fine. In Dahran you didn't know what the latest was because the latest was 150–200 miles away, or in Riyadh. So what was a perfectly respectable journalistic device – asking someone who was there – actually became completely down- graded and abused in the situation . . . I'm informed that such and such is going on. The only reason they knew that was because they phoned their office just before going on air and the office had read over to them the latest wire copy. I know. I did that.

That story was told on *Tales From The Gulf* (BBC 2, 19 July 1991) and was followed by a clip of Thomson doing it on 18 January 1991. 'But it was quite funny', he said, 'phoning up to find information from London. The only time it changed was during the Scud attacks.'

Thomson also described his attempts to hitch a lift with convoys to get nearer to the action. He was stopped. A British colonel told him to 'get off my land, like I was trespassing on his grouse moor or something. Absurd'. Journalists were assigned to pools, which were essentially coralled by the military. This gave them access to information the military were prepared to give them. Journalists not in the pool who tried to act autonomously were labelled 'unilateralists' and this could be a point of friction between journalists. When Robert Fisk of *The Independent* tried to report the battle of Khafji, which the Iraqis briefly held, the NBC correspondent, Brad Willis, reported him to the United States marines. Willis complained that Fisk's behaviour would prevent them from working. In the same place a French film crew obtained pictures which they were prepared to provide to others, as distinct from the official pool pictures. As Clive Ferguson of the BBC described it: 'They were spotted on the road and an American television reporter said: "Hey! They're not members of the combat pool. Arrest them." So when you get your own journalists acting against you in such situations it doesn't make life easy' (Miller and Allen 1991: 77).

Glyn Mathias of ITN has stated that they supplemented their participation in the pool with independent efforts. He cites, for example, Peter
Sharp's report on the oil slick off the Saudi coast and Sandy Gall's entry
into Kuwait with the Saudis, bringing back the first pictures of the ground
attack in Kuwait (ibid.: 75). So it appears that something of a cat and
mouse game was played between the military and the journalists. At risk
was the accreditation of the reporters and the threat of expulsion from the
country.

When we take into account the conditions under which news was gathered it is difficult to apply concepts of impartiality or objectivity to it. Kate
Adie and Martin Bell of the BBC, with the British pool, were regularly
filmed in military uniform, no doubt, at least in part, for operational
reasons and for their own safety if they were captured. But when that
happens, as they recognized, certain kinds of bargains are struck and
compromises reached with the military, on whom you depend for your
personal survival. So there were limits on what they could say. And, in
practice, when it came to the ground offensive, much of this was unre-
ported in visual terms, until the victory was won.

It is useful to bear this in mind when we think about the television
reporting from Baghdad. Once the Allied attack began, the presence of
reporters in Baghdad became controversial, especially when 310 civilians
were killed on 13 February when an air-raid shelter in Baghdad received a
direct hit. The accusation was that British television carried Iraqi propaganda. Yet the stories from Baghdad were always surrounded by caveats.
For example, on 26 January 1991 we hear this on ITN:

> The latest pictures to come out of Iraq show extensive damage caused,
> the Iraqis say, by allied bombers . . . . This is an image of life in Iraq
> that Saddam Hussein is anxious for the world to see and believe. . . .
> The pictures were supplied by the Ministry of Information . . . as
> propaganda it graphically illustrates the suffering . . . [the pictures are]
> being used as a weapon . . . as a means to influence world opinion . . .
> Iraqi supplied material draws natural suspicions about its authen-
> ticity. . . . These people are claimed by Iraq to be recent victims of the
> bombing but they have not been independently verified as such.

No doubt the bombing of the Baghdad shelter did shock many people. It
was the first coverage of the death of Iraqi civilians in any large numbers.
Reports hitherto had emphasized the surgical accuracy of the bombing,
and although there were reports of 'carpet bombing' of Iraqi troop positions, nothing was known about the numbers killed, or at least it was not
reported. Although the sophisticated military technology available to the
Allies included video film of Iraqi soldiers being killed by bombs and
shells, from which they vainly tried to escape, these were not shown. So
these reports must be set against the generally sanitized accounts of the war

that had prevailed hitherto. In the military press briefing that followed the bombing the spokesman described himself as 'comfortable' with the sortie.

The reporters in Baghdad tried to describe as accurately as possible what they had seen. This broke the frame within which the war was generally reported on television and may help to explain why they were subjected to such close questioning by the newscasters in the London studios. For, as Philip Knightley has pointed out:

> A new language was brought into being to soften the reality of war. Bombing military targets in the heart of cities was called 'denying the enemy an infra-structure'. People were 'soft targets'. Saturation bombing was 'laying down a carpet'. The idea was to suggest that hardly any people were involved in modern warfare, only machines. This explains the emphasis at Alliance press briefings on the damage 'our' machines have caused to 'their' machines, and the reluctance of briefing officers to discuss casualties – on either side.
>
> (1991: 5)

We did not know at the time, but the United States air force has now stated, that of the 88,500 tonnes of explosives dropped over Iraq and Kuwait during the forty-three days of the war, 70 per cent missed their targets. Nor did we know that only 7 per cent of the bombs dropped were so-called smart bombs and the rest were free-fall (Brittain 1991: xvii). Well, we know now and it may cause us to reflect on how uncritically some of the news was relayed at the time. And we may recall the interpretative framework that this could generate. So, a senior broadcaster like David Dimbleby, who served many hours as a BBC anchorman in the London studio could become fascinated with the video of smart bombs destroying a military headquarters in Baghdad and say to the American ambassador to Britain:

> Doesn't this suggest that America's ability to react militarily has really become quite extraordinary, despite all the critics beforehand who said it will never work out like that? You are now able to claim that you can act precisely and therefore – to use that hideous word about warfare – surgically.

He then linked this questionable technological point with a political one:

> Isn't it in fact true that America is, by dint of this and by dint of the very accuracy of the weapons we've seen, the only potential world policeman? You may have to operate under the United Nations, but it's beginning to look as though you're going to have to be in the Middle East, just as in the previous part of this century, we and the French were in the Middle East.
>
> (BBC 1, 18 January 1991)

In the end we did glimpse some of the victims in the bombed convoy on the road to Basra. It was, the military assured us, an operational necessity to obliterate a raggle-taggle fleeing army of tanks, charabancs, cars, jeeps and lorries, many of whom were Kurdish conscripts. What language could encompass such carnage?

As we now contemplate these events, can we say with confidence that we really know what it was about? For that we would surely need a strong grasp of history and geo-politics. But that is a million miles away from instant news.

SOME REFLECTIONS ON THEORY

A marker

A stimulus to my own thinking has been the work of C. Wright Mills. Although I part company with him at certain points I want to begin with him in this more theoretical part of the paper and indicate why I think reference back to his work is still useful. His primary point of empirical reference was the United States but there are a number of conceptual and analytical matters raised which justify continuing consideration.

Mills's essay on mass media and public opinion was written in the wake of the 1948 presidential election of Truman, when the opinion pollsters had predicted a clear win for his republican opponent Governor Dewey. Since Dewey had also received extensive backing in the mass media Mills felt able to conclude that:

> No view of American public life can be realistic that assumes public opinion to be wholly controlled and entirely manipulated by the mass media. There are forces at work among the public that are independent of these media of communication, that can and do at times go against the opinions promulgated by them.
>
> (1963: 577)

How can this happen? Part of his answer is to point to the pluralist character of the mass media themselves, which provide the opportunity for different voices to be heard:

> In the enormous flow of words, signs, images, sounds and entertainments there is much that is openly controversial, much that is critical and it does not add up to one, standardised official image of the world: it does not reiterate one standard set of norms for reality; it contains various images and, to a considerable extent, they compete with one another.
>
> (ibid.: 578)

In principle, therefore, one set of messages can be compared with another, even if some are more prevalent than others.

Yet, from the standpoint of democratic politics, there is, Mills suggested, a growing problem. If we distinguish between 'primary publics' – that is, the face-to-face groups where people may discuss, argue, listen and respond to one another – and the mass media, then there is the concern that media markets will gain ascendancy over primary publics: 'in the mass society of media markets, competition goes on between the crowd of manipulators with their mass media on the one hand, and the people receiving their communications on the other. "Answering back" by the people is systematically unavailable' (ibid: 584).

Against the concept of *democratic society* Mills juxtaposes – as an ideal type not an empirical reality – the concept of *mass society*. It carries with it the idea of the destruction of primary publics and voluntary associations and their replacement by the 'mass' and the 'crowd' – with connotations of manipulation from above and irrationality. Herein lie possibilities for manipulation, either because individuals become passive spectators rather than active agents in political life, or because they may be mobilized from above for collective purposes. In the extreme case the mass communications industry 'pumping opinions to huge media markets, displaces the face-to-face communications systems comprised of a multiplicity of primary publics' and, alongside this, there is 'a definite centralisation of the opinion process: discussion circles are necessarily small and decentralised; media markets are huge and centralised'. Consequently, 'the way opinions *change* is more authoritative and manipulative. There is little or no self-regulation on the part of the public' (Mills 1963: 577). It is as though public opinion – the pivot of democratic politics – is expropriated by the mass media. It has been subverted, but the rhetoric remains and, indeed, to criticize 'public opinion' would be to imply that you are a critic of democracy. That is quite a paradox.

In *The Power Elite* the arguments of his earlier essay are repeated, although perhaps with more pessimism about the drift of events. There is comment about the nature and significance of the 'opinion business':

> In the primary public the competition of opinions goes on between people holding views in the service of their interests and their reasoning. But in the mass society of media markets, competition, if any, goes on between the manipulators with their mass media on the one hand, and people receiving their propaganda on the other.
>
> (Mills 1959: 305)

And the picture he offers is of the owners and higher echelons in the media business as members of or servants to powerful élites. Moreover,

> Alongside or just below the elite there is the propagandist, the public

relations men, who would control the very formation of public opinion in order to be able to include it as one more pacified item in the calculation of effective power, increased prestige, more secure wealth.

(ibid.: 305)

The essential point Mills is making is that in an authoritarian society power may be used explicitly and nakedly and – in the extreme case – the mass media are simply a propaganda adjunct for policies with the use of physical and institutional sanctions anyway. But manipulation – the exercise of power behind the backs of the people, as it were – is a feature of a society which is shifting from a democratic base to a mass society. In such circumstances those in the commanding positions of power are able to nullify or bypass the checks and balances of democratic discussion and accountability.

One sociological sign of such a trend is when individuals are not able to connect their private troubles with public issues. Questions of war and peace, unemployment, poverty and sickness, racial and industrial conflict are public issues which have structural features. When individuals see themselves as victims, or hopeless and helpless in the face of these prob- lems, perhaps even blaming themselves, they may not have the knowledge to connect their experiences with what is happening in the world. Moreover, the capacity to act, to see oneself as agent and not victim, when it is blunted contributes to the subverting of the democratic process. Democracy, after all, implies the participation of an informed citizenry, actively contributing to and engaging in the processes of social change.

Mills himself, despite the strain of pessimism, remains convinced that threats to democratic life and practice can be dealt with:

Publics live in mileux but they can transcend them – individually by intellectual effort; socially by public action. By reflection and debate and by organised action, a community of publics comes to feel itself and comes in fact to be active at points of structural relevance.

(Mills 1959: 321)

Some modifications

Already you can see that by choosing that particular point of departure for reflections on theory I have adopted a rhetorical strategy – which is something sociologists share with journalists, though both groups on occa- sion are loath to admit it. There is a perspective – the concept of a democratic society peopled by a community of publics. There is a vocabul- ary – the public and the private, the mass, the authoritarian, the democra- tic society and the pervasive idea of the manipulation of media markets. This is part of a sociological stream of analysis which can be found in the work of the Frankfurt school and those influenced by it. I am thinking, for example, of Adorno and Horkheimer's essay, 'The culture industry: enlightenment as mass deception' (Adorno and Horkheimer 1979) whose very title tells its story. In considering the relationship between mass production in the culture industry and the needs of the consumer Adorno and Horkheimer delineate a technological system grounded in economic power, which is characterized by what they see as a circle of manipulation and retroactive need in which the unity of the system grows ever stronger. The critique is connected with the idea that needs are themselves subject to manipulation and that this process impinges on consciousness itself in a way that serves to strengthen the structure of domination, which generates this form of social and cultural control. Therefore, as they see it, 'the stronger the position of the culture industry becomes, the more summarily it can deal with consumers' needs, producing them, controlling them, disrupting them, and even withdrawing amusement. No limits are set to cultural progress of this kind' (Adorno and Horkheimer 1979: 144).

The same motif and pessimism can be found in Marcuse's once influential *One Dimensional Man* (1964) and more recently in Habermas's complex and extended theory of communicative action, where among other things he argues that consciousness and possessive individualism with their accompanying motivations of performance and competition join forces to shape conduct in advanced industrial societies. Administrative systems, the bureaucracies, are portrayed as taking away the political space for action and, by the same token, undermining independent sources of opinion formation (Habermas 1971, 1974). Hence politics becomes separated from the citizens – it happens over their heads – and the expert is separated from the public – information is not meaningfully accessible even in what is sometimes labelled an information society. Knowledge, therefore, is both simultaneously present and absent in such a society. It is differentially available and becomes an element in the control of societies, rather than routinely and publicly available for citizens as a basis for participation and decision-taking.

Now much of this sounds like a worried man singing a worried song. In part we may allow that it is the burden of critical theory to indicate that things are not always what they seem. Ironically, the language of critical theory can itself be mystifying and therefore its insights, if such they be, are restricted to a limited audience. But the general thrust of the argument can be appreciated. The image of society we are offered is of a powerful combination of people (not always clearly specified) reinforcing their power and social systems which are reproducing forms of social inequality and in which the political, economic and cultural spheres are inextricably mixed. Such systems seem impregnable and the forms of control irresistible. Leakages in the system or the possibilities of the structured intentions of the powerful not being fulfilled are usually presented in a minimal form, with or without some utopian flourishes as to how things might be in another social world.

It is here I turn to a central modification that is grounded in a reading of Alvin Gouldner's *The Dialectics of Ideology and Technology* (1976). While Gouldner's work treats the approach of the Frankfurt school with sympathy and has some affinity with it, there are some crucial differences which I want to call attention to and develop.

Gouldner reminds us not only of the Frankfurt school but of the Chicago school of sociology. Professor Robert Park had himself been a journalist and clearly saw that news was not a mirror image of what was happening in the world but a professional construction of social reality. In this sense news was not simply mediated but produced by journalists. The question then posed is how convincing an account of social reality is it. The visibility of the story does make it available to public scrutiny and in principle makes it open to challenge from those with particular interests or additional knowledge. That, in itself is a plus for the exercise of public rationality yet it does not exhaust the matter since newspapers can still be trivial. As Gouldner explains:

> To the extent that newspapers are concerned with being merely 'interesting' (in the subjective sense of capturing attention) this might be done by *diminishing* the information and by increasing the 'entertainment' content. To that extent, news and newspapers might then inhibit critical reflection, and constitute narcotising diversions from rationality or foster escapist, irrational fantasies.
>
> (1976: 121–2)

You will observe the crucial metaphor here, that of addiction, which almost by definition, bypasses rational judgement and free choice. It is here that we come to the decisive modification whereby discussion is moved away from a straightforward ruling class or power élite conspiracy model of the mass media, with its anti-democratic connotations. News and its relation to official accounts of reality is the pivotal example:

> It is *not* that officials cease promoting their own accounts of their management, nor even that they have no special credit in the media. Nonetheless, the media *mediates*, which means they select and edit, dramatising some and repressing other events according to their own standards and rules. They stand *between* the public, on the one side, and, on the other, the official managers of institutions, organisations, movements, or the society's hegemonic elites. Media develop their own machinery and rules for generating convincing accounts of social reality, and of what is worth featuring or reporting at all. To that extent, and quite apart from their 'objectivity', media must generate accounts that

differ in *some* measure (even if they do not 'expose' or criticise), from the accounts rendered by social managers.

(ibid.: 123)

What this suggests is that those in positions of power in society will certainly make attempts to control the media. When they are successful then conspiracy theories of the media have some credibility. But that is not the whole story, which is perhaps why some commentators have contrasted conspiracy theories with 'cock-up' theories of the media – the notion that what emerges from the media is more a product of unintended consequences and absence of planning, in relations between the state and the media. But let us pursue this matter of the relationship between the media and mechanisms of social control a little further before we accept too easy a contrast. It does not, after all, have to be either one or the other. In reality there may be different mixes. The point that Gouldner is emphasizing is that if the mass media are not to be understood simply as an appendage to the official management and definition of society, then, even if they are only partially independent of them, the official managers of society are in some measure vulnerable.

> A new historical situation has now been created for societal managers; their dealing with the public and with one another is now greatly affected by reports carried by the media. The problem of dealing with the media now becomes a central and special problem for all social institutions.
>
> (ibid.: 124)

So I want to suggest that the media occupy space which is constantly being contested, which is subject to organizational and technological restructuring, to economic, cultural and political constraints, to commercial pressures and to changing professional practices. The changing contours of this space can lead to different patterns of domination and agenda setting and to different degrees of openness and closure, in terms of access, patterns of ownership, available genres, types of discourse and range of opinions represented. Although it is intrinsically difficult to theorize the complexities which are implied in this formulation, the implications of the empirical outcomes of the struggle over this terrain are crucial for the ways in which they help or hinder the democratic process. This is so, not only because of the role which the mass media play in consciousness formation, but more specifically because public opinion, which we find crystallized and represented to us throughout the media, is itself affected by knowledge. It is an informed citizenry, not simply an opinionated one, that is a prerequisite for a mature democracy. The mass media, alongside other parts of our cultural apparatus, notably the education system, have a decisive role to play in this respect.

The essays in the present volume seek to address some of these complexities. The critiques developed by the Glasgow University Media Group have not always made for easy relationships with the BBC and ITN. At the same time we have always received a good deal of help and support from within the broadcasting organizations, including journalists. So while the hostility of some broadcasters is a matter of record, the assistance of others is something we are glad to acknowledge. This has continued and developed over the years. This itself is sufficient to remind us that we are not dealing with monolithic institutions. Again, it is too simple to depict the conflicts as media academics versus broadcasting professionals. The first research director of the group, Brian Winston, was himself a media professional, having worked with the BBC's *24 Hours* and Granada's *World In Action*. He was later to receive an Emmy Award for his work on *Heritage: Civilisation and the Jews*. He was insistent that any critique of 'objectivity' had to be grounded in an empirical delineation and understanding of professional practices.

This is precisely what he does in the essay for this volume in offering a detailed account of CBS *Evening News*, 7 April 1949. This is almost a kind of media archaeology. He is interested in the development of filmic and linguistic practices that establish television news as 'natural'. There is an important sense in which that achievement helped to lay the basis for claims to neutrality and objectivity. The ideological basis of those claims was obscured by the very naturalness of the product. Yet, as Winston shows, it took a great deal of professional labour to achieve this naturalistic quality. In this respect his paper serves as a prehistory to the Glasgow work. By the 1970s British television news had clearly defined formats with routine practices that were embodied in distinctive visual and linguistic codes. To examine these practices in detail was to make visible taken for granted assumptions. The claims to objectivity based upon these professional practices were indeed challenged. Since a central tenet of news production was questioned on the basis of detailed empirical research it is not too surprising that some disputes – private and public – between some broadcasters and the research group took place.

Howard Davis reminds us of the context within which the Glasgow University Media Group's analysis of television news took place in the 1970s. He references the relatively stable institutions and values of public broadcasting at that time against the technological, institutional and political changes that have taken place since then. This creates new problems for media professionals and new challenges for media research. For him, there are a number of issues raised by the Glasgow work which still need to be put in these changing times: the relationship between theory and method; between practitioners and researchers; between researchers and the funding bodies; between applied and critical research.

Given the strategy of work to which this volume gives witness his comments on the work of John B. Thompson (1984, 1988) are of particular interest. Thompson makes the case for a theoretical linking of production, content and reception in media studies as a way of understanding more precisely ways in which relations of domination are sustained or subverted. While, as Davis rather tartly observes, this is what many media researchers think they have been about for some time, it is good to have it articulated again and to recall how it bears upon issues of power and ideology in society. But turning it into a research agenda in a sustained way is difficult. This is because the theoretical and methodological problems involved in such a programme are complex and also costly in terms of research funding. Yet there is a way forward here that can allow space for critique and can claim to be relevant for media practice. The essays in the next three parts of this book seek to illustrate this contention.

Since our overall concern is to contribute to an understanding of the linkages between production, output and reception of media messages, the chapters grouped under one of these three heads do, not surprisingly, usually reference other parts of the communication process. The chapters on media production take widely differing topics – the Soviet media, the Northern Ireland Information Service and the Ethiopian famine of 1984. Each raises somewhat different issues of message production.

In the case of the Soviet Union, Brian McNair, with the benefit of an historical perspective, considers the changing societal context of message production and the altered legal framework. He reminds us that Lenin had seen the press as a crucial ideological and organizational weapon in the struggle against tsarism. It was to be a committed press because it was for the proletariat. But, because it was for the proletariat it would, by definition, be objective and truthful. However, the press as a form of revolutionary resistance to tsarism is one thing, the press as an instrument of social control, owned and controlled by the Communist Party in a one-party state is quite another. Once a party claims the monopoly of truth the suppression of other press activity outside the party becomes justified. It is denounced as counter-revolutionary, anti-proletariat and therefore, by definition, those who attempt to do this are enemies of the state. Censorship and repression thus came to be justified in the name of truth and freedom and this, of course, extended beyond the press to literature and the arts. This practice and experience was to spread to Eastern Europe in the postwar period. This was an enormous constraint on freedom of expression, yet it was not all powerful. So it was that literary works were sent secretly to the west and a samizdat literature and press developed. Moreover, as Schudson (1991) reminds us, an audience credibility problem can arise. He points out that in Eastern Europe readers had come to recognize that the only reading worth doing was 'between the lines'.

In 1975, Vaclav Havel wrote a courageous and costly letter to Gustav Husak, then President of Czechoslovakia, in which he described culture as the main instrument of a society's self-knowledge. He traced out the signficance for his own society:

> Where total control over a society completely suppresses its inner development, the first thing to be suppressed regularly is its culture: not just 'automatically', as a phenomenon intrinsically opposed to the 'spirit' of manipulation, but as a matter of deliberate 'programming' inspired by justified anxiety lest society be alerted to the extent of its own subjugation through that culture which gives it its self-awareness. It is culture that enables a society to enlarge its liberty and to discover truth – so what appeal can it have for the authorities who are basically concerned with suppressing such values? There is only one kind of truth they recognise: the kind they need at the given moment. And only one kind of liberty: to proclaim that 'truth'.
>
> A world where 'truth' flourishes not in a dialectic climate of genuine knowledge, but in a climate of power motives, in a world of mental sterility, petrified dogmas, rigid and unchangeable creeds leading inevitably to creedless despotism.
>
> This is a world of prohibitions and limitations and of orders, a world where cultural policy means primarily the operations of the cultural police force.
>
> (Havel 1987: 16)

Yet the late 1980s saw the unravelling of the authoritarian state systems in Eastern Europe. As McNair sees it, the glasnost campaign, in which the media were to play a leading role, was a response to the crisis of Soviet society. It was a special kind of radicalism which prompted Mikhail Gorbachev to suggest that a wrong turn was made very early on in the Russian revolution, embodied of course in Stalin and Stalinism. This was an attempt to find a way out of authoritarianism and to restructure an inefficient economy through encouraging the process of democratization. In a speech to the Soviet media in 1987, Gorbachev spoke of the need to maintain an atmosphere of openness through glasnost, democratization and criticism:

> We do not want things to be all quiet on the cultural front. On the contrary, we are all for the changes to continue in the same way that our political strategies are developing. . . . We sometimes lack a political culture, we do not have a cultural tradition of discussions or polemics, where one respects the view of an opponent. We are emotional people, and we shall, possibly, grow out of that. I maybe wrong about some things. I do not pretend to know the absolute truth. We have to search for truth together.
>
> (Walker 1987)

This rejection of absolute claims was a very important move and a prerequisite for the emergence of a pluralist media. Clearly, when in the wake of this Pasternak can be rehabilitated in the Soviet Union, when *Moscow News* could print criticisms of the health service and of the housing situation and admit that western views about human rights in the Soviet Union were sometimes justified real movement was taking place. But once pluralism makes its entrance it is not easy to predict its limits and directions. Thus Gorbachev himself had to learn that *Moscow News* could also criticize him in the spirit of glasnost, especially when, for whatever reasons, he appeared to move from a radical reforming to a conservative position. The break up of the Soviet Union has emphasized the role of press and broadcasting in the various states – Lithuania, Estonia, the Ukraine and so on. Competing accounts of the same events remind one sharply of the differing interests and audiences which are being addressed.

If, as I have argued, the media occupy a space that is constantly being contested, it is reasonable to look at the relationship between journalists and their sources (Chibnall 1977; Ericson, Baranek and Chan 1989). This is not a simple matter. The willingness and ability of journalists to interrogate their sources and compare one source with another is itself a critical variable and may be constrained by the organizational contexts in which they operate. Sources themselves vary in scope, size, power and influence. Reflecting on this area of media research Schudson has concluded:

> One study after another comes up with essentially the same observation, and it matters not whether the study is at national or local level – the story of journalism, on a day to day basis, is the story of interaction of reporters and officials.
>
> (1991: 148)

This is an important reminder of the bureaucratic context in which news is constructed. Yet the terms of trade within which information is exchanged may vary: sometimes it appears that the journalists are in the driving seat and sometimes the officials. Because we are dealing with social processes in which necessarily a good deal of linguistic labour is involved neither researchers nor actors can take too much for granted. This is another reason why simple conspiracy theories of the media are difficult to sustain. That does not mean that particular source-journalist practices cannot be discerned and their significance for powerful groups in society assessed.

David Miller's chapter on the role of the Northern Ireland Information Service (NIIS) in relation to the media is an instructive case in point. The recognition that Northern Ireland is the site of an intense propaganda war is, of course, not new. When three members of the IRA were killed by British security personnel in March 1988 in Gibraltar a story was put out that a 500 lb bomb had been planted in a car. The inference was that the killings were necessary to prevent the explosion which they could other-wise have detonated. Although the story was told on television and in the press it was not true. It was black propaganda – even when discredited it had served in those early hours to contextualize the action of killing unarmed people in the street. The later disputes concerning Thames Television's *Death on the Rock* programme in which official accounts of the Gibraltar killings were questioned remind us both of the extent and limits of political power in this area (Miller 1991). It is a real struggle with real costs and real consequences so far as open and democratic media are concerned, and illustrates the significance of Gouldner's point concerning the nature of media power which I noted above (pp. 19–20).

When we consider the Northern Ireland Information Service, therefore, we can see that as an official information source it is strongly placed to convey its picture of the world to the media. Miller draws attention to the way in which the office has operated a policy of hierarchy of access in relation to different journalists. This relates in part to a preference for broadcast over print journalists and in part to the audiences and readerships the journalists represent. So journalists working for British television national networks or lobby journalists get preference over local or Dublin-based journalists. Moreover, some messages are prepared with different audiences in mind. Thus the claim that the IRA is a Marxist conspiracy was made in information directed at the American media not the British. Clearly, these are attempts to control both the flow and content of the information/propaganda network.

Yet that is not the whole story. While the attempts at control have a clearly calculative rationale behind them and from the standpoint of the NIIS are not without success, there is an underlying dilemma. Information that stresses 'the wickedness of terrorism' is liable to undermine information that stresses the theme of Northern Ireland as a 'community on the move'. It is the second message which proves to be more difficult to get across. It is not in the interests of the NIIS to highlight violence at the expense of community stability, yet news values tend to relate to the former. In the end we need to be reminded that in this part of the UK the state's legitimacy is strongly contested. The Northern Ireland Office represents that state and is therefore part of the conflict, not above it. The role of the NIIS is to provide the kind of information that will sustain the credibility of the state's claims to legitimacy. While the underlying political conflict remains unsolved it will, at a day-to-day level, continue to put out contradictory messages – the good news and the bad news. In struggling to sustain its own credibility its denizens will need to work hard at their linguistic and visual labours.

Philo's chapter, 'From Buerk to Band Aid', shifts the focus to issues of information flow between the Third World and the west and the mediating character of news values and priorities. This provides us with an important example of what it means to talk about 'the power of the media'. The events which he refers to, the Ethiopian famine of 1984, had their own history in that country and in terms of media coverage. Jonathan Dimbleby's film, *The Unknown Famine*, had covered the Ethiopian famine of 1973. This, together with the spin-off journalism it generated led, among other things, to an estimated £15 million being raised by charity organizations concerned with famine relief (Harrison and Palmer 1986). There are grounds for claiming that the film contributed towards the subsequent coup, because the government of Emperor Hailie Selassie reacted to it by denying the existence of the famine. The Polish journalist, Ryszard Kapuscinski, in his book, *The Emperor* (1984), obtained accounts of this period from people who had supported the regime. One of them described the impact of the Dimbleby film:

> A month hadn't passed when a report came from our Embassy there (England) that Mr. Dimbleby had shown a film entitled *Ethiopia: The Unknown Famine* on London TV, in which this unprincipled calumnator pulled the demogogic trick of showing thousands of people dying of hunger, and next to that His Venerable Highness feasting with dignitaries. Then he showed roads on which scores of poor, famished skeletons were lying, and immediately afterward our airplanes bringing champagne and caviar from Europe. Here, whole fields of dying scrags; there, His Highness serving meat to his dogs from a silver platter. This, then that: splendour – misery, riches – despair, corruption. In addition, Mr. Dimbleby announced that hunger had already caused the deaths of a hundred thousand people, perhaps even two hundred thousand, and that twice that number might share their fate in the very near future. The report from the Embassy said that after the film was shown, a great scandal broke out in London. There were appeals to Parliament, the newspapers raised alarms, His Royal Highness was condemned. . . .
>
> (Kapuscinski 1984: 109)

But if the episode reflects something of the reality of media power within some more general organizational and political nexus, it also reminds us of the limits of it. Dimbleby himself has argued that the effects of the film were the creation of space to report and discuss Third World issues, including problems of famine and development, the setting up of the Independent Broadcasting Trust, with a Channel 4 commitment to development issues and a raising of public consciousness. None of this is to be gainsaid and yet, as Dimbleby puts it:

> The tragedy is that the momentum that was undoubtedly there in 1974 and 1985 wasn't maintained. What happened was that food stocks went marginally up, people stopped looking like skeletons, though they went on dying from malnutrition, and the infant mortality rates continued. The people who were on the edge of the precipice and

hadn't fallen over stayed where they were, ready to topple
time around.

(cited in Harrison and Palmer 1̅9̅0̅0̅.

It was a decade later, in 1984, that Michael Buerk of BBC News and
Mohammed Amin of Visnews went to Ethiopia and produced filmed
reports of the famine. This was shown on British television on main news
bulletins and elsewhere in the world, including the United States. The fact
that the story was there to be told was a chronicle of and testimony to
earlier failures to sustain the momentum, not helped, it must be said, by
the post-Selassie revolutionary government. Yet getting it on the bulletins
was by no means a straightforward matter, as Philo's account makes clear.
It was the specific report transmitted by the BBC on 23 October 1984,
while only one of a number of reports that had been shown elsewhere on
British television, that had the dramatic impact.

As we now know, this led to the charismatic intervention of Bob Geldof
and the immense fund-raising activities of Live Aid and Sports Aid. Yet
given the real struggle there was to get the news on in the first place,
rejection being based on assumptions about public opinion which turned
out to be wrong, this serves as a sharp reminder of the significance of news
values. These, however, are not immutable, nor, given the plurality of
news outlets, are they unquestioningly shared. Given the contests which
permeate the getting, presenting and shaping of news and the uncertainties
among professional media people as to how it will be received, we can
appreciate that relationship between the mass media, public opinion and
social consciousness does not admit of formulaic answers.

With Lucinda Broadbent's chapter on Nicaragua we shift continents, but
it is another important account of the coverage of a Third World country by
the media of the First World. In 1990, she worked in Managua as a videotape
archivist with NBC, a period which included the elections that led to the
replacement of the Sandinista government and its President Daniel Ortega
by the coalition alliance UNO and its leader Violeta Chamorro. In the early
part of her chapter she gives us a vignette of her experience. The videotape
editor, watching an Ortega speech at an election rally, says 'Who the hell
does he think he is, talking all that shit about American aggression? No-one
ever got anywhere by bad-mouthing the US.' He is speaking of a country,
which had for years supported the Contras in their armed conflict with a
democratically-elected government; the country which learned a new word,
Irangate, and the murky international dealings which led to the provision of
arms to the Contras, courtesy of the CIA.

Broadbent gives us a detailed analysis of how the American and British
press covered the 1984 elections. With the exception of a BBC *Newsnight*
programme, she points out that there was a significant absence in the
coverage: there is no clear indication of what the Sandinista, the FSLN,

stood for, Broadbent shows that in practice, although some dissent from President Reagan's policies at the tactical level was present in the American press, there was a high degree of news management. This was shown not only in the simple labelling of the FSLN as Marxist, without any elaboration of their policies on such topics as health and education, but also in the tendency to reduce discussion of the opposition to Arturo Cruz, a Washington-based, CIA-connected Nicaraguan banker. He said that his coalition group, the right-wing CDN, would not participate in the election because the Sandinistas did not provide democratic conditions for the election. The news management was not total because international observers were present at the elections and reported that they were conducted fairly. But there remained the tactic of disinformation. A security source in Washington leaked the story that Soviet MIGs were about to be unloaded in Nicaragua. The story became the basis for many other stories and swamped the election story. It was an unsubstantiated leak, later shown to be untrue. This is not treated as a simple conspiracy of the international press against Nicaragua, but does point to the power of the United States élites in the agenda setting of foreign policy in which their interests are at stake. In this she shares the view of Chomsky:

> the media do contest and raise questions about government policy, but they do so almost exclusively within the framework determined by the essentially shared interests of state-corporate power. Divisions among elites are reflected in media debate, but departure from their narrow consensus is rare. It is true that the incumbent state managers commonly set the media agenda. But if the policy fails, or is perceived to be harmful to powerful interests, the media will often 'contest government policy' and urge different means to achieve goals that remain beyond challenge, or, quite often, even awareness.
>
> (Chomsky 1989: 75)

We have encountered this perspective already in relation to Williams's chapter on public opinion and the Vietnam War. This, in turn, is in line with the work of Hallin (1986) on American media coverage of the Vietnam War. It is a theory of élite control that only breaks down when the élites are in conflict or disarray. It is close to the Wright Mills's view I have already discussed. This leaves somewhat problematical the questions of how and why élites lose control or whether there are any pressures from below that impinge upon them. The explanatory power and the limits of the approach are well illustrated by Robert Manoff's comment on élite opinion and the peace movement in the USA. Writing in 1984, he observed:

> Make no mistake about it: the press has become an essential component in the epistemological apparatus of the nuclear regime. For the press has proved responsive above all to government news leadership and to the

consensual militarism of elite opinion. Anti-nuclear movements do not interest the press until they begin to take notice. On that day the grass roots story moves from the category of human interest to that of politics, out of obscurity and onto page one.

(Manoff 1984: 11)

We can see that this perspective is an important corrective to a pluralist approach that rested on notions of a free press in which access and diversity are assumed rather than delineated. Yet, as Schlesinger has pointed out, referring particularly to the Herman–Chomsky propaganda model (Herman and Chomsky 1988), it is a highly deterministic version of how the media operate, linked with a functionalist conception of ideology (Schlesinger 1989). Moreover, as the subtitle of *Necessary Illusions – Thought Control in Democratic Societies* – suggests, the ways the messages are received are assumed. Yet it is one thing to recognize that there are inequalities of power, whether economic, political or cultural, but quite another to clarify how far the media modify or reinforce those inequalities. We continually need to ask questions about control through the whole process of production, content and reception. This is a conceptual, theoretical and empirical challenge.

Schlesinger, for example, has challenged the Marxist–structuralist assumption that 'official sources' constitute by definition the role of 'primary definers' in message construction:

One effect of this standpoint is that the sociological question of how sources organise *media strategies* and compete with one another is completely neglected. 'Primary definition', which ought to be an empirically ascertainable outcome is held to be an *a priori* effect of privileged access. For their part, empirical studies, although more sensitive to the reality of active source competition (a game played on unequal terms), have for the most part remained trapped within methodological frameworks that preclude direct investigation of source strategies.

(Schlesinger 1989: 284)

This point has been illustrated in our recent research activity on AIDS messages and the media. This project looked at the process of message production, content and reception. The three chapters in this volume on the project by David Miller and Kevin Williams, Peter Beharrell and Jenny Kitzinger deal in turn with each aspect of the process and point to a larger publication. What began as a limited exercise on the production side was extended as the researchers explored the ramifications of the processes of negotiation involved in the government's health education mass media campaign concerning HIV/AIDS in 1987–8. This entailed interviewing civil servants, health educators, advertisers and market researchers, a range of voluntary sector and pressure group workers, including professional organizations like the British Medical Association and AIDS specialist groups like the Terence Higgins Trust. Although an official campaign is produced it is not always easy to define an official source in an unambiguous way or to assume that such sources will always be in agreement with one another. Because there were different professional, political and moral perspectives there was a great deal of contention over the language and form of the advertisements. There were conflicts between advertisers who were primarily concerned about the message 'impact' and health educators who wanted to get the message, the information, right. The outcomes were a series of messages that carried their own confusions and language limitations. This, to put it mildly, is not a straightforward encoding process.

This did not mean that central government and medical establishment sources were without power in the matter. They did play a key role in the negotiating of the agendas that were followed. But not all official sources were able to use the media in the way they wanted. The Health Education Authority, for example, did not play the leading role it wanted to, partly because of its subordinate status within the Department of Health and partly because within the media there was a suspicion of 'experts'. Yet, conversely, non-official sources like the Terence Higgins Trust, despite limited resources and an initial credibility problem, as a representative organization of people with HIV/AIDS, developed an effective information strategy.

What we learn to recognize here is that power over the media, and in the media, is something which is contested. The very process of negotiation can teach us something about changing power balances. It is not a unidimensional or one-way matter. Thus, despite the media scepticism of health education expertise, noted above, some doctors involved in the treatment of AIDS became sources of expert information both for the policy-making community and the media. Their appearance on the media could be used as a pressure on the Department of Health. For some civil services this was a not unwelcome pressure, which they could use in their negotiations with other parts of the Whitehall bureaucracy.

The interaction between these sources and the journalists was then a complex matter. Not only were they negotiating within and between source organizations but also with journalists who were differentially placed in the media. Thus medical correspondents were in closer contact with routine sources on AIDS than general reporters and could find themselves in conflict with editorial viewpoints (and with the editors!). Beharrell, in his chapter, drawing upon a comprehensive content analysis of news coverage on AIDS in the media, shows that it is not homogeneous. For example, on an issue central to the government's campaign – that heterosexuals as well as homosexuals are at risk – the *Sun*, the *Daily Mail* and *Daily Express* published editorials and articles explicitly rejecting the health education campaign and questioning the truth of heterosexual risk. The *Daily Star* ignored the issue, while *Today* and the *Daily Mirror* supported the campaign. Moreover, an exploration of the content of different newspaper formats – editorials, news reports, features, signed articles, women's pages – each with their own codes and conventions led in practice to messages that were confused and contradictory, as well as representing different moral viewpoints.

It is in the light of these kinds of considerations and findings that issues relating to message reception need to be seen. In *Seeing and Believing* (1990) Philo developed a new approach to reception analysis in an attempt to delineate audience understandings of the 1984–5 miners' strike in the UK. A shorter account is given in this volume. He showed how, with the stimulus of a few off-screen photographs from TV news, a diversity of small groups were able to reconstruct news bulletins that bore great similarity to the actual bulletins, even though the exercise took place more than a year after the events themselves. This does say something about the power of the media, when the same kind of messages are repeated day after day, as in this case. Even so we are not left with the picture of a passive viewer since opinions expressing agreement or disagreement with the nature of the coverage could also be detected. Disagreements were noticeably present with individuals or groups who had direct experience of the events in question. Meanings and judgements are then negotiated by audiences even though, in this case, there were generally shared agreements as to what the message was. This itself can be related back to more general cultural stocks of knowledge – the nature of strikes, miners and coal-mining, the police, the government and so on.

This methodology was adapted and applied to the AIDS project and is reported in Jenny Kitzinger's chapter 'Understanding AIDS'. Again the ability to reproduce news accounts by a wide range of groups is shown. But she also argues that audiences are active participants in the construction of meaning. What she reminds us of, on the basis of very detailed audience accounts, is that both media and audiences are part of wider cultural and political contexts that may either facilitate or obstruct the acceptance of certain kinds of representations. So while the media and the audience may operate within a broadly defined consensus about 'reality' they are not themselves homogeneous entities. Yet again, we begin to learn something about the limits of media power, while treating its power potential with the utmost seriousness.

RERERENCES

Adorno, Theodore and Horkheimer, Max (1979) *Dialectic of Enlightenment*, London: Verso.
Brittain, Victoria (ed.) (1991) *The Gulf Between Us*, London: Virago.

Burns, Tom (1977) *The BBC: Public Institution and Private World*, London: Macmillan.
Chibnall, Steve (1977) *Law and Order News*, London: Tavistock.
Chomsky, Noam (1989) *Necessary Illusions*, London: Pluto.
Cockrell, Michael, Hennessy, Peter and Walter, David (1984) *Sources Close to the Prime Minister*, London: Macmillan.
Ericson, Richard, Baranek, Patricia and Chan, Janet (1989) *Negotiating Control. A Study of News Sources*, Milton Keynes: Open University Press.
Glasgow University Media Group (1985) *War and Peace News*, Milton Keynes: Open University Press.
Gouldner, Alvin (1976) *The Dialectics of Ideology and Technology*, London: Macmillan.
Habermas, J. (1971) *Knowledge and Human Interests*, Boston, Mass.: Beacon Press.
—— (1974) *Theory and Practice*, Boston, Mass.: Beacon Press.
Hallin, Daniel (1986) *The Uncensored War: the Media and Vietnam*, Oxford: Oxford University Press.
Harris, Robert (1983) *Gotcha! The Media, The Government and The Falklands Crisis*, London: Faber.
Harrison, Paul and Palmer, Robin (1986) *News Out of Africa*, London: Hilary Shipman.
Havel, Vaclav (1987) *Living in Truth*, London: Faber.
Herman, Edward and Chomsky, Noam (1988) *Manufacturing Consent: The Political Economy of the Mass Media*, London: Pantheon.
Kapuscinski, Ryszard (1984) *The Emperor*, London: Picador.
Knightley, Philip (1982) *The First Casualty*, London: Quartet.
—— (1991) 'Here is the patriotically censored news', *Index on Censorship*, April/May: 4–5.
Manoff, Robert Karl (1984) 'Journalism in the nuclear age', *Quill*, February.
Marcuse, Herbert (1964) *One Dimensional Man*, Boston, Mass.: Beacon Press.
Mercer, Derek, Mungham, Geoff, Williams, Kevin (1987) *The Fog of War*, London: Heinemann.
Miller, David (1991) 'The media on the Rock: the media and the Gibraltar killings', in Bill Rolston (ed.) *The Media and Northern Ireland: Covering the Troubles*, London: Macmillan.
Miller, Nod and Allen, Rod (eds) (1991) *And Now For The BBC*, London: John Libbey.
Mills, C. Wright (1959) *The Power Elite*, Oxford: Oxford University Press.
—— (1963) 'Mass media and public opinion', in *Power, Politics and People. The Collected Writings of C. Wright Mills*, edited by I. Horowitz, Oxford: Oxford University Press.
Morris, Colin (1986) 'What's so good about bad news?', *Listener*, 25 September.
Orwell, George (1954) *1984*, Harmondsworth: Penguin.
—— (1962) *Homage to Catalonia*, Harmondsworth: Penguin.
Philo, G. (1990) *Seeing and Believing*, London: Routledge.
Schlesinger, Philip (1987) *Putting Reality Together*, London: Methuen.
—— (1989) 'From production to propaganda', *Media, Culture and Society* 11: 283–306.
Schudson, Michael (1991) 'The sociology of news production revisited', in James Curran and Michael Gurevitch (eds) *Mass Media and Society*, London: Edward Arnold: 141–59.
Smith, Anthony (1976) *The Shadow in the Cave*, London: Quartet.

Thompson, John B. (1984) *Studies in the Theory of Ideology*, Cambridge: Polity Press.

—— (1988) 'Mass communication and modern culture: contribution to a critical theory of ideology', *Sociology* 22–3: 359–84.

Walker, Martin (1987) 'Gorbachev tells the media: we must never forgive Stalin', *Guardian*, 16 July.

Chapter 2

Media research: whose agenda?

Howard H. Davis

In the fifteen years since the publication of *Bad News* (Glasgow University Media Group 1976), the media landscape has been changing with increasing speed. Television news analysis in the 1970s took place against the background of relatively stable institutions and a still strong consensus about the values and goals of public broadcasting. However vigorous may have been the disagreements about their practical application, there was much common ground. The keenest debate at the time – lasting all of ten years – was about the form which one additional terrestrial channel should have within the system of public regulation. The subsequent acceleration of technical, economic and political change has made the work of researchers as well as practitioners more uncertain and complex. The field of media studies has grown and diversified during this period partly in response to these changes but the process of maturation still has some way to go. The main argument of this chapter is that sociology provides resources in the shape of concepts, theoretical approaches and forms of empirical analysis which the expanding field of 'media studies' has been neglecting to its disadvantage. I discuss reasons why this is so and try to identify some of the consequences. The second part of the chapter examines the question of how sociology, broadly interpreted, can inform media research in such a way as to contribute to a more coherent, critical and relevant field of study.

The chapter does not attempt to describe the 'proper' content of media studies, whether it can ever be a unified discipline, a catalyst for other disciplines, how it should contribute to professional formation or how it should be located in secondary, further or higher education. Such prescriptions tend to miss the point, as these issues are decided by circumstances and policies which teachers and researchers can do little to control. It is enough to recognize that the media have a permanent if not undisputed place in academic research and in the curriculum at all levels of the education system.[1]

No single discipline has colonized media studies and multidisciplinary teaching and research is the norm. However, it is interesting to note that social psychology, with its strong record of empirical research, is marginal to most media studies curricula because it sits uneasily with the qualitative and literary approach of the cultural studies tradition. Its theoretical orientation, its research designs and precise use of quantitative data – its uncompromising commitment as a discipline – prevents it from being incorporated further. Sociology has been more fully involved, particularly during its most expansionary phase in the late 1960s and early 1970s. It contributed the intellectual rationale for most of the research into media expressions of the (dominant) ideology at that time, including the work of the Glasgow University Media Group, but its influence has diminished as post-structuralism has flourished. One of the important consequences of the fluidity of the paradigms of media research and the marginalization of the most technical disciplines of research has been endemic uncertainty among the research funding agencies concerning the amount and direction of support. Where theoretical movements and shifts in research paradigms occur within disciplines they may actually stimulate research funding, but where there is less obvious continuity or focus, the same intellectual trends are interpreted as a sign of instability and immaturity. This chapter is concerned with the reasons for this state of affairs and the longer term prospects for research.

THE DEVELOPMENT OF MEDIA STUDIES

The object of media studies in Britain is conventionally described in textbooks and introductions to the field quite literally as 'the media' in the sense of the institutions and the messages they create. Successive media – the press, cinema, radio, television and, most recently, the 'new' information and communication technologies – are treated as the carriers of specific social, political and moral messages generated in a temporal sequence in response to developments in society. There is no conceptual core which corresponds to the field of 'communications' in North America, and with very few exceptions there is no well-defined institutional identity for research and teaching activities. Instead, there are distinct but overlapping clusters of activity which have roots in the social sciences, literary studies and philosophy.

The first notable social scientific media research in Britain dates back to the studies of the impact of television on the behaviour of children (Himmelweit, Oppenheim and Vince 1958). At this time, such approaches were already well established in the United States, where they flourished in response to the government's concern about the educational and propaganda uses of film, to political campaigns and to advertisers' attempts to influence consumers. However, the institutional position of media research and teaching was not destined to become as firmly established in Britain as it was in the USA, where the 'golden age' of empirical research was in any case about to falter (Katz 1977: 22–3). By the time the Centre for Mass

Communication Research at Leicester and the Centre for Television Research at Leeds were set up in 1966, the behavioural, cause–effect paradigm was meeting with a barrage of criticism for being too concerned with measuring effects at the level of the individual. Some of the significant early publications from these research centres (for example, Halloran 1965, 1970) appeared when interest was already growing in the wider implications of the media and the time was ripe for more sociologically-informed approaches.

The interaction between American communications research and the emerging field of cultural studies mapped out by Richard Hoggart (1958) and Raymond Williams (1958, 1961) is evident in Williams's *Communications* (1962). This uses content analysis and other empirical methods to examine popular culture. But this is not 'culture' simply as text abstracted from its origins in a social context; it is an approach which recognizes the 'solid, practical institutions' which embody the relations of cultural production. 'We cannot examine the process of general communication in modern society', he argues, 'without examining the shapes of these institutions' (Williams 1962: 20). The most significant institutional focus for cultural studies was the Centre for Contemporary Cultural Studies at the University of Birmingham. Stuart Hall, who succeeded Richard Hoggart as its director in 1969, presided over an expanded culturalist field which incorporated neo-Marxist, structuralist and semiotic theories and a distinct political commitment to the 'popular' in politics as well as culture.

The phenomenon which Hall aptly described (Hall 1982: 56–90) as 'the return of the repressed' in media studies, that is the rediscovery of ideology, language and politics, took time to take shape, but between 1970 and the end of the decade these themes became almost completely dominant. The confluence of Marxism, structuralism and cultural studies created a new and essentially 'European' intellectual field which set no boundaries for itself in terms of its theoretical scope or its methods of analysis.[2] Sociologists were quite central to these developments, although they borrowed heavily from political economy, linguistics, semiology and other disciplines. There is a temptation to exaggerate the vitality of this movement in sociology but there were definite signs (notably at Glasgow and Leicester) that sociology had rediscovered culture as an object of study and that it should have at least equal status with the popular concerns of the previous decade: namely class, stratification and the power of labour.[3]

The progress of research, however, was more erratic and its results more fragmentary. Differences of approach and emphasis generated their own research methods and techniques. Ethnography, production studies, audience surveys and content analysis all produced valuable results although work was heavily biased towards broadcasting. There was virtually no long-term investigation of changes in the media, no replication studies and few projects involving more than one or two types of media. Empirical studies generated a patchwork of information, not always consistent or comparable and only loosely linked to the development of theory. The Social Science Research Council committed less than 2 per cent of its funds to media research between 1970 and 1979 (thirty out of a total of 3,000 grants), so can hardly claim much credit for developments in this field (Advisory Panel for Mass Media Research 1980). The Research Council's reasons for dissatisfaction were expressed in a report which described the search for a research agenda. It noted that the field had developed in an uneven way, not just because of the pattern of funding but also because of the selection of 'negative' issues for academic scrutiny. They said:

> a picture emerges of a field of research, with no embracing discipline and with researchers working on a wide variety of topics. The appearance is however one of dispersion rather than healthy diversity and there is little evidence of positive collaboration or of steady accumulation of knowledge and understanding. . . . In general, academic research has tended to be fragmentary, repetitious rather than incremental and prone to fashion.
>
> (ibid.: 8)

The response, ironically, was to concentrate resources on the newly fashionable subject of information and communication technologies, which has done little to solve the underlying problem alluded to in the report, or to develop a strategy for reinforcing the surprisingly small community of about 100 researchers in the media studies field (Melody and Mansell 1986).

The growth of media teaching was not strictly dependent on the progress of empirical research and it gradually came to be integrated in the curriculum through an engagement with texts rather than through social scientific approaches. The British Film Institute's first national conference on studying the media in higher education, held in 1979, was a coming of age event – reflected in its themes of realism, authorship and cultural theory. Undergraduate courses in communication and media studies were taught in a number of polytechnics and a number of universities were soon to follow.

In sociological research and teaching the late 1970s were a time of theoretical stock-taking and reassessment, illustrated by the content of the British Sociological Association's 1978 conference on 'Culture'. The editors of the collection of conference papers described the theoretical inadequacy of much sociological work on culture and attributed this to the tendency towards theoreticism and the polarization between positions named as 'culturalism', 'historicism', 'economism' and 'Althusserianism' among others. 'Veering from the view that representation is an unmediated reflection of material conditions of existence to the view that representation is necessarily totally autonomous of those conditions, analysis has taken the ultimately futile path of theoreticism' (Barrett *et al*. 1979: 24). However, the impression given by the debates of this period was that the subject-matter had been identified correctly as the culture/ideology problem, and that the way ahead would be to concentrate more on the socially and historically situated process of the production of meanings. It was also felt that these issues (and therefore analysis of the media) should be closer to the mainstream concerns of sociology. Since then, the strength of the 'dominant ideology' paradigm has weakened, partly as a result of theoretical critiques (Abercrombie, Hill and Turner 1980; Williams 1981) and particularly because audiences are once again acknowledged to be active participants in the production of meanings. The general framework continues to be important, however, because there is no comparable social account of influence and effects, and perhaps also because it is in the interests of media researchers and teachers that their object of study should continue to be seen as inherently powerful and important. Cultural studies took an important turn when it began to prioritize the problem of the multiplicity or 'surplus' of meanings in popular cultural forms and to seek out the possibilities for subversive or anti-hegemonic readings. While much of this work is implicitly or explicitly critical of the notion of dominance, it has failed to give a good account of the relationship between the meanings of a text as set by the particular commercial, political or cultural circumstances of its production, and the meanings which it may have for audiences at different times and in different social contexts. With some notable exceptions (e.g., Morley 1986; Philo 1990) empirical studies of audiences have been neglected in favour of flights of interpretative fancy based on texts alone.

The 1980s therefore saw increasing differentiation between cultural analysis and those social scientific approaches which continued to subscribe to a notion of 'dominance'. Before moving on to examine the prospects for the latter, we can note the general consequences for sociology and media studies of the twenty-five years of growth and elaboration of what is sometimes called the 'critical' paradigm, in order to distinguish it from those approaches which have more in common with the American systems-based, empirical tradition (Gurevitch and Levy 1987). First, and most noticeably, theorizing has often been detached from empirical investigation and analysis. This may be because theories have been imported from countries (especially France) where empirical work is not regarded as an essential companion to theory; it is also because some of the basic theoretical propositions (for example, about ideology and the media's contribution to the reproduction of social relationships) are notoriously difficult to state in an operational form. Intermittent research funding also works against cumulative contributions to empirically grounded theory. Second, the critical paradigm seems to focus attention almost instinctively on issues of the state, power and those media which are most significant in terms of their size, audiences and political centrality. The currently dominant medium is the 'natural' candidate for studies of media power and it can too easily be made to act as a metaphor to embrace other media which may have quite different dynamics. The bias towards television broadcasting which I am referring to here may not necessarily contribute to a theoretical bias, but we will only know whether it does by paying more attention to other media and the relationships between media. Third, there is no apparent consensus about the kinds of social data which are essential for serious analysis of the media and even less concern about collecting them systematically in ways which would be useful for social analysis. Consider, for example, the problems of finding occupational data on the media industries, patterns of media consumption within households and indices of change in broadcast content or subcultural styles. The need for national archives of audiovisual material has long been recognized, but the issue is still unresolved. Fourth, the critical paradigm only partly avoided the lure of new technologies and the 1980s agenda for deregulation, although this may be explained by the feeling that the ideology of technological transformation had to be attacked on its own ground. Finally, the development of the cultural/ideological perspective in media studies has so far had only a marginal relationship to the media industries, whether in terms of critiques of output, policy proposals or contribution to education and training for media careers.

The pressures for institutional change in education, from student demand for more applied content and the need for more satisfying solutions to research problems, have all combined to bring the intellectual framework of media studies into question. Whose agenda will prevail and which is the likely future for sociologically-informed empirical research? It is not my intention to encourage or perpetuate a dichotomy between 'empirical' and 'theoretical' approaches to the sociology of the media. There is a tendency for the history of any discipline to be represented as the progress of its ideas and theories, but new sources of data, new technologies for research and new empirical methods can be just as significant as theoretical work for the development of the field of study. Usually they interact. In the 1970s, for example, new kinds of research into television news became possible thanks to relatively cheap video-recording technology. However, the new facility to process large quantities of news output also encouraged more subtle interpretations of 'ideology'; a more complete record of professional routines could be used to test hypotheses about the role of newsfilm, writing conventions and other features of news production (for example, Glasgow University Media Group 1976). In the following section I have selected certain authors for discussion because they have put forward proposals which could be the basis of an agenda for empirical research. They lend support to the observation that the breadth of sociology offers more possibilities of synthesis than, say, economics or politics or social psychology (Gurevitch and Levy 1987: 13–15). The approach of 'political economy' is discussed first, then a contemporary view of mass communications as ideology and finally there is some consideration of the relationship between media researchers and professional practitioners.

POLITICAL ECONOMY

The most consistent exponents of a political economy approach within sociology have been G. Murdock and P. Golding (for example, Golding and Murdock 1979; Murdock 1982, 1990; Murdock and Golding 1974, 1977) and, from a position of close proximity to the discipline, N. Garnham (for example, 1977, 1979, 1988). In the case of Murdock and Golding, the problem is located in the heartland of traditional sociological enquiry as the capitalism–culture relationship and the contribution which the media make to the legitimation of inequalities. Reacting against the culturalist tendencies of the 1970s they asserted the importance of the economic organization and dynamics of media production and its determining influence. Their statements of the thesis have usually been somewhat cautious, as in the following:

> We are not arguing that economic forces are the only factors shaping cultural production, or that they are always and everywhere the most significant. . . . We do not deny the importance of the controls and constraints imposed by the state and the political sphere, or the significance of the inertia exerted by dominant cultural codes and traditions. Nor do we deny the 'relative autonomy' of production personnel and the pertinent effects of professional ideologies and practices.
>
> (Golding and Murdock 1979: 198)

However, they have not been reluctant to use expressions like 'economic determination'. In a subsequent discussion of control in the communications industries, Murdock has clarified and expanded the concept of 'control' in relationship to ownership and the distinction between approaches which emphasize agency and those which emphasize structure:

> An adequate analysis needs to incorporate both [structural and action approaches]. A structural analysis is necessary to map the range of options open to allocative controllers and the pressures operating on them. It specifies the limits to feasible action. But within these limits there is always a range of possibilities and the choice between them is important and does have significant effects on what gets produced and how it is presented. To explain the direction and the impact of these choices, however, we need an action approach which looks in detail at

the biographies and interests of key allocative personnel and traces the consequences of their decisions for the organization and output of production.

(Murdock 1982: 124–5)

The charge of 'economism' certainly does not apply here, if it ever did. The way is opened up for a more sociologically-informed discussion between views which start from the patterns of media ownership and the general dynamics of capitalist economies and those which start from the organization of cultural producers. It is interesting that Murdock concludes his essay by saying that 'the central issues raised by these conflicts remain open both theoretically and empirically' (ibid.: 147). It is true that the complex linkages between the ownership of media companies, corporate strategies, forms of management and the production and sale of cultural goods have not been investigated sufficiently. In the absence of empirical investigation it is tempting to move from questions of economic organization to questions of cultural content as if the logic were transparent. Thus the concentration of media ownership leads some critics like Bagdikian to conclude that 'there is a growing gap between the number of voices in society and the number heard in the media' (Bagdikian 1985; cited in Murdock 1990: 7). This proposition deserves thorough empirical testing but it may be that, as the Glasgow University Media Group and others have found in studying the output of public broadcasting, *how* voices are heard can be as important as *how many* are heard. The intensification and internationalization of competition in media markets, combined with the re-regulation of public broadcasting to bring it more fully into the market sphere, makes these questions increasingly pertinent.

The desire to broaden the theoretical and empirical scope of the political economy approach in recent years is illustrated by the work of Nicholas Garnham. In 1979 he responded to the challenge set by Raymond Williams, who had called for a major revision in cultural theory in order to take account of the expansion of capitalist forces in media and cultural production (Garnham 1979: 123–46). True to the historical materialist tradition, Garnham asserts that cultural (re-)production is subject to material determinants, but adds that a distinction must be made between the 'material' and the 'economic'. The former is a general category which refers to essential characteristics of the social relations of production, whether they lead to commodities or cultural forms. The 'economic' refers to the specific, i.e., capitalist, form of the social relations of production and distribution. Since this capitalist form is incomplete and embodies a contradictory process, it is necessary to trace how, and to what extent, the cultural sphere has been absorbed into full-scale commodity production. Singled out for special attention are: increasing international competition; intensifying struggles over the productivity of labour; attempts to open up new markets; and the political debate and policies concerning the new media technologies.

In a more recent contribution, Garnham (1988) outlines a possible research agenda based on these principles. The industrialization of culture with its increasingly specialized, technologically-based institutions and practices, gives rise to the same two fundamental questions: what determines access to or control of scarce material and cultural resources?; and what determinate effect does that structured access and control have upon social structure and process in general? There is, however, a slight change of emphasis. The processes of determination include feedback at the level of appropriation or reception, the level at which the form of communication is interpreted as meaning, and also 'the level at which this meaning is *or is not* translated into social action, an action which is at the same time and always itself also a symbolic form' (Garnham 1988: 4; my emphasis). At this point, the political economy approach falls back on the general assumption that these processes are determined by the dominant contemporary social form, namely capitalism, and that there must be substantial conformity between it and the general system of culture and symbols. The proposed research agenda includes problems of the limits to global market dynamics, the formation of intellectuals, the changing status of information and, most significantly, a revival of the issue of citizenship and the 'public sphere' (see also Garnham 1986). This brings political issues back into the main agenda and raises the possibility of explanations which recognize longer-term processes and socio-political practices which do not have an exclusive economic motive. Recent changes in broadcasting regulation in Britain illustrate the continuing importance of other motives. To say, as Murdock and Golding have done, that public broadcasting behaves in many ways as though it were itself a commercial undertaking, while true, is to neglect the fundamental differences and why they exist. For example, the modifications included in the 1990 Broadcasting Act and the continuing role of the Independent Television Commission have confounded the worst fears of uncontrolled competition. With all the signs of compromise which accompanied the earlier phases of broadcasting, a system has emerged from the latest franchise round which gives as much status to 'quality' and 'public' good as to 'choice' and 'competition'. This expression of pluralism rather than market freedom undermines all simplistic forms of economic and political determinism.

The agenda for the political economy of the media is impressive in scope, especially as it has now apparently reinstated a number of connections to social and political issues which were only latent a decade ago. It is capable of generating a substantial quantity of empirical research and policy-related discussion. However, it can hardly claim to have displaced other concerns in media studies and the question remains: how does empirical research contribute to this understanding of the issues?

In Garnham's work, the concept of advanced industrial capitalism remains central. While there is a hint that this is an economy 'increasingly
dominated not by subsistence or functional material needs but by psychological and symbolic needs', this theme is not elaborated and he is naturally
dismissive of what he calls 'the relativist irrationalism of most post-
modernist discourse theory' (Garnham 1988: 8). Murdock and Golding, on
the other hand, have defined their view more explicitly against a sociological background. These differences are significant, but, at the risk of
overgeneralization, there seem to be a number of important themes which
are understated in the political economy approach as a whole but which are
none the less implied by its arguments. The first has to do with the material
differences between media themselves, in their technological and organizational aspects. While it is normal in the language of political economy to
distinguish between the different sectors of industry or forms of capital
there is, strangely, little reference to what the French author Miège
(writing from a political economy perspective) calls the different 'social
logics' of the cultural industries: namely, the distinctions between the
'editorial' production of cultural commodities; the 'flow' production of
broadcasting; the production of written information; the production of live
entertainment; and the production of electronic information (Miège 1987,
1989; Miège, Pajon and Salaün 1986). These 'logics' are heterogeneous,
they compete with one another and they entail far more than business
strategies. A second neglected theme is the social differentiation of
audiences and consumers. The usual categories for describing social structure, class, gender, generation and ethnicity are not deployed, only references to 'audiences' and 'consumers'. I have argued elsewhere that while it
may be quite correct to see the cultural sphere coming increasingly under
the influence of the capitalist market system, this does not remove the need
for an explanation of social differentiation and patterns of social consciousness which may have a quite different point of origin in social relations
(Davis 1987). Third, the mediation of culture through time has so far
received little attention in the political economy approach. There is more
to this than adding an historical narrative. The problem is reflected in the
fact that individuals participate in many different cultures over a lifetime,
that generations have identifiable systems of culture and that there is a
continuous succession of new media through time, each causing a transformation of what has gone before.

These are not fundamental flaws and, by drawing attention to them, I am
not making a theoretical criticism. Rather, I am suggesting that these
relatively neglected issues are ones to which empirical studies can usefully
contribute.

MASS COMMUNICATIONS AS IDEOLOGY

In a recent book and an earlier summary article, John B. Thompson has argued that mass communications are central to modern culture and that, as such, they belong among the core concerns of sociology rather than with a narrow group of media specialists (Thompson 1988, 1990). He also outlines a methodological framework for the study of culture and communication which he believes can assist the renewal of critical social theory. His proposals therefore provide some interesting points of comparison with those of political economy.

The approach begins with an abstract, 'structural' definition of culture as socially embedded symbolic forms ('meaningful actions, objects, and expressions of various kinds') which circulate in institutionalized channels of transmission and diffusion. In modern societies, these channels are increasingly those of 'institutionalised networks of communication . . . in which the experience of individuals is increasingly mediated by technical systems of symbolic production and transmission' (Thompson 1990: 11). But their characteristic is to act as filters as well as channels, so that the production and reproduction of cultural forms takes place *selectively*. The appropriation of media messages is likewise a selective and socially differentiated process.

The main features of this concept of the 'mediazation' of modern culture are easily recognizable as those of the dominant/critical paradigm of media studies, so does Thompson's methodological statement represent a useful elaboration? He describes three phases of analysis, beginning with the reconstruction of the specific social–historical context of communication. This involves an examination of specific social relations and institutions, and the distribution of power and resources, by virtue of which this context forms a differentiated social field. The second phase involves a formal analysis of relevant cultural objects and expressions, be they words, images or artefacts. The third, interpretative phase builds on the other two and requires entry into the 'risky', conflict-laden area of explaining and projecting meanings on to cultural constructions. The general method is given a special slant towards ideology by using the analysis to highlight the relationships between meaning and power: 'when our concern is with the analysis of ideology, then the role of interpretation is *to explicate the connection between the meaning of symbolic constructions and the relations of domination which that meaning serves to sustain*' (Thompson 1988: 372; emphasis in original). The application of this method to mass communication is simple because it relates directly to the three object-domains of the media, namely: the institutional arrangements for production; the messages themselves; and the reception and incorporation of messages by individuals and groups.

Thompson argues that previous efforts to understand the social process of the mass media have tended to focus on the first of these two 'moments' (production and content) and have made the mistake of subsuming the mass media within a general analysis of the 'culture industry' which is unsupported by empirical evidence, or working with a vague concept of ideology which fails to show the specific social and institutional conditions of message production. Only by attending to the complex ways in which the different aspects of communication relate to each other, says Thompson, can we hope to understand the ideological process. In particular, 'we must focus on the space of transformation within which the meaning mobilised by media messages is transformed in the process of reception, serving thereby to sustain or subvert, to reinforce or undermine, relations of domination' (ibid.: 380).

Many media researchers could be excused for thinking that this is essentially what they have been about for quite a long time. The hermeneutic approach, post-Marxist understanding of ideology and the distinction between three aspects of the communication process are certainly not new. However, Thompson's methodological advice has the definite merit of bringing these aspects into closer relationship with each other and of giving much greater importance to the reception process than has generally been the case.

The method clearly has an attractive simplicity and symmetry and helps to open up a major field of enquiry which for years had been left to a handful of pioneers (for example, Morley 1980, 1986) although it is now attracting widespread interest. In one form or another it is likely to be influential in media studies for a long time to come. Compared with the political economy approach, however, the understanding of 'modern society' remains implicit and there is some danger that the characteristics of power and domination in society will be read back from the study of its cultural objects and expressions; which would be ideological critique rather than sociology of culture. The problems of directing research activity into the recommended areas are also considerable because they are likely to be very costly (in the case of reception studies) or highly complex (if all three aspects of communication are to be studied simultaneously), or both. Unfortunately, prospects for research funding do not seem to have improved since the 1970s.

The culture/ideology approach reminds us that the interpretation of ideology necessarily involves claims and counter-claims, and that there is no intrinsic reason why the subjects who are involved in the production of media messages should not use it to reflect critically on their own practices. This leads to the general issue of the relationship between media research and teaching and practitioners.

MEDIA STUDIES AND MEDIA PRACTICE

It is well known that media studies have had a poor reputation in the practitioners' world, and that serious attempts to put research on a better footing in relation to broadcasters, for instance (for example, Katz 1977), have met with little success. But this is not an eternal truth. . . . In some areas, especially film, with the British Film Institute as an intermediary, relations are much closer. However, neither of the two general approaches discussed above (pp. 40–5) has much to say about the question, although both see a close connection between ideological critique and political struggle.

The issue can be stated in terms of the institutional changes in both education and the media industries. Both are undergoing structural changes and diversification: the old monoliths are being eroded or dismantled. In the first forty years of broadcasting, for example, most 'training' was corporate training within the BBC. The greater variety of recruitment and career paths in today's industry means that a new, and perhaps more positive, relationship between media organizations and educational establishments will emerge.[4] As far as the topics on the research agenda are concerned, they are increasingly likely to be set by the imperatives of new technology, the course of deregulation and the restructuring of audiences. The prospects for cumulative, theoretically-informed work will therefore depend heavily on the continuity of the centres of research activity, and their ability to train new generations of researchers. Few centres of research activity have had the regularity of research funding and institutional support to make a steady contribution to the field or to create lasting networks into media organizations. Some, like the Birmingham CCCS and Glasgow University Media Group, have always had to struggle for continuity, expanding and contracting with the intermittent flow of funding. Solid empirical work is unlikely to be guaranteed by any unified research policy, but it is hardly promoted by existence on a shoestring. Coordination (for example, to generate the types of data which have not been collected in Britain – such as panel data on patterns of media consumption in households) will need to come from the community of researchers itself.

If funded research has been under pressure to conform more closely to the 'administrative' rather than the 'critical' model, then education too is experiencing pressures in a similar direction. At present this is seen most clearly in the student demand for courses which have a 'practical' or 'skills' component, though not necessarily a vocational character. An issue for the future will be the extent to which the teaching of media studies, with its predominantly critical intellectual framework and ethos, should adapt to this student demand and the likely demand from employers looking for specific managerial or creative skills in the new media industries. If sociology continues to play as important a part in shaping the new generation of media studies as it has played in the past, there is every reason to believe that this field will flourish as a critical enterprise while becoming more closely involved with media organizations and practices.

NOTES

1 A full description of the development of media studies remains to be written. In a chapter on the history of media teaching, Alvarado and his colleagues claim that there is insufficient evidence for a detailed chronology and refer instead to 'four interrelated traditions of media education – sociological, cultural, "skills" and political' (Alvarado, Gutch and Wollen 1987:9). The approach here is similar in that it avoids a detailed chronology. However, I concentrate on the contribution of sociology in research as well as teaching and the institutional arrangements which have helped or hindered the process. Turner (1990) provides a useful history of cultural studies with observations about the role of sociological studies.
2 James Carey points out that this lack of boundaries meant that the media were identified as a '*site* on which to engage the question of social theory: How is it . . . that societies manage to produce and reproduce themselves?'(1989: 110), not as the object of a particular discipline.
3 At an academic seminar in 1975 two members of the Glasgow University Media Group presenting some of the preliminary results of their research were asked 'Which tradition of research would you say you are working in?' The (partly) joking response was 'We are creating our own'. The continuing distinctiveness of the group's activities in relation to both subject-matter and method has proved this to be more true than the group imagined at the time.
4 Desmond Bell, professor of media studies at the University of Ulster, commented on this issue in his inaugural lecture (1990). Narrow vocationalism or training in specific skills is inappropriate, he says, because of the speed of technical change which quickly renders such training out of date, the high cost of equipment and the variety of professional disciplines in the media industries. There is, however, need for a pedagogy which links practical work with criticism because it is through involvement with the practical problems of planning, executing and evaluating a project that students learn most effectively about the professional and cultural codes which shape media production. Most teachers of media studies would probably concur with this as a general view. However, there are likely to be new demands for specialized education in certain areas (for example, media management, media policy) at the postgraduate level.

REFERENCES

Abercrombie, N., Hill, S. and Turner, B. S., *The Dominant Ideology Thesis* (1980) London: George Allen & Unwin.
Advisory Panel for Mass Media Research (1980) *Report to the Research Board and Council*, London: SSRC.
Alvarado, M., Gutch, R. and Wollen, T. (1987) *Learning the Media: an introduction to media teaching*, London: Macmillan.
Bagdikian, B. H. (1985) 'The US media: supermarket or assembly line?' *Journal of Communication* 35(3): 97–109.
Barrett, M., Corrigan, P., Kuhn, A. and Wolff, J. (eds) (1979) *Ideology and Cultural Production*, London: Croom Helm.
Bell, D. (1990) 'On the Box . . .', *Times Higher Education Supplement*, 6 July.
Carey, J. (1989) *Communication and Culture: Essays on Media and Society*,

London: Unwin Hyman.

Davis, H. (1987) 'Class', in J. Seaton and B. Pimlott (eds) *The Media in British Politics*, Aldershot: Gower.

Garnham, N. (1977) 'Towards a political economy of culture', *New Universities Quarterly* 31(3): 341–57.

—— (1979) 'Contribution to a political economy of mass communication', *Media, Culture and Society* 1: 123–46.

—— (1986) 'The media and the public sphere', in P. Golding, G. Murdock and P. Schlesinger (eds) *Communicating Politics: mass communications and the political process*, Leicester: Leicester University Press.

—— (1988) 'Money, meaning and power. Notes towards the definition of a research agenda', ESRC/PICT Workshop, Cambridge (April). 27–9.

Glasgow University Media Group (1976) *Bad News*, London: Routledge & Kegan Paul.

Golding, P. and Murdock, G. (1979) 'Ideology and the mass media: the question of determination', in M. Barrett, P. Corrigan, A. Kuhn and J. Wolff (eds) *Ideology and Cultural Production*, London: Croom Helm.

Gurevitch, M., Bennett, T., Curran, J. and Woollacott, J. (eds) (1982) *Culture, Society and the Media*, London: Methuen.

Gurevitch, M. and Levy, M. R. (eds) (1987) *Mass Communication Review Yearbook*, vol. 6, London: Sage.

Hall, S. (1982) 'The rediscovery of "ideology": the return of the repressed in media studies', in M. Gurevitch, T. Bennett, J. Curran and J. Woollacott (eds) *Culture, Society and the Media*, London: Methuen.

Halloran, J. D. (1965) *The Effects of Mass Communication*, Leicester: Leicester University Press.

—— (ed.) (1970) *The Effects of Television*, London: Panther.

Himmelweit, H., Oppenheim, A. N. and Vince, P. (1958) *Television and the Child*, London: Oxford University Press.

Hoggart, R. (1958) *The Uses of Literacy*, Harmondsworth: Penguin.

Katz, E. (1977) *Social Research on Broadcasting: Proposals for Further Development*, London: BBC.

Melody, W. H. and Mansell, R. E. (1986) *Information and Communication Technologies: Social Science Research and Training Vol I: an overview of research*, London: ESRC.

Miège, B. (1987) 'The logics at work in the new cultural industries', *Media, Culture and Society* 9 (3): 273–89.

—— (1989) *The Capitalization of Cultural Production*, New York: International General.

Miège, B., Pajon, P. and Salaün, J. M. (1986) *L'industrialisation de l'audiovisuel*, Paris: Aubier.

Morley, D. (1980) *The 'Nationwide' Audience*, London: BFI.

—— (1986) *Family Television: Cultural Power and Domestic Leisure*, London: Comedia.

Murdock, G. (1982) 'Large corporations and the control of the communications industries', in M. Gurevitch, T. Bennett, J. Curran and J. Woollacott (eds) *Culture, Society and the Media*, London: Methuen.

—— (1990) 'Redrawing the map of the communications industries: concentration and ownership in the era of privatization', in M. Ferguson (ed.) *Public Communication: the New Imperatives*, London: Sage.

Murdock, G. and Golding, P. (1974) 'For a political economy of mass communications', in R. Miliband and J. Saville (eds) *The Socialist Register 1973*, London:

Merlin.

—— (1977) 'Capitalism, communication and class relations', in J. Curran, M. Gurevitch and J. Woollacott (eds) *Mass Communication and Society*, London: Edward Arnold.

Philo, G. (1990) *Seeing and Believing: The Influence of Television*, London: Routledge.

Thompson, J. B. (1988) 'Mass communication and modern culture: contribution to a critical theory of ideology', *Sociology* 22 (3): 359–83.

—— (1990) *Ideology and Modern Culture*, Cambridge: Polity Press.

Turner, G. (1990) *British Cultural Studies: An Introduction*, London: Unwin Hyman.

Williams, R. (1958) *Culture and Society 1780–1950*, London: Chatto & Windus.

—— (1961) *The Long Revolution*, London: Chatto & Windus.

—— (1962) *Communications*, Harmondsworth: Penguin.

—— (1981) *Culture*, London: Fontana.

Part II

Message production: strategies and tactics

Chapter 3

Reform and restructuring in the Soviet media

Before and after the August 1991 coup

Brian McNair

The task of keeping up with and recording the development of the Soviet media since 1986 has not been easy. Even journalists, who are paid to keep us informed of events on a daily and weekly basis, have been strained to follow the tortuous debates and multitudinous reforms which have accompanied glasnost and perestroika in the media. For an academic writer, who must timetable projects in terms of years, it is rather like the tortoise trying to catch the hare.

At the end of 1990, it seemed reasonable to say that the reform process in the Soviet media had reached a watershed, and would slow down for a time, allowing media professionals, their audiences and scholars both east and west to take stock. On 12 July 1990 a media law had been passed which, for the first time in Soviet history, guaranteed citizens and their representative organizations freedom of expression in journalism and the creative arts; broad rights of access to information and the means of its mass dissemination; specified the obligations of the authorities in respect of these rights; and defined the rights and responsibilities of journalists and editorial boards. In the words of Soviet commentator Fyedor Burlatsky, who played a major role in the drafting of the law, it was intended to transform the USSR into an 'open society', and establish 'a quite new approach to . . . both internal and international information . . . and a clear-cut notion of freedom of the press and freedom of information'.[1] Other changes in legislation concerning ownership and enterprise had created the conditions for media organizations to operate in conditions of economic independence from the party–state apparatus, and thus to become self-financing, profit-making bodies.

Then, in early 1991, events indicated that the glasnost project continued to be vulnerable to developments in the wider economic, social and political spheres. On 16 January Mikhail Gorbachev proposed to the Supreme Soviet of the USSR that it should temporarily suspend the media law, in response to what he saw as excessively critical coverage of his government's involvement in the killings earlier that month in Riga and Vilnius. Indeed, the attacks by Soviet paratroopers on the Baltic television centres, which precipitated the violence, were widely perceived as an assault by the conservatives not only on the secessionist elements of Lithuania and Latvia, but on the media who dared to support them.

Gorbachev's proposal went no further on that occasion, partly because it was intended as a 'shot across the bows' rather than a serious attempt to backtrack on legislation which had been several years in the making. It clearly signalled, however, that the conservatives were losing patience with dissenting journalistic voices.

Their patience finally ran out in August 1991, when, for a few tense days, an attempt was made to turn Soviet society, and its media, back to the Brezhnevian practices Gorbachev and the reformers had sought to eradicate.

The coup failed, and the conservatives were decisively defeated. When it was over, the curtain had come down on the seventy-year long experiment in media organization initiated by Lenin and the Bolsheviks, and a new era for the Soviet media had begun (if we can still refer to the media organs of Russia, Armenia, Latvia and the rest of the republics as 'Soviet').

This chapter will examine the options and paths for development now faced by the press and broadcasting media in what was once the USSR as they, like other sections of industry, seek to make the transition to a mixed market economy. Before that, however, it outlines the Leninist principles which shaped the Soviet media system, and the subsequent influence upon it of Stalinism. It then discusses the roots of the media law, its main features and its impact on the Soviet media up until the August coup.

THE SOVIET MEDIA: A BRIEF HISTORY[2]

The roots of the old Soviet media system lay in the materialist theory of Karl Marx. It was he who advanced the idea that political power was closely tied to the ownership and control of what he called 'the production and distribution of ideas'[3] – the media of mass communication (which in his time comprised the press and to a lesser extent the telegraph). For Marx, revolutionary class consciousness – consciousness *for* itself – on the part of the oppressed classes in capitalist society was dependent not least on their control of newspapers and other media. This belief led him in 1848 to form the first 'communist' newspaper, the *Neue Rheinische Zeitung*, which subsequently became the model for the Bolshevik press. Marx's view of the relationship between the media and class power underpinned Lenin's insistence, first expressed in his 1901 article 'Where to begin', that the Russian Social Democratic Labour Party (RSDLP) should have a strong, centralized media.[4]

Lenin argued that newspapers were the key organizational and ideological weapons available to the proletariat in its struggle against tsarism in

Russia. The press, in his famous phrase, would be the 'collective organiser, agitator, and propagandist' of the party.[5] The work of setting up, producing and distributing newspapers throughout Russia would bring into being the strong party organization which could overthrow tsarism, while at the same time politicizing and mobilizing the proletariat for struggle.

This press would be partisan, following the materialist thesis that all cultural production is reflective of the interests of one class or another. The capitalist press were partisan on behalf of the bourgeoisie, and thus for Lenin it followed that the workers' press should express and pursue the interests of the proletariat. His insistence on a 'committed' media was contrasted with what Lenin called the 'hypocritical notion of press freedom'. As he wrote in 1905 to:

> you bourgeois individualists . . . your talk about absolute freedom is sheer hypocrisy. There can be no real and effective 'freedom' based on the power of money, in a society in which the masses of working people live in poverty and the handful of rich live like parasites.[6]

In contrast, he proposed a concept of press freedom which stressed rights of ownership and control of media organs by the masses. As he put it shortly after the Bolsheviks' seizure of power:

> For the bourgeoisie, freedom of the press meant freedom for the rich to publish and for the capitalists to control the newspapers, a practice which in all countries, including the freeest, produced a corrupt press.
>
> For the workers' and peasants' government, freedom of the press means liberation of the press from capitalist oppression, and public ownership of mills and printing presses; equal right for public groups of a certain size (say, numbering 10,000) to a fair share of newsprint stocks and a corresponding quantity of printers' labour.[7]

Lenin stressed that the party, as the legitimate representative of proletarian class interests, should closely control and supervise the work of the media.

The communist press, then, had to be overtly ideological, and it had to be part of the party's organizational structure. But it was also to be objective, in so far as the partial world-view of the proletariat, which was to guide the workers' press, was also in Lenin's schema the basis of a scientific approach to the problems of human development. To be for the proletariat in journalism was to be, by definition, truthful.

These principles, it should be stressed, were originally applied only to the party press. Prior to 1917 Lenin and the Bolsheviks did not openly advocate the censorship or suppression of the non-party and bourgeois press in Russia. Like Marx, they opposed censorship in principle and tsarist censorship of their own press in particular. The emergence of a more

authoritarian Bolshevik policy towards the capitalist media coincides with
the so-called 'July Days' – July 1917 – when the Provisional Government
banned *Pravda*, smashed its offices and unleashed a smear campaign
against Lenin himself. Only after this did Lenin begin to advocate the
closure of bourgeois newspapers as a serious policy option.[8]

The subsequent 'Bolshevization' of the media system in Russia and its
transformation into the instrument of a single party paralleled the process
which took place after 1917 in the political sphere. Despite policy statements made prior to the revolution in which the Bolsheviks expressed their
opposition to the idea of a single-party state, they moved quickly to
monopolize political power. Confronted with civil war, economic collapse,
domestic resistance (including terrorism) and foreign intervention, the
banning of non-Bolshevik political parties was accompanied by the suppression of their media and the gradual erosion of civil society. The first
legislative act of the new Soviet government was the issuing of a press
decree prohibiting newspapers from publishing anti-Soviet sentiment.
Failure to comply meant the confiscation of printing equipment and newsprint stocks. Press advertising was transformed into a state monopoly, thus
depriving private newspapers of their main source of revenue.

Lenin acknowledged the unpopularity even within his own party of such
measures by insisting that they were temporary, and would be repealed
when circumstances permitted. Indeed, during the period of the New
Economic Policy (an historical experience upon which contemporary
Soviet reformers drew heavily in their formulation of the perestroika
programme) a measure of pluralism returned to the Soviet media with the
opening of private publishing houses.

The suppression of opposition parties was echoed in the discouraging of
inner-party debate. 'Factionalism', as Lenin called it, was outlawed at the
Tenth Congress. Thereafter, public debate between party members
became equated with subversion and disloyalty. The case of Alexander
Myasnikov, who argued against Lenin's policy on press freedom and
restricting non-party media in 1921, is illustrative. He was slapped down by
Lenin in characteristic fashion, accused of 'helping the class enemy'.[9] He
was expelled from the party in 1922, and later disappeared in Stalin's
purges.

The rest of the story is familiar. Lenin's 'temporary measures' were not
repealed in his lifetime (indeed, as the 1920s progressed he became more
hostile to the 'bourgeois falsehood' of press freedom), and the authoritarian media system which he created was subsequently commandeered by
Stalin and his supporters.

Regardless of Lenin's motives, and the undoubtedly severe problems
facing the young Soviet republic in its early years, by suppressing the non-
Bolshevik media and subordinating those that remained to the leadership
he rendered them vulnerable to their effective 'hijacking' by the Stalinists

who followed him. After Lenin's death his principles of partisanship and objectivity, consistent in themselves with a materialist approach to culture, were gradually emptied of their original meaning. By 1929, and the consolidation of Stalin's hold on the party, the Soviet media had become organs of social control, rather than socialist construction.[10] Notwithstanding the party's brief flirtation with cultural liberalism during Khrushchev's period as leader, this was still the media's primary role in 1985, when Mikhail Gorbachev emerged as the successor to Konstantin Chernenko and became General Secretary of the Soviet Communist Party.

THE GLASNOST CAMPAIGN

The glasnost campaign, which began shortly after Gorbachev came to power, was presented to the Soviet people and the world as the rediscovery of Marxism–Leninism's radical democratic potential; as an attempt to go back to some point before Stalinism, when the Bolsheviks could claim with some justification to be a revolutionary, progressive force. It was intended to establish, for the first time since the 1920s, a political culture of debate and difference, rather than uniformity and regimentation.

Developments since 1985 provide no reason to doubt Gorbachev's and the reformers' claims that they were motivated in the direction of glasnost by a genuine revulsion for the cultural policies and neo-Stalinist practices of the Brezhnev generation; by a desire to reclaim the ideological and moral high ground which, after all, communist parties had traditionally claimed to monopolize; to bring 'words and deeds into harmony', as party propagandists frequently put it in the late 1980s. But there were also important pragmatic reasons for the policy.

First, by the mid-1980s the party was finding it increasingly difficult to maintain the isolation of the Soviet people from western and capitalist influences. Anthony Giddens observes that contemporary societies are becoming ever more linked and interdependent as new information technologies break down the barriers of time and space which have previously divided communities, nations and states.[11] The Soviet Union tried with some success to resist this process for nearly seventy years, but by the 1980s it was becoming increasingly difficult to do so, as the Korean Airlines and Chernobyl tragedies clearly showed.[12]

The resultant cultural 'contamination' of Soviet society by ideas and imagery *za granitsu* (from abroad) was eroding the party's credibility as a source of information and knowledge, threatening its hegemonic position.

At the same time, the perception was growing that a resolution of the USSR's economic problems could not be achieved without the adoption of new technologies and entry into the world market economy. This implied a totally new approach to information. On the simplest level: how could enterprise, initiative or even computer literacy be encouraged in a population denied unsupervised access to such a basic piece of information technology as the photocopier?

Whatever else it may have been, therefore, the glasnost campaign was a necessary and long overdue response to crises in the political, ideological and economic spheres, implemented by people who had a genuine attachment to the principles upon which the USSR was originally founded.

In advancing their reforms Gorbachev and his supporters employed the party's traditional method of looking to Lenin for support and authority.[13]

Lenin, it was shown by historians, had been for 'the ruthless criticism of all shortcomings' in the economy and the state apparatus,[14] thus legitimizing the move towards 'openness' associated with the Gorbachev era.

In 1900, on the launching of *Iskra* (*The Spark*), the first RSDLP daily newspaper, Lenin had called for 'open polemics between comrades'.[15] This and similar statements were dusted down and interpreted as support for the Gorbachevian concept of socialist pluralism.

Lenin's appeal in the early 1920s for glasnost in the workings of the party, government and state machinery was used to legitimize the reformers' policy of granting journalists in particular, and citizens in general, free access to official information.

The conservative wing of the party rejected this reading of Lenin's approach to information and the media, or was resistant to it for reasons of self-preservation (the Soviet media in recent years frequently ran reports of intimidation of journalists by local party bosses, particularly in the regions), so a law was prepared which would codify relations between journalists and creative media workers, their organs, the public and the state. The law, when it appeared in draft form, was the outcome of a long process of discussion and evolution involving journalists, academics and lawyers. As a result it claimed widespread support inside the USSR, being widely perceived as the 'guarantor' of glasnost against any future attempts to return to the Brezhnevian and neo-Stalinist ways of old.

THE MEDIA LAW[16]

The Law on the Press and Other Mass Media, to give it its full title, enshrined, first, the right of all legally established organizations – be they political, religious or artistic – to establish media organs, subject to a simple registration procedure. This key clause effectively removed the party's power of veto over who should own and control media. To establish a television channel, a newspaper or a film journal the prospective founder would henceforth have to declare its title, language and location; the size and nature of its intended audience; the aims and objectives of its content; the intended frequency of its appearance; and the source of its finance. Provided this was done, registration would be a formality.

A registration fee was to be payable (in 1991 the sum required was 2,000 roubles), and applications dealt with by committees at the appropriate level of government. Thus, an application to register an all-union newspaper (one which is printed in Russian but distributed throughout the union republics) would be addressed to the Council of Ministers of the Supreme Soviet of the USSR. A local radio station (such as the recently established 'Eko Moskvy') would apply to the Moscow city council, while Russian Television applied for its registration to a committee of the Russian parliament.

The law established Soviet journalists' rights of access to all unclassified official information, and imposed an obligation on the holders of such information to supply it when requested. Failure to do so without good reason became punishable by heavy fines. In return the journalist took on the responsibility for ensuring accuracy and reliability when using the information. In the event of a demonstrable misuse of information, the law introduced a statutory right of reply for individuals and organizations who felt themselves to have been unfairly treated by the media.

Journalists were also granted important new rights *vis-à-vis* their employers, such as the right to refuse to have one's name associated with any item or article which one felt to have been distorted by the editor, or which was contrary to the journalist's convictions in one way or another. Soviet journalists (unlike their colleagues in the United Kingdom) were given the legal right to protect the anonymity of their sources.

Censorship, which was already in decline as a means of controlling information flows in Soviet society, was abolished, although certain categories of output were expressly outlawed. Clause five of the law, on 'Prohibition of abuse of freedom of speech', stated that:

it shall be prohibited to employ the mass media for the disclosure of state secrets or of information specially protected as secret under law; for calls for the violent overthrow of or alteration to the existing state and social system; for the glorification of war, violence or cruelty; for the promulgation of racial, national or religious superiority or intolerance; for the promulgation of pornography. . . .

The use of the mass media to interfere in individuals' private lives, or to infringe upon individuals' honour or dignity, shall be prohibited and punishable by law.

The Glavlit agency, previously responsible for censorship, but whose existence was never officially acknowledged, was reconstituted as a legal entity to safeguard against the public dissemination by the media of official secrets, and its activities were opened up to public scrutiny and accountability. Journalists, artists and all who used the mass media could no longer be censored on political or ideological grounds.

The combination of rights and responsibilities contained in the thirty-nine clauses of the law was intended to create the conditions for the emergence of a (socialist) pluralist media system in the USSR, which would reflect the range of class and ethnic group interests by then acknowledged by the party to have legitimate rights of expression in Soviet society. It also represented the recognition that freedom of information and expression was not merely of importance in itself, but would have a major role to play in the future economic development of the USSR. As such, it was justifiably regarded by Soviet observers as the single most important act of legislation in the cultural sphere since Lenin's Press Decree of 1917.

THE LAW APPLIED

The final draft of the media law was approved by the Supreme Soviet of the USSR in July 1990, after which time, with the exception of those categories of output listed in clause five of the law, organizations and individuals became free to print, broadcast and screen whatever they wished.

As a consequence, a pluralistic media system quickly began to take shape, for the first time in seventy years. The largely successful implementation of the registration procedure resulted in the appearance of several hundred new newspapers and journals in the first few months of the law's operation, including such organs as *Menshevik*, a monthly produced by the Social Democratic Party; *Democratic Russia*, which declared itself to be 'the newspaper of Russia's democratic forces' and took a broadly pro-Yeltsin line; *Nyezavisimaya Gazyeta* (the *Independent Newspaper*) whose founding body was listed as the Moscow city council but which, as its name suggests, proclaimed its independence from particular political positions; *Kommersant* (*Business Man*), the organ of the USSR co-operatives' union, which set out to represent the interests of the emerging petty bourgeoisie; and *Golos* (*Voice*), described as 'the free tribune of journalists' to distinguish it from the official organ of the Journalists' Union, *Zhurnalistskiye Novosti* (*Journalists' News*). The co-operatives' union re-established *Moskovskiye Vyedomosti* (*Moscow Gazette*), first published in 1756 and banned after the October Revolution.

A number of established titles were taken from their previous owners and transformed into independent publications. *Moskovskiye Novosti* (*Moscow News*), for example, a title which existed before 1985 when it was run by the Novosti news organization, became the property of an independent journalists' collective, which ran the newspaper on a self-financing, cost-accounting basis.[17]

As a result of these new publications coming into being there was an unprecedented explosion of political debate and commentary in the Soviet media, much of it hostile to Gorbachev's all-union government. Many of the independent newspapers adopted the western liberal pluralist model and positioned themselves in an adversarial relationship to the government. As the battles lines were drawn and redrawn between the central government, the governments of the republics, the military and the other key players in the ongoing political turmoil inside the USSR, the print media tended to identify themselves with the various sides. The 'official' press, such as *Pravda* (*Truth*) (the organ of the CPSU Central Committee), *Krasnaya Zvezda* (*Red Star*) (the Defence Ministry's newspaper) and *Sovetskaya Rossiya* (*Soviet Russia*) (the official organ of the Russian parliament) lined up behind the conservatives in their attempts to halt and reverse the reform process, while the 'unofficial', independent press sided to a greater or lesser extent with the reformers.

A practical illustration of this diversity was shown in coverage of events in the Baltic republics in January 1991. On the 13th of that month Soviet paratroopers, responding to a call by the self-styled 'Committee for National Salvation' in Vilnius, Lithuania, stormed the city's TV centre, killing thirteen people. On 16 January the official news agency TASS transmitted its account of events, which was carried in *Pravda* and other official organs. The TASS report supported the National Salvation Committee's call for direct presidential rule and the overthrow of the elected republican government. It reproduced without qualification the committee's castigation of the 'Landsbergis clique' as a 'bourgeois–nationalist group'. The (democratically–elected) Landsbergis government was accused of having provoked the paratroopers into attacking by carrying out a 'parliamentary overthrow' of Soviet power. The Lithuanian government was accused of trying to turn the republic into a platform from which the western secret services could restore capitalism in the USSR. The report ended by observing that 'today in Lithuania dual-power has been established: the authority of the bourgeois–nationalist Supreme Soviet and the authority of the Lithuanian Committee for National Salvation' (in fact, the Committee for National Salvation had no legal authority, as President Gorbachev himself made clear a few days after the killings took place). This situation, it was noted ominously, could not last long. The report ended with a call for the restoration of Soviet law and the Soviet constitution to the republic.

This was the line taken by the great majority of the established official media, including television. The independent media, however, covered events rather differently:

Today's issue of *Moscow News* is printed with black borders. We are mourning the Baltic victims, but not only them. On the bloody Sunday of January 13, guns were fired at democracy. For the first time in the Soviet Union, a blow was dealt to a government freely elected by the people.

A regime in its death throes has a last-ditch stand: economic reform has blocked, censorship of the media reinstated, brazen demagogy revived, and an open war on the Republics declared. . . .

> The right to self-determination of all Soviet nations has been violated. The events in Lithuania can be unambiguously defined as CRIMINAL [their emphasis]. . . .
>
> After the bloody Sunday in Vilnius, what is left of our President's favourite topics of 'humane socialism', 'new thinking' and the 'European home'? Virtually nothing.[18]

Here, and in several other publications, Gorbachev and his administration were labelled as 'criminal'. Indeed, along the outside walls of the *Moskovskiye Novosti* building in Pushkin Square posters, placards and slogans were pasted up bearing the simple message – 'Down with Gorbachev! Down with Bolshevism!'

Clearly, then, a diverse media was coming into existence in the USSR, politically independent and (to varying degrees) economically self-financing. Voices other than those of the party leadership were being heard. Journalists who wished to criticize the Soviet political establishment had no longer to fear beatings, imprisonment, and KGB harassment.

Soviet journalists often excused the continuing reticence and hesitancy of some categories of their coverage (particularly international news) by reference to their 'genetic collective memory' of Stalinism, and what it did to their professional standards. The media law put in place the preconditions whereby that genetic memory could begin to be erased.

In the sphere of television, the impact of the law was most clearly seen in the establishment of Russian Television, which began transmitting on 13 May 1991, on the second all-union channel, initially for 6 hours a day. Russian Television thus became the first TV channel to be operated independently of the All-Union State Television and Radio Broadcasting Company (formerly Gostelradio), and was able to circumvent the latters's relatively conservative, pro-party stance. While Gostelradio's Central Television was able to restrain, cancel and if necessary ban the more radical programmes which it produced such as *Vzglyad*, *TSN* and *Prozhektor Perestroiki*, Russian Television could pursue an adversarial relationship with the central government in its coverage of such issues as the Baltic killings, strikes and ethnic conflict.

As the director of Russian TV, Sergei Podgorbunsky, put it just before the channel went on air, Russian Television intended 'to defend consistently the rights of citizens to "receive through the mass media reliable information on the activities of state organs, public organisations, and official persons", as enshrined in the Media Law'.[19] In particular, noted Podgorbunsky, the programme *Vesti* (*News*) would compete with *Vremya* to provide 'objective, timely information about events, in all their complexity, taking place in today's world'.

1991 AND AFTER

The media law was intended to institutionalize and provide legal guarantees for a pluralistic media system and a culture of public debate. By the beginning of 1991 such a culture was taking shape. As one Soviet commentator put it in January 1991, the media law and the process of glasnost in general had let the genii of pluralism and debate escape from their bottles, and it was difficult to see how they could ever be forced back inside. As he put it, 'too much truth is out'.[20] However, the events of January 1991 in the Baltic republics had repercussions for the newly independent media which showed that such confidence was premature.

As the Soviet political system entered what turned out to be its terminal crisis, so the journalists came under intensifying pressure to moderate the tone of their coverage of sensitive issues, such as the shootings in the Baltic. Having called forth an independent media the central government, like those of many other countries, now found that its policies and actions were being subjected to unwelcome (and for the CPSU) unprecedented scrutiny, most of it far from sympathetic. In response, Gorbachev and his administration began to show signs of backtracking on the strategy of glasnost, and of mobilizing their still considerable array of weapons to force the media to become what Gorbachev called 'more objective'.

One should of course acknowledge that Gorbachev had been placed (and had placed himself) in an extremely difficult and thankless position. His policies in the cultural sphere had been highly successful, making possible the kind of sustained critical commentary on his government which became evident after the summer of 1990. But the failure of his economic policy, and the rising nationalism in most of the republics, meant that the cultural freedom which he was instrumental in creating was turned against him. In a liberal democracy this situation would have provoked an election. In the USSR, however, there was no coherent alternative to the CPSU at the all-union level, and no mechanism for an orderly transfer of power to that opposition if and when it came into being.

Consequently, Gorbachev was faced with the serious risk of civil war – or rather, civil wars between, on the one hand, the republics and the centre (complicated by proliferating ethnic conflicts *within* the republics) and, on the other, between conservatives and reformers within the state apparatus. We need hardly be surprised at his reluctance to allow increasing social discontent, expressed publicly through the media, to lead either to the destruction of the Soviet state or to the imposition of a right-wing military dictatorship, as was attempted in Lithuania in January 1991. Few governments, faced with such pressures, would have allowed a hostile media a free hand. In 1991, therefore, he adopted a policy of threatening, intimidating and heightening political control of the media with the aim of curbing what he saw as their excesses.

We have already referred to *Moskovskiye Novosti's* coverage of the Vilnius violence, and its description at that time of the central government as a 'criminal regime'. The impact of this particular attack was heightened by the fact that the paper had traditionally been a fervent supporter of Gorbachev, backing him every step of the way. Consequently, when he read this story he was especially angry. During a closed session of the Supreme Soviet of the USSR held in the Kremlin on 15 January Gorbachev began by suggesting that 'the Supreme Soviet take over control of all of TV, radio and newspapers, to ensure that they include all points of view'.[21]

He was suggesting that the Supreme Soviet – still dominated by forces loyal to the government – take upon itself responsibility for ensuring the 'objectivity' of the press.

One deputy responded that the media were already objective, in so far as they allowed for a diversity of viewpoints to be heard. Gorbachev replied:

> we are all worried that in the coming weeks and months we will be living through a very serious period, adopting the most far-reaching proposals. At such a time, those who are disposed to speculate can always find an object for their speculation. These decisions will not be simple, and society needs objectivity so that all points of view are presented. . . . A decision could be taken right now to suspend the Law on the Press. The Supreme Soviet will ensure complete objectivity.

Another delegate, Yuri Karyakin, expressed a powerful objection to Gorbachev's proposal when he noted: 'the President said that the Law on the Press should be suspended for at least one month. Let me remind you that this was done once before, in 1918 [a reference to Lenin's 'temporary' press restrictions contained in the Press Decree], and the law was not reintroduced for more than 70 years'.

Gorbachev then said that he wanted to see 'full pluralism of opinions and viewpoint' in all the media. To back up his argument he quoted the example of *Moskovskiye Novosti*, his former ally:

> in which they have written that today there exists a criminal regime, and they have included the President among the criminals. I don't only want this point of view, but other points of view reflected as well. I want every newspaper to present all of society's viewpoints, and not only the positions of narrow-minded political groups'.

As the then editor of *Moskovskiye Novosti*, Yegor Yakovlev, later pointed out:

> this is a mistake, and if Gorbachev had thought twice about the matter he would agree with me. A paper which contains the whole spectrum of public opinion is not a paper but a mailbox. All our experience tells us that a paper must have a tendency. I, for example, won't publish an

article by Colonel Alksnis [a leading conservative deputy in the Supreme Soviet] unless it is accompanied by a commentary.[22]

To the relief of the reformist deputies Gorbachev was persuaded to withdraw his proposal to suspend the law, but the incident demonstrated his readiness to retreat from the path of glasnost if he felt it necessary.

Cold feet on Gorbachev's part, however, was not the only or chief obstacle to the introduction of 'media freedom' and pluralist culture in the USSR. A greater constraint was the party's continuing domination of the media apparatus. Until the August coup, for example, the party monopolized 80 per cent of the Soviet Union's newsprint production so that, if there were a desire to do so, it was relatively easy for the government to make life difficult for troublesome newspapers.

The central government retained a high degree of political control over some key sectors of the Soviet media, in particular television. After the introduction of the media law, broadcasting in the USSR, unlike the press, remained highly centralized, under the control of the All-Union State Television and Radio Broadcasting Company, which had a relationship to the government akin to that of a ministry. At the end of 1990 the former director of the news agency TASS, Leonid Kravchenko, was appointed chairman. He was generally regarded by Soviet broadcasters as a 'Gorbachev man', and after his appointment the trend towards glasnost in Central Television was halted and indeed reversed. This was presented to the Soviet public not as 'censorship', but as the legitimate exercise of the managerial prerogative. Politically controversial programmes disappeared from the schedules not because they were controversial, it was said, but because they did not meet the high professional standards demanded of Soviet broadcasters.

Kravchenko, on behalf of Gorbachev, made it clear that, as one of his senior staff put it, Central Television:

isn't private television, it's state television. So of course we have to support the state we serve, which pays our wages. Although we do have the right to criticise at every level, even the government, we only criticise constructively, for the good of the state.[23]

Kravchenko's reward for such loyalty was to be allowed to continue broadcasting during and immediately following the August coup. While the majority of independent newspapers and broadcasting organizations were immediately closed down, those on whom the conservatives could depend, such as Gostelradio, TASS, *Pravda*, *Sovetskaya Rossiya* and *Krasnaya Zvezda*, continued to appear.

But when the coup plotters were rejected by the Soviet people, so were their media organs. The day after Gorbachev returned from the Crimea the pro-coup newspapers were summarily closed down by decree of the Russian president Boris Yeltsin, and their assets 'nationalized'.

The Russian government's response to those newspapers which it felt had betrayed glasnost and perestroika was perhaps understandable, but not universally welcomed. The staunchly anti-coup Union of Journalists, and the prominent radical newspaper *Komsomolskaya Pravda*, were among those voices which declared unambiguously against the wholesale confiscations of assets and the bannings of titles such as *Pravda*, claiming that such policies contradicted the triumphant reformers' stated intention to encourage the formation of a genuinely pluralist political culture.

It can be argued that those who have successfully resisted an attempted military overthrow have the right, and indeed the responsibility, to deprive the enemy of its propaganda apparatus. Lenin would certainly have thought so, which is why in 1917 he moved swiftly to ban all 'anti-Soviet' newspapers and confiscate their printing presses. 'At times such as this' he said in justification of his authoritarian press decree, 'words are more dangerous than bombs and bullets.' Unfortunately, his restrictions remained in place for seventy-three years, playing a central role in the process by which the Stalinist party machine was able to silence and suppress its opponents without fear of criticism.

Few Russian observers would suggest that Yeltin's 'decree on the press' was the harbinger of a Bolshevik-style media clamp-down, or that his restrictions will last quite as long as Lenin's, but it is a useful reminder that the authoritarian streak still runs strong in Russian politicians.

As for *Pravda* and the rest of the old establishment titles, with their employees, real estate holdings and printing presses, it was decided to follow the example of *Moskovskiye Novosti* and place at least some of them in the hands of 'independent editorial collectives', made up of progressive journalists and editors, who would run them as going concerns in the media market-place now developing. This looks set to be a process fraught with difficulty, since the legal machinery to resolve disputes about who owns a title, or the buildings in which it is produced, has not functioned well thus far, leading to many messy disputes about the rightful ownership of this or that publication.

Two weeks after the coup, however, and notwithstanding legal difficulties, *Pravda* reappeared as an 'independent', under the editorship of a leading progressive, Ivan Seleyev.

As regards broadcasting, following the failure of the coup Gorbachev's appointee as head of the state broadcasting network, Leonid Kravchenko, was sacked and replaced by the leading reformer Yegor Yakovlev, the very man, indeed, who as editor of *Moskovskiye Novosti* had so incensed Gorbachev in January with his newspaper's coverage of the Baltic crisis.

As with the press, 'independence' is the keyword in discussions about the future of Soviet television. When Russian Television came on air it was hailed as the first independent television service in the USSR. In fact, Russian TV was and remains a broadcasting organization bound to a political institution – the Russian parliament – and reflecting the balance of forces existing there. If Central Television under Kravchenko's leadership was the creature of the party, so Russian TV was from the start allied with Yeltsin and his supporters.

Of course it was perfectly proper, in the circumstances, for a democratically-elected president and his party to have a platform from which to present their arguments against the undemocratic, unrepresentative and (as it turned out) potentially homicidal Communist Party leadership. In the post-coup atmosphere, however, with the Yeltsin forces now firmly in control, pressure is growing for the establishment of a genuinely independent television service, free of all political ties.

Two models are currently being advanced for such a system. On one side are those who advocate state television, along the lines of the British public service system. This is referred to by its supporters as the 'BBC model'. Like the BBC, the service would be funded by the state from the proceeds of a licence fee or some other form of public taxation. Unlike the present Gostelradio, however, it would have its political independence and journalistic autonomy guaranteed by the constitution.

The advantages of such a system are clear: secure funding for clearly-defined public services such as information, education and entertainment, and the capability to speak to the country as a whole. Such a system, its supporters believe, would be a force for consensus and unity in the difficult times which lie ahead.

The opponents of state television point to the fact that Gostelradio had formal independence from the party, but that this did not prevent it being taken over by the coup leaders. Instead, they favour a path of commercial development, in which political independence would be guaranteed by financial autonomy.

One of the advocates of this approach has been Eduard Sagalayev, a former producer of Gostelradio's *Vremya* news programme. In his view, state television will always be political television. For this reason, he declined to follow those of his colleagues who moved from Central to Russian TV in 1991, and began to mobilize support for a television system which would be financially and politically independent from all state structures. In London before the coup, Sagalayev outlined his plans to establish a commercial television channel, initially on the Moscow region's sixth channel, serving a potential audience of 8 million people with 4 to 6 hours of programming per day. Start-up capital would be provided by issuing shares to the public (51 per cent), the Moscow city council and the Ministry of Communication (10 per cent each). Twenty-five per cent of the shares would be made available to foreign investors. Running costs would be met by a combination of viewers' subscriptions, advertising revenue and sponsorship by foreign companies. Income would also be generated by the provision of production facilities for western programme-makers working in Moscow.[24]

By the beginning of August, Sagalayev had already raised 100 million roubles for the new channel, but, as those who prefer the public service solution point out, major difficulties lie ahead for any Soviet commercial media operation. By Sagalayev's own admission, 100 million roubles will not buy much broadcasting equipment at today's (hard currency) prices, and the Soviet consumer market is not at present large and stable enough for the foreign investor to be prepared to make up the difference.

Even if it were, many producers and consumers of the Soviet media are concerned about the likelihood of wealthy foreigners and multinational corporations using their economic power to buy into and dominate the newly independent media industries. In the debate which accompanied the progression of the media law through the Soviet parliament it was argued that allowing individuals to own media would risk the creation of commercial media empires of the kind which exist in capitalist societies. The right of individual ownership was approved none the less by 213 votes to 84 in the Supreme Soviet, on the grounds that Soviet media law should reflect in all respects the provisions of the Universal Declaration on Human Rights. As a safeguard, the law prohibited the monopoly control of any single media form by individuals or organizations.

It will be of considerable interest to see if and how, in the circumstances now prevailing, the CIS in the 1990s can avoid the concentration of media ownership and control witnessed elsewhere in the world during the 1980s. CIS media organizations (and the independent sector in particular) are naturally torn between the need for investment and the fear of foreign domination and 'cultural imperialism'. They are now required to operate in a commercial environment, in many cases without state subsidy, in which many of the materials required for normal working (newsprint, state of the art film equipment, etc.) are available only with hard currency. Co-operation with foreign capital will be necessary, and need not lead to domination by Murdoch- and Maxwell-style predators, but the fear of take-over is more than justified, as borne out by the experiences of other former Soviet-bloc countries, such as Hungary.

Zolton Jakob, senior adviser to Magyar Television in Hungary is reported recently as stating:

> 'when the Hungarian press allowed foreign investment, 50 per cent of it was bought by west European companies. We now have the situation where Maxwell owns 50 per cent and 41 per cent of two national daily papers and country press. News International owns 50 per cent of two national tabloid papers and our largest popular weekly.'[25]

With Hungarian broadcasting now in transition to a commercial market-based system, Jakob expresses the hope that foreign ownership of new channels can be restricted to 35 per cent. But, he says, 'we do not yet know if Hungary can support the proposed expansion with such restrictions in place'.

The CIS media industry faces a comparable dilemma: to what degree should it enter into sponsorship, investment and co-production deals with companies from the capitalist world, and the United States in particular? As in Poland and elsewhere in Europe, CIS media organizations, film-makers and producers find that the transition to a market economy has had one great disadvantage – the ending of the financial security which was provided by the centralized, state-run system.

The problems of transition which face the media industries are echoed throughout CIS industry, of course, which is in a chaotic state of restructur-ing and reorganization. One can sympathize, nevertheless, with the desire of CIS journalists and film-makers (as of their colleagues in the other formerly neo-Stalinist European states) to retain a healthy national media sector, not only in the Russian Federation, with its large and potentially lucrative consumer market, but in the Caucasian, Baltic, and Central Asian republics, where the small size and linguistic diversity of the popu-lations makes the commercial viability of indigenous media production more problematic.

Fortunately, the European Community appears to recognize the difficul-ties facing the eastern European film industry in the coming period, and has launched a number of initiatives designed to facilitate co-production which respects and promotes national industries. It remains to be seen if these initiatives can succeed in the face of what is already shaping up to be a determined onslaught from western media corporations.

CONCLUSION

Finally, what does the August coup portend for what has been called in this essay 'the Bolshevik experiment in media organization'? Is there anything worth preserving in the Leninist approach? Is there a valid distinction between Lenin's authoritarian approach to the early Soviet media, formed and shaped by perceived threats to the world's first socialist state, and Stalin's transformation of them into organs of his own personal power?

Before the coup, Soviet intellectual opinion was split. On the one hand were those who stressed the continuity between Lenin's policies towards the media and those of Stalin, arguing that the latter merely refined and radicalized a process of stifling dissent and discussion which had begun with Lenin himself. For this group, the return to 'authentic Leninism' espoused by the Gorbachev government was a totally misconceived project. For them, nothing short of liberal pluralism on the familiar western model would do.

On the other hand, the view of Gorbachev and his supporters was, as suggested above, that one could find in Lenin's thinking all the concepts and principles which underpinned the modern glasnost campaign, and that the party's task was to rediscover and reclaim the radical, progressive kernel of his thinking on this and other matters.

From a materialist theoretical perspective, and from the experience of capitalist media development, it is hard to disagree with Lenin's critique of the liberal pluralist concept of 'press freedom'. One can also find sympathy with his definition of an alternative freedom, founded on positive rights of access to the mass media for the majority. And it is certainly true, as the Gorbachev wing of the party argued, that Lenin did at various times, both before and after the October Revolution, support the pursuit of 'open polemics', of criticism and self-criticism in the media and elsewhere, and of openness in all affairs of the state and government.

Yet he failed to ensure the survival of any of these concepts, just as he failed to prevent Stalin's bureaucratic take-over of the party apparatus, even while he was still alive. In media and cultural policy the Leninist approach can be said to have failed, since it demonstrably gave birth to Stalinism. The question still to be answered (and this applies to all aspects of the Marxist-Leninist experience) is: did it have to do so, or was there an alternative road which might have avoided bureaucratic despotism, and which might still assist in the formulation of a democratic socialist media policy, relevant not only to the people of the CIS but to those of other societies?

Even before the coup, it might be thought that, for the Soviets, the answer to this question was contained in the decision of the inhabitants of Leningrad to rename their city St Petersburg. After the coup, and the final collapse of Communist Party authority, it hardly seems relevant even to pose it.

There are those, none the less, who will continue to argue for systems of media organization which are neither completely 'free market' nor subordinated to authoritarian political systems. One suspects that, for some time at least, they will not be heard with a sympathetic ear in what remains of the Soviet Union.

NOTES

1 From an interview broadcast by the Moscow Home Service, 6 October 1989, and published in *Summary of World Broadcasts*, 11 October 1989. The 'freedom of the press', in this context, may be taken to incorporate the freedom of the media as a whole, including television and film.
2 A fuller account of some of the material presented in this essay can be found in B. McNair, (1991) *Glasnost, Perestroika, and the Soviet Media*, London: Routledge.
3 From 'The German ideology', in Karl Marx and Friedrich Engels (1976)

Collected Works, vol. 4, London: Lawrence & Wishart.
4 Lenin's writings on the theme of communication are collected together in *Lenin v Pechati*, Moscow: Politizdat 1958; and *Lenin About the Press*, Prague: International Organisation of Journalists 1972.
5 From 'Where to begin?', *Collected Works*, vol. 5, Moscow: Progress Publishers 1961: 24.
6 *Lenin About the Press*: 149.
7 *Collected Works*, vol. 24, Moscow: Progress Publishers 1964: 283.
8 In September 1917 Lenin wrote that it would be necessary for a Soviet government to suppress the bourgeois counter-revolutionary papers, to confiscate their printing presses, to declare private advertisements in the papers a state monopoly, to transfer them to the paper published by the Soviets, the paper that tells the peasants the truth. Only in this way can and must the bourgeoisie be deprived of its powerful weapon of lying and slandering, deceiving the people with impunity, and preparing a counter-revolution. (*Collected Works*, vol. 26, Moscow: Progress Publishers 1972: 67)
9 From *Lenin v Pechati*: 644.
10 For the best and most detailed account of Stalinism and its impact on Soviet society, see Roy Medvedev (1989) *Let History Judge*, London: Hutchinson.
11 Anthony Giddens (1988) *The Consequences of Modernity*, Cambridge: Polity Press.
12 For a discussion of the impact of these events on western media images of the USSR see B. McNair, (1988) *Images of the Enemy*, London: Routledge.
13 In 1989 the party's publishing house, Politizdat, produced a volume entitled *Lenin o Glasnosti* (*Lenin on Glasnost*) which in traditional CPSU fashion reflected the view that no doctrinal reform of Marxism–Leninism is legitimate unless it can be shown to have been personally endorsed by the founder of the Soviet state himself.
14 Leonid Onikov (1988) 'Glasnost i demokratiya', *Pravda*, 19 June.
15 *Lenin About the Press*: 61.
16 This section is based on the text of the law published by *Izvestia* on 20 June 1990.
17 The introduction of the law produced some confusion about rights of ownership of media organs, leading in several cases to protracted legal actions. *Literaturnaya Gazyeta* (*Literary Gazette*), for example, once the official organ of the Writer's Union, was effectively 'hijacked' by a collective of the production staff, and now announces itself as the 'free tribune of writers'.
18 *Moscow News* 3, 20 January 1991.
19 S. Podgorbunsky, (1991) 'Televideniye Rossii', *7 Dnyei* 20.
20 From the transcript of the Supreme Soviet session of 16 January 1991, as reported by *Moscow News* 4, 27 January–3 February 1991.
21 ibid.
22 From an interview conducted by the author in January 1991. In the course of this interview Yakovlev clarified *Moscow News*'s position as regards Gorbachev's 'criminality':

> We have a long-standing relationship with Gorbachev. He got used to us always supporting him, and he was offended by the fact that our position has changed. He thinks that *Moscow News* has changed, and we think that he has changed . . . . But we don't think [Gorbachev is a criminal]. We think that Gorbachev acts within a regime which has existed for seventy-three years, and he has done a lot to overcome this regime. But none the less he is now acting foolishly.

23 Reported on *Newsnight*, BBC 2, 19 March 1991.
24 E. Sagalayev (1991) 'News on Soviet television: breakthrough to independence', paper delivered at the International Television Studies Conference, London, July.
25 S. Turner (1991) 'West looks set to dominate Hungary', *Broadcast*, 7 June.

Chapter 4

The Northern Ireland Information Service and the media

Aims, strategy, tactics

David Miller

Media images of Northern Ireland have been the subject of critical analysis by researchers since the early years of the current period of 'troubles'. Many have argued that the media concentrate on violence at the expense of background or contextual information (Curtis 1984; Elliot 1977; Schlesinger 1987; Schlesinger, Murdock and Elliot 1983). The continuing flow of decontextualized and seemingly irrational violent incidents are assumed by many critics to 'fit' unproblematically with the psychological warfare strategies of the state and thus to allow official sources to dominate the news. Schlesinger has argued that one-dimensional coverage of this type 'reflects, at least in part, the effective long-term strategy of attrition waged by the British state in its psychological-warfare campaign, one which has involved increasingly sophisticated public relations techniques' (1981: 92). However, these 'sophisticated' public relations techniques have, in fact, come in for very little study. Additionally most critical analysis has itself concentrated on how violence is reported with a consequent neglect of the role of other images of Northern Ireland. One reason for this focus on the coverage of violence by media critics is clear. National television and press reporting *is* dominated by violence or conflict-related incidents (Elliot 1977). A further reason is the 'media-centric' (Schlesinger 1990) approach of many studies which concentrate on the production of news or on news content, with a consequent neglect of the perspectives and media strategies of powerful (and less-powerful) source organizations. Once we begin to investigate them it becomes clear that it is indeed only 'in part' that the coverage of violence reflects the long-term strategy of the British state. For example, the Northern Ireland Office (NIO) itself has criticized media portrayals of Northern Ireland in terms which are similar to some academic critiques: 'Most people, dependent on the media for their information, see Northern Ireland as a community in turmoil – wracked by violence, bitterly divided, socially regressive. That perception is wrong' (NIO 1989: 72). Apparently, then, the NIO itself is not *always* keen on the type of reporting which is current in British news coverage of Northern Ireland.

The Northern Ireland Information Service (NIIS) is the press and public relations division of the NIO, the British government department responsible for running Northern Ireland. The Information Service is a major source of political news on Northern Ireland. It delivers press releases to news desks in Belfast three times a day and in 1991–2 employed fifty-eight staff in its Belfast and London offices (*Hansard*, 7 May 1991: 429 (w)). In 1989–90 it spent £7.238 million on press and PR, administering a population of 1.5 million (*Hansard*, 2 April 1990: 451–2 (w)). In the same year, by comparison, the Scottish Office, which administers 5 million people, spent £1.4 million (*Hansard*, 30 April 1991: 158–9 (w)).

This chapter will examine NIO public relations aims, strategy and tactics.[1] First, after a short introduction to interpretations of the conflict in Ireland, I will look at the broad strategy of the Information Service. Using the example of a publicity booklet issued in 1989 I will illustrate the general picture of the conflict the NIO attempts to paint. Second, I will examine some key themes which have been emphasized by the NIO and demonstrate how they are targeted. Third, I want to look at the different tactics the NIO uses in its relations with different sets of journalists. A key problem for much contemporary media research is the assumption that the media are homogeneous. In this view the process of news negotiation is similar regardless of the type of news outlet or source organization(s) involved (Ericson, Baranek and Chan 1989: 24). But as Ericson, Baranek and Chan note, different sources have different requirements of publicity and secrecy. I will suggest that it is also the case that the NIO operates a 'hierarchy of access' in relation to different groups of journalists in order to influence various audience agendas.[2]

LEGITIMACY AND THE STATE

The central dispute in interpretations of the conflict in Ireland is the question of the legitimacy of the Northern Ireland state and of the British presence. The official view of the conflict is based on an assumption, rarely made explicit, that the state is legitimate. While it acknowledges that the civil rights protests in the late 1960s against the systematic discrimination, gerrymandering and repression of the Unionist government had some justification, it sees the introduction of Direct Rule in 1972 as having fundamentally reformed the Northern Ireland state. From that point on, the causes of the conflict had been removed and any manifestations of unrest could only be explained as initiating from 'extremists'. This view denies the political motivation of the Irish Republican Army (IRA) who are seen simply as terrorists. The IRA is held to be a criminal conspiracy which is similar to organized crime networks such as the Mafia (thus the use of the term 'godfathers' in some official propaganda). It is also presented to some audiences as part of an international network of 'terrorists' with connections to Marxist revolutionaries in Europe, anti-western feeling in the Middle East, particularly Libya, and was until recently linked to the global ambitions of the Soviet Union.

The role of the British army and Royal Ulster Constabulary (RUC) in all this is seen as being to counter the 'terrorist threat' and keep the peace between the warring factions. The governmental apparatus exists solely to oversee a return of 'normality'. Thus we have seen media coverage of a large number of attempts by the British to 'facilitate' a negotiated settlement between the two communities. When these fail the responsibility rests, in the official version, solely with the deep and irreconcilable historical antagonisms which bind the unionist and nationalist communities in conflict.

But there are other views of the conflict. The most widely held of these stresses that Britain is not 'above' the conflict but is actually an intimate part of it. In this view the question of the legitimacy of the state is central. The conflict in Ireland is seen as rooted in the creation of the statelet of Northern Ireland in 1921 specifically to ensure a protestant majority in perpetuity. The cause of the conflict in Ireland is therefore seen as the existence of the border. In this view the maintenance of the border is guaranteed by both the presence of British troops and the funding of the current administrative set-up by the British government. The cost of this British subvention to Northern Ireland in 1988–9 was £1.9 billion (Gaffikin and Morrissey 1990: 49). Versions of this view are shared by many politicians in the south of Ireland, the Social, Democratic and Labour Party (SDLP) in the north as well as by some politicians in Britain. It is also current in some parts of the media. The *Daily Mirror*, for example, has put this view since 1978. In an editorial, signed by former proprietor Robert Maxwell, following the collapse in the summer of 1991 of the latest round of talks sponsored by the NIO, the *Mirror* repeated its view that the conflict continues because it is funded and underwritten by Britain:

> Once again, a well-meaning attempt by the British government to solve the unsolvable in Ulster has ended in failure. It will always be so. The Northern Ireland Secretary, Peter Brooke, as so many decent men before him, tried to win from the leaders of the Protestant majority and the Catholic minority an agreement on some measure of power sharing. *He was doomed to failure, as were all the other Government Ministers who have tried before him.* The Protestant Unionist leadership will never concede an inch to the Catholic republicans as long as they believe they have a Big Brother in Britain to protect and finance them. The nationalists will remain obstinate while they believe the Dublin Government is always in their corner.
>
> (*Daily Mirror*, 5 July 1991; emphasis in original)

Arguments like these recognize that the conflict in Ireland is essentially a political one for which there is no military solution. Contrary to the logic of much *public* official thinking some senior figures in the British establishment also accept that this is the case. General Sir James Glover, the former Commander-in-Chief, UK Land Forces, who had previously served as an intelligence officer in Northern Ireland, has put this view:

> In no way can, or will, the Provisional IRA ever be defeated militarily . . . . The long war will last as long as the Provisional IRA have the stamina, the political motivation – I used to call it the sinews of war – but, the wherewithal to sustain their campaign and so long as there is a divided island of Ireland.
>
> (*Panorama*, BBC 1, 29 February 1988)

Some unionists in Northern Ireland also question the idea that Britain is neutral in the conflict. Many are distrustful of the motivations of British policy and often suspect their interests are being ignored or that they will be 'sold out' to the south. This was one of the main loyalist objections to the Anglo-Irish Agreement of 1985. As a result of such uneasy feelings, some unionists now advocate either an independent Northern Ireland or closer integration with Britain in order to lessen the chances of being 'cut loose'.

The NIIS has sought to present its view of the conflict as the legitimate and rational perspective in opposition to that of the paramilitaries and other 'extremists'. Yet it is clear that both nationalists and some unionists in Ireland as well as some powerful voices in the media and, indeed, the British military do not altogether share their perspective. Instead they see the presence or role of the British as part of the problem.

'THE WICKEDNESS OF TERRORISM' VS 'A COMMUNITY ON THE MOVE': THE STRATEGY OF THE NIO

The central strategy of successive British governments in Northern Ireland has been one of containment. Home Secretary Reginald Maudling provided an early illustration of this when he memorably revealed that the aim of the British government was to reduce the violence to 'an acceptable level' (*Sunday Times* Insight Team 1972: 309). But as O'Dowd, Rolston and Tomlinson have pointed out the strategy of containment is not simply one of repression or counter-insurgency. When the British introduced Direct Rule to Northern Ireland in 1972 they followed a dual strategy in which they 'Accelerated the drive for reforms and the reconstitution of the rule of law, while at the same time drawing upon the latest repertoire of counterinsurgency thinking and practices derived from colonial experiences elsewhere' (O'Dowd, Rolston and Tomlinson 1980: 201). This strategy developed over time and has been inflected according to both the party in power and perhaps more importantly the balance of forces at any one time. For example, the strategy of criminalization adopted by the British state following the collapse of the power sharing executive in 1974 stressed the essential criminality of the assault on the state by abolishing 'special category status' for political offences. During Roy Mason's term as secretary of state, in the late 1970s, this was supplemented with an attempt to portray the problems of Northern Ireland as not simply emanating from 'terrorism' but also from the evils of unemployment. Thus in 1979 Mason could claim that 'We have created a package of financial inducements which is one of the best in Europe' (cited in ibid.: 77). This compares with the approach of the Thatcher government, at least in the early 1980s, which introduced the rhetoric of self-reliance as well as cut-backs and increasing unemployment. More recently there has been a much greater emphasis on social and economic matters and particularly on industrial regeneration and development. This priority runs in tandem with the campaign against 'terrorism'. However, economic regeneration is often not seen as an end in itself. Instead the creation of jobs is seen as contributing to counter-insurgency strategies. As Richard Needham, minister for the economy at the NIO, has put it:

> It has to be in our interests . . . for us to try and get more jobs in West Belfast . . . that is the way in which we will reduce the terrorist menace. By making people economically independent from terrorism, that is the prime strategic objective of the government.
>
> ('Newsbreak', BBC Radio Ulster, November 1989;
> cited in West Belfast Economic Forum 1990: 38)

Most research studies which have concentrated on the analysis of news coverage or on the production of news have tended to ignore or play down attempts to communicate the reform part of the NIO strategy. Nevertheless, it has assumed a very important role in the approach of the NIIS which stresses two basic messages: on the one hand, that the problem is the terrorist 'assault on democracy' (NIO 1989: 20), and, on the other, that the people of 'Ulster' are 'a community on the move' in which local 'entrepeneurial flair' and 'Ulster generosity' are 'rendering bigotry irrelevant' (ibid.: 72).

The attempt to convince the world that Northern Ireland is getting 'back to normal' has been massively funded. A large proportion of all NIO expenditure on press, public relations and advertising is spent on this approach.[3]

Because of the perceived difficulty of getting good news into the media, the Information Service itself has two staff who produce 'good news' stories for an international market, partly working through the Central Office of Information (COI) and their London Press Service. They attempt to 'place' these stories in suspecting and unsuspecting magazines and newspapers. Naturally, they are free of charge or copyright restrictions. Additionally, in 1990 the Industrial Development Board replaced their PR consultants Burson Marstellar with PR firm Shandwick and paid them £3.5 million for the first year of a contract, which included supplying the world's media with good news stories from a news bureau set up in Belfast.

The day of the men and women of peace

To illustrate the dual approach of the NIO I want to give some examples from the publicity booklet produced by the Information Service, in July 1989, for the twentieth anniversary of the redeployment of British troops.[4] Ten thousand copies were produced and, according to the NIO, distributed to 'MPs, the media, opinion formers and those interested in Northern Ireland' (*Fortnight*, September 1989). It is a large glossy publication full of photographs and reproductions of press clippings and is divided into five chapters which address the 'perceptions and realities' (NIO 1989: 1) of Northern Ireland. Opening with a review of the civil rights campaign of the 1960s, a list of campaigners' demands is counterposed with a list of 'reforms' to suggest that civil rights grievances have been met (Figure 4.1). Since then British governments have 'worked to create sufficient cross community consensus to restore an agreed measure of self-government to Northern Ireland' (ibid.: 7) Once it has been established that the British are simply trying to bring the two sides together we can move on to the 'real' problem of Northern Ireland which is 'terrorism'.

In chapter 2 ('Attacking the community') the message on the 'terrorists' comes to the fore with a series of images of the death and destruction caused by the IRA (although loyalist 'terrorists' are mentioned there is only one photograph of identified loyalist violence compared with eighteen of victims of the IRA) (Figure 4.2). The conflict in Northern Ireland is due, in this version, to the 'evil dreams of evil men' who manipulate people so that:

> Young men and women with the normal aspirations of marriage and family and the ability to hold down good jobs needlessly spend years in prison as the penalty for listening to the evil dreams of evil men. And some die. That, too, represents part of the tragedy of Northern Ireland. Not only do PIRA kill, they do so with a cynicism which is a total perversion . . . .

> (NIO 1989: 14)

We might then ask what the government is doing to combat these 'evil' men. Chapter 3, 'Protecting the community', gives us the answer: 'keeping the peace and maintaining law and order' (ibid.: 32). The 'wickedness of terrorism' requires that the police and army be portrayed as able to deal adequately with the 'terrorist threat', while at the same time the presentation of the army and police as peacekeepers requires that the police are seen as part of '*the* community'. As one commentator noted: 'The major

CIVIL RIGHTS DEMANDS (1969)	THE RESPONSE
One Man — One Vote	✓ One Man—One Vote Introduced
New Electoral Boundaries	✓ Electoral Boundaries Redrawn
Ban Religious Discrimination	✓ Religious Discrimination Banned
Fair Housing Allocation	✓ Housing Executive Established
Disband 'B' Specials	✓ 'B' Specials Disbanded
Repeal Special Powers Act	✓ Special Powers Act Repealed

The Civil Rights campaign—students confront the police in Belfast

Figure 4.1 According to the Northern Ireland Office, civil rights grievances have been met

problem for the authors of chapter three was how to make the RUC appear tough enough to cope with the boys in chapter two and still be friendly local bobbies' (Odling-Smee 1989: 14–15). The way the NIO tries to resolve this tension is to deploy visual images of friendly, helpful-looking police men and women. As well as one photo of policemen carrying a coffin there are four of officers helping children or giving directions, patrolling the streets or chatting with pedestrians (Figure 4.3). There is only one photograph in the whole booklet in which members of the police appear armed. In a bizarre expression of this tension between the

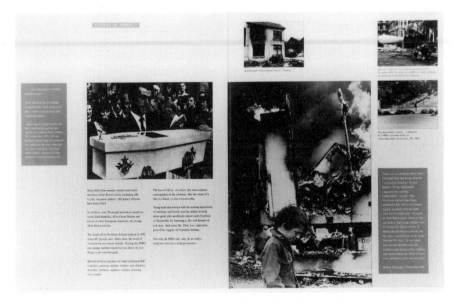

Figure 4.2 The 'evil' activities of the IRA contrasted with, *Figure 4.3,* the friendly bobbies of the RUC

'anti-terrorist' and 'local bobby' images, the officers are seen wearing plastic red noses and laughing as they point their guns at the camera (Figure 4.4).

The point of such images, as the text makes clear, is to reinforce the notion that Northern Ireland is a society getting back to 'normal'. This is why there is such an emphasis on the low crime rate and the repetition of a common official normalizing anecdote about deaths on the roads being twice as common as deaths 'at the hands of a terrorist' (NIO 1989: 36).

By the end of chapter 3 we have already started to shift to the images of what is called a 'community on the move'. Chapter 4 deals with Ulster's achievements in industrial development and employment, agriculture, innovation and culture. It argues that successive British governments have shown a 'high degree of commitment' to Northern Ireland by subsidizing public expenditure and trying to attract overseas investment (ibid.: 44). There are many colour photographs showing some of the developments supported by the Industrial Development Board (Figure 4.5) while the text reveals the 'excellent job' done by the board in attracting investment. There are no images of poverty or underdevelopment in this section. What is not mentioned is that, according to the Northern Ireland Economic Council, much United States investment does not stay very long and that investment by some companies, for example the Ford Motor Company, has led to net job losses (Obair 1991). Ironically for a chapter titled 'a community on the move' there is no room to mention the problems caused

RUC river-rescue hero

A Londonderry-based RUC sergeant was the hero of a daring river rescue yesterday.

He dived into the freezing waters of the River Foyle and swam several hundred yards to bring a semi-conscious woman to safety.

The officer, who has not been named, is back on duty today declining to talk about the incident.

The drama began when the officer spotted a woman in mid-stream being carried away by the current.

They drove immediately to the dockside and when they discovered they could not get a boat launched in time to effect a rescue, the sergeant dived in and swam to the woman who was then about 100 yards off-shore.

He dragged her to the bank and both were taken to hospital for observation.

The woman, who is 19, was detained. The officer was discharged after.

Measured against the 1987 crime statistics for England and Wales only two police areas (Surrey and Dyfed-Powys) show fewer than Northern Ireland's 4,075 recorded crimes per 100,000 of population. This figure is much less than half the highest United Kingdom rates, recorded in London and Manchester, of about 10,250 offences per 100,000 persons. The 1989 survey of regional trends showed that Northern Ireland is the most law-abiding part of the United Kingdom.

And with the detection or "clear-up" rate of about 43 per cent and rising, the RUC compares impressively with other British police forces.

So, alongside the priority of combating terrorism, Ulster's police more and more are performing basic police duty; walking beats in country villages, patrolling shopping areas, working with local schools and communities and trying to instil a new sense of road safety in the population.

Red Nose Day. Every year policemen and women help the less fortunate in the community by raising thousands of pounds for charity.

Figure 4.3

by the large physical movement of population out of Northern Ireland via emigration.[5] Chapter 5 relays rosy images of the 'new spirit' through which 'new attitudes and new frameworks for equality and mutual understanding' (NIO 1989: 64) will be created with the help of the British government.

The conclusion sums up the twin approach. After arguing that the public, media induced, perception of Northern Ireland is wrong, it goes on to stress the official version of the counter-insurgency strategy of the state:

In reality, the community, together with Government and the forces of

Red Nose Day. Every year policemen and women help the less fortunate in the community by raising thousands of pounds for charity.

Figure 4.4 The laughing policemen

> law, order and justice, is determined to succeed. It resists the small band
> of terrorists with a resilience which is impressive. It is coming to grips
> with its historic legacies, resolved to break their stranglehold. The
> economic and sectarian chains which have bound it for too long are
> slowly but inexorably being loosened.
>
> (NIO 1989: 72)

Here we have the familiar themes of the 'community' upon whose backs
the 'small band of terrorists' prey. The government in this construction is
on the same side as '*the* community' which is coming to grips with '*its*
historic legacies'. The key proposition here is that the problems of
Northern Ireland are nothing to do with the British government or the
NIO. The position of the NIO in all this is that of a neutral observer or at
most a facilitator for the Irish to sort out *their own* problems. The only

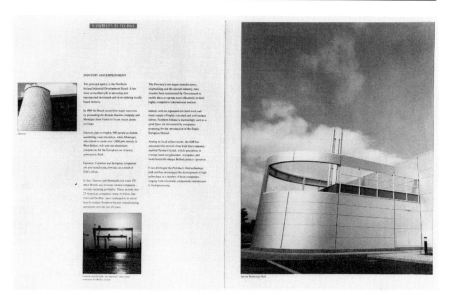

Figure 4.5 'A community on the move'

reason for the continued British presence is the democratic wish of the protestant majority to remain British.

Once this definition of the British role is laid out the argument moves on to the reform strand of NIO strategy emphasizing the 'nice' side of 'Ulster':

> The future begins to look brighter. Civic, family and personal pride are still intact. Space is being created to allow Ulster generosity to express itself in an ever increasing number of ways. Mutual respect and a willingness to appreciate the other's point of view are rendering bigotry irrelevant.
>
> Faith in the future is stronger than ever.

(ibid.: 72)

In this view the solution to the conflict is an end to bigoted attitudes which are to be replaced by cross community co-operation. The existence of the border, the presence of British troops and indeed the overall role of Britain in Ireland are evidently not at issue.

SOME KEY THEMES

A key claim of official propaganda and of counter-insurgency theorists has been that IRA propaganda delivers variable messages to variable audiences (e.g., Tugwell 1981). The evidence for this is often Maria McGuire's 1973 memoir, *To Take Arms: A Year in the Provisional IRA*. It is quoted, for example, in an unattributable Foreign and Commonwealth Office (FCO) briefing paper which starts by arguing that:

> The claim of the provisional IRA to be the champion of Irish Nationalism overseas is accepted by many Americans of Irish origin, from whom it derives considerable support. . . . Elsewhere, however, support comes largely from Communist, Trotskyist and other extremist and anti-western groups – a fact which the Provisionals are careful not to publicise in America.
>
> (FCO 1981:1)

Some politicians apparently believe the briefings they are given and reproduce them in their memoirs. Jim Prior for example, who was Secretary of State for Northern Ireland from 1981 to 1984, has argued that what the IRA 'really want' is: 'The destruction of Democracy, and its replacement by a Marxist Irish state, which in time might threaten the whole of Western security' (Prior 1986: 221). But claims like this were apparently only meant for certain eyes. The case of the 'Marxist conspiracy' was, according to a senior information officer, 'a purely American oriented projection', which:

> was fairly calculated and cool, simply that just telling America that an actor, for example, has communist tendencies, and he ain't going to work any more. Tell them that the IRA is a Marxist-Leninist conspiracy and people are going to say 'Well. . . .'
>
> (interview with author, December 1990)

The aim of this type of material is clearly to suggest the dishonesty and hypocrisy of the republican movement. It is ironic that briefing documents like this one are themselves mainly intended for United States and international distribution and that the Marxist revolutionaries line is not for distribution in Britain or Ireland nor is it promoted by the Information Service to British journalists (see also Rolston 1991: 161).

Another view promoted by the FCO and NIO has been the 'terrorist international' favoured by some counter-insurgency theorists (Sterling 1981; Wilkinson 1977). An analysis of unattributable briefing papers issued by the information department of the FCO reveals that this theme is often returned to (see, for example, FCO 1981, 1984, 1988b). This view tends to rest on two sorts of evidence. First, when the IRA were found to be in possession of weapons manufactured in the (former) eastern bloc it was implied that these countries supported the IRA (McKinley 1987), although when the IRA use arms manufactured in western countries this argument is not advanced. Second, the existence of 'Irish solidarity' groups in European countries is often taken to imply connections between 'terrorist' groups in France, Spain, Holland or Germany and the IRA.[6]

Following the killing of WPC Fletcher outside the Libyan Peoples' Bureau in London in 1984 and the United States bombing of Libya in 1986, the Libyan connection became one of the major themes of official propaganda (FCO 1984, 1986a, 1986b, 1988a, 1988b). Evidence of IRA attempts to obtain arms from Libya first surfaced in 1973 with the interception of arms aboard the *Claudia*. In the run up to and aftermath of the 1986 bombing of Libya, the United States government had constructed Libya as a major threat to western security. President Reagan had included Libya in his list of 'outlaw states' run by the 'strangest collection of misfits, looney tunes and squalid criminals since the advent of the Third Reich' (cited in Jenkins 1988: 7).

At the NIO and FCO the climate in the United States was seen as a good opportunity to influence United States opinion. As one information officer observed, the Libyan connection had 'bugger all to do with internal government or policy' (interview with author, December 1990). The capture of the *Eksund* in 1987, followed by reports that between 1985 and 1987 four shipments of arms and explosives had reached the IRA, gave a further boost to the campaign (Taylor 1988). The fact that these shipments included arms and plastic explosive of Czech manufacture allowed the NIO and FCO to imply eastern bloc involvement although there was, and remains, precious little evidence of this. The Libyan/Czech connection, though, was not only used in the United States. But when it was used in Britain this was partly in order to maintain the belief in the United States that it was not simply a 'line'. As one information officer argued: 'It was more or less to give credibility to emphasising it abroad. . . . It would look bloody stupid if we were talking about Libya and Czechoslovakia in America and nobody here [in the UK] was informed about it' (interview with author, December 1990). Another important reason for emphasizing the Libyan connection in Britain was the possible secondary effect of this in the United States. As well as targeting different audiences through different groups of journalists and emphasizing different themes (where appropriate) to each, a long established technique of NIO publicity has been the importance attached to who is perceived to be delivering a message. It is to this approach that we now turn.

Who speaks?

If the lobby system or off-the-record briefings are useful in disguising the source of an official statement, they may still indicate that information emanates from official sources and as such, to a suspicious audience, they may be tainted (Cockerell, Hennessy and Walker, 1984; Margach 1978). How much better it would be to be able to put over your view by using the public words of other people, who might be thought to be independent or even critical of the state. Early NIO broadsheets and leaflets often used this device to attempt to show that influential opinion was on their side. For example, the then director of British Information Services in New

York told the expenditure committee of the House of Commons in 1973 that:

> Some of the most effective material in this context comes from Dublin: from the statements of the last Prime Minister, Mr Lynch, the Cardinal, Cardinal Conway, and the former Irish Minister of Justice, Mr O'Malley, particularly on such matters as denouncing the support given in the USA to the IRA in way of funds.
>
> (Commons Expenditure Committee 1973: 18)

More recently, the glossy booklet issued by the NIO in July 1989 for the twentieth anniversary of the redeployment of British troops in Northern Ireland uses an assortment of quotes from politicians, religious figures, an American businessman and even George Bush. The title itself uses the words of Cahal Daly the then Bishop of Down and Connor: 'The day of the Men and Women of Peace Must Surely Come' (NIO 1989).[7] The philosophy of this approach was explained in the confidential planning notes of the film *Northern Ireland Chronicle* which were leaked in 1981. It argued that statements about the criminality of those convicted for 'scheduled' offences would be: 'far more cogently made by, say, a Catholic bishop than . . . by any on-or-off-screen Government spokesman'. But it was not just interviewees from the British government who might not be convincing. Unionist politicians too were out, particularly since the target audience for the film was (and remains) the United States.[8] The unionists:

> are the people whom the film's target audience . . . would be most inclined to reject. That Molyneux would speak out against the IRA is obvious; that, say, John Hume or Bishop Daly would might be a revelation. These are the people who, in terms of the film, will carry the most authority and have the most 'muscle'.
>
> (cited in Curtis 1984: 200)

More recently the Information Service has attempted to have their message carried by Irish diplomats, SDLP politicians and Northern Ireland trades unionists as well as former politicians such as Paddy Devlin, particularly in relation to the British campaign against the MacBride principles of fair employment. Sometimes these approaches are done without the permission of the people who are used. Curtis notes that John Hume and Edward Daly were 'furious' when they found out they were being used in *Northern Ireland Chronicle* (Curtis 1984: 201).[9]

Academics are another potentially valuable resource for the information manager. If they can be supplied with detailed information which is then reproduced in books this lends more credibility to the arguments of the Information Service. Many of these writers are ex-military and some have had first-hand practical experience of 'psychological warfare' campaigns in Ireland (see, for example, Clutterbuck 1981; Evelegh 1978; Hooper 1982;

Kitson 1971, 1987; Tugwell 1973, 1981, 1987). The reproduction of the arguments of the NIO or FCO is sometimes not even accompanied by rewriting and whole passages of briefing documents have found their way verbatim into published work. For example, volume 1 of Barzilay's four volume study of the *British Army in Ulster* (Barzilay 1973) includes large sections of a Foreign Office, Information Research Department (IRD) briefing, *The IRA: Aims, Policy, Tactics*.[10] The NIO or the FCO can then use the writings of academics as impartial and independent commentaries. The academics themselves may then be called upon by journalists as 'experts' on 'terrorism' (see George 1991; Herman and O'Sullivan 1989, 1991; and Schlesinger 1978, for more details on 'terrorology').

In the case of the Libyan connection the usefulness of plugging the line in Britain was not only to ensure that it was convincing for United States journalists. There was a potential secondary pay-off in personal and business contacts. It was seen as important that people in Britain and Northern Ireland were 'informed' about the Libyan connection in the event of visiting the United States. Members of the business community were seen as particularly useful in this area:

It was useful that [a business person] felt that there was a Libya/ Czechoslovakia connection, so if he were talking as an independent businessman in America to people he would have a line that was credible to him as well as to Americans to whom he spoke.

(interview with author, December 1990)

The constant attention paid to the right message delivered by the right person was also influenced by the mode of delivery. For many years the perceived problem for both the Northern Ireland government and latterly the NIO in presenting themselves in the United States was that there was no full-time officer devoted to Northern Ireland in the diplomatic service. In addition the officers who did deal with Northern Ireland were British. In the late 1940s the Unionist administration of Basil Brooke attempted to have an 'Ulsterman' positioned in the United States in an information role in order to mitigate these two obstacles. The Foreign Office was not keen and rejected the advance. It was not until the H-Block crisis in 1980 that the FCO relented. According to its then head, Patrick Nixon, this was partly because British Information Services in New York found that Northern Ireland became 'the biggest single item of government policy' they were called on to explain ('File on Four', BBC Radio 4, 23 November 1982). As Jenkins and Sloman point out: 'For years the Foreign Office was criticised for failing to put across the government's case on Ulster, sending diplomats with plummy accents to defend the thesis that Ulster people really did want "the British to stay" ' (1985: 83). The solution was to send the press officer from the Northern Ireland Department of the

Environment in Belfast on a four-year secondment. Cyril Gray was clear about the advantages of not having a 'plummy' accent:

> I find it quite remarkable the impact that an obvious Irish accent has on often very difficult Irish-American audiences. They may be many generations out from Ireland, they have a very imperfect, inaccurate knowledge of Ireland. Nonetheless, they do ask very detailed questions at all times and, to be frank, it's the only kind of detail you could know if you are yourself Irish and have been there.
>
> (cited in ibid.: 83)

TACTICS – TARGETING THE AUDIENCE

The differential targeting of some messages implies that the NIIS recognizes and exploits the varying work routines of different groups of journalists. It operates what we might call a 'hierarchy of access'. However, this general hierarchy is traversed by media type and by professional and personal relationships. For example, there have periodically been complaints from writing journalists that better facilities are offered to broadcast journalists. Indeed, in late 1981 the then Northern Ireland Secretary Jim Prior was threatened with a news black out by the National Union of Journalists if the practice continued (*Belfast Telegraph*, 30 September 1981; *Sunday World*, 1 November 1981). Additionally, there are clear differences within as well as between media types, for example, between news reporters and features writers or TV documentary-makers. Journalists may move between different positions as their careers progress or they may be simultaneously working in more than one capacity. The relationship of any given group of journalists with the NIO is also constantly in flux. Nevertheless it is possible to categorize four main politico-geographical groups of journalists who are treated in distinct ways in relation to the hierarchy operated by the Information Service: Dublin journalists; local journalists, who work for regional newspapers, or broadcast outlets; journalists for London-based media outlets (including both Belfast and London resident news reporters and TV current affairs and documentary-makers); international journalists both London- and home-based.

Dublin

Carrying on a tradition which goes back at least thirty years, Dublin journalists seem to be the least favoured of all those who cover the situation in Northern Ireland. This can perhaps best be illustrated by the treatment accorded to Garret Fitzgerald, the former Taoiseach (prime minister) of the Republic of Ireland, when he worked as a journalist. In

1960 the NIIS was approached by Fitzgerald in his position as the Dublin correspondent of the *Financial Times* for information on economic affairs in Northern Ireland. The Information Service was not keen and tried to exert pressure on the *Financial Times* to drop Fitzgerald in favour of their existing Northern Ireland correspondent, who unsurprisingly worked for a unionist paper in Belfast. The director of the Information Service was moved to write a memorandum for the Cabinet Publicity Committee of the Northern Ireland government giving details of Fitzgerald's background and arguing that:

> Any Dublin writer wishing to become a commentator on Northern affairs should be discouraged as far as can tactfully be managed and that no special arrangements should be made to supply him with press releases. The fact that Fitzgerald is a very able economist and writer and that he has got a firm foothold in the *Financial Times* and the *Economist* Intelligence Unit as well as a link with overseas papers makes it all the more important tht we should keep our services to him to a minimum in an effort to restrict his scope to the South. Whatever about economics being non-political, Fitzgeralds viewpoint and sympathies are Southern and this must colour all his writings.
>
> (Public Record Office of Northern Ireland CAB9F/123/72 Memo from Eric Montgomery, 18 March 1960)

The publicity committee chaired by the Prime Minister Basil Brooke agreed with the director of information and concluded that: 'the Director should continue to provide only the basic minimum co-operation with Dublin writers as at present' (PRONI CAB9F/123/72, Minutes of 97th Cabinet Publicity Committee meeting, 23 March 1960).

In the last twenty years there have been many allegations from Dublin journalists that they are denied information given to others. When the director of Information Services tried to set up a lobby system in the mid-1970s it was Dublin journalists who got the blame for breaking it up. From the point of view of the NIO, a group lobby system was impossible because while: 'the locals and to a great extent the Nationals obeyed the rules . . . there were others, particularly from the South of Ireland who simply didn't obey the rules and you got shopped' (interview with author, August 1989).

The practice of the Information Service has been shaped by the perception that Dublin journalists are more likely to be critical of the NIO. They are, in effect, a lost cause. This perception is related to the history of the Information Service as much as it is to the practice of Dublin journalists. In 1970, for example, four new appointments were made to the Information Service. Three of the four were reported as having family connections with either the ruling unionist party or with existing information officers. *Private Eye* reported scathingly that their job would be 'to tell the world that the days of Government-sponsored favouritism, discrimination and nepotism are over' (2 February 1970). By 1972 there was apparently only one Catholic member of staff in the Information Service (*Irish News*, 9 May 1972) The NIO, perhaps more than any other government department has had great continuity of staffing in its press office. In 1987 when the director, David Gilliland, retired, the top four posts at Stormont were occupied by information officers who had been in the Information Service since at least 1970 when the Northern Ireland government was still in existence. Nevertheless one experienced British journalist has recounted his 'shock' when he encountered 'what I would call racism from the Northern Ireland Office in the way they spoke about Dublin journalists. . . . Oh "it's him from another country" sort of old-fashioned Protestant racism really. . . . Their calls aren't returned. I witnessed that' (interview with author, January 1991).

But it is not simply individual attitudes which determine this practice. Rather it is a complex blend of the perceived critical nature of Dublin journalists, the relative lack of importance of public opinion in the south to the NIO, and the general political orientations of British policy.

Local vs British journalists

When journalists who work for media in the north of Ireland are denied access by the NIO it is often in favour of journalists working for British national outlets, particularly TV current affairs or lobby journalists. I will therefore deal with local and British journalists together. Because the audience for the local media is by and large limited to Northern Ireland a journalist on a local paper is likely to be well down the hierarchy of access of the Information Service. As one senior information officer related:

> Local journalists with the best will in the world are simply local journalists. Their interests are in the Northern Ireland scene and just occasionally they will ask, how is Northern Ireland going to be affected by Nuclear legislation, or whatever, and so briefings for local journalists were simply about the nitty gritty of every day Secretary of State and Ministerial life and there was never any deep political probing. . . . I haven't met one single Northern Ireland Journalist who was worth five minutes of my time.
>
> (interview with author, August 1989)

In an early, and less than subtle, example of the practice that goes with this view, recounted here by Henry Kelly, William Whitelaw's PR officer, Keith McDowall, attempted to exclude all but correspondents for London papers.

> For several days towards the end of last week, Mr McDowall gave confidential 'lobby' briefings about what the Secretary of State had been

doing during the day. But these were confined to English reporters only. No Belfast based papers were invited to send reporters, never mind Dublin based Irish dailies or evenings.

(*Irish Times*, 6 April 1972)

Local journalists often resent this treatment. Some protest to the NIO about the facilities they are offered. For example, in 1989 one Belfast-based journalist proposed a TV programme which would have involved filming on patrol with the Ulster Defence Regiment (UDR). Following initial briefings the proposal was apparently referred to the top of the UDR and then to the NIO, who turned it down. Some months after this BBC 1's *Panorama* team were allowed the access to the UDR denied to the local journalists. But they did not come up with a cosy portrait, suggesting instead that members of the UDR have close links with loyalist paramilitaries. The programme revealed that at least 197 members of the overwhelmingly protestant regiment had been convicted for 'terrorist', sectarian or other serious offences, including seventeen convicted of murder (*Panorama*, BBC 1, 19 February 1990). *Panorama* also revealed that only NCOs and above are briefed on loyalist paramilitary suspects, 'on the grounds that if the Other Ranks were given the information they would tip off the suspects' (*Observer*, 25 February 1990).

The Secretary of State for Northern Ireland, Peter Brooke, was moved to write to the UDR commanding officer and release the letter to the press, arguing in morale-boosting fashion that the programme was a 'smear' on the whole regiment (*Guardian*, 20 February 1990). The access given to *Panorama* led to complaints to the NIO by local journalists. One recounted: 'My argument was that we were much more sympathetic to the local situation, from whatever side, simply because we knew the nuances and the delicacies of the situation much better' (interview with author, August 1990).

The proximity of local journalists to the NIIS means that they are much more often in touch with it as a regular source than journalists who work for network current affairs programmes. Because of their work-cycle with daily deadlines, news reporters on the three Belfast dailies are more frequently in touch with their major sources than their colleagues who work on BBC Northern Ireland or Ulster Television current affairs programmes or even on the Belfast Sunday press. Local daily news reporters tell of their daily routine involving the regular 'ring-round' of sources and half-hourly 'check calls' to the police press office.

This close daily contact for staple items of news and the latest events to follow up means that the availability of a regular flow of news items is more crucial on a day-to-day basis. This often means that British or overseas journalists view local journalists as more easily manipulated. As one London-based television producer put it:

Sometimes you do upset them [the NIO], and we can afford then to let them go and not talk to them for a year, that's happened. . . . If you're local you have to deal with them on a daily basis, you can't do it. Therefore the room for manipulation and abuse by the Northern Ireland Office with local journalists is much more acute.

(interview with author, January 1991)

Indeed, in his study of the Information Service, Hardy found that, over a three-month period, the three Belfast dailies used between 57 and 68 per cent of NIO press releases as the basis for news stories (Hardy 1983: 49), and that the transformation process they were put through was often slight. As he has related:

Attached to each press release there are things called Notes to Editors, which are supposed to be a government analysis of its own facts and figures and quite often I found that, in fact very often, you have journalists using these Notes to Editors as their own analysis.

(*Hard News*, Channel Four, 19 October 1989)

When access is denied to local journalists, it may be in favour of London-based media outlets, with the emphasis on television current affairs programmes. In the hierarchy of access, media outlets which cover all of the 'United Kingdom' are more important for many messages. But public opinion in general may sometimes be an incidental target for image-conscious ministers. The suspicion of thwarted local journalists is that Northern Ireland ministers, none of whom are actually elected by Northern Ireland voters, can sometimes be more interested in their profile in government or in their own political party or constituency than the content of the message. More centrally, though, the local media in the six counties of Northern Ireland is not read by the British establishment or the 'opinion formers' which the Information Service targets.

But 'national' newspapers are not such a captive market for regular press releases. Because they devote less coverage to Northern Ireland they are also likely to put a press statement through a greater process of transform-ation before it hits the paper or screen. Other researchers have pointed out that journalists throw most press releases in the bin (Tiffen 1989: 74) but it also depends on which journalists and whose press releases they are.

In London being frozen out from a particular government department is not nearly as great a hardship as it is in Belfast. According to some journalists this *relative* lack of power is recognized by the Information Service who are 'more cautious' with London journalists 'because [the journalists] would write the story of how the Northern Ireland Office tried to manipulate me. [The Information Service] don't want that story, they are very sophisticated in their judgement' (interview with author, January 1991). Nevertheless, this does not mean that British reporting *is* more critical than local reporting. Some researchers have pointed to the relative openness and higher proportion of political news in the local news media compared with national news (Elliot 1977). Indeed, Belfast-based journalists (on the local media as well as for London outlets) are often sceptical about their London-based colleagues' lack of knowledge about Irish events or the ease with which they are taken in by official briefings. In this view London journalists who fly in for irregular and brief assignments are referred to as 'fire brigade' units or 'parachutists'. When Secretary of State, Peter Brooke, said in an interview, to mark 100 days in office, that the IRA could not be defeated militarily many London journalists, following briefings from the NIO, interpreted his remarks as a deliberate indication of a policy change. But, as the NIO later privately acknowledged, Brooke's remarks were a 'gaffe' (*Sunday Tribune*, 20 August 1989). Belfast-based political correspondent Eamon Mallie, who was actually present when Brooke made the remarks, thus referred scathingly to the London press as 'remote control' writers (*Fortnight*, December 1989).

The point is not whether journalists on national media do or do not push harder for information, nor is it a question of which group of journalists are the 'best'. These differences between the various local and national media can be partly explained by the strategies and priorities of sources like the NIO which release information selectively. Thus a front-page lead on Northern Ireland in the *Belfast Telegraph* might not be accepted by the *Daily Telegraph* which would require a different type of Northern Ireland story to feature it on the front page.

International journalists

A final key area of interest for the NIO is international opinion. Information work for journalists from other countries involves additional tactics not used for British or Irish journalists as well as messages which emphasize more heavily the 'positive aspects' of Northern Ireland.

Interest in overseas journalists is again subject to a hierarchy of access. Journalists from western countries are seen as more important than journalists from what was the eastern bloc or the Third World. Indeed, journalists from eastern Europe have, on occasion, even been refused official co-operation and prevented from setting foot in Northern Ireland. At the time of the H-Block protests two Soviet journalists were told by the British authorities that they were 'Unfortunately unable to make available the facilities for interviews at the time requested and, in these circumstances . . . it was probably best that they should not make the trip' (*Irish Times*, 19 March 1980). Even among western journalists degrees of access can depend on the importance to the British government of the country they are from. French and German journalists, for example, are higher up the priority list than their counterparts from Norway, Denmark, Sweden or

Finland. When confronted with a Scandinavian TV crew, one information officer explained:

> That gave me a real pain in the head, because I have no interest in what Sweden or Norway thought. I really don't care, because it isn't going to affect the situation of HMG one little bit. . . . But Paris is different. French, Germans, in particular Parisian journalists, I make a fair bit of time for.
>
> (interview with author, August 1989)

But the main target for information efforts overseas has long been the United States of America. This is because of the large Irish-American community in the United States and its effect through elections and lobbying on United States politics. America is an ally and can exert some influence on British government policy. It is also because the republican movement has many supporters in the United States. One information officer explained the thinking of the Information Service:

> The prime target as far as I was concerned were American journalists, because they were the people . . . we had to get to . . . because they really could influence policy in terms of [the] United Kingdom. Because here was the leading nation in the Western world [and] if the US government had thought that the United Kingdom was wrong in their policy towards Ireland . . . then somehow one had to get the opinion formers onside. And so I devoted a great deal of my time to the American journalists . . . to see if we couldn't possibly influence opinion there. And if you could influence the media then you could influence the senators, Congress and eventually perhaps, the White House.
>
> (interview with author, August 1989)

In London the major targets among American reporters were the heads of bureaux because:

> I took the view that . . . they were high flyers in their own papers and if one got to know them while they were in London and if you never sold them a bum steer – some day somewhere at some time you might get to see them in America when they were bigger guys . . . And I must say that proved a very effective thing to do.
>
> (interview with author, August 1989)

Activities in the United States

In the United States itself editorial boards of the major newspapers and business people have been the most visible targets of information officers and politicians. One typical journey for Tom King, when he was secretary of state, took him from 'the World Trade Centre, where he hosted a lunch for businessmen in the 107th-floor restaurant, downtown to meet the editorial board of the *New York Times*' (McKittrick 1989: 21). The targeting of editorial writers, rather than news journalists who visit Northern Ireland more routinely, has meant many trips by successive secretaries of state to the United States accompanied by press officers and other officials. In the view of the Information Service this tactic has been a great success. The long-time director of the Information Service, David Gilliland, has argued that:

> Although the wire service reporting of events in Northern Ireland still tends to concentrate on the sensational, the *editorial* comment which is very important in the United States in the more serious newspapers and indeed on television and radio displays a much greater understanding of the problems and a greater sympathy with the policies of Her Majesty's Government than was apparent in previous times . . . . Where, as we frequently have done, we have sat down and patiently explained the background to the problems and the policy measures that have been adopted, we have found a sympathetic and responsive audience and that has been reflected in editorial comment throughout the United States.
>
> (Gilliland 1983: 7)

DISCUSSION – PROBLEMS OF CONTAINMENT

I have argued that the approach of the NIIS embodies the dual strategy of the British state to the Northern Ireland problem. There are a variety of public relations techniques available to any organization, but while I have not explored many of the techniques used by the NIO, I have tried to explore the broad tactical way in which they are used. However, even the most powerful source cannot always be guaranteed the profile in the media that it would like. The NIO experiences many problems in its encounters with the media even at the broadest level of strategy. While strategy is inflected according to the government in power or in relation to the balance of forces at any given time, there is a sense in which the major contradiction at the heart of NIO public relations remains the same. It is to this problem that I now turn.

There is a practical difficulty for media strategies in the dual approach which simultaneously emphasizes the 'wickedness of terrorism' and a 'community on the move'. There is evidence that this was recognized by the NIO in the month of its creation in March 1972. The first (and last) major piece of propaganda produced by the NIIS for the Unionist government was a booklet, *The Terror and the Tears* (Figure 4.6), published in March 1972 in the aftermath of Bloody Sunday when British troops shot and killed thirteen unarmed civil rights marchers. In the words of one information officer: 'We thought that the IRA were being portrayed as

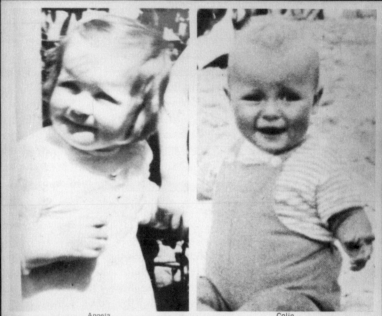

THE TERROR – AND THE TEARS

The facts about IRA brutality and the sufferings of victims

Angela   Colin

"one of the hazards of urban guerilla war"

"It was ..... one of the hazards of urban guerilla warfare."

These words by Rory Brady, political leader of the provisional IRA, related to the death of little Angela Gallagher.

Angela was seventeen months old. She lived with her parents and family at Cavendish Street, Belfast. On 3rd September, 1971, she was toddling along Iveagh Street beside her eight year-old sister when she was shot in the head. The child died instantly, victim of an IRA gunman's burst of automatic fire.

Colin Nicholl, of Elimgrove Street, was even younger—only seven months old. He was killed as he lay asleep in his pram, victim of a bomb tossed indiscriminately by a terrorist into a furniture store which Colin's pram just happened to be passing.

Angela was a Catholic and Colin was a Protestant—only two of the tragic victims of the indiscriminate terrorism of the IRA. Altogether 252 people have died. Hundreds more have been injured, some of them seriously.

Behind the grim statistics are stories of ruthlessness and atrocity by the IRA and suffering and loss by ordinary people of all creeds and classes. Some of these are told in the pages that follow.

Figure 4.6 The Terror and the Tears: British officials thought it distasteful

freedom fighters – glamour boys in trench coats. We hope this dossier will show them to be what they really are – thugs with blood dripping from their hands' (*Daily Mirror*, 4 March 1972). The sixteen-page booklet did this with a series of photographs of victims of the IRA.[11] Around 100,000 copies were printed with the Unionist government ordering a further 150,000 just before Direct Rule was introduced (*Irish Times*, 22 March 1972). One hundred and twenty thousand copies were distributed much to the apparent 'distaste' (The *Times*, 27 August 1974) of the British government, which ceased general distribution of the booklet from 24 March, the very day of the introduction of Direct Rule.[12] Loftus reports that advertisers were then 'restrained' by a government/army/police committee which believed that 'at times overstressing security gave the government a poor image and that it was advisable to soft pedal' (Loftus 1980: 73).

More recently in a rare public speech in 1983, the then director of the Information Service spelt out the tensions within their approach:

> If we are to impress upon people abroad that the channelling of money or equipment to organisations within the province on one side of the community or the other which will contribute to violence is wrong, then we do have to show publicly the uses to which that money or equipment is put. By doing so we run the risk of leading people in industry or business to conclude that Northern Ireland is not a sufficiently stable community within which to commit their resources. It is a very real dilemma.
>
> (Gilliland 1983: 7)

In practice the attempt to resolve this dilemma is to emphasize that the 'terrorists' are only a tiny minority. It was something of an embarrassment then, when, in the early 1980s, Sinn Fein started contesting elections and winning around 40 per cent of the nationalist vote. Despite these difficulties of strategy the NIO and other official sources (most notably the RUC) continue to promote the anti-terrorist image. It is therefore somewhat disingenuous of the NIO to omit to mention their role in the creation of the 'bad image' of Northern Ireland when they argue that 'the violent images that have shaped the world's perception of the Province have also made it more difficult to achieve economic and industrial regeneration' (NIO 1989: 44).

CONCLUSION

While there may be a range of techniques and tactics available to source organizations, the evidence here suggests that the particular tactics used depends partly on the aim and strategy of the source rather than on which techniques are available. Some research attempts to catalogue the skills and stratagems sources use (even if they explicitly reject such an approach)

(Chibnall 1977; Tiffen 1989). But these general pictures of the available range tend to see the media as homogeneous and do not differentiate between the different audience agendas which sources attempt to influence. We have seen that the NIO adopts quite distinct strategies and themes for dealing with distinct groups of journalists and operates what I have called a hierarchy of access.

One advantage of an approach which analyses the strategies of particular government departments or power blocs in parallel to considerations of their media profile is that we can much more clearly assess their relative strengths and, at least as importantly, their relative weaknesses (Bruck 1989). This approach also allows for a consideration of the *developing* strategy of the NIO and moves us away from the narrow and static snapshot which is the result of some theoretical approaches based on content analysis.

The NIO does not just highlight violence. They also want 'good news' coverage which does not automatically fit with the news values operated by many media outlets. In other words there are real problems and dilemmas of strategy for the NIO. In addition there are a number of factors which potentially limit the ability of the NIO to dominate the news in all the ways they would wish.

More broadly, though, the fact that the war is not called a war is testament to the power of official sources. The NIO is not above the fray, instead it has pursued a strategy which bolsters certain conceptions of the conflict and marginalizes others, such that certain solutions follow. The presentation of Britain as neutral in the conflict is part of a deliberate counter-insurgency strategy in which the NIIS plays a key role. However successful the Information Service is in managing the media, in the end the political problem of the legitimacy of the state remains. It is precisely this problem which the information management of the NIO attempts to obscure. In as much as it is a diversion from the question of legitimacy the strategy of containment is itself a major obstacle to peace in Ireland.

ACKNOWLEDGEMENTS

Thanks to all the journalists, information officers, civil servants and other sources who spared the time to talk to me. Thanks to Robert Bell and Bern Kane at the Linenhall Library in Belfast for being a continuous mine of information and to Kevin McNamara MP. Thanks also to Kevin Williams, Liz Curtis and Mike Tomlinson and my colleagues at Glasgow University, John Eldridge, Jenny Kitzinger, Greg Philo and Jacquie Reilly for comments on earlier drafts. Finally, thanks to the Deputy Keeper of the Records, Public Record Office of Northern Ireland for permission to publish from Crown papers.

NOTES

1 These findings are based on over fifty interviews and conversations with, first, former and serving civil servants and information officers in the Northern Ireland Office, Foreign and Commonwealth Office (FCO), Central Office of Information (COI) and Ministry of Defence and, second, journalists from media outlets in Belfast, Dublin, London and internationally. I have also drawn on newspaper cuttings and other documents including publicity material and press releases issued by the NIO, COI and the FCO.

2 This chapter is part of ongoing work on the production and content of media messages on Ireland and their impact on audience beliefs. I am focusing on questions of source strategy and tactics in this chapter partly for reasons of space. Questions of techniques, the range of activities of the NIO and of source power will be addressed elsewhere. The question of the relative power of sources and media is often posed in terms of the ability of certain views to dominate the media. But this is only part of the equation. The struggle over the reproduction of powerful ideas also depends partly on audience belief. Consequently the research also examines the role of the media in the formation of public knowledge in an attempt to recentre the 'Macro structures of Media and Society' which have been displaced by an 'increasing emphasis on the micro-processes of viewing relations' (Corner 1991: 269). This work develops recent methodological advances outlined elsewhere in this volume by Philo and Kitzinger (Chapters 10 and 11), see also Miller (forthcoming).

3 Details of expenditure in 1989–90 is as follows:

NIO	
'Press, PR and advertising'	£12,276,545
Industrial Development Board	
'Promotional expenses'	£5,234,000
Northern Ireland Tourist Board	
'Press and public relations'	£976,181
Total spending	£18,486,726

Adding the spending of the IDB and tourist board to the press and PR spending of the Department of Economic Development (DED) (£3,477,000), the department concerned both with running IDB and countering the MacBride principles campaign in the United States gives a total of £9,687,181 which is over half the total of NIO spending. Obviously we should be cautious about these figures because those given for advertising by NIO are not broken down by department, nor is there any indication of the use to which other funds are put. Additionally the only data available on the RUC, recently released in a parliamentary answer, is not comparable. The RUC press-office was merged with its command centre in 1982 to create the Force Control and Information Centre (FCIC) and figures given do not indicate the amount of expenditure specifically on press and PR work. The figures given are an estimate for the whole of FCIC and cover the whole year of 1989 rather than the financial year 1989–90. The figure for advertising is given for the financial year:

Royal Ulster Constabulary
Force Control and Information Centre   £2,380,000
Advertising   £22,000

(Sources: *Hansard* 2 April 1990, col. 451–2; Industrial Development Board,

Northern Ireland 1990: 93; Northern Ireland Tourist Board 1990: 21; *Hansard* 9 December 1991, col. 454–5).

4 Publicity broadsheets were a favoured form of communication with journalists and others in the 1970s. During the time of the H-Block crisis a large number of glossy booklets and fact-sheets were issued (see NIO 1980a, 1980b, 1981a, 1981b, 1981c, 1981d), but more recently less of such material has emerged (see NIO 1985a, 1985b). What has been published has mainly followed a theme of normalization in playing down violence and emphasizing the 'nicer' side of Northern Ireland (NIIS n.d.; NIIS/Arts Council of Northern Ireland 1985; NIO 1989). Much 'grey' propaganda in the form of unattributable briefing papers is also issued, mainly produced by the Foreign and Commonwealth Office (see, for example, FCO 1981, 1983, 1984, 1986a, 1988b).

5 Thanks to Mike Tomlinson for this observation.

6 Thus a January 1988 briefing document, 'The Provisional IRA: international contacts outside the United States', from the information department of the FCO includes information about support groups in, for example, the Netherlands. Some of this information was then reproduced by counter-insurgency journalist Christopher Dobson (see *Irish Independent*, 2 May 1988; *Daily Telegraph* 3 May 1988; cf. Dobson and Payne 1982). Much of the information was inaccurate and the Foreign Office was forced to withdraw some of it. British author Liz Curtis was among those named in the document (see Curtis 1984). Although inaccurate information about her was withdrawn, the Foreign Office refused to remove her name from the briefing, thus smearing her as an 'international contact' of the IRA (*Guardian*, 11 May 1988; *New Statesman and Society*, 1 July 1988).

7 This phrase is an inversion the Irish republican slogan 'Tiocfaidh ar la!', which translates as 'Our day will come!'.

8 An updated version of *Northern Ireland Chronicle* was made after the signing of the Anglo-Irish Agreement in 1985 and is still in the catalogue of the London Television Service at the COI which produces films for the FCO to distribute overseas.

9 In a recent example of this tactic pictures were used. Two pictures (one before and one after) of a man whose face was disfigured by serious burns after his bomb exploded prematurely were used as 'a visual epitaph to the wickedness of terrorism' (NIO 1989: 27). The man concerned commented 'I have served my prison sentence and I don't need to be reminded of this' and related that because of his injuries he had been the victim of British army harassment. According to the *Sunday World*: 'He received a newspaper photograph of Falklands veteran Simon Winchester, who was also badly burned, with the words "Toastie – The Boys are Back in Town" cut out of newsprint written below it' (6 August 1989).

10 This briefing document which is ostensibly anonymously produced was among others circulated to selected journalists. Pages 119–24 of Barzilay's *British Army in Ulster*, vol. 1 (1973) are lifted almost verbatim from the IRD produced document, sometimes with only spelling mistakes or typographical errors to distinguish it from the original (see also *Time Out*, 14–20 October 1977 – thanks to Duncan Campbell for pointing out these passages). IRD subsequently became the Overseas Information Department and then the Information Department. The present day Information Department still produces 'grey' propaganda material similar to that produced by IRD. See Bloch and Fitzgerald 1983; Dorril and Ramsay 1990; Fletcher 1982; Smith 1979 for material on IRD.

11 Although not all of the victims were actually killed or injured by the IRA. A

photo of the bombing of McGurks bar was included. McGurks was bombed by a loyalist group, but was blamed on the IRA by the army and police (see Curtis 1984: 91–2 for a full account). *The Terror and the Tears* is introduced with photographs of two very young children, one catholic, the other protestant, who are described as 'only two of the tragic victims of the indiscriminate terrorism of the IRA. Altogether 252 people have died. Hundreds more have been injured, some of them seriously'. There is no mention of deaths caused by either loyalist groups or by the army/RUC, although these accounted for a significant portion of the 252 dead. The message is plain – any violence is the work of the IRA. The army only responds to the situation.

12 The 80,000 remaining copies were kept in stock until 19 June when David Howell announced in the House of Commons, in response to repeated questioning from unionist Jim Kilfedder, that copies were available on request. Between then and 3 July 15,000 copies were distributed apparently following requests. See *Hansard* 9 May 1972, col. 352, 7 June 1972, col. 109, 19 June 1972, col. 38–9, 3 July 1972, col. 43, 5 July 1972, col. 179–80, 11 July 1972, col. 324, 24 July 1972, col. 233, 31 July 1972, col. 33, 9 August 1972, col. 495, 26 October 1972, col. 378, 19 December 1972, col. 352–3 for details of the saga.

REFERENCES

Barzilay, David (1973) *The British Army in Ulster*, vol. 1, Belfast: Century Services.

Bloch, Jonathon and Fitzgerald, Patrick (1983) *British Intelligence and Covert Action*, London: Junction Books

Bruck, Peter (1989) 'Strategies for peace, strategies for news research', *Journal of Communication* 39(1) (winter): 108–29.

Chibnall, Steve (1977) *Law and Order News*, London: Tavistock.

Clutterbuck, Richard (1981) *The Media and Political Violence*, London: Macmillan.

Cockerell, Michael, Hennessy, Peter and Walker, David (1984) *Sources Close to the Prime Minister*, London: Macmillan.

Commons Expenditure Committee (1973) *First Report from the Expenditure Committee: Accommodation and Staffing in Ottawa and Washington*, 22 November, HC 29, London: HMSO.

Corner, John (1991) 'Meaning, genre and context: the problematics of "public knowledge" in the new audience studies', in James Curran and Michael Gurevitch (eds) *Mass Media and Society*, London: Edward Arnold.

Curtis, Liz (1984) *Ireland: The Propaganda War*, London: Pluto Press.

Dobson, Christopher and Payne, Ronald (1982) *Terror! The West Fights Back*, London: Macmillan.

Dorril, Stephen and Ramsay, Robin (1990) 'In a common cause: the anti-communist crusade in Britain, 1945–60', *Lobster* 19 (May): 1–8.

Elliot, Philip (1977) 'Reporting Northern Ireland: a study of news in Britain, Ulster and the Irish Republic', in UNESCO (ed.) *Media and Ethnicity*, Paris: UNESCO.

Ericson, Richard, Baranek, Patricia and Chan, Janet (1989) *Negotiating Control: A Study of News Sources*, Milton Keynes: Open University Press.

Evelegh, Robin (1978) *Peace-Keeping in a Democratic Society: The Lessons of Northern Ireland*, London: Hurst and Co.

Fletcher, Richard (1982) 'British propaganda since World War II – a case study', *Media Culture and Society* 4: 97–109.

Foreign and Commonwealth Office (1981) 'Irish terrorism's overseas supporters', *Greyband Brief*, October.
—— (1983) 'The IRA and Noraid', *Greyband Brief*, October.
—— (1984) 'Libya and Irish terrorism', *Background Brief*, June.
—— (1986a) 'Libya: Second International Conference Against Imperialism', *Background Brief*, April.
—— (1986b) 'Qadhafi and Irish terrorism', *Background Brief*, April.
—— (1988a), 'Libya: external relations and activities', *Background Brief*, October.
—— (1988b) 'The Provisional IRA: international contacts outside the United States', *Background Brief*, January.
Gaffikin, Frank and Morrissey, Michael (1990) *Northern Ireland: The Thatcher Years*, London: Zed Press.
George, Alexander (ed.) (1991) *Western State Terrorism*, Cambridge: Polity Press.
Gilliland, David (1983) speech to Meeting of the Belfast Chamber of Commerce and Industry, Forum Hotel, Belfast, 31 January.
Hardy, Eamon (1983) "Primary definition" by the state: an analysis of the Northern Ireland Information Service as reported in the Northern Ireland press, unpublished dissertation, Queens University, Belfast.
Herman, Edward and O'Sullivan, Gerry (1989) *The 'Terrorism' Industry*, New York: Pantheon.
—— (1991) ' "Terrorism" as ideology and cultural industry', in Alexander George (ed.) *Western State Terrorism*, Cambridge: Polity Press.
Hooper, Alan (1982) *The Military and the Media*, Aldershot: Avebury.
Industrial Development Board, Northern Ireland (1990) *Annual Report and Accounts, 1989–1990*, Belfast: IDB.
Jenkins, Philip (1988), 'Whose terrorists? Libya and state criminality', *Contemporary Crises* 12: 5–24.
Jenkins, Simon and Sloman, Anne (1985) *With Respect Ambassador: An Inquiry into the Foreign Office*, London: BBC.
Kitson, Frank (1971) *Low Intensity Operations*, London: Faber & Faber.
—— (1987) *Warfare as a Whole*, London: Faber & Faber.
Loftus, Belinda (1980) 'Images for sale: government and security advertising in Northern Ireland, 1968–1978', *Oxford Art Journal*, October: 70–80.
McGuire, Maria (1973) *To Take Arms: A Year in the Provisional IRA*, London: Quartet.
McKinley, Michael (1987) 'The Irish Republican Army and terror international: an inquiry into the material aspects of the first fifteen years', in P. Wilkinson and A. Stewart (eds), *Contemporary Research on Terrorism*, Aberdeen: Aberdeen University Press.
McKittrick, David (1989) *Dispatches from Belfast*, Belfast: Blackstaff.
Margach, James (1978) *The Abuse of Power*, London: W. H. Allen.
Miller, David (forthcoming) *The Struggle Over and Impact of Media Portrayals of Northern Ireland*, Glasgow: Glasgow University.
Northern Ireland Information Service (n.d.) *Northern Ireland Observed*, Belfast: NIIS.
Northern Ireland Information Service/Arts Council of Northern Ireland (1985) *Images: Arts and People in Northern Ireland*, March, Belfast: NIIS/Arts Council.
Northern Ireland Office (1980a) *H-blocks: The Facts*, October, Belfast: NIO.
—— (1980b) *H-blocks: The Reality*, November, Belfast: NIO.
—— (1981a) *Day to Day Life in Northern Ireland Prisons*, March, Belfast: NIO.
—— (1981b) *H-blocks: What the Papers Say*, July, Belfast: NIO.
—— (1981c) *Scope for Further Improvements in Prison Life*, July, Belfast: NIO.

— (1981d) *The Tragedy of Terrorism*, October, Belfast: NIO.

— (1985a) *Armagh Prison Strip Searching: The Facts*, Belfast: NIO.

— (1985b) *Life Sentence Prisoners in Northern Ireland: An Explanatory Memorandum*, January, Belfast: NIO.

— (1989) *'The Day of the Men and Women of Peace Must Surely Come . . .'*. July, Belfast: NIO.

Northern Ireland Tourist Board (1990) *Annual Report, 1989*, vol. 42, Belfast: NITB.

Obair, The Campaign For Employment in West Belfast (1991) 'US investment in the North of Ireland', *Briefing Paper No. 5*, June, Belfast.

Odling-Smee, James (1989) 'Making histories', *Fortnight*, September: 14–15.

O'Dowd, Liam, Rolston, Bill and Tomlinson, Mike (1980) *Northern Ireland: Between Civil Rights and Civil War*, London: CSE Books.

Prior, James (1986) *A Balance of Power*, London: Hamish Hamilton.

Rolston, Bill (1991) 'Containment and its failure: the British state and the control of conflict in Northern Ireland', in Alexander George (ed.) *Western State Terrorism*, Cambridge: Polity Press.

Schlesinger, Philip (1978) 'On the scope and shape of counterinsurgency thought', in G. Littlejohn *et al.* (eds) *Power and the State*, London: Croom Helm.

— (1981) ' "Terrorism", the media and the liberal-democratic state: a critique of the orthodoxy', *Social Research* 48 (1) (spring): 74–99.

— (1987) *Putting 'Reality' Together: BBC News*, 2nd edn, London: Methuen.

— (1990) 'Rethinking the sociology of journalism: source strategies and the limits of media centrism', in Marjorie Ferguson (ed.) *Public Communication: The New Imperatives*, London: Sage.

Schlesinger, Philip, Murdock, Graham and Elliot, Philip (1983) *Televising 'Terrorism': Political Violence in Popular Culture*, London: Comedia.

Smith, Lyn (1979) 'Covert British propaganda: the Information Research Department: 1947–1977', *Millenium: Journal of International Studies* 9 (1): 67–83.

Sterling, Claire (1981) *The Terror Network*, New York: Holt, Rhinehart & Winston/Reader's Digest.

Sunday Times Insight Team (1972) *Ulster*, Harmondsworth: Penguin.

Taylor, Peter (1988) 'The unanswered questions about the IRA's Libyan connection', *Listener*, 3 March: 4–5.

Tiffen, Rodney (1989) *News and Power*, Sydney: Allen & Unwin.

Tugwell, Maurice (1973) 'Revolutionary propaganda and the role of the information services in counter-insurgency operations', *Canadian Defence Quarterly* 3 (autumn): 27–34.

— (1981) 'Politics and propaganda of the Provisional IRA', *Terrorism* 5 (1–2): 13–40.

— (1987) 'Terrorism and propaganda: problem and response', in P. Wilkinson and A. Stewart (eds) *Contemporary Research on Terrorism*, Aberdeen: Aberdeen University Press.

West Belfast Economic Forum (1991) *Is West Belfast Working?*, the report of a conference held at Whiterock College of Further Education, 2 June 1990, Belfast: West Belfast Economic Forum.

Wilkinson, Paul (1977) *Terrorism and the Liberal State*, London: Macmillan.

Chapter 5

From Buerk to Band Aid

The media and the 1984 Ethiopian famine*

Greg Philo

INTRODUCTION

There has been much criticism of the way in which western audiences are informed about the Third World. As the UNESCO study *Many Voices One World* commented: 'The imbalance in the flow of news and information between industrialised and developing countries [has been] a major topic in international meetings . . . . Today virtually no-one disputes the reality of this imbalance.' It went on to note that 'It must be acknowledged that the way in which the public in the industrialised countries is informed about the Third World is not very effective' (UNESCO 1980: 36, 180).

As a case study, this report examines the television coverage of the Ethiopian famine of 1984–5. Since it is generally accepted that it was British television companies that first broke the news of the famine in Ethiopia, this study centres on the UK experience. In the first section we look at how news organizations operate, how they gather information and what their news priorities are. We ask why it was that the famine, which was predicted well in advance, took so long to be generally publicized. In the second section we look at the content of what was said in news reports, and finally we examine the impact that reports had upon mass audiences. From this we shall be able to draw conclusions about the manner in which information flows between the developed and the developing world.

THE ORGANIZATION OF NEWS AND NEWS VALUES

There was a horrifying sense in which the famine in Ethiopia and Sudan was avoidable, and had somehow been allowed to happen. In November 1984 a British Member of Parliament, Russell Johnston, stated in the House of Commons that:

> The entire aid world has been screaming from the rooftops for the last eighteen months that what has happened in Ethiopia was about to

occur, yet it was only when we saw it in colour on the screens in our living rooms that the Government acted.

(*Hansard*, 68 (1984–5), 22 November 1984: 418)

As Mary Magistad writes:

Warnings not only from the RRC [Ethiopian Relief and Rehabilitation Commission] but also from British aid agencies working in Ethiopia, and from research organisations like the International Disasters Institute, began in 1982 and increased in quantity and intensity throughout 1983 and the first half of 1984.

(1986)

The story of the impending disaster had been carried in the 'quality' press in the UK and other European countries since at least the beginning of 1984, yet it made no international impact on television until October of that year. Many journalists are willing to recount how difficult it was to get the major news organizations to take up the story. Once the catastrophe had happened, Kenya-based cameraman, Mohamed Amin, was able to film it for Visnews and his pictures were then carried by the BBC. Yet Mohamed Amin had in fact travelled in the area in April 1984 and in May had published material which predicted that millions of people would starve. The story was picked up by Reuters news agency, but again failed to produce any immediate and major response from the broadcasting organizations. Lloyd Timberlake of the International Institute for Environment and Development (IIED) told us that he had gone on a United Nations Environment Programme-sponsored 'Earthscan' field trip to the affected areas in May 1984 with twenty-four journalists. Their copy had been prominently carried in some western European newspapers, but this had 'sunk without a trace in terms of exciting interest in the organisations'.

It is little wonder then that by November 1984 the UNICEF representative in Addis Ababa was prepared to go on record saying: 'We have been asking for help since early 1983. It seems you have to have thousands of corpses before people will sit up and take notice' (*Time*, 12 November 1984). The media have a crucial role here. For although it is government and relief agencies which provide aid, the media are central in galvanizing an international response and in pressuring governments to provide more adequate levels of aid.

The story breaks

In practice, despite all the early warnings, the story of the 1984 famine did not begin to break through into television until July of that year. The catalyst for this was a television documentary, *Seeds of Despair*, which recorded the first wave of famine victims into the relief camps at Korem. The programme-makers at Central Television considered that the situation was sufficiently grave that it should go out on television with an appeal for aid. Consequently, they approached the UK Disasters Emergency Committee which decided on such issues. The BBC has representatives on this committee and the decision was made within the corporation that it should produce its own report to go out on the same day as the appeal on the Independent Television network. Writing in the *Listener*, Brian Phelan describes the genesis of the first BBC report:

> On the same day, 17 July, partly in competition, partly in co-operation, BBC Television News showed the first Michael Buerk report from Ethiopia. It was a rushed job, a direct response to *Seeds of Despair*, which the BBC had seen as a member of the Disasters Emergency Committee. Buerk was dispatched hot-foot to get in-house footage. The Ethiopian Government refused to give him a visa, so he hitched a ride with a relief mission. This meant he missed Korem, the epicentre of the famine, and had to film in the south, which was still green compared with the brown desiccation of the north. Above all, it means that this was a typical 'fireman's' piece, with the correspondent flying in and out again in a day, staying just long enough to give a snap judgement to camera.
>
> (*Listener*, 28 February 1985)

At this stage, the story was still not given 'lead' status by television. This first Buerk report in July came midway in the main BBC news bulletin between a story on the French prime minister resigning and one on Israeli involvement in Lebanon. That there was public interest in the story was shown by the response to the BBC and ITV appeals for donations for the Ethiopian famine. The amount raised was over £9 million which was considered high, given the timing of the appeal, in mid-summer, and the amount of publicity which the disaster had so far received.

None the less, the story faded from the news. As Mary Magistad writes:

> 'the coverage fizzled to almost nothing in August, September and early October. After its July pieces and before October 23, for instance, the BBC ran only one famine-related story – on Ethiopia's need for grain – and that amounted to two minutes on the September 19 news only. ITN's summer famine docket was only slightly more crowded: two stories in late August, and one in early October.
>
> (1986)

On 23 October there came the BBC report which finally treated the disaster as a major news story.

The second Buerk report

In the period after July, Mohamed Amin, chief of Visnews' African bureau, secured the consent of Visnews to follow up the first BBC story.

He eventually gained the permission of the Ethiopian authorities to film in areas outside the capital, Addis Ababa. The party consisted of Mohamed Amin, his sound recordist and the BBC radio correspondent, Mike Wooldridge. At the last moment Mohamed Amin received a call from Michael Buerk asking if it would be possible to obtain another permit so that he might travel with them. Mohamed Amin gave us a detailed account of the events which followed: 'The BBC heard about the story from their contacts with Visnews. Buerk telephoned me from Johannesburg and put a lot of pressure on to be able to come'. They were to have gone on Monday, 15 October, but because of the addition of Buerk there was a delay of two days while Amin contacted the Ethiopian authorities to obtain another permit. There was then a further delay of two days taken up in arguments with the Ethiopians over whether they could film in Makalle, a militarily sensitive area. Eventually they left Addis Ababa on 19 October and filmed in Makalle that day, travelling to Korem and filming there on 20 and 21 October. They flew back to Nairobi and edited the material there on the 22nd. That evening Buerk flew back to London with the videotapes and the material was first transmitted by the BBC on 23 October.

We asked Mohamed Amin whether there had been any problems in getting the media organizations to take up the story. He told us:

> The pictures were the property of Visnews not the BBC. There was no trouble with Visnews as they are usually interested in what comes from the field. Visnews offered the material to Eurovision on 23 October and they rejected it; it was offered to NBC in the States the same day and they rejected it.

The head of NBC's London bureau, Joe Angotti, then persuaded the New York office to take the pictures over by satellite to at least look at them. Mohamed Amin continues:

> Joe Angotti was putting a lot of pressure on them to take the pictures – he persuaded them to look at the pictures so they took them over on the 23rd. When they had seen the pictures they re-cut them and put them in as the last item on their nightly news. . . . NBC ran full page ads in the New York Times after they had seen the public responses. Eurovision asked for the pictures the following day.
>
> (17 September 1986)

Joe Angotti told us:

> The initial reaction was: 'ship it in and we'll have a look at it in a week or so because we can't get it into the show'. . . . At the risk of sounding callous, when you say over the telephone that we have a story on the Ethiopian famine, there's nothing compelling about that in terms of rushing to get on the air – because everyone has seen the pictures and

the swollen bellies before. . . . I made repeated calls but they said there was just too much material to get it in that night. I went off and came back and saw the BBC Nine O'clock News and decided to try one more time. I told them that I was going to feed it into the satellite and they were to look at it and it came through to New York an hour before they went on. . . .

(25 September 1986)

Robert Lamb, who was part of a Central TV team filming debates at the UN General Assembly in New York, told us that 'the effect of the NBC report was electrifying. Suddenly the *New York Times* and other newspapers were running front-page stories. From nowhere, the crisis in Africa became the lead agenda item at the General Assembly'.

In the UK the BBC's decision to use the Visnews pictures as a major story had a huge impact upon the rest of the media coverage. Figure 5.1 shows the effect upon the popular press in Britain.

The effect on the relief agencies in Ethiopia was equally dramatic, as Mary Magistad writes:

Literally overnight, it seemed that *everyone* wanted to cover Ethiopia. Reporters deluged Addis Ababa by the hundreds: many aid workers who had been trying for more than a year to pull the news media's attention to the famine were now finding themselves so busy briefing journalists that they barely had time to do their normal relief work.

(1986)

The news of the impending disaster had been featured fairly consistently in the quality press. The question is why did it take so long for it to be treated as a major news issue by television?

News limits

There are many limits which journalists point to when discussing the constraints which can operate on news stories – limits, for example, of time, space and resources. More concretely, in the case of the famine, the Ethiopian authorities were criticized for limiting the movement of journalists beyond Addis Ababa during the period in which the regime was celebrating the tenth anniversary of the Ethiopian revolution. It was an additional delay of two months. Charles Stewart, the maker of *Seeds of Despair*, argued that one of the reasons for the opposition to filming the famine was that the Ethiopian authorities believed the western media would simply use it to attack them as a Marxist regime. It is noteworthy that their attitude changed markedly when Peter Gill of Thames Television suggested a different approach for his film, *Bitter Harvest*. He suggested contrasting the overproduction of food in Europe with the poverty of

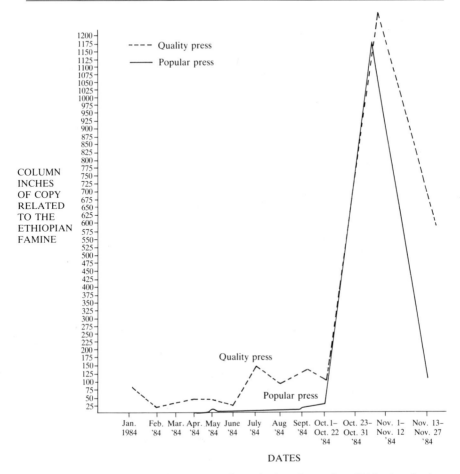

Figure 5.1 Quality vs popular press: column inches devoted to Ethiopian famine coverage. Reproduced from Magistad (1986)

Ethiopia and this met with much greater approval (Harrison and Palmer 1986: 106).

Speaking with us, Mohamed Amin commented that an additional reason for the limit was that the Ethiopians were afraid that journalists would report on military operations or focus on political questions in relation to the on-going civil war. There can be little doubt that *Seeds of Despair* had already partly convinced the Ethiopian authorities of the constructive power of the medium. Mohamed Amin was allowed in when he finally convinced them that he wanted to focus exclusively on the question of the famine. There were still arguments, but he was then allowed into the front-line military areas, accompanied by Ethiopian officials. It might also be said of the Ethiopians that for years previously their Relief and

Rehabilitation Commission (RRC) had been appealing for aid to combat the growing crisis. For example, *Seeds of Despair* had featured footage of the RRC commissioner making an impassioned appeal early in 1984 for food aid before the UN General Assembly. The Ethiopian authorities did not realize the impact that the pictures would have in generating a larger aid response. When this did become apparent, they went to some lengths to increase the facilities that were available for the production of material on the crisis. It does not seem enough in accounting for the lack of coverage to simply blame it on the Ethiopians. Mohamed Amin told us there was no pressure at all from the BBC to go back after the July story. In a separate interview with us, Michael Buerk commented that there was some interest in the BBC in London for the story, but only in the sense that they had featured the appeal in July and thought it might be interesting to do a follow up on how the money was being spent. He told us:

> [After the July appeal] there was a lot of impact and the BBC were rather anxious to return to Ethiopia and find out, in their rather naive way, how the money was being spent – less so from my point of view as I was rather tied up in South Africa and communications between South Africa and the rest of black Africa are rather poor. But on our joint behalf Mike Wooldridge who is the BBC Radio Correspondent in Nairobi and Mohamed Amin – they work in adjacent offices – started pestering on behalf of the BBC and Visnews to be allowed to go back in to Ethiopia to see how the situation had developed. . . .

As Michael Buerk comments, the interest in London in the story about how the appeal money was being used to solve the famine was, to say the least, naïve. The perspective of the reporters in the field such as Mike Wooldridge and Mohamed Amin was quite different, as Michael Buerk told us: 'From the point of view of the fieldworkers, the story was [that] . . . the situation there had got markedly worse' (22 September 1986). This perspective had apparently not been grasped by London despite all the warnings from the aid agencies. In 1973 Jonathan Dimbleby had made a film about the terrible famine which had afflicted Ethiopia at that time. The film and the publicity which it attracted contributed directly to the downfall of the emperor, Haile Selassie. In October 1984, Dimbleby castigated the west for the neglect which had allowed the tragedy to occur again. He wrote:

> In June, Ethiopia had pleaded for half a million tons of grain. This is a quarter of what Egypt and Bangladesh are each given each year, a fiftieth of what the Russians have bought from America and still only a small fraction of that vast stockpile harvested in the Western World.
>
> It is inconceivable to me that the governments of the United States, Australia, Canada, Britain and the other EEC countries could have

been unaware of what was by now a major emergency. Yet between them they had pledged only enough grain to feed all the victims for thirty days.

Even in September, when every international relief agency in Ethiopia called for 'immediate and massive action', those Governments still insisted that there was no more grain available. That was, and is, an unforgivable nonsense to which those tiny rag doll corpses now bear terrible witness.

Now, when it is too late, Western Governments had been driven by public opinion into a belated and inadequate response, although they have the temerity to present it to us as though it were a swift and generous reaction to a dramatic and unexpected crisis. And we are bombarded with excuses: Ethiopia can't handle any more grain, the Government is incompetent or corrupt, the distribution system would collapse. That just is not true. The excuses simply do not wash: they are based either on ignorance of what is possible, or reluctance to act.

(*Mail on Sunday*, 28 October 1984)

This is not to say that the Ethiopian government was above reproach. It was severely criticized for the level of its military spending, for the conduct of its resettlement programme and for failing to move what grain there was into the war-torn provinces. But it is clear that they were issuing urgent appeals well before either the mass media or western governments took any serious notice. The priorities of most western governments can be explained by their hostility to the political complexion of the Ethiopian regime. But why did Ethiopia come so low in the priorities of news?

News priorities

A simple truth underpins the everyday practice of the media institutions and the journalists who work within them – that they are all at some level in competition with each other to sell stories and maximize audiences. From the point of view of the programme-makers they must do this at a given cost and at a set level of resources. To justify the resources and for an issue to be featured, the story has to be 'big' in terms of what the journalists imagine will appeal to their audience. It has to be said that their perception of their own audiences is sometimes wide of the mark. Many television professionals were genuinely surprised at the intense and prolonged level of public interest in the problems of Africa. Mohamed Amin, speaking to us about the difficulties of getting the story taken up in the first place, commented: 'it was the American elections and no-one was interested in a few starving kids'.

The inherited journalistic wisdom is that for the story to count the disaster has to be big and the pictures have to be dramatic. Wendy Riches, the public relations director of Save the Children Fund, described the problems that they had:

> In early 1984, a reporter from *News at Ten* [Independent Television News] visited our headquarters for a briefing on the situation in Ethiopia. He was knowledgeable about the problems and sympathetic to our fears. He promised to do what he could and shortly visited Korem, where he filmed. But the reports he filed focussed on the political involvement of the USA and the guerilla war in the North, with only a passing reference to increasing food shortages. When he came back to England, he was genuinely disappointed he hadn't been able to do more about the impending famine but, he explained, there were no acute cases of starvation to film so it wasn't *news*.
>
> (cited in B. Phelan, *Listener*, 28 February 1985)

Even if we assume that television needs terrible pictures to generate interest this still does not seem altogether credible as a reason. For example, when television news wishes to stress the impact of strikes, they have used library film of previous disputes to show the consequences of industrial action. In this way they have shown the dangers to public health caused by disputes involving groups such as refuse workers and have done so in the very first days of the dispute, before the alleged effects have actually occurred (Glasgow University Media Group 1976). By the same token, it would have presumably been possible to use library film of the previous Ethiopian famine and to say that this was about to happen again unless something was done to stop it. But featuring a huge potential disaster in the Third World does not warrant the same research and commitment needed to illustrate much smaller potential problems at home. This is not always the fault of individual journalists in the field – it is more to do with the priorities set by the organizations within which they work. Brendan Farrow dealt with Ethiopian story for Visnews, London. He told us that:

> There is no such person as the BBC: there are individuals there, some of whom will have seen the story and are interested in it. But overall the priority of an organisation like the BBC is their own national news and interests, and Third World issues come behind that.
>
> (17 September 1986)

Consequently, the view has persisted that if the resources are to be committed the story has to be 'big' and successive stories have to be bigger and bigger to justify attention. Nick Cater of the *Guardian* quotes the comments of a BBC team filming in Sudan in June 1985: 'But it has to be good, as a BBC team made clear in June in Sudan. "What happens if what you find isn't worse than Ethiopia?" they were asked. "There's no story", they replied' (*10.8 Quarterly Photographic Magazine*, 19).

Robert Lamb of the Television Trust for the Environment argues that Central Television, the company which actually broke the story with *Seeds of Despair*, was in a different position. The United Nations Environment Programme had provided director/cameraman, Charles Stewart, with a three-month grant in 1983 to research a TV documentary on desertification in Ethiopia. Central had commissioned Stewart to make a film series exploring the link between soil erosion and food shortage. He had begun to film the series early in 1984 as the situation began to deteriorate. Stewart was therefore on hand to see the crisis develop. Stewart and Lamb himself were on hand to convince Central's programme-commissioners that Stewart should break off the desertification series to film in Korem. Even then there was a debate lasting for several weeks within the company – which has no international news-making mandate – over whether to make the film that became *Seeds of Despair*. It required considerable commitment in time and resources and would take up one of Central's limited quota of slots on the national network. One producer commented that 'the situation was analogous to covering a bombing blitz – you could not do the story until the bombs had dropped'. But eventually the view prevailed that the story should be made because some 'bombs' had dropped already and that a lot more were about to.

That debate could have gone on in any one of hundreds of media organizations, and the more commercial its priorities, the sooner the conversation would have turned to how many people would watch and what would the impact on the audience be? To Central's credit, they did send the team in. This decision had a crucial impact because of the way in which news organizations operate in relation to each other.

News organizations

A good reason for covering a story is that someone else might do it before you. There were strong suggestions in 1984 that such concerns had influenced the BBC's decision to go into Ethiopia. As *The Economist* noted in a development report: 'What put Ethiopia in the front page in October? Most cynically, competition between two television channels. This is the second time this year that a BBC news team has scooped a long-planned ITV programme on the famine' (November 1984).[1] Competition between channels can mean that they will all suddenly pursue a story if it is judged to be sufficiently important, or in different circumstances it can mean that some organizations will reject the story if they decide that it has already been covered by their competitors. Television is so competitive that even bulletins on the same channel compete with each other over the treatment of specific stories. Michael Buerk told us how this had affected the treatment of his second report from Ethiopia. The *Six O'clock News* on the BBC had led with the story as a 6-minute piece, giving it maximum impact. By contrast, the *Nine O'clock News* had downgraded the story to fourth position and led with a story on the continuing British miners' strike, which was then in its seventh month. Buerk commented to us that:

> The Nine O'clock News began on some miner accretion in the miners strike of no consequence and [The Ethiopian report] was the fourth story on the Nine O'clock News. The Six O'clock News was intended to be a programme rather than simply a bulletin – so their instinct was that, if they had a big story, to go to town on it. There are rivalries between the bulletins and possibly [the *Nine O'clock News* editor] thought that he had better be different.
>
> (22 September 1980)

Even with the *Six O'clock News*, the decision to use the Buerk/Amin piece first was not immediate. By chance, it was a slack news day, but even then there was a discussion about whether to use other possible lead stories. John Simpson of the BBC, who was part of the discussion, commented that 'We could have led with any of a handful of fairly substantial stories . . . in the end it was decided to try an imaginative lead' (cited in Magistad 1986). Mike Wooldridge's radio report fared worse. He had filed it while the team was still in Ethiopia. It was a strong report but was not even given peak time exposure as it did not receive the necessary support in London (Harrison and Palmer 1986: 121).

Another feature of the way in which television companies tend to be organized is that they are all physically separate from each other. There is no special reason why, for example, a documentary-maker from Central Television would have any contact with either BBC Television News or even with Independent Television News. When the makers of *Seeds of Despair* returned from Ethiopia to London, their initial response was simply to wait until their alloted programme slot came round, though they did manage to achieve an earlier showing for it than had originally been planned.

But it was their decision to link the programme to a public appeal which seems finally to have instigated the response from the BBC. The view expressed in Central was that as programme-makers they were a little put out by being scooped by the BBC, but that, from the point of view of the Ethiopians, it was the best thing that could have happened, as the BBC would then put out the story through its whole organization – on everything from the World Service through to current affairs programmes such as *Newsnight*.

The competition between companies meant that there was then an undignified rush to claim credit for the story. Visnews put out press releases talking of their 'exclusive coverage' (30 November 1984) while the BBC ran 'anniversary' pieces on their breaking of the story.

This drew the following comment from Peter Fiddick of the *Guardian*:

there were those who found the 'first anniversary' element of some BBC presentations just a touch jarring. Someone who was working for one of the aid agencies in Britain in the period before the West awoke, observed that in fact there was a disaster appeal several months before the Buerk/Amin film hit the peak time television audiences where it hurt, and that it too followed a television programme, *Seeds of Despair*.

(28 October 1985)

One conclusion from all of this is that the decision to feature the story of the famine and the manner in which it was treated were largely directed by the internal logic of the media institutions.[2] This is not to say that there was no commitment on the part of individual journalists to the story. Indeed the impact of the October report from Buerk was heightened by the personal commitment he evidently felt.

But overall it is clear that the priorities and internal logic of media organizations can differ sharply from those of relief agencies and field-workers who are seeking to highlight the genesis of problems in the Third World and to find solutions before the catastrophe strikes.

Media priorities and relief priorities

The difference in perspective between media workers and relief workers can even lead to quite different understandings of what is actually occurring. As we have noted, before making *Seeds of Despair*, Charles Stewart had filmed for an extended period in the Ethiopian Highlands. He wrote of this that:

One of the aid workers told me right at the beginning that people don't understand. . . . We were there for a year before the famine. . . . In that first year, people were short of food for three months but that was normal. In the villages we were in, you couldn't see any malnutrition. We thought everyone was telling us lies. But then you began to notice that the children were a bit thin, a bit small. People live short lives, they die quicker. All that's normal. There's a lot of blindness. One out of every ten is blind in one eye. One out of two hundred is blind in both eyes. Starvation at that level doesn't strike you.

(*Listener*, 28 February 1985)

The likelihood of it striking a journalist is probably lessened if the style of reporting is to rush in and out of an area, with a few hours on the ground (the so-called 'fireman's approach').

How can these differences be resolved? Courtnay Tordoff, the BBC's foreign news editor, told us that the BBC talks to various relief organizations regularly. But Pam Pouncey, the secretary of the Disasters Emergency Committee, believes that there is a need for a closer liaison with the controllers of news. She told us that she now accepts the view that if relations with the media are not changed, then the whole situation could simply recur.

TELEVISION CONTENT

What kind of images of the Third World are offered to western audiences? The UNESCO study, *Many Voices One World*, commented that 'chauvinist attitudes and ethnocentricity in some professional communicators may warp their selection and interpretation of news from foreign environments' (UNESCO 1980: 159). Television is relaying images to an audience whose beliefs are already partly formed, and who share in different degrees a common cultural inheritance. This includes assumptions about who lives in the Third World, how they live and what their problems are. Some of these assumptions derive from the history of colonial contacts, from 'racial' generalizations and indeed from the images provided by television and the press as well as those found in children's comics, school books, films and magazines. It is this common history which we will look at first.

Our cultural heritage

History is written by the victors. In an important study of children's literature, Jennie Laishely commented:

It is unusual for a child to be given any information on pre-colonial Africa, India, the Caribbean or America, and this is the fault of the curricula as much as the books. Everything that is deemed to be of significance starts when the Europeans arrive.

(1975: 82)

In the books that she examined, she noted that the selection of events once the whites have arrived:

is skewed totally to the British or European standpoint. White explorers 'discover' Africa, missionaries 'civilise' Black Peoples, white educators, administrators and the miliary obliterate existing cultures under the premise that the British way is the best. The military victories are those won by the British, the atrocities and perfidies, like the Black Hole of Calcutta, are perpetrated by the other side.

(ibid.: 82–3)

She also examined textbooks which were written in the 1930s but which were still appearing in classrooms in the 1970s. Of one entitled *Work in Other Lands*, she commented that:

Exploitation by whites of black people is often explained away. In [this] book, it is said:

'the darkies who grow cotton are happy people with few cares. The planter looks very carefully after his darkies . . ., long, long years ago many of the darkies were slaves. Even then, very many of them were happy, for they are an easy going people'.

(ibid.: 84–5)

On this Laishley commented that:

For the black child, the history and geography lesson, not to mention other subjects, can become a lesson in inferiority and this information is not from fiction but supposed reliable school books. Think how an African child would feel reading something like this: From *People and Homes in other Lands*:

'Besides being the home of many wild animals, the African grasslands are the home of many different tribes of Negroes'.

(ibid.: 85)

She also showed how such images find a resonance in popular culture. In her analysis of children's comics, she noted that:

An example of the type of treatment Africa and Africans receive appeared in the boy's comic *Smash*. This serial, 'The Fighting Three', told of three white main characters who were described as being 'in darkest Africa'. Africans appeared as the Obijoes, stupid and ineffective savages, who were referred to as 'natives' and once as 'you big ape'. They were tamed by one of the white men, whom they worshipped for his resemblance to their idol. . . . A one issue story in *Princess Tina*, called 'Warrior's Child', told of a Boer Trek in the 1830s. The black characters were 'fierce Hottentot warriors' of whom it was said 'even among themselves these terrible people made war'. The happy ending to this story was engineered by the kind act of a white girl and the story, not very surprisingly, made no comment on white hostility in Africa, on the fact that whites were taking over land that did not belong to them or that the course of subsequent race relations in this part of the world is nothing to be proud of.

(ibid.: 72–3)

Another key component of popular culture is, of course, television itself. Mark Tully, the respected New Delhi-based BBC correspondent, has commented that:

I find that there is a great deal of misunderstanding about India amongst quite ordinary people. I mean, remember once I was at a meeting – it was a political meeting – and I asked a question, I said 'Was the candidate happy about the amount of aid that Britain was giving to the developing countries', and a woman turned round to me and she said: 'What do you want to give them aid for, it's all their own fault – they are lazy – if they worked hard they would be as well off as we are'.

But of course that is a total misunderstanding of the situation – and judging by the way that woman talked I fear she must have got most of her opinions from the media.

We tend, I think, to give listeners and viewers the impression that poverty is a crime committed by the country in which that poverty occurs and that it would perfectly easily be eradicated if the country really tried to do so. And I just don't think that is true.

(1986)

It is not hard to see how such images of the Third World can correspond with other popular beliefs about the 'reasons' for poverty, for example, blaming it on a lack of education and ability or simply blaming it on over-population. There are now attempts being made to change both the images given by television as well as the content of much of what is taught.[3] Local authorities in Britain, for example, have set up major projects to alter both the content and style of teaching. The leader of one of these projects commented in a BBC programme that:

If we want to teach children about [where they live] we teach them its history which is about dead people. If we want them to know about the wider world, we teach them about Hottentots or Eskimos. That's what we've got to change.

(*Brass Tacks*, BBC 2, 19 September 1986)

The above examples do not represent the whole content of television or indeed everything that goes on in classrooms. There have been serious attempts to offer more diverse accounts. But the evidence suggests that these are likely to be overwhelmed within a popular culture and television images which focus upon very simplistic explanations. For example, the Inner London Education Authority (ILEA) had begun to analyse the attitudes of school children to the Third World. Of this study, Anne Simpson wrote:

A group of third form pupils in an ILEA secondary school, when asked about their images of the 'Third World' listed the following:

'poverty, babies dying, monsoons, war, devastated crops, starvation, disease, drought, refugees, flies, death, Oxfam, dirty water, India, Cambodia, curry, beggars, malnutrition, bald children, large families, insects, stealing, poor clothing, bad teeth, kids with pot bellies, mud huts, injections.'

When asked where these images came from the class said that *Blue Peter* (a BBC programme) had many appeals for blankets and water pumps to help poor people in poor countries; *John Craven's Newsround* often showed pot-bellied children eating rice; TV programmes about war and refugees provided some more of the images. One girl wrote: 'Our images came from programmes like *Blue Peter*, the News, *Village Earth* and special films. In most of these films they show sickening sights of poor people . . . they always show screaming pot-bellied kids having injections from white doctors in short sleeved shirts with other kids waiting in queues for the same thing, or screaming babies getting weighed by nurses that looked like nuns.'

(Simpson 1985)

One of the problems with such images, whether they appear in the advertisements of aid agencies or on the television news, is that they show the population of the Third World simply as victims. But they do not take in causes of poverty such as the prevailing political and economic relationships between the rich and poor world. Neither do they show Third World populations or governments doing anything on their own behalf to resolve the problems. These have been key elements in the criticisms that have been levelled at the television coverage of the Ethiopian famine.

Ethiopian news

Michael Buerk's first report on Ethiopia in July 1984 went as follows: 'There is a simple and a complicated truth about what is happening here. The simple truth is that the rains have failed. The complicated truth is that the land can no longer support the number of people on it.' Writing about this in the *Listener*, Brian Phelan commented that:

In other words, it is a natural disaster in which over-population has conspired with the weather to produce a major tragedy. The implication is that it has little to do with us, watching at home. It is, rather, an Ethiopian problem of too many people on too little fertile land.

This is a well trodden stereotype of the Third World, hardly likely to create a stir.

(28 February 1985)

But, in fact, Michael Buerk's first report and *Seeds of Despair* did raise over £9 million in donations. We might note, then, that even the simplest descriptions of the effects of a famine does have some purpose. The showing of the terrible pictures of suffering plus a simple appeal to Christian values of fellowship and 'love thy neighbour' was an important and effective way of mobilizing a response within television audiences. The impact of Michael Buerk's second report in October 1984 was heightened on BBC news by juxtaposing it with a commentary on the European grain mountain. This theme was then taken up by other media commentaries and carried clear political overtones, by raising questions of allocation of resources and consumption in the west relative to the Third World. The account is still simplistic in the sense that Africa's problems could not be solved in the long term by simply moving the grain mountain from Europe to Africa, but it was an important beginning. Some current affairs programmes went beyond this to openly question the political issues which underpinned the famine. A *World in Action* programme on the 'Politics of starvation' began as follows:

> Tonight with the people of Ethiopia in desperate need *World in Action* reveals a growing conflict between those who have been trying to get aid to Ethiopia and the politicians who they say, refused it. It's what's becoming known as the Politics of Starvation.
>
> (12 November 1984)

Michael Poole, writing in the *Listener* argued that the typical images of starving people, moving as they are, inadvertently misrepresented the nature of the problem. Television images, he commented:

> shared one thing in common: they presented the Ethiopians pouring into Korem and other centres in search of food as the victims of some 'natural' disaster, like an earthquake or a flood. A perspective also shared by most of Fleet Street. The vocabulary chosen by *The Daily Express* was especially revealing in this respect: 'drought and starvation have taken up residence once more in this impoverished, cursed, land. . . . A malevolent Nature can be thanked for this.' In fact, what has been happening in Ethiopia, though drought has undoubtedly been the catalyst for it, is really of a different order in so far as it was predictable – was indeed *predicted* – and could therefore have been averted. . . . As Oxfam put it in their almost totally ignored July report warning of the danger of widespread famine in the northern provinces of Wollo and Tigre: 'poor people live at the margin of existence even at good times; the weather can easily tip them over . . . because it's the weather that tips the balance, it is easy to assume that it is the *main* cause of disasters such as famine. But the weather doesn't cause poverty. It merely focuses attention on it.'
>
> (8 November 1984)

The essence of Michael Poole's argument is that famine is a problem of underdevelopment. To see the problem in its proper context we need to analyse international trade, colonial ties and other factors which make developing countries dependent on world markets which are controlled by and oriented to the needs of the developed economies. If, however, we rely on the western media to inform us about the Third World, then we face the problem that media priorities will determine whether or not we are told anything, and journalistic assumptions will shape what is included within the story. Having said this, once the media did decide to treat the Ethiopian famine as a major issue, the results were dramatic.

News Impact

We can assess the impact on television of the news story by simply looking at the number of stations which carried the story in its different phases and at the potential audiences which they could reach. The first Michael Buerk report on the famine in July 1984 was syndicated to sixty-three television stations by Visnews (*Television Weekly*, 27 July 1984). The Buerk/Amin report in October 1984 was carried by 425 of the world's broadcasting stations, with a potential audience of 470 million people (*The Times*, 13 March 1985). The story was taken up in the popular press and then given a huge further impetus by the intervention of Bob Geldof. His Band Aid record was released for Christmas 1984 and he then toured Ethiopia in January 1985 with a plane load of journalists. This movement climaxed in July 1985 with the Live Aid concert, which was shown in 120 nations with an estimated audience of 1,500 million viewers. In May 1986, Sport Aid was staged as a deliberate 'consciousness raising' event, to involve large numbers of people in simultaneous athletics, to demand action for Africa. Two hundred and seventy-four cities in seventy-eight countries around the world staged simultaneous runs involving in all up to 20 million people worldwide. Perhaps because of the non-participation of the USA it was less of a television event, being picked up by forty-nine television stations in forty-seven countries.

Impact on governments

News pictures from October 1984 and the public interest that they aroused had some impact on the pledges for immediate food aid by governments.

The United States government announced that it was adding $10 million to its existing commitments, while the British government announced that it was adding £5 million and 6,000 tonnes of grain to Ethiopian relief efforts. The western television reports also influenced the Soviet Union. As an ally of Ethiopia it had thus far supplied mainly military equipment, but it now announced that it was sending 400–500 trucks, sixteen planes and twenty-four helicopters to distribute foodstuffs (*Time*, 12 November 1984).

These levels of aid came nowhere near to meeting the actual needs of Ethiopia either in terms of immediate relief or in providing long-term development aid. Mary Magistad has argued that the British government's concern was in fact largely rhetoric:

Even when the government *did* appear to be responding to the famine, its 'humanitarian' concerns were, it seems, less genuine than its political ones. This was highlighted by the contradiction of the government's rhetoric that it was committed to helping starving Africans, and the fact that it was at the same time cutting its aid budget by an average of 6 per cent per annum.

(1986)

Government aid had unexpectedly become a hot political issue. In November 1984 the *Observer* broke the story that the government was planning to cut its overseas aid budget. In an editorial the paper commented:

The aid cuts now being contemplated by the government demonstrate how far out of touch it can be with public sentiment. It takes a special degree of ineptitute, or insensitivity, to consider taking millions of pounds off the government's aid budget at the very time when the public . . . is flooding the relief agencies with notes and cheques to save lives in Ethiopia.

(18 November 1984; cited in Magistad 1986)

In the event, there was a back-bench revolt in the British parliament and it is a testament to the power of the moment that the proposal to cut aid was voted down.

Public impact

One way of measuring the impact of the media coverage on the general population is by looking at the increases in charitable donations. In the case of Oxfam, in the year from May 1984 to April 1985 the total donated was £51 million. In the previous year the total donations had been £23.9 million and in the year after April 1985 the donations were £45.2 million. Other charities such as Save the Children and Christian Aid also experienced dramatic rises in donations. All this was additional to the extraordinary fund-raising efforts of Band Aid, which by September 1986 had raised $110 million (this excludes Sport Aid donations).

There was also a huge increase in the number of enquiries to government departments and charitable organizations such as Oxfam. The switchboard at Oxfam was jammed for three days after the Buerk/Amin reports, while the other charitable agencies also reported similar increases in public concern. The public response was clearly affected by the degree of media interest, but it was also conditioned by the specific history and culture of various audiences. For example, the group which gave the most per capita were the Inuit in Canada (more crudely known as Eskimos). Their overwhelming response clearly related to their own cultural history and to the privations which they had endured in the past. It is difficult to measure whether the media coverage of 1984 and its aftermath had any major effect upon beliefs and opinions within the general public. One of the problems is that aid and Third World issues have been judged traditionally to be so low on the political agenda that there is very little data compiled about what people actually believe. The Harris Research Centre told us that such issues were not judged to be in the 'top ten' upon which questions were asked. However, it did seem clear that after 1984 aid and the Third World took on a higher profile. More concrete evidence comes from Oxfam which commissioned a Nielsen Research Poll in the UK in November 1984. They found that 76 per cent of the population either wanted to spend more on aid or to leave the level as it was.[4] They also found that 74 per cent of the public thought that the main purpose of British government aid should be long-term development projects.

On the surface these figures suggest a much higher level of commitment and knowledge among the public than had hitherto been believed by either politicians or broadcasters. If anything the effect on the public was cumulative and increased over the next year. Why should this be so?

One answer is that Band Aid and the work of Bob Geldof extended the life of the story and the range of its impact upon the public. Bernadette Prat of Oxfam's press office commented to us that Band Aid had motivated groups of people with whom the established agencies had experienced only limited success. But if this is so, then why did the news images not work as dramatically for younger people? The answer is probably that these groups in general do not watch the news. With the BBC children's news (*John Craven's Newsround*), only about a quarter of those watching it are actually aged 15 and below. Over 60 per cent of those watching it, in the same week as the Live Aid concert, were over 25 years old. In television terms its audience is relatively low at 3 million. For the *Nine O'clock News* on the BBC 71 per cent of those watching it were aged over 35. But in the same week as these figures, the first 6 hours of the Live Aid concert were watched by an audience of whom 68 per cent were below the age of 35. By 3.00 a.m. there were still nearly three times as many people under the age of 16 watching it as there were over the age of 55 (BBC Broadcasting Research Department).

The extraordinary impact of the story can partly be explained by the interaction between the news and the Band Aid/Live Aid/Sport Aid events. These events provided a further rationale for extending media coverage and, acting in tandem with the news, they generated what was an almost unique *national* audience.

Conclusions

The western media did not have a very deep interest in the issue of famine or a sustained commitment to explaining its causes. Once the disaster had reached catastrophic proportions in Ethiopia, the BBC took the story and finally treated it as a major issue. But even then it was in conditions which owed something to chance and, even then, some of the biggest organizations actually turned down the story. The final assessment depends on what we mean by the 'western media'. If we mean by it a few individuals such as Mohamed Amin of Visnews and Mike Wooldridge of BBC Radio and programme-makers such as Charles Stewart and Peter Hill, then of course there was interest. There was also a smattering of news items during 1984. But if we take 'interest in the western media' to mean the commitment of major resources by major organizations, then this simply did not happen until the tragedy had already struck. On 23 October 1984, the day on which the Buerk/Amin report was first shown, the BBC offered a full set of pictures to the *Sun*, the largest newspaper in Britain with 11 million readers. The response was: 'We're actually not interested in famine' (Harrison and Palmer 1986: 100). Five days later, when the story had broken, the *Sun* ran two inch headlines on: 'RACE TO SAVE THE BABIES' (cited in Magistad 1986). We can share some of the despair of Peter Cutler, a relief worker, who returned from Ethiopia in September of that year after assessing the state of food supplies: 'I remember coming back in September 1984 and literally giving up. We were just banging our heads against a brick wall. I'd tried all the donor agencies and the media. People were sick of my going on about it' (cited in Gill 1986).

The western media were late in coming and what they had to say was very limited. They were anxious to take the glory for helping Africa, but are more reticent in examining the news values and production processes which meant that they could have missed covering the story altogether.

The everyday practices of television will have to be rethought if it is to show a more consistent commitment to the problems of the Third World. In reply, the broadcasters might answer that it is not their job to do this – they are there simply to report the stories. But the broadcasters do want to take credit on humanitarian grounds for finally bringing the deaths of tens of thousands of people to the world's attention. They might then also wish to ask whether they could have done so sooner and more importantly ask how they can apply a rational and humane response to present and future crises.

NOTES

* This chapter was originally prepared for UNESCO and included a section by Robert Lamb of the Television Trust for the Environment, on the setting up of a clearing house for films on development and environmental issues and the promotion of news features by Third World programme-makers.

1 The 'second scoop' referred to is a reference to Peter Gill of Thames Television and his programme *Bitter Harvest*. This would have gone out before the second BBC report but was delayed by a technicians dispute.

2 This is further illustrated by the spasmodic way in which stories can be taken up and then left. For example, the BBC's *Newsnight* did three reports on famine in April and May 1984 (cited in Magistad 1986). In June 1984 ITN showed parts of a film made by Fr Mike Doheny and Paul Harrison for the Irish charity, Concern. In July, ITN featured the Ethiopian government's appeal to the west for help. In early October 1984, Save the Children gave a press conference with fieldworkers who had just flown in from Ethiopia and who were able to give graphic accounts of the disaster. ITN carried an item on its news about it, and in effect had the story which was launched with much greater impact later in the month by the Buerk/Amin report (see *Media Week*, 8 March 1985; and Harrison and Palmer 1986: 101).

3 This is not to say that racism in our society could be removed or the problems of the Third World be solved simply by changing the images that exist in the media or in the classroom. It is clear that the images are partly rooted in the actual relations of dominance and dependence which exist between the First and Third World. But it is also clear that the simplistic images that are at present offered do little to challenge popular assumptions about the reasons for the differences between the rich and poor worlds.

4 41 per cent wanted to spend more, 16 per cent wanted to spend less and 2 per cent wanted to spend nothing.

REFERENCES

Gill, P. (1986) *A Year in the Death of Africa*, London: Paladin.

Glasgow University Media Group (1976) *Bad News*, London: Routledge & Kegan Paul.

Harrison, P. and Palmer, R. (1986) *News Out of Africa*, London: Hilary Shipman: 106–13.

Laishely, J. (1975) 'The images of blacks and whites in the children's media', in C. Husband (ed.) *White Media, Black Britain*, London: Arrow.

Magistad, M. (1986) 'The Ethiopian bandwagon: The relationship between news media coverage and British foreign policy toward the 1984/85 Ethiopian famine', LMA thesis, Sussex University.

Simpson, Anne (1985) 'Charity Begins at Home', *10–8 Quarterly Photographic Magazine* 19.

Tully, Mark (1986) *The Black and White Media Show*, BBC, 27 August.

UNESCO (1980) *Many Voices One World*, Report of the International Commission for the Study of Communication Problems, Paris: Kogan Page.

Chapter 6

Negotiating HIV/AIDS information
Agendas, media strategies and the news

David Miller and Kevin Williams

INTRODUCTION

The interaction between the news media and the social institutions they report is a key issue for the sociology of journalism (Schlesinger 1989a: 283). What appears in the news is the outcome of a process of *negotiation* between the reporter and the source of information. In the 'dance' between reporters and official sources some see the officials as leading (for example, Cohen 1963; Hall *et al.* 1978), while others argue that reporters do (for example, Hess 1984). However this dance is subject to a number of agendas, personal, organizational and political, that are brought to bear on the reporter and the source within their own organization.[1] Although we are aware of the factors that shape the behaviour of the reporter within his or her organization, we are less aware of the factors that determine source behaviour. What we do know about the latter is often based on accounts provided by those in the media and hence these are coloured by their perceptions of source's activity.[2] In our work on HIV/AIDS we have started to examine how such agendas have shaped media–source interaction from the point of view of the source as well as the reporter.

Studies of news media coverage of HIV/AIDS have found that the portrayal of the infection has been limited and distorted (see, for example, Albert 1986; Baker 1986; Naylor 1985; Watney 1987; Wellings 1988). Explanations usually focus on two general areas: first, that media representations of HIV/AIDS are dominated by 'official' definitions and perceptions of the disease; and second, that the workings of the media result in inaccuracy and sensationalism in the reporting of HIV/AIDS. What these explanations share is a tendency to treat 'the news media' and official accounts in an undifferentiated way. Consequently, there is little discussion of the social struggles that take place around meaning in the process of production prior to the 'moment of definition' (Schlesinger, Tumber and Murdock 1991: 398).

However, the news media 'do their work in differing ways at different times, depending, among other things, upon the topic, political circumstances and . . . the alternative social and discursive pressures exerted at a given time' (Bruck 1989: 113). Official sources do not always succeed in setting the news agenda. It has been shown that 'resource poor groups' face many problems in gaining news coverage (Goldenberg 1976), and compromises and accommodations may have to be made for such groups to gain access to the news media (Gitlin 1980). However, there has been little systematic study of the production process to obtain some idea of how and why dissenting or alternative perspectives can appear in news media accounts. It should not come as a surprise that official perspectives tend to dominate news accounts, but what is of interest is how this task of reproduction is accomplished and what factors are at work when it fails (Bruck 1989). Besides building up a more complete picture of the workings of the news media, such analysis is of practical value. It helps those wanting to provide alternative opinions to 'assess the chances for, and measures of, effective work through the mass media' (ibid.: 112).

News is not a reflection of a world 'out there' but, as Molotch and Lester have said, is a product of the 'practices of those who have the power to determine the experience of others' (cited in Schudson 1991: 148). This chapter is a preliminary discussion of how such 'practices' have shaped and influenced news media accounts of AIDS.

Our central argument is that the process of media production is an arena of contest and negotiation in which official sources cannot always take it for granted that they will be able to set the agenda. This is why powerful organizations such as the Department of Health actively organize media strategies to influence relevant agendas. However, even when official sources do organize media strategies, they can be hampered by a number of factors in gaining access to the media. In our research on AIDS we focused on the Health Education Authority (HEA) because, since 1987, it has had the main statutory responsibility for HIV/AIDS public education in Britain and Northern Ireland.[3] In the first section of this chapter we consider some of the difficulties the HEA found in putting its media strategy into practice, as well as some of the factors which allowed non-official bodies to use the media.

In the second section we look at some of the negotiations within media organizations which illustrate the impact of media factors on source accounts and show that the process of negotiation does not always run smoothly once information is fed into the media system.

SOURCE FACTORS

The HEA's campaign placed great emphasis on the mass media. Its strategy for using the mass media as part of its education efforts involved two components: advertising and press and PR. The HEA recognized the importance of targeting individual media outlets, editors and reporters to create a positive climate to support its advertising campaign. This was spelled out in the 'Total public communication strategy' drawn up for the HEA by the advertising agency Boase, Massimi, Pollit (BMP). A proactive public relations campaign was envisaged which sought to 'brand' the HEA the 'most useful source of AIDS information' (Boase, Massimi, Pollit 1988). However, the implementation of this strategy was influenced by several factors, including health educators' distrust of the mass media, the HEA's relationship with the Department of Health (DoH) and the low status of health education in the eyes of the mass media.

Distrust of the media

Health educators have tended to be suspicious of the media, resulting in a certain reluctance to deal with journalists. As Holmes has noted they regard the media as 'untrustworthy' and 'sources of conflict and misinformation' (Holmes 1985:18). This suspicion of the mass media was illustrated by the way in which some health educators in the HEA reacted to enquiries from journalists. A public affairs division employee said that for many health educators: 'Their idea of a journalist was somebody from the *Sun*. . . . A journalist to them was a hack of the lowest order.'

Because of this suspicion the HEA's public affairs division – who were responsible for formal relations with the press through its press office – had to educate many of its senior staff on the need to be open and accessible to journalists. Attempts were made to encourage them to read the newspapers and watch TV regularly in order to gain some understanding of the differences between media outlets. But, as one member of the HEA said, 'there was a resistance' from health educators.

Public affairs personnel told us about having to impress on health educators the importance of prompt responses to media enquiries. According to some HEA members this distrust, compounded by the bureaucracy of the HEA, resulted in it taking 'a long time to get the simplest piece of information'. The cautious approach of many HEA staff influenced journalists' perceptions of the HEA's usefulness as a source of both HIV and health education information. Although many correspondents had what they described as valuable *informal* sources inside the HEA they would refer disparagingly to formal contacts. As one tabloid medical correspondent said: 'They never really had anything I wanted.'

Inside the HEA a tension existed between those with a media or advertising background and those with a research or health education background. This meant that the public affairs division, which dealt with advertising and publishing as well as press relations, was often at loggerheads with the AIDS division – and other programme divisions. The former director of the AIDS division, Susan Perl, has characterized the differences as a 'clash of cultures' in which the public affairs personnel were concerned with 'impact' while the health educators were concerned with 'sensitivity' (Perl 1991: 15). The differences resulted in the drawing up of the 'ten commandments' which governed what could and could not be said in advertising, with the objective of avoiding 'victim blaming, stereotyping and stigmatising' (ibid.: 14).

Such internal differences and suspicions of the media emphasize that the time and energy of the press office – the formal point of contact between organizations and the media – can be devoted as much to dealing with internal matters as it is to handling enquiries from journalists.

HEA/DoH relations

Another factor influencing the development of the HEA press and PR strategy was its relationship with the Department of Health. The HEA took over responsibility for HIV/AIDS campaign information from the department which did not look favourably on the HEA trying to established itself as the 'most useful source' of HIV/AIDS information. The department, according to some HEA sources, got 'shirty' about this strategy, being unwilling to give up its 'expert' role. These concerns were formalized in a 'Memorandum of understanding' drawn up between the DoH and the HEA in 1990. While accepting that the HEA has a right to give advice in public and private where appropriate, the document circumscribes the conditions under which the HEA can put out public statements.

> The HEA was not established to be, nor is funded as, a campaigning 'pressure group', although it is conceivable that issues might arise on which it would attempt to influence strongly the direction of government policy through 'pressure' and be seen to be doing so. It must judge such instances carefully. *It is important that Ministers, through the Department, are informed in advance of advice to be given in public.*
>
> (DoH/HEA 1990: 7; emphasis in original)

Clearly, this had implications for the HEA's information strategies. For example, it was almost impossible for the HEA press office simply to put out a press statement. Press releases had to be checked by administrative civil servants and clearance to put out a statement was often delayed. Quite often a 'terribly straightforward and anodyne press release' which the HEA press office wanted to get out quickly would 'disappear down a black hole in the Department of Health'. Sometimes, according a former employee of the public affairs division, 'press releases didn't get out at all'.

Such delays discouraged the issuing of statements by the HEA press office. The pithy quote wanted by journalists to bolster a good story was not always forthcoming from the HEA. As one senior member of the HEA told us, it was:

A very hard part of my job to give interesting quoteworthy comment, which wouldn't have the government down like a ton of bricks. It was a very difficult line to tread. Sometimes I erred on the side of being too bland, and sometimes I erred on the side of finding a ton of bricks on my head.

The lack of quotable material and the restrictions placed on the HEA in making firm statements on AIDS policy made it difficult for the HEA's press office to establish effective relations with journalists who despaired of what they saw as the authority's 'fence sitting'.

Status of health education

Health education as a profession has relatively little status (Ling 1986). Health educators are near the bottom of the journalists' 'hierarchy of credibility'. Doctors and scientists have much greater authority and therefore credibility for journalists. As Karpf points out:

> It seems as if being part of the scientifico-medical establishment is itself sufficient in the media's eyes to make you a medical expert, even on an issue on which you have no specialist knowledge. Leading doctors and medical researchers become 'Anything Authorities'.
>
> (1988: 111–12)

Because journalists have no objective standard for verifying what they are told they value authority and status over other criteria in assessing the reliability of information they receive (Lett 1986). In spite of the particular problems the news media face in sorting out the disputes or uncertainties around HIV/AIDS, health educators, with their low degree of perceived authority and status, have difficulty in being included in news accounts.

Credibility

There have always been disagreements among doctors and medical researchers on the aetiology of AIDS as well as the best form of prevention. Media professionals are often criticized for their reporting of conflicting claims. Wellings (1988), for example, complains about the reporting of Royal College of Nursing (RCN) figures predicting 1 million AIDS cases by 1991. The problem here is the high credibility of the source – the RCN. In reporting the figure the journalist made his or her assessment on the basis of who is telling, not on what is being told. Thus journalists can defend themselves on the basis that they were only reporting what they were told.

Who does the telling

Sources of AIDS information have a highly developed understanding of the importance of who does the telling. The official response to AIDS was hampered by division inside government and the cabinet over what course to take. The Department of Health and Social Security (DHSS), in the early days prior to the HEA inheriting the education campaign, was involved in much coalition building to surmount cabinet and prime ministerial objections to discussion of anal intercourse and condoms in the public education campaign. The media played an important role in their efforts. Berridge notes that Peter Jenkins was briefed by a 'very senior government official' as to the 'catastrophe' posed by AIDS (Berridge 1992: 18). The resulting column, which appeared in the *Sunday Times* on 9 November 1986, is now seen as having played an important part in the government's emergency response to AIDS. We found on occasions the Department of Health would use or encourage pressure groups or others to say what it felt it could not. One clinician said:

> When there were things they [DoH] couldn't deal with because of their position they would ask, would you do this broadcast because the CMO [Chief Medical Officer] can't do it and we want you to front it because we know you could put across the message that we would like.

The HEA also found itself in a position where it was difficult to comment. What it did was to prime other sources who were sympathetic to the HEA line and use them to talk to journalists. One HEA official said: 'Very often when a story was breaking I'd set people up and say OK if the press are going to call me I'm not going to answer and I'll put them on to you.'

It is not only official organizations which recognize the importance of who does the telling. Voluntary sector AIDS organizations are sometimes happy to see more activist groups (whether specifically AIDS organizations such as ACT UP or more broad based lesbian and gay groups such as Outrage! or Stonewall) stage actions or make statements that might damage their credibility. One voluntary sector worker said about the demonstrations and sit-ins outside news organizations: 'We tend to assume ACT UP are going to do those . . . ACT UP is so important because it can do things we can't do, just as we can do things the government can't do.'

Organizations, therefore, which have differences over AIDS policy can and do negotiate or co-operate with each other in developing strategies to use the news media. Such activities do not often show up in media coverage, but they do represent part of the negotiation process of agenda building.

Self-publicity

Sources which may be used as experts by the media can use their credibility with journalists to push their own agendas. It is often forgotten that even eminent scientists and doctors sometimes can be their own best publicists (Check 1987). One senior AIDS doctor talked of having used his authority as an 'expert' to use the media to 'exert leverage on the government'. He also said that media interventions in the early 1980s 'were very effective, not in getting money personally for research or anything, but in getting money put into health education and into services'. Berridge points to the media not always being receptive to the advances of the AIDS experts (1992: 17). However, while media practitioners do complain about certain experts receiving too much coverage we found that these complaints were usually overridden by other assessments of a source's value.

Other factors

Other criteria that can play a part in assessment of sources' worth include the need for quotable material, presentable interviewees and personal empathy. One medical correspondent told us what he found useful about a doctor who, while not a HIV/AIDS specialist, was a widely used source comparatively early on in the HIV/AIDS epidemic: 'He was fluent, articulate, always ready with a good quote and prepared to speculate in a way more careful scientists weren't.' Such factors allow alternative sources to have some input into news media accounts.

Within 'alternative' organizations there is a debate about the efficacy of using the media (see Goldenberg 1976). Some feel that the mainstream media is always antithetical to their efforts. Others argue that by packaging and presenting their message they can have some influence. Peter Tatchell of Outrage! has argued that gay organizations can establish greater credibility with the news media by the quality of information they provide: 'We produce very good quality press releases that back up what we say with hard facts and statistics. It makes it much easier for people to take us seriously' (cited in Garfield 1991:5).

The success of an organization may also be affected by the image it presents. In the view of one voluntary sector spokesperson several factors contributed to successful intervention in the media:

> I'm not threatening in a way. I am 35, I'm middle class, I speak in BBC type English, I'm very acceptable. I am the kind of homosexual you'd want to take home to your mother and that is a great relief to them, especially the ones who are desperately trying to show their liberalism.

The Terrence Higgins Trust (THT), for example, established itself as a key source of AIDS information partly through a creative information strategy even though initially it lacked credibility as an authoritative source. THT, along with other voluntary bodies representing the needs of people with HIV and AIDS have had an influence on news media coverage. One THT spokesperson argued:

> One of the important things that we've done is . . . we've created, or helped to create a three way debate about what in the past would have been seen solely as a medical issue and would often have been debated between an interviewer . . . and a doctor and we've always managed to make that a three way debate in which you've had an interviewer, a doctor and somebody affected one way or another by HIV.

The THT has not found itself, in the words of one AIDS worker, 'coming up against a brick wall of silence in the media'. In fact the trust's success with the media proved a problem for the organization. As a THT spokesperson said:

> One of the problems that we suffered from, particularly around 1987, was that the public image of the Trust was much bigger than we were as an organisation. And the commonsense and dignity of Tony Whitehead and the other people we put up to talk meant that we were rapidly established as a sensible organisation to go to and I haven't had to go around pushing the Trust at all.

The success of the trust has not, however, been even. It has clearly had more impact on television and the quality press where, it can be argued, a more developed sense of 'social responsibility' exists than with the tabloid press with its more overt political agenda (see Chapter 9). What can or cannot be said does not only vary according to the news media outlet; it is also a product of conditions at a given time. The governmental response to AIDS has, as Berridge and Strong point out, gone through a number of stages: the initial period between 1981–6 saw no formal co-ordinated government response to the disease; 1986–7 was a period of 'wartime emergency' when, with the first government television advertising campaign, tackling AIDS became a national priority; and since 1988 there has been a period of normalization of policy (Berridge and Strong 1991). The policy arena during each stage posed a different set of circumstances and political configurations for the interaction between the media and the social institutions charged with responding to the disease. The access of the THT was at its height during the period of 'wartime emergency' in 1987 when the pressure for more open programming and information about the disease was at its greatest. During the period of 'routinization' established in the wake of the emergency there has been a reining in. Nevertheless, it can be said that there has been a long-term impact on the media's discourse on sex and sexuality. According to a voluntary sector spokesperson:

We managed to do things that never happened on television or radio before . . . talking about masturbation on *Women's Hour* . . . or about fist fucking on DDC 1 with a huge audience – that has never happened before and incidentally it has never happened since. I think 1987 was a blip which has now been screwed down tight but we have been able to extend talking about sex on TV and radio a great deal, to the point where certain things such as *Sex Talk* would never have been possible without the kinds of things we did on *Open Air* and others did elsewhere on the need to talk about safer sex.[4]

The strategies of source organizations are not the only factors affecting news coverage. Journalists too have their own agendas. They may select sources according to the particular story-line they are taking or the political line of their organization. Sources not fitting the preferred line can be excluded from an account. One medical correspondent told us why she had dropped a particular doctor as a source of HIV/AIDS information. He had been:

very, very helpful but later on he got a funny bee in his bonnet – it had all been started off deliberately in laboratories and it was either the Russians or the Americans – at which time we decided he'd gone completely over the top, and left him alone.

However, sources themselves can help to bring to or keep an issue at the forefront of the news. It has been noted that if sources do not continue to draw the media's attention to an issue, that issue can become invisible (Check 1987). The decline of the news media's interest in HIV/AIDS in late 1990 was not simply the responsibility of the media. One British Medical Association (BMA) press officer argued that AIDS had:

become less fashionable because we've stopped parading it as an issue. It's become less fashionable because the Department of Health has deliberately run it down as an issue, and therefore it is not so much guaranteed a good run as far as journalists are concerned. So yes, we unwittingly conspired to downgrade a subject that matters to us very much indeed.

Finally, the influence of sources is not necessarily indicated by their appearance in news texts. A distinction should be made between formal and informal influence. Often alternative or oppositional sources, while not appearing directly in media accounts, can influence those accounts through contact with journalists. Most of the correspondents to whom we talked have a small circle of tried and trusted sources they talk to regularly to check out information or to trawl for ideas for stories. These circles include people inside official organizations such as the Department of Health or the HEA, doctors as well as representatives of alternative opinions whose influence may not be commensurate with their appearance in the reporting.

MEDIA FACTORS

It is important to distinguish between different types of journalists and media outlets. Many have co-operated with health educators over HIV and AIDS, defining their reporting in terms of social responsibility. Among these one HEA employee classed 'people who write for women's magazines, which are very influential, and the agony aunts, and the whole pop culture which has been very supportive of us, music magazines'. We should also distinguish between specialist reporters covering health and medicine and general reporters. Meldrum (1990) notes that specialist correspondents have been appalled at some of the antics of general reporters or national press stringers. Our interviewees made similar distinctions seeing them as important in dealing with the news media. As one Department of Health press officer saw it:

> Health correspondents were very responsible and good but because AIDS became a headline story you got a lot of general reporters who really didn't know what they were writing about . . . and just went for the easy line and they didn't bother to check with us.

Journalists are often wary of accepting that their job has great effect on the formation of public knowledge, preferring instead the mantle of disinterested observer dependent on influencers of opinion (Loshak 1986). But, significantly, some medical or health correspondents have a much more committed view of their role. They recognize that what they write may affect their readers (either with or without HIV), and regard themselves not simply as reporters but as socially responsible educators. Consequently, some medical correspondents have rejected the central ideological motif of impartiality which for many other types of journalist remains a strategic legitimator. One broadsheet medical journalist defined her role in this way:

> Certainly it's always first to inform. I think we do have a strong public health role in this one, probably more than anything else. Well maybe in the same way that we do with smoking . . . as a smoker I am diligent about writing stories about how pernicious, disgusting and unhealthy it is.

This role definition allows the journalist to play a more active part in the construction of news accounts than the professional ideology of neutral reporter of facts would allow. Thus when Lord Kilbracken was reported by the *Sun* as confirming that 'Straight sex cannot give you AIDS – official' (*Sun*, 17 November 1989) the problem for concerned journalists whose editors followed this line was how best to counter it. One such tabloid journalist told us the strategy was to 'try and get as many experts on the phone to rubbish it. You can't just sit there rubbishing it yourself, you're a reporter of other people, but you're selective about who you're picking up the phone to get'.

Although many specialist medical and health correspondents would stress their social responsibility in covering an issue such as HIV/AIDS the occupational culture of journalism provides a countervailing pull. For example, the difference between an 'AIDS victim' and a 'person with AIDS' was lost on one otherwise sympathetic journalist whose concern focused on the news account being 'watered-down': 'I mean they are AIDS victims if they've got the disease and they're certainly suffering if they're carrying that virus and knowing it. Victim is an over-used word but you can't water it down too much.'

Other problems stem from personal reasons. We found that some male medical journalists seemed to have great difficulty relating to out gay men. One gay voluntary sector spokesperson told of a TV journalist who 'just doesn't understand at all'. The journalist asked him:

'Were you born homosexual, because I've got my two young children and they're coming up to 13, 14 and it does worry me one of them might be gay' . . . and this is the man who's done programmes in which he'll show a throbbing disco floor and talk about the homosexual underworld. That's who you're dealing with. So of course there are going to be problems there.

News values

Fears that news accounts would lose their impact are closely connected with another criterion of journalistic action – news values. If a story is 'newsworthy', goes the argument, then journalists are powerless to prevent themselves writing it. This concept of news values may run counter to a conception of journalists as educators. One tabloid journalist explained how she saw the difference between being an educator and a 'reporter':

Being a reporter doesn't always help other people. That's a terrible thing to say isn't it? If something happens . . . there could be someone whose whole family has got AIDS or something. Well that is an amazing story. That wouldn't really educate people. But it is a good story that should be told. Or you could look at it with your halo on and say 'Oh yes it will because it can educate people that they are all at risk.' But you wouldn't really be telling 100 per cent the truth.

Journalists will often appeal to news values when challenged on their coverage although there may be conflict between newsworthiness and other conceptions of their role.

Subs and editors

News accounts are the outcome of a process of negotiation between reporters, the news desk and the editorial line of the news organization. The news desk is responsible for what goes in the newspapers or programme everyday. It is the ultimate guardian of what is considered the 'news value' for the particular media outlet. The versions of news values which media outlets operate combine conceptions of what is an appropriate style of address for their audience and the editorial priorities of the paper. The health or medical reporter's input is only part of the equation. Andrew Veitch won a THT award for his reporting of HIV/AIDS when he was the Guardian's medical correspondent (*Guardian*, 23 November 1989). He highlighted the failure to educate news desks about HIV/AIDS:

> I think that we, in turn, have failed to get through to the people who really make the papers – the editors, the sub-editors, the guys who decide what goes in the pages, the guys who write the headlines you hate so much.

(Veitch 1986: 128)

The failure to make a distinction between medical and health correspondents and others involved in the news production process was acknowledged by those responsible for the HEA's press and PR strategy. A senior HEA official said:

> I think we make a mistake in the sense of always talking about journalists because it is the people who control what is actually printed who are crucial and this is an almost shadowy group we don't get to in the normal course of events.

Besides the news desk there are the subeditors whose job it is to write the headlines and to cut a journalist's copy to fit the space available in the paper. This often means headlines which are markedly different from the text beneath them. Because of their smaller area of news coverage the subs on tabloid newspapers tend to intervene more in news stories. Yet even on broadsheet papers there are clear tensions between journalists and subeditors. Andrew Veitch spoke of his experience at the *Guardian*.

> I've been trying to use the words 'anal intercourse' for two years now and I can't get them in to the newspaper. The usual reason I am given it's too boring. So I try the words 'receptive anal intercourse' to get a bit of flavour into it and my editors say 'What's that?'. I think next time we will try 'buggery' and see what happens.

(Veitch 1986: 128)

In considering the use of language in HIV/AIDS stories news editors and subeditors depend on the conceptions they have of their audience. Edgar,

Hammond and Freimuth (1989) note that in early HIV/AIDS coverage editors considering using direct language would always ask themselves whether their subscribers would like to read this or that at the breakfast table. Answering questions like these resulted in inconsistencies within media outlets as well as between them. As Veitch pointed out:

> We have another little rule. You can get 'fuck' into the *Guardian* as long as it is on the arts page and the theatre reviews and it is artistically justified. So you can say 'fuck' to your readers over the corn flakes in the morning but you can't say 'anal intercourse'. It's a bit of wonderful hypocrisy.
>
> (Veitch 1986: 128)

It is not only supposedly self-evident 'news values' or considerations of space and lay-out which determine what an editor sees as important. Political considerations also intervene. One tabloid reporter found that following the Kilbracken row, the news desk was keen on the 'straight sex is safe' line pursued by the *Sun*. The reporter said:

> He [Kilbracken] did a lot of damage because a lot of people were only too willing to believe that man and you find yourself here saying, 'It's garbage . . .'. You're trying to tone down the coverage and [the news editor says] 'Yes but it is a story'. . . . So you have this, I won't say conflict, but differing interests.

The intensity of these contests and their resolution varies between media outlets depending on the influence of the specialist correspondent. A number of factors come into play including the personality and status of the correspondent, the tradition of the news outlet, the importance of the health 'beat' and the attitude of the editor. Ultimately the pressure for the correspondent to conform is considerable. As a member of the AIDS division at the HEA found out when they phoned a medical reporter to complain about an article which:

> was one of the worse pieces of gay bashing and junkie bashing that you can imagine, and I called up [the journalist] and said 'what the hell is this about?' . . . she said, 'It was that or my mortgage because the editor . . . said, "I am not having any more of your gay loving, junkie loving pieces. We are going to tell it like it is".'

A feature of the reporting of HIV/AIDS has been the tension between news desks and specialist correspondents over the representation of illness.

CONCLUSION

In this preliminary discussion of our research we have tried to identify some of the factors that have shaped the production of news media messages on HIV/AIDS. We argue that in order to understand the routine news coverage of HIV/AIDS it is necessary to examine both the strategies formulated by sources of information to influence and use the news media as well as the strategies deployed by the news media to gather and process information about HIV/AIDS. To explain the output of the news media it is necessary to examine the nature and process of negotiation between the reporter and his or her sources of information. This examination has to be located in the context of the competition between sources as well as the organizational pressures on the reporter and the political–economic context of media production.

Our study of the process of source–media interaction over HIV/AIDS information suggests that the media strategies of official sources do not automatically succeed. There were a number of factors that shaped the nature of the media messages that the HEA sought to communicate to the public. There were also a number of sites of contest in the production process, on the source side as well as within the media, which influenced the outcome. Conversely, the strategies of less powerful groups do not automatically fail. Alternative voices were able to intervene at different points within the production process to impact on the messages the public received on HIV/AIDS. Their degree of influence depended on a number of factors including the professional and political climate, their knowledge and expertise, their understanding of media practices and their personal contacts with media practitioners.

We would not disagree that powerful sources play a crucial role in determining the output of the news media. However, we would argue that if there is a wish to shift the balance of the debate and actual policy in favour of people with HIV and of preventive campaigns then there is a need to formulate media strategies which recognize the variations within and between the media and the process by which their representational practices are shaped.

ACKNOWLEDGEMENT

We would like to acknowledge the help of the ESRC and of our colleagues, Peter Beharrell, Lorna Brown and Jenny Kitzinger and the grant holders – Mick Bloor, John Eldridge, Sally MacIntyre and Greg Philo.

NOTES

1 This discussion is based on a series of interviews carried out between 1988 and 1991 as part of an ESRC-funded project based at Glasgow University – the AIDS Media Research Project (award no. A44250006). The project is a study of the production and content of media messages on HIV/AIDS and their reception by audiences. To examine the production of HIV/AIDS information over ninety interviews have been carried out with medical correspondents, news editors,

health educators, press and information officers, market researchers, advertisers, civil servants, researchers, doctors, TV producers and executives, voluntary sector workers and pressure groups. These interviews were done to inform a content analysis of the news reporting of HIV/AIDS by the press and television between 1986 and 1990. The study describes and analyses the nature and sources of specific statements on 'risk groups' and their activities, routes and modes of transmission of HIV and methods of prevention. Throughout this chapter quotations come from our interviews unless otherwise specified.

2 This approach has recently been criticized as 'media centric' (Schlesinger 1990) although some researchers have started to document the 'strategies' which source organizations use to influence media (see, for example, Cook 1989; Ericson, Baranek and Chan 1989; Schlesinger and Tumber 1991).

3 We have also carried out research at the HEA's related national bodies in Scotland and Wales (the Health Promotion Authority in Wales and the Scottish Health Education Group, now renamed the Health Education Board for Scotland). We were refused an interview with the newly-created Northern Ireland body.

4 This view raises the problem of what constitutes alternative or oppositional perspectives on HIV/AIDS. Our discussion is simply an attempt to outline some of the sites of struggle over meaning around HIV/AIDS rather than a celebration of the success of any particular alternative view. The predominant response to the HIV epidemic has been the promotion of 'safer sex' including the use of condoms. To advocate this approach clearly involves a degree of explicit discussion and description of sex and sexuality in public. This has meant AIDS workers together with journalists and programme-makers have had to struggle against media hierarchies reluctant to breach conventions on describing and discussing sexual acts (cf. Diamond and Bellitto 1986; Kinsella 1989 for similar processes in the USA). The debate around the representation of HIV/AIDS has predominantly been shaped and described as the opposition of a moral absolutist perspective which is sometimes referred to as an 'anti-sex' position with a 'radical', 'sex positive' approach (Segal 1989: 136). In this struggle the groups representing the 'anti-sex' position have had relatively little success in influencing the media agenda on HIV/AIDS. Groups such as Family and Youth Concern or the Conservative Family Campaign are particularly critical of the lack of media response to their calls to cut off funds to the THT. Meanwhile, some of the insights derived from the feminist debate on pornography and representation tend to be marginalized. Some writers have criticized AIDS public education materials for their failure to challenge dominant accounts of (hetero) sexual practice (for example, Wilton 1992). Thus Bea Campbell has written that some HIV/AIDS campaigns contain little more than 'penetration propaganda' (Campbell 1987).

REFERENCES

Albert, Edward (1986) 'Acquired Immune Deficency Syndrome: the victim and the press', *Studies in Communication* 3: 135–58.

Baker, Andrea (1986) 'The portrayal of AIDS in the media: an analysis of articles in the New York Times', in D. Feldman and T. Johnson (eds) *Social Dimension of AIDS: Method and Theory*, New York: Praeger.

Berridge, Virginia (1992) 'AIDS, the media and health policy' in Peter Aggleton, Peter Davies and Graham Hart (eds) *AIDS: Rights, Risk and Reason*, London: Falmer Press.

Berridge, Virginia and Strong, Philip (1991) 'AIDS in the UK: contemporary history and the study of policy', *Twentieth Century British History*, 2(2): 150–74.

Boase, Massimi, Pollit (1988) BMP/HEA, *Total communication package* 25 August.

Bruck, Peter (1989) 'Strategies for peace, strategies for news research', *Journal of Communication* 39(1) (winter): 108–29.

Campbell, Bea (1987) 'Taking the plunge', *Marxism Today*, 9 December.

Check, William (1987) 'Beyond the political model of reporting: nonspecific symptoms in media communication about AIDS', *Reviews of Infectious Diseases* 9(5) (September–October).

Cohen, Bernard (1963) *The Press and Foreign Policy*, Princeton, NJ: Princeton University Press.

Cook, Timothy (1989) *Making Laws and Making News: Media Strategies in the U.S. House of Representatives*, Washington DC: Brookings Institute.

Department of Health and Health Education Authority (1990) 'Memorandum of understanding', June.

Diamond, Edwin and Bellitto, Christopher (1986) 'The great verbal cover up: prudish editing blurs the facts on AIDS', *Washington Journalism Review* (8) (March): 38–42.

Edgar, Timothy, Hammond, Sharon Lee, and Freimuth, Vicki S. (1989) 'The role of the mass media and interpersonal communication in promoting AIDS-related behavioral change', *AIDS and Public Policy Journal* 4(1): 3–9.

Ericson, Richard, Baranek, Patricia and Chan, Janet (1989) *Negotiating Control: A Study of News Sources*, Milton Keynes: Open University Press.

Garfield, Simon (1991) 'The age of consent', *Independent on Sunday Review*, 10 November: 2–6.

Gitlin, Todd (1980) *The Whole World is Watching*, Berkeley, CA: University of California Press.

Goldenberg, Edie (1976) *Making the News*, Lexington, Mass.: D. C. Heath.

Hall, Stuart, Critcher, Chas, Jefferson, Tony, Clarke, John and Roberts, Brian (1978) *Policing the Crisis: Mugging, the State and Law and Order*, London: Macmillan.

Hess, Stephen (1984) *The Government–Press Connection*, Washington DC: Brookings Institute.

Holmes, Pam (1985) 'How health hit the headlines', *Nursing Times* 10 April: 18–19.

Karpf, Anne (1988) *Doctoring the Media: The Reporting of Health and Medicine*, London: Routledge.

Kinsella, James (1989) *Covering the Plague: AIDS in the American Media*, New Brunswick, NJ: Rutgers University Press.

Lett, John (1986) 'Anthropology vs. the media: it's in the epistemology', *Newsletter of the National Association of Science Writers* 34(1): 13.

Ling, Jack (1986) 'Media and health must forge a partnership', *Hygiene* 5(1): 23–6.

Loshak, David (1986) 'Medical journalists in society', *THS Health Summary*, February.

Meldrum, Julian (1990) 'The role of the media in the reporting of AIDS', in Brenda Almond (ed.) *AIDS – A Moral Issue: The Ethical, Legal and Social Aspects*, London: Macmillan.

Naylor, William (1985) 'Walking time bombs: AIDS and the press', *Medicine in Society* II(3): 5–11.

Perl, Susan (1991) 'Reflections on using mass media for AIDS public education', *AIDS and Sexual Health Programme Paper* 13, London: Health Education

Authority.

Schlesinger, Philip (1989) 'From production to propaganda', *Media Culture and Society*, vol. 2, London: Sage: 283–306.

—(1990) 'Rethinking the sociology of journalism: source strategies and the limits of media centrism', in Marjorie Ferguson (ed.), *Public Communication: The New Imperatives*, London: Sage.

Schlesinger, Philip and Tumber, Howard (1991) 'Crime and criminal justice in the media', *Reseaux*, Colloque Sociologie Des Television en Europe, Paris: Centre Georges Pompidou, 24–5 January: 205–24.

Schlesinger, Philip, Tumber, Howard and Murdock, Graham (1991) 'The media politics of crime and criminal justice', *British Journal of Sociology* 42(3) (September): 397–420.

Schudson, Michael (1991) 'The sociology of news production revisited', in J. Curran, and M. Gurevitch (eds) *Mass Media and Society*, London: Edward Arnold.

Segal, Lynne (1989) 'Lessons from the past: feminism, sexual politics and the challenge of AIDS', in Erica Carter and Simon Watney (eds) *Taking Liberties: AIDS and Cultural Politics*, London: Serpents Tail and ICA.

Veitch, Andrew (1986) Comments on 'Education and communication: enhancing public understanding and fostering disease prevention', in AIDS: impact on public policy, *Proceedings of a Conference* 28–30 May, New York: New York State Department of Health and the Milbank Foundation.

Watney, Simon (1987) *Policing Desire: Pornography, AIDS and the Media*, London: Comedia.

Wellings, Kaye (1988) 'Perceptions of risk – media treatments of AIDS', in Peter Aggleton and Hilary Homans (eds) *Social Aspects of AIDS*, London: Falmer Press.

Wilton, Tamsin (1991) 'Feminism and the erotics of health promotion', paper presented to the 5th *Social Aspects of AIDS Conference*, South Bank Polytechnic, March.

Part III

Message output: content and formats

Chapter 7

Backyard on the front page
The case of Nicaragua

Lucinda Broadbent

INTRODUCTION: NICARAGUA AND THE FIRST WORLD NEWS MEDIA

> Blessed is the man that reads not advertisements
> nor pays heed unto broadcasts
> nor yet gives credence unto slogans.
> For he shall be like a tree, planted by the rivers of water.
>> (from 'Blessed Is The Man', by Ernesto Cardenal poet,
>> priest, and Nicaraguan Minister of Culture 1979–80)

The principal complaint about First World media coverage of the Third World is that there is very little of it. And when Third World nations do break through the invisibility barrier to appear in the media of the richer countries, the news is only of war, famine, coups and earthquakes.

Nicaragua provides a counter-example: a scrap of a Latin American country that has scored extraordinarily highly in terms of international column inches and broadcast minutes. The Sandinista revolution of 1979 carried Nicaragua to pride of place on President Reagan's hit-list. This in turn swept Nicaragua from obscurity on to the world's front pages; and the media became one of the chief battlegrounds in Washington's war on Nicaragua. At stake was the image of the revolution: in the eyes of the State Department the Sandinistas held Nicaragua in the grip of a Marxist dictatorship; for the Roman Catholic peasants of Nicaragua, the revolution was an authentic attempt by the poor to build the Kingdom of God on earth.

Within the west, Nicaragua has been taken up as a cause by both left and right. The struggle to define, to eliminate or to celebrate Sandinismo was carried on far beyond the tiny country's borders. This chapter used comparative content analysis of media coverage to assess how such a hotly-disputed issue has been handled by our media, and the quality of information made available to the consumers of news.

February 1990 saw the downfall of the Sandinista administration, when Washington's candidate Violeta Chamorro won elections as a result of massive United States intervention. These were hailed as the 'first free elections' in Nicaragua. At this point, when the United States seems to have achieved its objectives in this rebellious corner of its backyard, it is a fruitful exercise to look back at the path the United States followed and some of the sophisticated ideological weapons it employed. The murky waters between the mainland of news coverage and islands of editorial comment are explored in a search for the limits of dissent permitted in the western media.

Conflicting images: the history

With the foundation of the Frente Sandinista de Liberacion Nacional (FSLN) in 1961, the Sandinistas took on the name and the ideology of Sandino – a national hero who had held out for Nicaraguan sovereignty against United States army occupation of the country in 1928–33. The FSLN plan for national salvation stood on the three pillars of political pluralism, the mixed economy and non-alignment.

At the head of a popular insurrection, FSLN guerrillas marched triumphantly into Managua on 19 July 1979. Thus fell the last of the Somoza dictators, a dynasty installed by the USA in 1936. Somoza fled in a United States plane, having ordered the bombing of his own capital in a last vain attempt to crush the uprising against him. The country lay in ruins; 50,000 people had lost their lives during the eighteen-month insurrection.

As leaders of the new revolutionary government, the Sandinistas broke the hoops of steel that had bound Somoza's Nicaragua to the USA. The dictatorship had, for example, allowed the 1961 Bay of Pigs invasion of Cuba to be launched from Nicaragua; meanwhile, United Fruit and the Rosita Mining Company helped themselves to Nicaragua's natural resources.

Sandinista social policy was based on the 'logic of the majority', or the needs of the poor. The Nicaraguan revolution's efforts received widespread praise. In 1983 Managua won a World Health Organization prize for introducing an 'exemplary' free health service. Development agencies were similarly impressed:

> Nicaragua stands out because of the positive climate for development based on people's active participation, which Oxfam has encountered over the past five years. . . . Since 1979 the scope for development has been enormous, with remarkable progress achieved in health, literacy, and a more equitable distribution of resources.
>
> (Oxfam Public Affairs Unit 1985: 15)

And in terms of the human rights record:

> In Nicaragua there is no policy of torture, political assassination, or

disappearances. . . . The allegations of human rights abuses have become an important theme in the [United States] government's campaign to overthrow the government of Nicaragua, but . . . we have found that the most violent human rights abuses in Nicaragua have been committed by the Contras, whom President Reagan calls our brothers, freedom fighters, and the moral equivalent of our founding fathers.

(America's Watch 1985)

The Contra forces which so horrified America's Watch were a proxy army founded, trained and armed by the United States administration with the aim of putting an end to what Oxfam called the 'threat of a good example'. United States aid to the Contras began with a covert allocation of $19m from President Reagan to the CIA in 1981, for the purpose of uniting the scattered remnants of Somoza's guard into a mercenary force sent to attack 'soft targets' such as schools, health posts and farming co-operatives. By 1990 over 10,000 Contras were still at large, funded by a labyrinthine web of public allocations from the administration, private United States fundraising by anti-communist crusaders and illegal funds from drugs and arms trading masterminded from within the CIA (as partially revealed by the 'Irangate' hearings). Unstinting support for the Contras and the entire United States panoply of aggression against Nicaragua – military, economic, diplomatic and ideological – were justified in the following terms by President Reagan in his address to Congress in April 1983:

The Sandinista Revolution turned out to be just an exchange of one set of autocratic rulers for another, the people still have no freedom, no democratic rights, and more poverty. Even worse than its predecessor, it is helping Cuba and the Soviets destabilize our hemisphere.

In terms of world opinion, the United States evaluation of the Nicaraguan revolution found few supporters. Indeed, when the Contra war against the Sandinistas brought the USA to the dock, the International Court of Justice at the Hague condemned United States aggression against Nicaragua and ordered the USA to pay $17 billion in reparations.[1] This chapter sets out to study how successful the United States administration has been in imposing its vision of the Sandinista revolution on the international news media, despite the lack of supporting evidence for the United States case that Nicaragua was suffering under a Marxist dictatorship and threatening the hemisphere.

The Sandinistas have always been aware of the importance of the mass media; and equally of the weakness of their own position in the world information order. The first ever FSLN broadcast was made in Managua in 1974, after a guerrilla commando stormed a Somocista Christmas party, demanding the transmission of their communiqué to the Nicaraguan people in exchange for the hostages' lives. Daniel Ortega, president of Nicaragua until 1990, spent part of the 1978 insurrection in the back of an unmarked truck in the streets of Managua, beaming revolutionary slogans and coded military messages from the illegal transmitter 'Radio Sandino'. However, it was the international media that took the decisive role. In June 1979 Bill Stewart, ABC News reporter covering the insurrection, was gunned down in the street by one of Somoza's guards. Public outrage at his death – especially because it was shown on network television in the USA – finally forced President Carter to withdraw support from the crippled Somoza regime, which fell a month later.[2]

In 1981, in the very early days of Sandinista rule, the Minister of Culture, Father Ernesto Cardenal, made this heartfelt plea for fairer media coverage to the United States Congress on Peace and Disarmament. He begins by talking about how the revolution dealt with its enemies, in this case with the members of Somoza's National Guard, who were held for rehabilitation in model prisons after the Sandinistas abolished the death penalty:

> In Mina Rosita the Somocista prisoners are taken to the village cinema once a week, to the local billiard hall and the town dance – and on Sundays they are allowed to go home. I know this is true, because one of their guards now works with me in the Ministry of Culture; his name is Gerardo Torrentes. I imagine that these things would simply not be believed if they were just published in the papers; I hope you will believe them in the mouth of a priest like myself. . . .
>
>   But there is one powerful enemy against whom we have no defence – the international news agencies. What can we do, when they hide the beautiful reality of the Nicaraguan Revolution, when they lie, distort the truth and libel us with every day that passes?

News production: eyewitness NBC

For a cameo picture of the production process of news about Nicaragua, I invite you into a darkened room in central Managua. Lights twinkle in the gloom from stacked video recorders and monitors, the air-conditioning is on full, Hershey's Chocolate Kisses and Evian water are served; while outside the city steams, women queue for water and the electricity supply has been cut off again. We are in the editing suite of NBC's Managua office (where I worked as a temporary videotape archivist), putting together reports on Nicaragua's 1990 elections for a live satellite feed to NBC Miami for broadcast across the USA.

'I want some poverty! I want some suffering!' is the anguished cry of the videotape editor, who is on $125,000 a year himself, but right now wants some appropriate footage for the point where the script tells how the

Sandinistas have reduced Nicaragua to economic ruin. He describes it as 'a piece on why people wouldn't vote for the Sandies'. His boss commiserates: 'We did poverty yesterday. . . . Can we use the same poor family, or was that a Univision exclusive?'. They take delivery of a fresh tape of Daniel Ortega belting out his electoral address to a crowd of some 300,000 gathered in the plaza. (Marchers have been making their way past the NBC office all afternoon en route to the plaza. Unused to mass popular demonstrations and tired of their chanting, the cameraman jokes, 'You know why it sounds like so many people? It's the same ones going round and round the block.') As Ortega's speech to the FSLN election rally is rapidly translated for him, the editor bursts out:

> Who the hell does he think he is, talking all that shit about American aggression? No-one ever got anywhere bad-mouthing the US! Look at Cuba! What's he [Ortega] ever done for the people? When did the US ever invade?[3] We'd go through this place in half the time it took us in Panama! Just wait until the US sends in the 82nd Airborne!

In the end the Ortega tape goes back on the shelf. 'If something big had happened, like someone had taken a shot at him, we'd broadcast tonight' the editor comments regretfully.

NBC's film crew returns in a good mood from the funeral of some Nicaraguan *campesinos* murdered by the Contras. The cameraman announces gleefully: 'We got some good crying on this. . . . We were the only crew, ABC had to split for a feed.' As the pallbearers come into view, the desk officer relieves the boredom with a joke: 'It's not a coffin, it's a barbecue set!' He proposes enthusiastically: 'I'd like to end with the shot of her crying. You can't lose going out on crying.' Pause. In a quieter voice he muses 'I just don't know what she was crying about.' However, the sweat and tears are not enough. 'Couldn't you have put in some blood?' he complains irritably to the crew.

The next incoming tape is from a freelance cameraman who was out in the hills early that same morning, filming the Contras on patrol in the north. Contra forces are operating inside the country as 'armed canvassers' for the United Opposition Union (UNO). 'I didn't know we had that many Contras out there in the hills.' The editor corrects himself: 'Sorry, I didn't mean to say "we".' The tape shows Contra soldiers relaxing; they are interviewed. Again he is outraged: 'That's what our taxes go on – what do they ever do? Why don't we just send in the 82nd and get it over with?' The desk editor's disappointment with the effectiveness of the Contras is more specific. In a tone of frustration, he asks 'Don't they teach these people to speak in sound bites?' His final decision: 'If it wasn't Friday, I'd say shoot, let's do a piece on this [the Contras].'

Ex-President Jimmy Carter, official observer of the Nicaraguan election process, gives a press conference. As the tape rolls, Carter is saying 'we've financed a war that's had over 50,000 casualties'. Puzzled, the editor comments 'Now he's bringing in Vietnam.' His boss sets the record straight, 'No, that's here.' There is general annoyance when Carter breaks into Spanish to address his Nicaraguan host.

In a more reflective mood, the videotape editor expands on his experience: 'I've been in wars in 70 countries. I've been shot at and arrested . . . . I'm old-fashioned: I believe we have a duty, like a doctor, to give unbiased news, a duty to the public. They believe what they see, we have to educate them.' And what has he learned from his experience? 'It couldn't get any worse here unless they nuked it. You know the thing about these countries, nothing works except the laundry service. You go to Cuba – fantastic laundry service! You get your shirt back the same day!'

On election day, 25 February 1990, tapes are delivered showing Nicaraguan citizens queuing excitedly to cast their votes. The script says that there were delays and the voters were frustrated. 'Why are they so happy?' screams the editor at the figures on the screen. 'Don't smile bud – look frustrated!'

When the NBC report is beamed to Miami that night, all the indications are that the FSLN will win the elections hands down. The piece closes with top NBC journalist Ed Rabel speaking to camera on the roof of the NBC office. He makes an interesting point: 'People are eager to know how a freely-elected Sandinista government would be treated by the US.'

After making sure the satellite feed goes smoothly, the news team gathers around the swimming pool to discuss the following day's assignments. Which crew will go to Ortega's victory speech, who will get the UNO candidate Violeta Chamorro saying 'we tried hard, but . . .'? To everyone's surprise, when the results come out the Sandinistas have lost. This time, the United States strategy of intervention in Nicaragua's elections has paid off. Rabel's question – how would the USA treat a freely-elected Sandinista government – seems to be left hanging in the air.

However, there is a well-kept secret in Nicaragua's recent history. Virtually unmentioned in mainstream media coverage of the 1990 elections are the previous Nicaraguan elections of 1984. The first ever free elections in the country were won by the FSLN, with 67 per cent of the popular vote. In other words, the way the USA has treated the Sandinistas since 1984 – sponsoring a mercenary army to attack the country, imposing a crippling economic blockade, slandering Sandinista rule in every possible forum – is precisely how the USA treated a freely-elected Sandinista government.

It is instructive at this stage, now that the USA has its own candidate installed in the Nicaraguan presidency, to look back at the way Nicaragua under Sandinista rule was portrayed in the international media. The 1984 Nicaraguan elections themselves provide an excellent case-study.

Although it is revealing and entertaining to eavesdrop on the cracks and asides of journalists and editors as they go about their business of assembling news reports, it is clearly not sufficient to back up a critique of the news coverage of Nicaragua. As individuals, they have every right to give free rein to their own ignorance and prejudices in the privacy of the darkened editing suite. The NBC news team quoted above is useful as a fairly typical example of the foreign TV news crew at work. But to be fair, many other individual journalists and stringers went to report on Nicaragua with a position of sympathy or even support for the beleaguered Sandinistas. The individual reporter or editor is not in control of the news business. What really matters, after all, is what ends up on television screens and in newsprint. Or to put it another way, whether the Washington angle on Nicaragua, shared by the State Department and in practice by many of the press corp, is in fact the angle presented to the public under the guise of 'unbiased news'.

Thus the following critique of the international media coverage of Nicaragua's 1984 elections is based on detailed content analysis of a wide range of news media.

THE CASE STUDY: 'BALLOT-BOX MARXISTS'[4]

Nicaragua's presidential and national assembly elections of November 1984 offered a good testing-ground for the media's performance.

Technical conditions for reporting the elections were unusually good from the foreign correspondents' point of view. They were scheduled in advance, according to a familiar timetable, and (deliberately) just two days before the United States presidential election, while Nicaragua was a hot domestic political issue in the USA. This ensured that it was not left to stringers and the 'budget bang-bang' crews often responsible for filing central American copy.

Instead, senior reporters and Latin America experts were dispatched to the scene, to make up the biggest foreign press corps ever seen in Managua (the press office issued credentials to some 1,500 journalists, roughly one for each 1,000 of the electorate). In addition, the Nicaraguan cast of Sandinistas and opposition politicians were unusually well-prepared for press conferences, interviews, briefings and photo-calls. So news-gathering conditions were not typical, but represented a 'best case' for the media.

Politically, the 1984 election race presented a serious challenge to the official United States image of Nicaragua. If the FSLN government was a totalitarian dictatorship, why was it holding open elections contested by seven different political parties ranging from the traditional conservatives

(PDC) and liberals (PLI) to the Trotskyist Popular Action Movement (MAP–ML)?

To the discomfort of Washington, the whole electoral process was widely endorsed by observers and witnesses from the USA itself and from abroad:

> The Reagan Administration is absolutely wrong when it describes no genuine opposition and a rigged electoral process; the process appears to be open and honest. The parties participating in the election represent a full political spectrum, and they have substantial freedom to make their platforms known.
>
> (Delegation of US lawyers guild)

> The electoral law was adequate to cover secret elections. I was able to observe unhindered the electoral process, and could detect no suspicion of malpractice. The elections were properly carried out. . . . In fact in many ways a good deal more fair, more precise, than we have in England.
>
> (David Ashby MP, Conservative Party member of the British parliamentary delegation)

The Reagan administration responded by branding the elections a farce and pushing its own client, Arturo Cruz, as the 'true democratic opposition'. Cruz, a wealthy banker from Nicaragua who had made his home in Washington, had been invited by the new government in 1979 to represent them as ambassador to the USA. However, by 1981 he had openly rejected the Sandinistas and aligned himself with counter-revolutionary forces. Neither Cruz nor his far-right coalition, the CDN, had any genuine basis of support inside Nicaragua.[5] His rise to the position of civilian 'opposition leader' was engineered in Washington, just as the CIA promoted him the following year to the role of political head of the united Contra forces. Cruz obligingly declared that he would not participate in the elections because the Sandinistas had not provided proper democratic conditions. The international media then faced a choice between accepting the 'Washington candidate' Cruz as the main opposition, or exposing his role in the administration's campaign, and reporting honestly on the real election race between the FSLN and the participating opposition.

The following analysis takes a sample of United States newspapers (prestige and tabloid, east and west coast), plus prime-time network television newscasts for the two weeks before and immediately after the elections in Nicaragua. It also encompasses British press and TV network coverage for the same period, in order to investigate the Sandinistas' charge that Washington mounted an *international* propaganda campaign against them.

Table 7.1 lists the media included in the sample and shows the distribution of news stories about Nicaragua.

Table 7.1 United States and British coverage of Nicaraguan election 1984: distribution of stories by date and medium

	October								November						
	24	25	26	27	28	29	30	31	1	2	3	4	5	6	7
US MEDIA															
New York Times	/	/		/			/	/		x		//	///	///	/
										x	x				x
Washington Post		/				//			x	/	/	/	/	//	/
Los Angeles Times	/		/		/		/					/	//		x
					x										
Charlotte Observer												/	/	/	/
Boston Globe							/	/		/	/	/	/	/	/
															x
Richmond Times-Despatch					/			/				//			/
New York Post												/	/		
USA Today												//	/		
Washington Times					/							/			
					x										
Daily News								/				/	/	//	/
												x			
ABC *World News Tonight*												/	/		
NBC *Nightly News*						/					/				
CBS *Evening News*			/								/	/			
BRITISH MEDIA															
Financial Times							/		/						/
Guardian		/	x				/			/	/	x	/	/	//
															x
Daily Telegraph			/				/					/	/		
The Times		/					/	/		/	/		/	/	/
Sunday Times				/											
Observer												/			
Channel 4 News									/			/			
BBC 1 *Nine O'Clock News*						·						/			
ITN *News At Ten*												/	/		
BBC 2 *Newsnight*										/		/			

Key: / = news story; x = editorial or feature article; total = 97

Note: The other national British papers, the *Daily Mirror*, *Sun*, *Daily Express*, *Daily Mail* and *Daily Star* were included in the sample but did not print any stories on Nicaragua's elections.

Screening the Sandinistas

The analysis begins with coverage of the Sandinistas themselves, who are after all at the heart of Nicaragua's newsworthiness, having led the 1979 insurrection, instituted the revolution and called the elections.

Strangely enough, the FSLN remains remarkably shadowy after sifting through all the United States and British news reports in the sample, especially when it comes to the question of what the party was offering Nicaragua's electorate. I assembled all the descriptions and accounts of the

Sandinistas given throughout the sample, dividing statements made directly by journalists in the course of their reports from opinions quoting or citing other sources. First, the journalists' own statements: these tend to carry the most weight since they are presented as accepted fact or eye-witness observation. A small selection of descriptions appears again and again across the various papers and newscasts – Table 7.2 lists these recurring terms, showing the frequency of each over the whole sample. It gives some sense of the monotony of the coverage and the dominant image of an unpopular, left-wing, Soviet-sponsored regime. Note that while journalists concede three times that the FSLN 'have majority support' (a fact borne out by their 67 per cent share of the vote in the elections), to 'balance' this single positive description the reports state on six occasions that they 'are not popular' or 'have lost support' or 'won fewer votes than predicted'. The other recurring descriptions fit in with the official United States model.

Table 7.2 Recurring journalists' statements on the FSLN in United States and British media sample on elections

Leftist/left-wing	used 16 times
Marxist	12
Hoping to bolster their legitimacy/trying to legitimate their rule	9
Monopolize state institutions	8
Celebrated victory before the vote was counted	7
Not popular/lost support/won fewer votes than predicted	6
Have close links with Cuba and the Soviet bloc	4
Have majority support	3

The remaining one-off acounts use different phrases but follow similar lines, for example:

> Their revolutionary brand of power-to-the-people politics is seen by opponents as leading to a one-party state.
>
> (*Channel 4 News*)

> have absolute power.
>
> (*Daily Telegraph*)

> acted secretly to ensure opponents would take certain positions.
>
> (*Boston Globe*)

> face a long and still-growing list of problems.
>
> (NBC)

A sinister picture is built up of Marxists clinging to power, and very little detail is added. The descriptions 'Marxist' and 'left-wing' are notoriously value-laden and content-free terms in the western journalists' vocabulary. Asked what most United States journalists understand by 'Marxism-Leninism', ex-*New York Times* journalist Ray Bonner said 'Nothing. None of them would be able to tell you what it means. It's used simply as a term of abuse' (interview with Anne Jones 1984).

Moving on from direct statements by journalists to the quoted and reported statements about the FSLN, by far the most common point made is the charge that the Sandinistas 'harass the opposition' or 'stacked the deck in their own favour', reflecting the views of the boycotting opposition. There is also more on the Marxism–Leninism theme: 'I'm satisfied that the regime that presumably wants to get itself re-elected wants to be what they call Marxist-Leninist' (Fred Tuckman interviewed on BBC 2 News). A new note comes in only once, when a candidate from the Trotskyist opposition party, the MAP–ML, is quoted describing the Sandinistas as 'too bourgeois'.

Newsnight

In the whole sample, the fullest account of the FSLN comes on BBC 2's late-night news/current affairs magazine, *Newsnight*. *Newsnight*'s background piece on 2 November 1984 is worth analysing in some detail: it comes closest to outlining Sandinista policies, and running at 12.5 minutes had a uniquely generous slice of time to do so. With the title 'Revolutionary Elections' emblazoned behind the newscaster's right ear, the report begins with a punchy studio introduction:

> Well, the ballot boxes will be out in Nicaragua on Sunday. But the Marxist Sandinista government is warning the people that they may soon be facing American bullets instead. Although the revolutionary government is holding the first election since overthrowing the right-wing dictatorship of President Somoza in 1979, the Reagan Administration regards these elections as sham. On the face of it, they're not one-party elections in the best communist fashion, other parties are taking part, but some leading opposition parties are boycotting the elections on the grounds that they can't be fair and that strong-arm tactics are being used against them. These incidents have helped to ensure that the Reagan Administration will not alter its view of the Sandinistas as dangerous revolutionaries.

The familiar ingredients are there: the drama of a potential United States threat, elections with the leading opposition missing, alarming charges that the Sandinistas are 'dangerous revolutionaries'. The newscaster is mainly reporting what other people have said about the Sandinistas – journalists cannot be criticized for reporting the views of the relevant actors. But it is interesting to unravel the way this is done, since the newscaster's introduction has an important role in framing the story. Whereas the Sandinista perspective is not at this point reported at all, the newscaster picks up on the charges levelled by the Reagan administration. He describes the government as revolutionary, which is accurate, but lends unfortunate authority to the 'dangerous revolutionaries' judgement, which is something else. After reciting the accusations of the 'leading' opposition, that the Sandinistas have prevented fair elections, he says that 'these incidents' have helped to ensure that the Reagan administration will not alter its view, as if the CDN's allegations of Sandinista 'strong-arm tactics' were true. (By contrast the overwhelming majority of foreign observers saw ample freedom for opposition campaigning, and there were only five recorded 'incidents' in 250 campaign rallies.)

He closes on: 'What is certainly clear is that Washington's relations with Nicaragua will be high on the agenda of the new American President', echoing another persistent assumption, that Nicaragua is only interesting in relation to United States policy, and not as a country in its own right.

The reporter in Managua who takes over from the anchorman refers only once to anyone else's view of the FSLN: 'The US has been unremitting in its accusations that . . . Nicaragua is essentially a one-party dictatorship trying to look respectable.' His own comments reveal a particular (professional) interest in the way the Sandinistas use the media – although he has nothing to say about how the media use the Sandinistas. He refers sarcastically to the 'revolutionary chic' of 'media-smart' campaign posters, and accuses the FSLN party political broadcasts of 'indulg[ing] in revolutionary romanticism'. He neglects to mention the television broadcasts by the opposition political parties, although all seven contenders were allocated equal air-time. Later he adds:

> Nicaragua's limitations include the fact that the entire state is created in the image of the ruling party: evocations of Sandino are everywhere, they fulfil much the same function here that Marx and Lenin do in the Soviet Union. . . . The institutions of the state are all Sandinista. The Sandinistas made the revolution and to the victors went the spoils.

He has indeed put his finger on a potential weakness in the Nicaraguan system. With the reconstruction of the country by the Sandinistas after the corrupt Somoza dictatorship was overthrown, the lines between party and state have been blurred on occasion and this would no doubt have been a problem for any other party taking office if it had won the elections. Yet, in saying that 'the entire state is created in the image of the ruling party, evocations of Sandino are everywhere' the BBC journalist betrays a serious misunderstanding of the role of 'Sandinismo' in Nicaraguan politics. The

FLSN is by no means the only party to follow Sandino or to lay claim to his heritage. Sandino is truly a *national* hero. If the journalist had known Spanish (his reports show him using an interpreter), he might have noticed that many of the 'evocations of Sandino' on Nicaraguan walls were adorned with graffiti proclaiming 'I am a liberal'. (Sandino *was* in fact a member of the Liberal Party in the 1920s.)

The right-wing newspaper *La Prensa*, which maintained a stubborn opposition to the FSLN and supported the CDN, hangs a portrait of Sandino in the office lobby. Even some of the Contras claim to be the true heirs of Sandino; the radio station run from Costa Rica by Contrafaction ARDE was called 'Voz de Sandino'. So to equate respect for Sandino with the dominance of the FSLN is a fundamental mistake. To add 'he fulfils much the same function here that Marx and Lenin do in the Soviet Union' is thus a very shaky comparison indeed, while 'to the victors went the spoils' implies a corrupt, self-serving government.

The remainder of this report leaves viewers with two images of the Sandinistas. There is film of another FSLN rally, with more mass yelling and cheering and raised fists. Second, there is the regulation story of 'Sandinista mobs harassing the opposition', an endlessly recurring theme in all the election coverage. A group of CDN supporters is shown, and the commentary continues: 'the crowd chanted "democracy yes, communism no", equating Sandinism with Marxism. Within minutes crowds of Sandinista counter-demonstrators had their revenge. They stormed through the streets putting the Cruz supporters to flight and damaging their property'. This is accompanied by dramatic footage of 'storming' Sandinistas wielding sticks, the camera zooming in from below on their shouting faces, making them appear as threatening and violent as possible. Although the journalist continues his commentary with 'such violence hasn't been seen again', this phrase is almost drowned out by the shouting before and after it. The interesting thing about the use of this strong image of Sandinista violence is that it was actually filmed in July, *over three months previously*, and before the election campaign had begun.

Yet it was presented as election 'news', presumably because it was seen as visually stimulating 'action footage', and because there was no contemporary Sandinista disruption of opposition rallies to illustrate the story. Just because it wasn't happening, that did not mean it could not be featured in living colour on the news to present an ugly picture of the FSLN.

So late-night *Newsnight* with all its flaws is the exceptional best: in all the United States and British press, and on prime-time TV, there is only a yawning gap to be found when looking for information about what the FSLN stands for.

Altogether this style of reporting leaves the audience with a mystery: why should 67 per cent of the Nicaraguan electorate have voted for such an unattractive party of power-hungry Marxists? The implication is that the election must have been rigged.

Cruz and the CDN: the boycotting opposition

The real focus of election coverage in the USA and Britain was not the FSLN, nor even the parties standing against it, but Reagan's favourite Nicaraguan, leader of the boycotting CDN, Arturo Cruz. The media were in almost total agreement about the CDN's status: it was identified as 'the main opposition' nineteen times in all across the coverage, plus thirty-five synonyms (Table 7.3). One or other of this narrow range of terms was used

Table 7.3 Journalists' statements on the CDN (United States and British media)

Main opposition	19 times
Major opposition	8
Largest	5
Strongest	3
Leading	3
Important	2
Principal	2
Most significant	2
Key	2
The opposition	2
Best known	1
Most stable	1
Represents the bulk of opposition to Marxist rule	1
Attracting most attention	1
Most of the opposition	1
Prominent	1

by all nine of the United States papers studied, and by all of the British press as well, with only two exceptions, the *Guardian* and the *Observer*. The latter carried one election story, and chimed in without specifically naming the CDN: 'Although a Sandinista victory has never been in doubt, a meaningful participation by opposition groups would have strengthened the Government's claims to legitimacy' (*Observer*, 4 November 1984). A little more originality and variation came in when describing the CDN's composition and politics (see Table 7.4). To the careful reader, taking more than one newspaper and with a head for figures and the complexities of Latin American politics, this confusion among the journalists about basic facts like the number of parties in the CDN coalition (there were actually three) and their political alignment ('far-right' is closer to the mark than 'moderate'), might undermine their firm statements about how 'major' it is. More plausibly, the journalists' confusion would simply add to the prevailing impression that politics outside the western democracies is an impenetrable mess.

Table 7.4 CDN's composition and politics

A coalition of three parties	13 times
A coalition of four parties	8
Moderate	1
Centrist	1
Centre-right	5
Right-wing	7
Conservative	2
Far-right	1
Anti-Sandinista	2
Ranging from centrist to conservative	3

There was no thorough exposure of the CDN's links with the Reagan administration and the Contras, no discussion of how such minute parties with no national organization inside Nicaragua could pose as a popular opposition, in sum, practically no attempt to go beyond the United States embassy's press hand-out.

To appreciate the power of this perspective on Cruz and the CDN, it is important to move back from counting the overall lists of descriptions and look at the context. Cruz appears in every single election report on all three United States TV network programmes; for example, NBC's election preview on 29 October 1984, which begins briskly with 'Now it's the battle of the ballots in Nicaragua', as the anchorman firmly draws the battle-lines: 'the main opposition parties have pulled out, complaining they were harassed by the Sandinista press and gangs. So, the Sandinista government will be elected'. In the first few minutes of the report from Managua, NBC's correspondent paints a depressing if rather one-sided picture of what he calls 'deepening disillusionment with the Sandinista revolution'. He interviews a draft-evader, complaining about national service, car drivers complaining about the oil shortage (one can imagine the disturbing impact of this image of drivers having to queue for fuel on sympathetic car-owners in the United States, although it means a lot less in the Nicaraguan context where only the tiniest minority of the population has a private car), then shows footage of a Managua market, where 'you find that simple goods have become luxury items. Powdered milk from the Soviet Union . . . the most serious shortage is food . . . which means more rationing'. It goes without saying that his image of disillusionment – fitting into the classic United States media stereotype of 'socialism = shortages' – could have been reversed if he had interviewed instead one of the 400,000 volunteers in the Popular Militia, explained that the oil shortage was due partly to the CIA blowing up the fuel depot at Corinto, admitted that the poorest Nicaraguans had far more access to simple goods than before the revolution or mentioned any of the country's astonishing advances in literacy, health, education or human rights.

Against this gloomy backcloth of deprivation he brings out Arturo Cruz, as 'candidate of the coalition of the *major* opposition parties', for the following exchange:

> *Cruz*: It is my opinion that the Sandinistas have suffered a tremendous disfiguration in public support. If there was true elections, with all the necessary freedom, and the people could express their dissatisfaction through their vote, I have serious doubt that the Sandinistas could win the election.
>
> *NBC correspondent*: But that is why there will not be free elections, and why Cruz and his coalition are boycotting the vote.

He continues to pick up on Cruz's point of view through at the remainder of his report: the only reference to the actual election campaign is the brief concession that 'some small opposition parties are running' over film of a Liberal Party rally, leading to this damning summing up: 'To observe what is happening here in Nicaragua is to see what was a popular revolution being squandered by its Marxist leaders. Whatever they may claim, the fact is, they are losing the support of the people, the masses.'

CBS and ABC follow a similar pattern: in fact the 'Cruz perspective' is so well integrated into the plot that when the results are announced on ABC News (5 November 1984) the possibility of the Sandinistas winning 67 per cent *simply because they were popular* is not even considered. The figures are no surprise to the world-weary experts at ABC: the newsreader, unruffled, opens with 'It is already clear that the Sandinistas have won a sizeable majority. *Not surprisingly, perhaps, since there was only token opposition on the ballot*' (emphasis added). Lavishing this sort of uncritical attention and air-time on Cruz and the CDN is a direct attack on the legitimacy of the elections. The media are doing much more than misrepresenting the domestic following of one Nicaraguan politician: they are swallowing and regurgitating the central plank of Washington's disinformation campaign against Nicaragua's election process.

Credibility of the election process

If Arturo Cruz was the United States and British journalists' first preoccupation, the credibility of the electoral process was probably a close second, since they started from the assumption that an election run by the Sandinistas must be suspect. 'How democratic will the elections be?', enquires one TV anchorman rhetorically (Channel 4, 1 November 1984). Another, *after* announcing that the FSLN won 68 per cent of the vote, asks 'So how well did the Sandinistas do, and were the elections fair?' (BBC 2, 5 November 1984) – his scepticism seems to be specifically reserved for elections in 'unfriendly' or Third World nations. Some of the reports on the election process are downright misleading:

HUGE TURNOUT SEEN ELUDING SANDINISTAS

is the front-page headline in the *Washington Times* after election day (5 November 1984). 'There were indications', claimed the report, 'that the Sandinistas might not get the "massive" turnout they wanted as a show of support by the populace'. In a rare example of investigative journalism in the *Washington Times*, a check on polling stations by the paper itself is cited as evidence of low turnout. In fact, 82 per cent of the registered electorate voted – higher than the Sandinistas' predictions and unimaginably higher than the best turnouts in the *Washington Times*'s home country. From a Nicaraguan point of view, it was the final proof of the elections' legitimacy. No correction to the story was published.

The lively election debate inside Nicaragua between the seven competing parties was virtually invisible in the United States and British media, allowing the image of a muzzled or scarcely-existent opposition to thrive unchallenged by the reality of their campaigns. It seemed that the best way for an opposition party to attract the attention of foreign journalists was to look as if it might leave the race. Some media clearly could not wait for this to happen; the *Daily Telegraph*, for example, reported without foundation that five parties were joining the boycott (30 October), ITN that 'most of the opposition parties boycotted the election'. Others contented themselves with guesswork: 'There is speculation that the Democratic Conservative Party and the Popular Social Christian Party will leave the discredited contest' (*The Times*, 25 October 1984). In place of concrete information about the scrupulous fairness of the electoral process, the media built up its impression of the elections by means of quoted or reported statements from the actors involved. The clear winner for the most-quoted description of the elections is 'a farce', used seventeen times and in almost all the media; followed by 'a sham', quoted ten times, including a few references to the full 'Soviet-style sham'. The main source of these remarks is the United States administration, which provided forty-seven of the reported statements in the United States media and twelve for Britain, the commonest after 'farce' and 'sham' being:

Phoney	7 times
A piece of theatre	6
It wasn't an election	4
No credible opposition	4

United States newspaper editorials: freedom of expression?

The ground rules for editorials and opinion articles are very different from the news pages: here 'neutrality' slackens its grip, writers are cut loose from mere facts and set free to interpret, analyse, make jokes, set contexts, pass judgement. I have been arguing that the gulf between all this and 'hard news' is not as wide nor as clear-cut as the lay-out of the papers suggests, that the fabric of 'news' too includes interpretation, analysis, context, judgement (even jokes sometimes). But editorials and opinion pieces are worth looking at on their home ground to see, apart from anything else, how opinion expressed as opinion tallies with opinion incorporated in news.

Almost all the United States papers in my sample found the Nicaraguan elections worthy of comment, printing thirteen pieces in all (Table 7.5).

Table 7.5 Titles of US press editorials on Nicaragua's 1984 election

Nobody won in Nicaragua	*New York Times*	7 Nov 84
Expect a farce	*New York Times*	2 Nov 84
Success undercut	*New York Times*	2 Nov 84
Going through the motions in Nicaragua	*New York Times*	4 Nov 84
Elections in Managua	*Washington Post*	1 Nov 84
The differences are clear	*Washington Post*	29 Oct 84
Bring forth the Octotal accords	*Washington Post*	29 Oct 84
Nicaragua: why quibble?	*Los Angeles Times*	7 Nov 84
Clouds over Nicaragua	*Los Angeles Times*	29 Oct 84
Vote early, vote often	*Daily News*	4 Nov 84
Nicaragua's non-election	*Richmond Times Despatch*	8 Nov 84
Democracy now	*Boston Globe*	7 Nov 84
The Nicaraguan jumble	*Boston Globe*	9 Nov 84

All the comment on Reagan and United States policy in Nicaragua from these editorial and opinion articles, is extracted in Table 7.6 and divided into 'positive' and 'negative' columns. It makes surprising reading after the news pages.

Table 7.6 United States press editorials on Reagan and United States policy

Newspaper	Positive	Negative
New York Times		'Ronald Reagan's charge . . . is malicious and inaccurate'
		'Mr. Cruz's coalition now acknowledge that they were under pressure from the CIA to find a pretext for abstention'
		'the election . . . cannot serve as justification for recent US policy'

'the Somoza's fraudulent elections produced little outrage from Washington'

'the struggle for democracy in Nicaragua should not be confused with the security interests of the US'

'it does not warrant US-sponsored invasion or terrorism'

Washington Post
'American pressure has had a visible if modest moderating impact on Sandinista militancy'

'Few would claim that the US has made good use of all the conventional economic and political sticks available to it'

Boston Globe, 7 November

'American complicity with Pinochet renders hypocritical the White House complaints about phoney elections in Nicaragua'

Boston Globe, 9 November

'fair, tough-minded criticism is the last defence against a needless, historically tragic American military adventure'

Washington Times
'under a second Reagan Administration, renewed US aid should help a growing guerilla army to prevent the Sandinista regime from perpetuating itself'

'Washington needs to be clearer about present objectives'

'difficult as it is for many Americans to believe, not everyone highly prizes our advice on the proper management of their affairs'

'the Reagan Administration's wrong-headed campaign to pressure the Sandinistas through covert war'

'the most specific thing tried by the Reagan Administration, the CIA's campaign to overthrow the Sandinistas by covert means, has been a tactical and political failure'

Richmond Times-Despatch
'only under international and domestic pressure, fuelled though far from fabricated by Washington, did the Sandinistas agree even to go through the motions'

'the Reagan Administration's effort to destroy the Managua government by political manipulation, slander, and two-faced diplomacy' 'the Reagan Administration is positioned to indulge in the low-cost blood sport of punishing Central American leftists'

'the massive Administration effort to discredit those elections is the mirror image of past campaigns to whitewash elections in "democratic" El Salvador that were far more deeply flawed'

'American policy hasn't helped. With the CIA financing gangs of terrorists across the border, mining the harbors, blowing up power stations and planning to murder local officials . . . the Reagan Administration's support for the Contras is building up a legacy of anti-Americanism that will last for years'

Editorial comment is overwhelmingly and virulently hostile to Reagan's policy; and the attacks do not just appear in 'liberal' papers like the *Boston Globe* or 'vote Democrat' papers like the New York *Daily News*, but come from the right-wing too. The *Washington Times* (a paper which was to launch its own appeal to help fund the Contras in spring 1985), criticizes the United States foreign policy establishment for being too keen on democracy and human rights in the Third World, arguing single-mindedly that 'We should not care greatly whether the government in Managua is headed by a democrat or a monarch, so long as the Communists, whose chief purpose is making trouble for us, are excluded from it' (29 October 1984). There is no sign of timid, sycophantic support for Reagan's policy in the press; on the contrary, there is every sign of lively disagreement and debate, with the editorial pages reflecting and taking part in a dispute on foreign policy towards Nicaragua that was going on inside the foreign policy establishment, in Congress and in campaigns across the country.

Is there not a contradiction here between the virtual passive acceptance of Reagan's line on the news pages and passionate rejection of his policy on the opinion pages? Lest we celebrate too soon the rediscovery of the United States newspaperman's critical faculties, we should look back at the same editorials to see what they say about Nicaragua's elections (Table 7.7). The comment shows the same approach as the majority of the news reporting, only rather more nakedly expressed.

Table 7.7 United States press editorials on the Nicaraguan elections

Newspaper	Positive	Negative
New York Times 2 November 'multiparty'		'Regrettably, the election will be a farce'
		'Voter turnout is likely to be as high . . . as in Poland and the Soviet Union. The reason is the same: coercion'
		'another fraudulent election'
		'rigged in advance'
		'a travesty of what they might have been'
		'the Sandinistas have seen their electoral experiment crumble . . . have undermined any chance that those elections could succeed'
		'in effect a referendum'
		'significant opposition groups have been denied such basic requirements as free and regular access to the media, and opposition rallies have been harrassed and broken by Sandinista thugs'
New York Times, 7 November		'Only the naive believe that Sunday's election was democratic or legitimising proof of the Sandinistas' popularity'
		'will not end the struggle for pluralism in Nicaragua'
		'the Sandinistas made it easy to dismiss their election as a sham'
		'the Sandinistas defending their election sound much like the dynasty they overthrew'
Washington Post		'will resolve nothing'
		'Managua's mock vote'
		'Managua has kicked away one good opportunity to start settling differences by American-style elections'

Boston Globe
'The partial opening for a pluralistic opposition that was created during the election process'

'Administration charges that the elections were a Soviet-style sham and that Nicaragua is a totalitarian dictatorship are gross overstatements'

'the Sandinistas surely do not deserve the good government seal of approval for the recent elections'

'the Sandinistas must . . . step past the elections into a substantive dialogue with the opposition, and schedule freer elections'

Washington Times

'The November 4 election in other words will be a farce, which is less than startling news'

'it is doubtful that Nicaragua would be capable of self-government'

'One by one the Nicaraguan opposition is dropping out of the campaign, leaving only the Sandinistas and a handful of obdurate holdouts'

'[the Sandinistas] have stripped away every last vestige of credibility these elections might have had'

'this crude manipulation of the electoral process'

'a fraud'

Los Angeles Times, 29 October

'won't bring stability'

'the Sandinistas have stacked the deck in their own favour'

'the Sandinistas' tough stance over election procedures will lead many people . . . to question how legitimate the new Nicaraguan government can be'

Los Angeles Times, 7 November

'There are many reasons to criticise last weekend's elections in Nicaragua'

'the electoral deck was stacked in the Sandinistas' favour'

Richmond Times-Despatch

'If elections are about choices, Nicaragua has yet to have one'

'Tammany couldn't have done
it better'

'Sunday's demonstration of the
Sandinistas' contempt for
democracy'

'Will they allow the Sandinista-
dominated Assembly to
develop into a democratic
alternative? Not likely, by their
record'

It seems that we are looking directly at the limits of acceptable debate. *Within these limits*, within the framework that the Sandinistas are just another Soviet-leaning anti-democratic regime, a genuine debate on policy rages wild and free. Should the United States intervene or not? Should the CIA back the Contras or not? The papers can trumpet their opinion and positions on these important questions, and on this level there is no doubt that they actually participate as the 'fourth estate' in policy formation, for instance by urging public opinion against a particular option, so restricting the administration's freedom of manoeuvre and making its supporters feel they are hemmed in by a vicious, overweaning 'liberal' press. But all this, however uncomfortable for the administration, goes on *within* the definitions set by the administration itself. To use a media researcher's cliché, the media are still following Reagan's agenda. It is a very long way from actually looking at Nicaragua in Nicaragua's terms, or opening the door even a crack to the possibility that the Nicaraguan revolution (and the 1984 elections as part of it) has been building something new, something the USA could even *learn* from, instead of just debating whether to destroy it now or later, by proxy or directly, by this method or that.

The following editorials, from the two very different papers, show how hard-hitting anti-Reaganism and meek adoption of Reagan's picture of Nicaragua coexist. The first is from the New York *Daily News*, a brash tabloid paper with a pro-democrat line on United States politics. On 4 November 1984, Nicaragua's election day, it produced an editorial that looks at first glance like a slice of the classic Reagan position: 'VOTE EARLY, VOTE OFTEN' is the cynical headline. A cartoon depicts Ortega as a fearsome Latin gaucho holding a rifle over the ballot box.

Vote Early, Vote Often
Today is election day in Nicaragua, and the odds favor the Sandinistas. Their presidential candidate, Daniel Ortega, may not achieve that democratic marvel, the 99.999% vote won by candidates in Albania or North Korea, but we can be sure he will have a comfortable majority.

There have been no free elections in Nicaragua in decades (elections run by the US Marines in the 1920s don't count) so it can't be said the

Sandinistas are violating any local traditions. On the contrary, they are clearly far more popular and deserving than the Somozas they over-threw in 1979. The problem is that a popular and justified revolution is being used by a group of dedicated Marxists to impose an undemocratic and inefficient government upon a country that has already suffered more than its share of misfortunes.

American policy hasn't helped. With the CIA financing gangs of terrorists across the border, mining the harbors, blowing up power stations and planning to murder local officials, Nicaraguans naturally support the government. The Reagan administration's support for the Contras is building a legacy of anti-Americanism that will last for years.

Ortega's victory won't change anything, but Tuesday's result might. If Walter Mondale wins, he will call off the Contras. If Ronald Reagan wins, he will have the opportunity to reconsider his policies toward Central America without fretting about being held responsible to the electorate for 'losing' Nicaragua – as though that country is ours to lose.

What either could do is proclaim victory and come home. The Sandinistas have discovered they can't get away with subverting their neighbors and have found that their Cuban and Soviet friends can arm them but can't feed them. Their only hope for a decent future is peace with their neighbors, including the US. We should offer them an olive branch, with strings. Chances are, they'd grab it.

(4 November 1984)

The text of the *Daily News* editorial starts by comparing Nicaragua with Albania and North Korea, and presenting electoral fraud as sad but inevitable: 'There have been no free elections in Nicaragua in decades . . . so it can't be said that the Sandinistas are violating any local traditions.' The standard anti-Sandinista refrain continues, without any evidence being produced: 'The problem is that a popular and justified revolution is being used by a group of dedicated Marxists to impose an undemocratic and inefficient government on a country that has already suffered more than its share of misfortunes.' The background assumptions are therefore firmly established when the paper turns to the question of United States policy. Here, though, the initial impressions are belied, and the argument is passionately anti-Reagan:

American policy hasn't helped. With the CIA financing gangs of terror-ists across the border, mining the harbors, blowing up power stations and planning to murder local officials . . . The Reagan administration's support for the Contras is building up a legacy of anti-Americanism that will last for years.

No doubt the piece would be read by any of the president's staff as a disloyal diatribe; none the less the backbone of Reagan's argument is accepted, repeated, illustrated and reinforced, even while the specific policies are attacked.

The second example is from the *New York Times*:

Nobody Won in Nicaragua

Only the naive believe that Sunday's election in Nicaragua was democratic or legitimising proof of the Sandinistas' popularity. The result was ordained when opposition parties tamely accepted terms that barred them from power. This plebiscite will not end the struggle for pluralism in Nicaragua. But neither can it serve as justification for recent American policy.

The Sandinistas made it easy to dismiss their election as a sham. Their decisive act was to break off negotiations with Arturo Cruz, an opposition democrat whose candidacy could have produced a more credible contest. He sought delay until January but was denied a truce from the US-armed 'contra' rebels.

The opposition to Daniel Ortega, the Sandinista presidential candidate, was finally shrunk to four small left-wing groups and factions of two traditional parties. Even so, after five years of unchallenged power, the Sandinistas appear to have won less than two-thirds of the vote. That means a 90-member National Assembly could begin to provide a forum for real debate – if the regime honors its promise to hold periodic elections and to respect press freedom and political assembly.

Nicaraguans know to be skeptical about such promises. The Sandinistas defending their election sound much like the dynasty they overthrew. 'The trouble with Americans is that they judge everything by United States standards', President Anastasio Somoza once declared. 'The people voted for me because I have won their affections. . . . There is sanitation, schools and communications and mechanization of agriculture.'

One crucial fact of history, however, is that the Somozas' fraudulent elections produced little outrage from Washington. The United States' tolerance then is not an argument for silence now, but it does require greater respect for Nicaraguan sensibilities about the past.

The struggle for democracy in Nicaragua should not be confused with the security interests of the United States. Whether Mr Ortega and his more rigid associates can still be lured from the Cuban model is unclear. But the political contest can be fought by diplomatic and economic means. It does not warrant US-sponsored invasion or terrorism.

More serious American action would be appropriate only if the Sandinistas become a security threat to the region. Until they clearly are, they should be dealt with as ideological adversaries, not military enemies.

(7 November 1984)

The *New York Times*, a heavyweight 'prestige' paper, is very different from the *Daily News*, but its editorial 'NOBODY WON IN NICARAGUA' on 7 November 1984 is remarkably similar in content. Again the message is that, on the one hand, the Nicaraguan elections were undemocratic, but on the other hand, this cannot justify recent United States policy. The *New York Times* is uncompromising in its judgements against United States policy – the Sandinista regime 'does not warrant US-sponsored invasion or terrorism', and Nicaraguans are 'not military enemies'.

While not trying to minimize the importance of these forceful anti-administration points, it is important to recognize exactly where the paper parts company with the president. The editorial accepts the grossly misleading assertions that the Nicaraguan elections 'will not end the struggle for pluralism in Nicaragua', were 'easy to dismiss . . . as a sham' and that Cruz's boycott was the Sandinistas' fault. The Sandinistas, according to this editorial, 'sound much like the dynasty they overthrew' and are set on following 'the Cuban model'. The *New York Times*'s point of disagreement is very specific: 'More serious American action would be appropriate only if the Sandinistas become a security threat to the region. Until they clearly are, they should be dealt with as ideological adversaries, not military enemies.' Rather than rejecting the idea of a United States-sponsored invasion of Nicaragua, it sets conditions on when such an invasion would be 'appropriate', assuming the right of the USA to engage in 'the struggle for democracy in Nicaragua', i.e. to interfere in the domestic politics of a sovereign nation.

Close the ballot box, open the MiG crate

On 6 November 1984, while the final results of the Nicaraguan voting were still coming in on horseback from remote polling stations, national elections took place in the USA. On the CBS newscast that night, the report of Ronald Reagan's election victory was interrupted by a dramatic newsflash. Soviet MiG fighter aircraft were said to be arriving in Nicaragua.

Thus broke the 'MiG crisis'. For the next five days, the media that had found but a small corner to report on Nicaragua's elections were swamped with stories about Nicaragua as an aggressive Soviet satellite. Library pictures of MiG planes abounded, headlines screamed: 'REDS SENDING GUNS GALORE TO NICARAGUA' (*Washington Times*); 'CRISIS IN NICARAGUA – PREZ: KEEP MiGS OUT!' (*New York Post*); 'US STEP UP THREAT ON RED JETS ALERT' (*Daily Express*); 'MiGS MENACE UNITES AMERICA' (*Daily Mail*). Even the relatively sedate BBC News joined in: 'US CLAIMS THAT SOVIET ARMS ARE ON THEIR WAY TO NICARAGUA' (BBC).

Virtual saturation coverage of the 'MiG scare' was scarcely affected by the inconvenient fact that no MiGs had actually been spotted. Speculation flourished. The *New York Times* spoke of 'The imminent arrival of a Soviet

freighter in Nicaragua with a cargo suspected of containing MiG 21's.'
Television news headlines continued on days two and three with leading
questions: 'THOSE RUSSIAN WAR PLANES – ARE THEY OR AREN'T THEY IN
NICARAGUA?' (BBC); 'AN EXPLOSIVE QUESTION REMAINS UNANSWERED
TONIGHT – DID THE SOVIET UNION SEND MiG FIGHTER PLANES TO NICARAGUA?'
(NBC); 'WE BEGIN AGAIN TONIGHT WITH THAT SOVIET FREIGHTER IN A
NICARAGUAN HARBOR – WHAT DOES IT HAVE ON BOARD?' (ABC).

In 111 news reports over five days, some ingenuity was shown on the part
of journalists, keeping the story running despite a severe shortage of
evidence. *Channel 4 News* (8 November 1984) resorted to an interview
with an expert to help interpret the smudgy satellite pictures of crates on
the quay of a Black Sea port, which formed the United States Intelligence
Center's case for the MiG claim:

Cratologist: Often these crates are of a distinctive custom-made size to
fit the weapon, so the whole science of cratology, which is a humorous
term to describe this type of research, is based on the comparative size
and shape of boxes.
Channel 4 interviewer: How often is that proved to be wrong?
Cratologist: Normally you have more things to go on which are more
important than the size of the crates, after all what we look for is a
picture of the weapon itself after it's been taken out of the crate.

The BBC's roving correspondent in Nicaragua filed reports from the
Nicaraguan port of Corinto for three nights running, where he was waiting
for the suspected MiGs to be unloaded. There are repeated close-ups on
the hammer and sickle on the side of the docked Soviet ship and increasingly absurd interviews. On day three he is seen venturing into the local
shipping office:

BBC correspondent: No weapons?
Port official: No, no, no.

Even when the existence of the MiG planes was severely in doubt, the
aggressive picture of Nicaragua was still painted, as in the example of this
Daily Express editorial:

RED ALERT FOR REAGAN
Whatever is in those crates at the Nicaraguan port of Corinto, the
United States is right to warn now that it will not allow the country's
Marxist Sandinista Government to use warplanes in its attempt to
spread revolution throughout Central America . . . President Reagan is
alert to the danger of Communist subversion in America's own
backyard. . . .

In the end, it emerged that the whole 'MiG crisis' was a hoax. There were
no MiGs. In the words of one Nicaraguan official, they were 'an American

dream'. Washington sources deliberately leaked the lie that Nicaragua was importing advanced Soviet jets, with the twin aim of overriding any positive impression of the Sandinista regime that their 67 per cent victory at the polls might have created, and mobilizing United States public support for Reagan's hard-line foreign policy.

What is most remarkable about the story is the way that the British and United States media swallowed it so easily. One unsubstantiated leak from a security source in Washington alleging that MiGs were on their way to a Nicaraguan port was all that was needed. As if by magic the papers and television news were obligingly filled with images of Nicaragua as a military aggressor, a Red stooge, a Soviet beachhead in the heart of the Americas. None of the resources or journalistic enthusiasm exhibited in the search for the phantom MiGs were employed in investigating the hoax. Nicaragua's denials (beginning with a phone call from Managua's foreign ministry to CBS on the night they broke the story) were routinely dismissed by the media. Again, Nicaraguans were shown to have little or no credibility when it comes to reporting on Nicaragua.

The MiG story was based on the assumption that receiving foreign fighter planes into central America was newsworthy because new wea-ponry would dangerously upset the regional balance of power. For the record, it is worth noting that Nicaragua under the Sandinistas had no foreign military bases at all. In fact, the Nicaraguan air force had only twelve combat aircraft – compared to thirty for neighbouring Honduras and fifty-nine for El Salvador. If a serious search is on for central American countries which are a threat to regional stability because of superpower intervention, Honduras and El Salvador are much more convincing candi-dates than Nicaragua. Honduras, for instance, next door to Nicaragua and with about the same population, is host to eleven United States military bases and five airstrips. In 1984 alone, some $250 million-worth of joint exercises and manoeuvres were carried out by the United States and Honduran armies. As final proof that the media are not automatically captivated by news of high-performance aircraft being sent to central America, see the case of the F5 fighter jets sent by the USA to Honduras in October 1985. The F5s are not only more advanced than MiG 21s – but also they actually arrived. It was an exact parallel to the MiG story of 1984; yet the United States planes provoked no headlines, no 'crisis'.

CONCLUSION: THE INFORMATION WAR AND ITS CONSEQUENCES

The Washington perspective

The starting point of this chapter was the question 'How have the western media portrayed the controversial revolutionary process in Nicaragua?'

The foregoing analysis of news coverage of the 1984 elections and the 'MiG scare' demonstrate that the United States administration has a solid history of effective domination of the news media. It was the Washington vision of Nicaragua and the State Department framework of world relations that were adopted by the press and broadcasters both within the USA and in Britain.

The United States 'backyard' appeared on the front page as a scarcely recognizable travesty of itself. The Sandinistas were presented as power-hungry Marxists without popular support, using violent mobs to intimidate the opposition and cheat their way to victory in sham elections. Archive film was used to back up claims of alleged intimidation. Arturo Cruz was portrayed precisely in the terms of the United States Embassy press hand-out. The Sandinistas were held to blame for all the country's problems, with no allowance made for the impact of United States-sponsored war and the United States economic blockade, nor any recognition of the revolution's remarkable achievements. The democratic debate between the eight Nicaraguan parties running in the elections was ignored, as was the testimony of hundreds of independent observers who witnessed the freedom and fairness of the country's first clean elections.

A common complaint about the news media is that they distort news by simplifying it – because of the pressure of time and limitations of space and the commercial need to produce punchy and entertaining copy, they are forced to gloss over the complexities, skimp on the background and so end up with a superficial and misleading version of events. But this excuse does not hold water in this case. It is true that the coverage failed to give much insight into significant historical background, but the basic flaw was not simplification. The Nicaraguan reality was no more complicated than the Reagan administration story-line. Set the two side by side:

According to Managua, the country is having elections, all political parties can participate. The USA, as part of a consistent campaign against the revolution, tries to discredit these elections by pretending that a marginal figure who is not even standing is the 'real opposition'.

According to Washington, Nicaragua is a Marxist dictatorship, that is holding elections but only mock elections to con world opinion, because Marxist dictatorships do not believe in democracy. There is no real opposition. Although six opposition parties are standing, they do not constitute the true opposition because Cruz is barred from the elections. Although the Sandinistas invited him to participate, it is the FSLN's fault that he has had to refuse. He is popular in Nicaragua even though the parties in his coalition have virtually no organization, nor visible support in the country. There is popular demand for concessions to be made to the Contras who are currently attacking the country. Foreign election observers who claim to have seen a free and fair contest have been duped by communist propaganda. Cruz does have contacts in Washington but there is no truth in the claims that the administration influenced his decision to withdraw from the elections (in which he was never a candidate).

There is nothing fundamentally simple about the Washington version. The problem is not just that the media are superficial, but *whose version* they choose to simplify. In spite of their claims to neutrality, it is Washington's version that consistently appears.

Finally, the 'MiG crisis', which received far more media attention than the elections, displayed the media's craven willingness to swallow an unsubstantiated and untrue report from the USA, to the absurd extent of believing that tiny impoverished Nicaragua represented a threat to the national security and safety of the mighty USA.

The Sandinistas were right to charge the USA with mounting a propaganda campaign against their revolution. Washington did indeed mobilize the news media – along with their military onslaught, the economic blockade, diplomatic pressure and political intervention – as a package of measures to bring the Sandinista regime to an end. The United States National Security Council (responsible for 'news management') noted with satisfaction after the 1984 Nicaraguan elections that: 'our handling of the Nicaraguan election issue . . . has shifted opinion against the sham elections'. (Washington Post, 7 November 1984). The close match between United States and British news coverage of the 1984 elections and the 'MiG scare' indicates that Washington's disinformation campaign had a successful international dimension.

Although clearly victims of high-powered news management, the United States media can hardly be described as 'unfree' – my analysis of United States press opinion and editorial pieces shows how the press actively relishes its freedom to participate in policy debate. But the crucial point is that neither does information flow freely: dissent in the area of policy choices only takes place within a very narrowly defined world-view. The uniformity of news reporting about Nicaragua is suffocating: the same perspective and the same language are used across media as outwardly diverse as the *Boston Globe*, the *New York Post*, CBS and the BBC. If the United States administration can succeed in selling a package of untruths in order to justify illegal intervention aimed at overthrowing the democratically-elected government of a sovereign nation, and get away with it with scarcely a whisper of contradiction, despite the unpopularity of its policy and the easy availability of counter-evidence, then how can it be claimed that the news-reading public enjoys freedom of information?

I am not arguing that there was a conspiracy of newspaper and TV news editors against Ortega's Nicaragua. Nor that the Sandinistas are angels, or beyond informed criticism. The stifling uniformity of misleading news reports points, rather, to a collusion with the interests of the United States élite which is valued far higher than freedom of information. As Noam Chomsky puts it bitterly in *Necessary Illusions*, 'the media are vigilant guardians protecting privilege from the threat of public understanding' (Chomsky 1989: 14). The structure of news coverage of Nicaragua rests on an imperialist attitude to the Third World which the media already share with the administration. They take it as 'objective' fact. This smooths the path for individual campaigns of news manipulation, such as the rewriting of the script of Nicaragua's 1984 election, and its subsequent disappearance.

Meanwhile in Managua

The Sandinistas were condemned for denying freedom of expression in their own country. In his televised address to the nation in May 1984, President Reagan claimed that

> From the moment the Sandinistas and their cadre of 50 Cuban covert advisers took power in Managua in 1979, the internal repression of democratic groups . . . began. The right to dissent was denied. Freedom of the press and freedom of assembly became virtually non-existent.

The only aspect of Sandinista media policy that attracted widespread attention was censorship. It is true that the FSLN government was guilty of both prior censorship of military news and of temporarily shutting down the main opposition newspaper *La Prensa*. This undeniably restricted the freedom of the press. However, a sense of proportion is required: censorship of military news is common to all countries at war, and Nicaragua was fighting a long and bitter war against the United States-backed Contras. Nicaraguan measures were mild indeed when compared, for instance, to United States or British control of the media when those countries were fighting the Second World War. The fact is that during almost the entire period of proxy United States aggression, the Sandinista allowed *La Prensa* to publish. *La Prensa* gave aid and comfort to the enemy by openly supporting the United States administration and the Contras themselves in its pages; while its domestic news coverage ignored the war and failed to report on the horrific damage wrought by Contra attacks. Furthermore, the paper accepted funding from the National Endowment for Democracy, a foundation wholly funded by the United States administration, set up by Reagan in 1983 for 'anti-communist operations'. In other words, *La Prensa* was funded by the same government that was making war on Nicaragua. The notorious temporary close down came on 26 June 1986, in response to a particularly acute provocation: the United States Congress voted US $110 million of new aid to the Contras in order to step up the aggression. *La Prensa*'s editor Jaime Chamorro had not only backed the campaign for this new instalment of Contra aid in *La Prensa*'s editorials, he also lobbied actively in Washington and published an article in the *Washington Post* (3 April 1986) calling on Congress to grant the $110 million 'to save democracy in Nicaragua'. Mark Cook of the Jesuit Central American University in Managua commented: 'The US couldn't expect to hang on to its domestic political assets inside Nicaragua at the same time as declaring war on the country' (Envio, UCA, Managua, July 1986). I repeat that during almost all of the ten years of Sandinista rule *La Prensa* continued to circulate, freely maligning and undermining Sandinista attempts to bring social justice and popular participation to the government of the country. Chomsky concludes from his three-month survey of *La Prensa*: 'There is no pretence of meeting minimal journalistic standards. Rather, the journal follows the standard procedures of US psychological warfare to a degree that is almost comical' (1989: 325). An example can be taken from the period of the case study above to illustrate *La Prensa*'s style and sympathies. The day after Nicaragua's 1984 elections (5 November 1984), *La Prensa* reported the 82 per cent turnout at the polls with the withering headline 'HUGE APATHY – 18% ABSTENTION'. Two days later when the results were announced for the elections in the USA, with a 45 per cent abstention rate, *La Prensa* produced the headline, 'OVERWHELMING VICTORY FOR REAGAN'.

The point I am trying to make is that although the Sandinistas did practise censorship, this was not a symptom of totalitarian control of the media. Censorship, however regrettable, was strictly limited and was used as a weapon of last resort in a grossly unequal battle, in this case against an enemy mouthpiece inside the country. Sandinista measures against *La Prensa* contrasted starkly with those taken against opposition media in the neighbouring states of El Salvador and Honduras, praised by the USA as fledgling democracies, where bombing newspaper offices and assassinating journalists were the preferred methods. The use of censorship is in fact a sign of weakness here rather than a signal of excessive state power. The Sandinista state clearly did not have the sort of informal, unspoken institutional power over the media that makes crude censorship unnecessary – the sort of power that the United States administration enjoys and makes expert use of.

In reality, the Sandinista revolution in Nicaragua embraced a genuine attempt to democratize the media. Sandinista commitment to openness and the free flow of information is evident in the way Nicaragua's borders were always kept open to journalists, observers, politicians and researchers from abroad. Apart from military escorts in combat zones, journalists were given free access throughout the country. The reports on Nicaragua's 1984 election analysed above are testimony to foreign correspondents' freedom of expression. (The pity is how few of them seemed willing to open their eyes to what was in front of them.)

As for the domestic media, there was an extraordinarily healthy variety of political standpoints available. Of the three national dailies, *Barricada* was unabashedly the FSLN party organ, blazing with revolutionary analysis and aiming to mobilize the masses. *La Prensa*, as we have seen, took an openly counter-revolutionary stance. *El Nuevo Diario*, an offshoot from the old *La Prensa*, offered 'critical support' from a basically pro-Sandinista position.

Considering high illiteracy rates and patchy newspaper distribution, radio rather than press is the most important medium of communication in Nicaragua. With some 274 receivers per 1,000 inhabitants (UNESCO figures 1982), it is to the radio that most Nicaraguans turn for information. When the Sandinistas were in power, there were a record forty-three radio stations broadcasting, and the majority were in private hands, including three out of the five stations with national coverage. There was real pluralism in programme content as well as ownership: most private radios were virulently anti-Sandinista, over half the private local stations regularly broadcast programming from the United States 'Voice of America'. The radios under Sandinista control undertook innovative experiments in opening the airwaves to the public: 'Voz de Nicaragua' gave 4 hours daily to the immensely popular 'Contacto 620', an open access programme with callers' complaints and denunciations of state malpractice broadcast live and investigated by the radio journalists. Television, reaching fewer people, was nationalized in 1979 and so came under state control; but here, too the broadcasters strove for greater democracy. The weekly *De Cara Al Pueblo* brought President Ortega and his cabinet face-to-face with the citizens, and called to account on air. In both the 1984 and 1990 elections all political parties were granted equal free air-time for electioneering broadcasts, and their leaders were invited to participate in live televised debates. So even under Sandinista control, the television was not monopolized by the FSLN party line. The plethora of small-circulation publications by political parties, religious and community groups, and the new outpouring of small-scale independent video productions were further signs of a striving towards freedom of expression.

Experiments in media democracy during the Sandinista years were no doubt partial and flawed. Like the rest of the revolution's initiatives, they were certainly stunted by the impact of the war and starved of resources. None the less, on balance, the Sandinistas did advance the cause of media freedom rather than crush it. Under the Somoza dictatorship, with the collusion of the USA, freedom of expression was a distant dream and public dissent could be fatal. The most celebrated case is Pedro Joaquin Chamorro, assassinated by Somoza's henchmen in 1978 for publishing in his paper an exposé of Somoza's blood-plasma racket. (Chamorro became a posthumous hero, launching into politics his widow Violeta, now president of the country.) The Sandinistas, in contrast, launched the most successful crash literacy campaign in history as one of their first acts in government. The idea of teaching poor *campesinos* to read and write was to give the people the tools to enable freedom of expression to take root. I would argue that there is still merit in the fledgling attempts of the Sandinista revolution to introduce a new democracy in the media, and to face up to the politics of the ownership and distribution of information. The tragedy is that this imaginative experiment was so crushed by war and political intervention, imposed by the USA.

It may seem absurd to compare, for instance, the cheaply-produced, relatively primitive newspapers of Nicaragua, usually only twelve pages long, with the prestigious press of the USA (like the *New York Times*, often over 120 pages in length). In glossiness and sophistication, in technology and style, the United States news media probably lead the world. And as I pointed out above, there is a fine and flourishing tradition of unbowed dissent in the United States press, as far as editorial discussion of government policy is concerned. But I want to make a comparison on a different plane.

What is notable about Nicaragua's humble media for our purposes here, is that their political affiliation is laid bare: there is no attempt to pose as 'neutral'. The media know they are instruments of political struggle. So do their audience. While the number of news sources is smaller than for the well-resourced United States or British press, the range of angles is wider – from anti-imperialist class analysis in the FLSN daily *Barricada* to counter-revolutionary agitation in *La Prensa*. The Nicaraguan media, weighed down by all the handicaps of a Third World country, made an authentic attempt to reflect the full range of ideological positions in the country, to play their role in the arduous struggle to build a new society. Nicaraguans were able, at least to some extent, to use their media to speak their own truths about the experience of their revolution, whichever side they were on. They had begun to see what freedom of information and freedom of expression might mean, and to recognize the role of the media in any information war, without being led astray by the western myth that news can be wholly 'objective' and 'value-free'.

The United States and British media, on the other hand, reported on Nicaragua in such a way that they played their own small part in the United States administration's campaign against the Sandinista revolution. They allowed the news to be so moulded as to bury the revolutionary message of the Sandinistas' achievements, and allowed themselves to be orchestrated into the chorus of attacks on Nicaragua's self-determination. And all along, while acting as unpaid agents for the United States disinformation machine or the Contras' 'war effort', the media protested their own objectivity and neutrality: 'I believe we have a duty, like a doctor, to give unbiased news, a duty to the public', said the NBC editor.

In the end the United States campaign against the freely-elected Sandinista government of Nicaragua was successful. The long-term strategy, combining the bullet, the blockade, the bribe and the press release, ousted the Sandinistas at their own polls in the 1990 elections. As Chomsky sums it up in *Deterring Democracy*, 'Nicaraguan voters were informed that they had a free choice: vote for our candidate or watch your children starve' (1991: 141). The information war was only one part of the campaign, but I would judge that the compliance of the United States media in presenting Washington's view of the Nicaraguan revolution was one element in its success. The media do indeed have a duty to the public, but on the evidence I have presented here, they failed in this duty. One voice predominates in the media coverage of Nicaragua, and the Nicaraguans' own voices were largely silenced. I leave the last word on objectivity and journalistic ethics to Mario Espinoza of the Managua daily *El Nuevo Diario*: '[Western journalists'] idea of objectivity is that everything has two sides. But that's wrong – things have more than two sides; they have a history, a value, causes, and consequences' (interview with author).

ACKNOWLEDGEMENTS

The author wishes to acknowledge the support of the ESRC for the research in this essay; to thank everyone in Managua who co-operated with my investigations, and Mike Gonzalez and Jenny England in Glasgow for their help.

NOTES

1 The USA refused to recognize the jurisdiction or the verdict of the World Court and to date has made no war reparations.
2 At Bill Stewart's memorial service, United States ambassador to the United Nations, Andrew Young, took the opportunity to express the administration's image of the United States's own mass media. He said 'It is a mark of progress in our civilisation that our journalists are our front line of defence, that we have learned to mobilise the power of truth through the mass media.'
3 United States forces have invaded Nicaragua six times between 1855 and 1934. United States funded and directed Contra forces made countless incursions and attacks between 1981 and 1990.
4 'BALLOT BOX MARXISTS' was the backdrop headline used on BBC 2 *Newsnight*'s report on the Nicaraguan elections on November 1984.
5 A similar strategy was used much more successfully six years later. The CDN was made up of three tiny pro-United States parties; whereas Chamorro's UNO coalition that stood against the FSLN in 1990 was a much broader alliance of fifteen parties. Coalition members ranged from well-established parties that had run alone in the 1984 elections (such as the PLI), to such unlikely anti-Sandinista bedfellows as the Communist Party and the MDN (a demobilized Contra group). It was a political coup for the United States embassy to keep this disparate group together for the duration of the campaign. (Now in government, the alliance has effectively broken up.)

REFERENCES

Most of the sources used are newspapers, television news broadcasts and the author's own interviews, as referenced in the text. Other published sources are listed below.

America's Watch (1985) *Human Rights in Nicaragua: Reagan, Rhetoric and Reality*, Washington DC: America's Watch.
Chomsky, Noam (1989) *Necessary Illusions*, London: Pluto Press.
—— (1991), *Deterring Democracy*, London: Verso.
Oxfam Public Affairs Unit (1985) *The Threat of a Good Example*, Oxford: Oxfam.

Chapter 8

The *CBS Evening News*, 7 Apr

Creating an ineffable television for

Brian Winston

The news, better perhaps than any other genre of television programming, illustrates that tendency, identified by Barthes, whereby bourgeois ideology 'completely disappears', leaving its productions as 'ineffable' (Barthes 1973: 138, 142).

By the mid-1970s, when the Glasgow University Media Group began its examination of television news, every last aspect of news presentation had been developed in professional usage and fixed by public acceptance. The point had been reached where the programmes' forms were perceived by professionals as 'natural'. The reality of the world as represented on television had indeed been transformed 'into an image of the world. History into Nature' (ibid.: 141). For instance, an early and not untypically overwrought official BBC reaction to the work of the group claimed that there was no meaning to be attached to the fact established by the group's visual analysis of the news that economics stories used more graphics than did labour dispute stories. It was merely, asseverated the BBC, 'natural' (Glasgow University Media Group 1980: 305).

Achieving the clear ideological advantage of transparency was television news' first and arguably greatest triumph. This was done largely in America during a formative period in the late 1940s. It was no mean feat, given that the solutions which looked so 'natural' by the mid-1970s were elusive, not to say vexed and complex, three decades or so earlier.

THE RADIO, THE RADIO NEWSREEL AND THE NEWSREEL

Before the Second World War, the issue confronting broadcast news personnel on both sides of the Atlantic as they turned to the new medium of television was quite clear: how to blend the techniques of the radio, then coming of age as an information channel, with the theatrical newsreel, by no means so secure a form of journalistic enterprise.

News had made an early connection with electronically transmitted speech. In 1893 the Budapest Telephone Service established a *Telephonic newspaper* (Marvin 1988: 222ff.; Woods 1967: 202). A pioneering radio broadcast station in San José was reading the news over the air in 1909 (Greb 1958–9: 3). The broadcasting of election returns, in effect the generation of news rather than its repetition, began in 1916. The Harding–Cox presidential election of 1920 'marks the generally acknowledged inaugural of regular radio broadcasting in the United States' (Bohn 1968: 268).

Radio news was both constrained and stimulated by relations with the press. On the one hand, the actual news bulletin was limited to specific news agency copy. In the UK this constraint was enshrined in the original BBC licence (BBC 1930: 159; A. Smith 1974: 41f). In the USA, where the situation was complicated by newspaper ownership of local radio stations, the actions of the Newspaper Publishers Association were primarily directed against the networks (Lott 1970: *passim*). But in each case, the result was similar; both the BBC and the networks had attenuated internal news operations into the early 1930s (Barnouw 1968: 16ff.; Briggs 1985: 116ff.).

On the other hand, these attempts in the 1920s and 1930s to limit the radio news to modest 'rip–and–read' operations encouraged other forms of factual coverage to develop. These included direct live inserts from remote studios (including international hook-ups), feature documentaries (including studio-based interviews), 'talks' (developed by the BBC but copied by the United States networks) and, in the USA, the rise of the radio commentator (Briggs 1985: 119; Scannell 1986: 7; R. Smith 1957: *passim*; Sperber 1986: 86). Thus it was that the organization of actual newsrooms followed the establishment of other factual programming production departments.

(The press was not the only inhibitor of these developments. There was also the failure to exploit the emerging technology of location recording devices. Although some attempts were made to use recorders, the on-site interview was unknown before the Second World War (Scannell 1986: 24). Instead, independent of the technological possibilities, there was a hostility to 'bottled programmes'. The result was a general insistence, 'almost on moral grounds', on the superiority of the live transmission, a fetishizing of 'liveness' (Briggs 1985: 121f.). As the 1941 *BBC Handbook* put it: ' "You have been listening to a recording . . . ." Some listeners cannot escape a feeling of disillusionment at these words' (BBC 1941: 25).[1]

As the 1930s advanced, the popularity of the medium and the march of events combined to establish radio news in a firmer position. The other modes of factual coverage that had been developed enhanced it, leaving it with a perhaps wider repertoire of presentational techniques than it might otherwise have had. For instance, the BBC covered the Saar plebiscite live on the 9 o'clock bulletin and, during the Anschluss, Ed Murrow and his colleagues at CBS created the montage of worldwide 'eyewitness' reports from correspondents – although, initially, the correspondents broadcast from overseas studios rather than locations. This was to be the most significant form of American radio network news broadcasting throughout the Second World War (Briggs 1985: 119; Sperber 1986: 116).

The Second World War brought an increase in the United States network time allocated for news and talks – from 16.4 per cent (October 1942–April 1943) to 18.6 per cent (May–September 1943) (*Broadcasting* 1944: 30). By 1940 the BBC's 9 o'clock news audience was anything from 13 to 16 million adults, compared with under 11 million for the most popular entertainment show *Saturday Night Variety* (BBC 1941: 76ff.).

Although it is clear that the press exerted the dominant external influence on the structure of these radio developments, nevertheless the existence of the cinema's news capacity was also acknowledged. Significantly, the Murrow show, *CBS World News Round-Up*, was generally referred to as a 'news*reel*'. This term had also been used as a programme title by BBC radio in the early 1930s.

Newsreels were, however, a quite distinctly tainted source of news. From the very beginning their response to the impossibility of covering the breaking story had been a tolerance for 'reconstruction' and a taste for trivialization. These tendencies were compounded by an unwillingness to tackle controversy and, by the 1930s, a madcap pursuit of 'exclusives' which resulted in a virtual war between production companies. The newsreels were something less than journalism of record. Indeed, in most informed contemporary opinion, they were something less than journalism, period.

In July 1936, for instance, the five major British companies devoted 44 per cent of their coverage to sport and the royal family. (This was sixth months after Edward VIII's coronation and sixth months before the abdication crisis.) In the USA, a parallel study of the big five in 1939 revealed that 51 per cent of items were devoted to disasters, fashion, sports and 'miscellaneous' (Aldgate 1979: 77f.). Pianist and wit Oscar Levant, summed up decades of disdain when he defined the form, even as it was on its last legs in 1965, as: 'The newsreel: A series of catastrophes, ended by a fashion show' (cited in Fielding 1972: 228). It is no wonder that a 1938 UK Mass Observation poll, in asking the question, 'On what do you base your opinion about the danger of war?', did not even bother to list newsreels as a possible source (Lewis 1977: 69). By 1940, 35 per cent of Mass Observation interviewees were spontaneously complaining that the newsreels had 'no news' (Aldgate 1979: 62).

Despite some nods towards the press, professional newsreel producers and technicians did not see themselves as journalists nor their product as journalism. There was little or no shared culture. Newsreel people were largely film industry personnel who had no experience of newspaper work. The nearest some got was to have worked in radio. The press barons, with the exception of Hearst in the USA and Rothermere in the UK, neither owned nor held interests in the newsreel companies (Aldgate 1979: 35; Fielding 1978: 4). The Hearst product was so unpopular as to invoke pickets from progressive forces outside the cinema and boos within (Fielding 1972: 248).

Fielding cites *Kino Pravda, Die Deutsche Wochenschau* and *The March of Time* as exempla of roads not taken by the newsreel companies (ibid.: 230).[2] Any of these might have yielded elements of a pictorial format that could have been of more direct use to radio personnel experimenting with television news. As it was, the most potent legacies of the newsreel were a very rough and ready aesthetic expectation plus a lingering doubt as to how serious a visual news could hope to be.

The newsreels did however confirm the radio pattern for a news broadcast, including a tendency to cram items into a short span and, most importantly, an ordering of stories which moved from the serious to the trivial:

> the American newsreel, with the fragmented succession of unrelated 'stories', the titles composed in the manner of front page headlines, and the practice of beginning each issue with the major news event of the day, followed by successively less important subject matter.
>
> (Fielding 1972: 135)

Fielding compares this to the weekly newsreel *Wochenschau*'s reversed structure where the most important story 'topped the bill', as it were, in a carefully constructed climactic sequence.

Despite the overall difficulties the newsreels raised, they did share enough with both press and radio news to be of service when the television experiments started in earnest in the mid-1930s. Newsreels, not radio 'rip-and-read' bulletins, were the first response. When the television stand was unveiled at the RadiOlympia show on 26 August 1936, the 100-minute demonstration included a Gaumont British newsreel, but not a newscast (Norman 1984: 14).

Much the same happened in the United States. NBC, televising via W2XBS, New York from 7 July 1936, included Pathé newsreels. The so-called RCA–NBC inaugural television programme on 10 May 1939 contained 'an especially made newsreel' (Slide 1987: 111).

However, the Americans did go a lot further than the British in experimenting with the radio format as well. NBC televised the Lowell Thomas radio news three times a week starting in 1940. Thomas was the news 'star' of the NBC Blue network. NBC thus began what was to turn into a long, if interrupted, series of such transmissions using a newsreader and still photographs. Standard Oil sponsored these early attempts to televise the radio news and a well-established (CBS) radio title was adapted: *The Esso Television Reporter* (Brunovska Karnick 1988: 27). After American involvement in the hostilities, NBC added *The Face of War*, a regularly scheduled summary of war news. Fronted by Sam Cuff, it used detailed maps to explain the situation on the fronts.

CBS and Dumont (NBC not yet having been forced to spin off ABC) were also continuing with experimental newscasts that relied more on radio models than on the newsreel. CBS, for instance, had a local 30-minute news on its New York station every week night and heralded the outbreak of war on 7 December 1941 with a 9-hour special transmission. But by the following year all these efforts had ceased.

It should also be noted that the German experimental period, which continued throughout the hostilities, so privileged television news production that *Tagesschau* was coined as a neologism to describe the daily show (Hempel 1990: 138; Uricchio 1989: 49).

One is, therefore, particularly struck by the absence of any parallel experimentation at the BBC's Alexandra Palace television studios. While it is true that the BBC was fettered by the press, it was slowly breaking free. A radio news department had been established in 1934. The corporation was still prohibited from broadcasting news before 6 p.m., but it was allowed to do so in emergencies. This restriction was thus being swept away by the deepening international crisis even as TV transmissions were beginning (Paulu 1981: 191). Anyway, television was an evening phenomenon with only demonstration films being transmitted during the day and could, on these grounds alone, have avoided the restrictions. Instead it continued to use a newsreel.

At Alexandra Palace, much creative energy was devoted to probing the full range of the studio, including what must have been quite complex attempts to create televised drama and dance. Paradoxically, it is this effort that might have inhibited the exploration of studio-based news presentations. It took at least 15 minutes to reset the studio for the scheduled dramatic and entertainment programmes. The newsreel film (and the Disney cartoon) provided this critical turn-round time (Norman 1984: 155). Be that as it may, the fact is that the British prewar television service closed down on 1 September 1939 without any attempt to televise the news having been undertaken.

In America, after a period when virtually no programming was transmitted, both CBS and NBC renewed the exploration of news on television in 1944. NBC started a non-nightly (i.e., newsreel-style) 10- or 15-minute programme transmitted at various times between 8 p.m. and 9 p.m. In May 1945 it established its own newsfilm operation. By 1946 the nascent three station NBC network was carrying *The Esso Television Reporter*.[3]

It was the fourth network, Dumont, then in better shape than the new-born ABC, which tried a regular networked week night news first. Spurred by the coming presidential election race, it began in August 1947 *News From Washington*. The programme, largely a to-camera recital of wire stories read by Walter Compton, lasted till the following May. But in January 1948 Dumont also began transmitting at 7.45 p.m. a more extensive film-newsreel-style programme. Yet Dumont, pressed by the FCC and AT&T long-line charges as well as its on-air competitors, could not keep up. It was without regular news broadcasts by 1950.

Of longer-term significance then was the development of TV news operations at NBC and CBS. In February 1948, a month after Dumont expanded its offering, NBC began its own in-house nightly production. To do this, it took over a show, *Camel Newsreel Theater*, which was already in its own schedule but produced by a sponsor, R. J. Reynolds, and 20th Century Fox's newsreel company. (This sponsored production pattern was the norm for radio soap opera, for instance, but not for radio news and current affairs.) The network, exploiting Reynolds's dissatisfaction with the newsreel company, offered its services instead (Brunovska Karnick 1988: 27). A year later, expanded to 15 minutes, the show became *Camel News Caravan*. Fronted by John Cameron Swayze, it was to last until 1957.[4]

The CBS network was not far behind. Rather than its own newsreel department, it had contracted with Telenews, a subsidiary of the Hearst-MGM newsreel, for film.[5] It began its regular nightly bulletin in May 1948. This was sponsored by General Motors but, significantly, it did not have a company plug in the title. Instead, on-screen and in the listings, it was just *CBS News with Douglas Edwards*. Edwards had been the on-camera talent for the network's experiments since 1944. He was to occupy the chair until he was replaced fourteen years later by Walter Cronkite.[6]

In these first years the days, times and lengths of these programmes on all networks varied. The week night news slot did not finally stabilize until 1949, from which year dates the first surviving telerecording. I propose examining the very earliest of these with a view to suggesting the degree to which, as the second decade of endeavour approached, the television news had, and had not, taken its modern form.

OLDS BRINGS THE NEWS: 7 APRIL 1949

The *CBS News with Douglas Edwards* was, on 7 April 1949, into its eleventh month of continuous transmission. For film it used the Telenews reel and, according to the closing credits, CBS film as well (*Newsweek* 1949: 59). Edwards, who wrote his own scripts, was supported by a full-time staff of sixteen and fourteen part-timers. It took, as a somewhat wondering *Editor and Publisher* headline put it, '148 Man-hours Produce 15 Minutes of TV News' (Walker 1949b: 50). The *CBS Evening News* was already, as this article also stated, 'a prize-winning pace-setter in video news reporting since 1944'. However, despite the team's some five years of experience, the broadcast to hand exhibits, by no means uniquely as viewings of other early surviving telerecordings confirm, considerable presentational tentativeness.

7 April 1949 was not a big news day. Civil wars were being fought in Greece and China. The US was still trying to reconstruct Europe, including establishing a form of government for the western half of Germany. (The Berlin airlift would end in May.) Domestically, Truman was a few months past his unexpected electoral victory. McCarthy's attack on the State Department was less than a year in the future but the corrupting effects of Truman's own loyalty oath executive order were being felt. All in all, though, an average day; one in which the news did not hit unexpected rocks but rather flowed smoothly over what American medical insurers would call 'pre-existing conditions'. In Manhattan one of the biggest things to happen was the premiere of *South Pacific* at the Majestic for which the crowd was gathering as the *CBS Evening News* was being transmitted.

Let me first deal with those elements that appear to have been fixed by this date.

Overall, CBS were producing something that was obviously a television news. After some false starts, it had been established that the news would be an in-house production with external sponsors, not, as was the case with other programming and some earlier TV news broadcasts, a sponsored production carried by the network. Thus the show was a network production and, in modern American fashion, had an opening title, followed by headlines, followed by a commercial. Thereafter came the body of the bulletin, concluded by another commercial, pay-off stories to camera and, finally, the closing credits.

The show came from a TV studio, not, as had been tried and abandoned the previous year on NBC, an outside broadcast from the radio news studio (Brunovska Karnick 1988: 27). CBS had already constituted Edwards in the ways that Morse notes as a mark of modern news production, where the newscaster is ' "a speaking subject" against an abstract map' (1986: 70, 59ff.). The 1949 CBS set, with its desk, map on the back wall surmounted by a 'CBS TV NEWS' sign and the top of a typewriter just visible in the foreground, is clearly a precursor of current practices. The two basic shots of the newscaster, a medium shot framed below the breast pocket and a close-up framed below the tie knot, are still the basic shots.

No human beings were credited with producing the programme. Already, the TV news was just ineffably happening, Edwards's thirty helpers and the film crews being invisible. (The closing captions simply acknowledged that newsfilm provided by CBS and Telenews was used and that 'This is CBS'.) The film did not noticeably 'stale' the bulletin, despite the professional discourse of the day which was making much of that medium's slowness. In fact, Telenews, which had began in February 1948, sent out prints nationwide by air and some stations would get the reel in time to transmit the same night (*Broadcasting* 1948: 19). This was certainly the case at the network and allowed it to meet the cultural expectations of news, rather than newsreel, topicality in its filmed stories.

Surprisingly perhaps, the crude measure of pacing – shot duration – was not that far from modern norms. The whole programme consisted of 130 shots, again including commercials and closing cards. There were 106 shots in the news proper, an average 6.75 seconds per shot. Newsfilm was being cut for an average shot of 4.41 seconds. The studio shots were some 13.28 seconds in duration on average. Although this rate compares reasonably with, for instance, British practice in the 1970s, the measure ignores the enriched visual environment of the today's basic studio shot (Glasgow University Media Group 1980: 198f.). Nevertheless, this fundamental of production, shot length, was already, in most regards, close to modern practice.

The editorial policy of network news, as the selection of the twenty-two stories presented in the edition attests, was also well established. In terms of the tension between newsreel and radio traditions, the radio, with its emulation of the quality newspaper, had already won.

The programme covered stories on national politics, United States international relations, the Cold War, other foreign events, domestic and local news and some human interest material. In terms of current practice only business and sport are missing (Glasgow University Media Group 1976: 269ff.)

Here then is the running order of this bulletin.

A National politics:

1 New farm subsidy program
2 Army Day celebrated
3 Truman still wants more taxes
4 Truman holds weekly press conference
5 New defense undersecretary named

B American international relations

6 Republicans blocking Euro-recovery bill
7 Allies OK new West German government
8 Extra budget to rearm Europe
9 Airfield aid pact signed in Panama
10 Brazilian war minister at West Point

C Cold War

11 Athens denies communist success in north
12 Communist Icelanders riot against Nato
13 Chinese nationalists seek peace with communists
14 UN to debate Soviet priests' case
15 Soviets claim Russian invented TV

D Foreign news (other than Cold War)

16 Earthquake-rent Fukui (Japan) recovers

E Domestic and local

17 Miners' retirement age reduced to 60
18 New York special congressional election set
19 New York City taxi strike continues
20 FBI raid corrupt banker's home

F Human interest

21 Bank opens window for pram-pushing mums
22 Prince Charles is 19 weeks old

Of these twenty-two stories, twelve were carried by the *New York Times* between 6 and 8 April. All but one of the stories 'headlined' by CBS were also given significant play in the *Times*. Three of the stories were carried by the *Times* on the morning of 7 April and repeated on CBS that evening, including a report on the Army Day parade which had been held in Washington on 6 April. As the film was to hand the same day as the story ran in the paper this is a good illustration of how the slowness of film was not necessarily that disastrous.

Seven of the stories were in the *Times* the morning after the transmission, CBS thus taking the lead. The *Times* even agreed with CBS about the newsworthiness of the one shared crime story, that about the corrupt banker.

Other stories covered by the *Times* but omitted by CBS were of a similar sort to those chosen by the TV news personnel – a riot in Hong Kong, rather than a riot in Reykjavik, more on clerics in other communist countries, etc.

The converse is also true. Human interest apart, the ten stories the *Times* did not report could have been carried by the paper, with the possible exception of the Brazilian war minister's visit to West Point. These were largely the filmed stories so the divergence was to be expected. What is surprising was that the news values of the newspaper held up in CBS' choice of newsreel material.

Moreover, we began with the most important story of the day, the farm subsidies plan, packaged by being topped and tailed with other Washington news. We progressed through the six categories in a fairly orderly fashion and certainly we finished with a (supposedly) jocular pay-off. The CBS agenda closely corresponded with that of the contemporary quality press and placement within the broadcast was thus largely in accord with modern norms.

So, the programme was produced in-house, sponsored, lasted for fifteen minutes, had shots that lasted for less than 7 seconds each, newsfilm markedly 'fresher' than newsreel norms, a newscaster using direct address from a studio with a map at his back and a news agenda shared with the quality press and shaped in a modern order. Nevertheless there were significant deviances from modern practice, all of which illustrate the degree to which the form was still in flux.

Let us now turn to these departures.

AA Title/commercial message   (0′23″)

BB 'The news picture tonight'   (0′44″)

    A 1   New farm subsidy program
    A 5   New defense undersecretary named
    C 14   UN to debate Soviet priests' case
    C 11   Athens denies communist success in north
    E 20   FBI raid corrupt banker's home

AA Commercial message   (0′52″)

CC 'The rest of the story'   (10′08″)

    A 4   Truman holds weekly press conference
    B 8   Extra budget to rearm Europe
    A 3   Truman still wants more taxes
    A 1   New farm subsidy program*
    B 6   Republicans blocking Euro-recovery bill
    B 7   Allies OK new West German government
    A 2   Army Day celebrated
    B 10   Brazilian war minister at West Point
    B 9   Airfield aid pact signed in Panama
    C 14   UN to debate Soviet priests' case*
    C 11   Athens denies communist success in north*
    C 12   Communist Icelanders riot against Nato
    C 13   Chinese nationalists seek peace with communists
    D 16   Earthquake-rent Fukui (Japan) recovers
    F 21   Bank opens window for pram-pushing mums
    F 22   Prince Charles is 19 weeks old
    E 19   New York City taxi strike continues

AA Commercial message   (0′52″)

DD 'A little late news'   (1′04″)

    E 17   Miners' retirement age reduced to 60
    E 18   New York special congressional election set
    C 15   Soviets claim Russian invented TV

AA Commercial message/credits   (0′22″)

    (* = 'headlined' story)

The first thing to note is that there were significantly more stories than is the current norm. This CBS edition lasted for only 14 minutes 25 seconds including commercial messages and closing captions. The twenty-two stories were headlined and reported in 11 minutes 56 seconds. By contrast British news broadcasts of this sort of length in the 1970s contained only nine or ten stories (Glasgow University Media Group 1976: 87). Today twenty-two stories would fill a United States commercial 22 to 24 minute news-hole, the *CNN Headline News* service for instance.

The dispatch with which many of these stories were treated is but the first factor leading to a certain overall sense of discontinuity. This incipient incoherence is compounded by three further elements.

First there were the rather curious 'headlines' at the outset of the programme.

= shot number

	/*Edwards* (to camera)
#4 Edwards M/S (top of breast pocket); f/g typewriter; b/g map on wall	(A 1) Good evening everybody, here's the news picture tonight. The Administration announces a new farm program calling for subsidies and price supports for food products.
	(A 5) Steve Early, former aide to FDR, has been named the undersecretary of defense. In effect he'll be the general manager of the armed forces.
	(C 14) United Nations has voted for a full-dress Assembly debate on the trials of the clergymen – this over bitter Russian protest this afternoon.
	(C 11) The Athens government says the guerilla offensive has been broken; 'not so,' says the communist side.
	(E 20) Here in New York the FBI has recovered a cache of bonds allegedly taken by banker Richard Kroll. Found them in an attic in Kroll's home.

> Well, in just a moment the rest of
> the story. Now a message from our
> sponsor, your Oldsmobile dealer.

This balanced choice of headline meshed with the news agenda since all but one (the Steve Early appointment) were carried by the *Times*. However, two of them did not function as headlines at all; rather they defeated expectations (if such expectations then existed) that more details would be given subsequently by not being returned to in the rest of the programme. In fact, the twenty-five words on Secretary Early and the twenty-six words on the FBI's raid in New York constituted the total reports on these topics. Further, when Edwards came back to one of these stories, the farm subsidy, he called attention to the fact that it had been headlined: 'this new and very broad farm program we mentioned'. It would seem as if the idea of electronic headlines was rather tenuous and confused.

To this, then, add a second element of dislocation. The overall structuring of the bulletin is less ordered than it at first appears. Although the categories moved, as might be anticipated, from national and international affairs at the top to local and human interest at the end and were treated almost completely as wholes, there are significant deviations from the associative logic of category clustering.

Two of these deviations arose because the geographical source of the story was being privileged over its content category. B 8, the international relations story about the budget for rearming Europe, came up at the president's press conference in the White House, as did the national story on Truman's desire for a tax increase that follows; so the group A 2/B 8/ A 3 was, in effect, a White House package. (There was no film of the president's press conference since this was not to be opened to non-print media until January 1955 (*Broadcasting* 1982: 128).) A potential thematic package about United States relations to and involvement with Europe (B 8/B 6/B 7) was thus broken by two domestic stories – a short note, A 3, on tax plans and A 1 the farm subsidy plan which was the long, 1 minute 35 second, main story of the night. The effect was to hop to Europe, then back to domestic concerns, then back to Europe again simply because all these stories emanated from the White House.

The same sort of problem can be seen with the placement of the Army Day (A 2) coverage. Although putting it in the middle of American international relations package (B) was not too surprising, the script revealed that another logic was at work. Following the farm subsidies A 1, which was introduced as the day's 'biggest one [*sic*] Washington development', B 6 and B 7, the two USA/European items, were similarly introduced: 'With other Washington news'. This led to the thematically misplaced Army Day film (A 2): 'Well, it was a very big day in Washington yesterday'. Thus there was a Washington package – A 1/B 6/

B 7/A 2 – following the White House package – A 2/B 8/A 3. This Washington package then segued, without returning to the studio but using instead a newsreel style caption, into a second filmed military report, the Brazilians at West Point.

The only question raised by third story isolated from its category, the Cold War joke C 15, is exactly that it should be in the Cold War category rather than the more expected human interest pay-off. The tone of the report, which Edwards delivered to camera, explained its placement:

#127 continued (as #4)

Edwards (to camera continued) Well now, here's one for the books and it comes to us tonight from Moscow. The Russians you know have been on a recent rampage claiming that they have invented this, that and the other thing all the way from the telephone to the nickel cigar. Today a Moscow claim . . . get set for it . . . a Moscow claim that television was invented by a Russian whose name shall here go unmentioned. Well that's the news from Moscow and this is Douglas Edwards saying goodnight for Oldsmobile.

(The name Edwards could not bring himself to utter was that of Boris L'vovich Rozing who, in 1911, transmitted a signal to a cathode ray tube, the first time this feat was recorded. Before the revolution Rozing numbered among his pupils at the St Petersburg Institute of Technology both Zworykin (later of RCA) and Schoenberg (later of EMI). Thus, his claim to television's paternity is no worse than anybody else's and a good deal better than most (Gorokhov 1977: 75; Waldrop and Borkin 1938: 213).)

There is a fourth story, not so much isolated from its category, as separated from it because of a commercial break. E 19, developments in the on-going New York City taxi strike, came after the human interest stories and before the second commercial. The other E domestic and local stories followed this break as a 'little late news', their topicality reinforced by Edwards's reading tapes, as news agency print-out is called in America. The taxi story was different in that it had been carried by the *Times* that morning.

So, there was a certain breathlessness in the number of stories covered, a degree of broken logic in some juxtapositionings and a certain roughness in the way some packages of stories were structured. However, most significant in this litany of deviances from the modern norm is the third element –

presentational form, and specifically the degree to which radio and news-reel were, or were not, melded together.

Adding information as to whether the stories were (a) delivered to camera without illustrative material (Edwards to camera), (b) delivered to camera with illustrative material, i.e., film, graphics and stills (Illus) or (c) on film alone (Newsfilm) reveals the extent to which radio and newsreel forms had yet to gel:

AA Title/commercial message   (0'23")

Main title film

BB 'The news picture'

Edwards to camera   (0'44")
    B 1   New farm subsidy program
    A 5   New defense undersecretary named
    C 14 UN to debate Soviet priests' case
    D 11 Athens denies communist success in north
    E 20 FBI raid corrupt banker's home

AA Commercial message   (0'51")

Ad-film

CC 'The rest of the story'

Edwards to camera   (2'43")
    A 4   Truman holds weekly press conference
    B 8   Extra budget to rearm Europe
    A 3   Truman still wants more taxes
Illus A 1   New farm subsidy program
    B 6   Republicans blocking Euro-recovery bill
    B 7   Allies OK new West German government
    A 2   Army Day celebrated

Newsfilm   (1'59")
    A 2   Army Day celebrated
    B 10 Brazilian war minister at West Point
    B 9   Airfield aid pact signed in Panama

Edwards to camera   (0'43")
    C 14 UN to debate Soviet priests' case
    C 11 Athens denies communist success in north

Newsfilm   (3'47")
    C 12 Communist Icelanders riot against Nato
    C 13 Chinese nationalists seek peace with communists

D 16 Earthquake-rent Fukui (Japan) recovers
F 21 Bank opens window for pram-pushing mums

Edwards to camera   (0′56″)
Illus F 22 Prince Charles is 19 weeks old
    E 19 New York City taxi strike continues

AA Commercial message   (0′51″)

Ad-film

DD 'A little late news'

Edwards to camera   (1′04″)
    E 17 Miners' retirement age reduced to 60
    E 18 New York special congressional election set
    C 15 Soviets claim Russian invented TV

AA Commercial message/credits   (0′21″)

Here is the rub: five years after Edwards himself started there was still little evidence that what might be described as the radio portions of this broadcast (Edwards to camera) were meshed with the newsreel portions (Newsfilm). In effect the first 4 minutes 21 second (including commercials) of the programme was in the radio style with only one story, A 1, having any illustrative material.

There followed for 1 minute 58 seconds a newsreel, complete with lower third captions ('West Point'/'Panama'), whip pans between stories and continuous non-sync. music on the soundtrack. The march for the Army Day parade, the Brazilian visit to West Point and the Panama pact signing was not just continuous – it was the same piece played by the same band, one track in true newsreel style. (Sync. film equipment was to (in Morse's phrase) 'virtuously expunge' such 'emotional keys' from the news (Morse 1986: 57). The lackadaisical date-lining in Edwards scripts, however, is still with us despite modern image gathering technology.)

After a brief Cold War bridge to camera without any illustrative material, C 14/C 11 (43 seconds), the newsreel resumed for a further 3 minutes 47 seconds with the Iceland footage, C 12, which segued to China C 13 via a full-screen title 'The Far East' with 'Far Eastern' newsreel music. This music continued under the Japanese story, D 16, which was also introduced with a whip pan and a location lower-third caption, 'Fukui'.

The transition to the next newsreel story, the babies at the bank piece, was particularly abrupt. The Far Eastern music stopped, the screen went to blank and a full-frame still of skyscrapers with a 'New York' supered on the upper third appeared. It would seem as if the Telenews was being crudely joined, via this still, to the suburban New York bank footage, which is perhaps CBS's own, on another reel being played into the programme from another telecine machine. This then meant, given the associative logic of story clustering, that Prince Charles, being a baby, had to go next to the banking babies and cause a foreign incursion into what would otherwise have been a purely domestic section of the broadcast.

With Prince Charles we returned to the radio mode for five stories lasting 3 minutes 12 seconds including commercial and closing commercial message. Only one story was illustrated, with baby pictures. The last stories, E 17/E 18/C 15, had the greatest 'rip-and-read' quality, not least because of the wire-service tapes. Edwards put the pieces of paper aside for the Russian television pay-off.

In effect, what we have is a (largely foreign) newsreel inserted into a (largely domestic) radio news. We begin with an American radio news which segues into a foreign newsreel via the Army Day film. The newsreel is interrupted by two radio-style foreign news stories, and then segues back, hiccupping over Prince Charles, to the domestic scene via the baby carriage film. The newsreel is thus introduced and interrupted; the radio news has two illustrated stories and, most importantly, the radio newscaster is also the newsreel narrator – but that is the limit of integration. The two traditions, radio and newsreel, remain clearly and obviously distinct. This is the most striking presentational characteristic of the broadcast.

The show also reveals this in another way – through the paucity of stories which did move towards modern presentational modes.

There were not more than four of these: two which had Edwards introducing, to camera, a piece of film; and two more which integrated Edwards's performance with other illustrative material (ILLUS in the list on pp. 194–5). Both these mixes (to camera/film and to camera/film: graphics: stills/to camera) were the shape of things to come, the norm of the modern newscast. They were the exceptions in 1949.

The Army Day film, the lead story in the martial music newsreel, was introduced by Edwards from the studio:

#26 (same as #17 continued *Edwards*) (BCU, cut off below tie-knot)	*Edwards to camera continued*
	(B 6) With other Washington news: Republican senators are still balking attempts to speed passage of the European recovery bill. The final vote is still in doubt.
	(B 7) The State Department announces that the foreign ministers of France, Britain and our own Secretary of State have reached an accord in principle about the future of Western

	Germany. It's expected to smooth the way for establishing a separate Western German government some time in the late summer.
	(A 2) Well, it was a very big day in Washington yesterday / full of
martial music in under	pomp and circumstance and bands
Fade	*Edwards v/o* /and parading. Big
#27 EST parade	time for the army and also a memorable one. For this is very likely the last / Army Day Parade.
#28 GV units	Lewis Johnson Secretary of Def/ense says from now
#29 MS marching legs; 6 files	on there will be only Armed Forces Day. /
#30 MCU soldiers walk through shot /	(music)
#31 WS TRACKING head of parade /	
#32 MLS files walk through shot /	
#33 GV crowd	*Edwards v/o* (music continued) /President Truman and Mr
#34 MS LOW ANGLE Truman and Johnson	Johnson watch from the President's box on Con/stitution Avenue.
#35 MLS 5-SHOT Truman and party	Representatives from all three serv/ices take part.
#36 MLS transports	Tanks, / guns and even the
#37 GV band led by mascot dog	canine corps. /
#38 MLS 3 SHOT REVERSE President's box /	(music)
#39 LS Honor Guard through shot /	
Whip pan	*Edwards v/o* (music continues) /The day before the army at
#40 MLS 3 SHOT 2 generals and priest, walk through SUPER (lower 1/3rd) '*WEST POINT*' #41	West Point played host to the Brazilian Minister of Wa/r. . . .

The second part of the newsreel was introduced thus:

	Edwards to camera
	(C 12) Well, now we have /
#53 (as #17) continued	some very very dramatic pictures made by Telenews on recent Atlantic Pact riots up in Iceland. These are scenes
	Edwards v/o
Fade	/of communist demonstrators
#54 EST HIGH ANGLE square	as they battle police in Parliament Square in / the capital of
music in under	Reykjavik. A real pitched battle,
#55 GV HIGH ANGLE police and people	stones against night
f/x crowd noise	sticks. Parliament meanwhile was debating joining the pact. /
#56 LS ditto	(music/ f/x)
	/
#57 LS (JUMP) ditto	*Edwards v/o* (music f/x continued) One officer caught alone
#58 WIDER LS scuffle around man	mobbed and downed by agitators. /Ah! there goes the teargas
#59 GV HIGH ANGLE sq etc.	and it finally disperses most of the crowd. Iceland has a population of only 130,000 1,000/of
#60 MLS HIGH ANGLE 2 riot police	whom are said to be communists all very much opposed / apparently to the
#61 GV HIGH ANGLE sq + gas	Atlantic pact. / But even
#62 CU broken window	as rocks were hurled into their chamb/er Iceland's
#63 LS Façade	parliament voted to join the Atlantic alliance.
#64 INTERTITLE	/
'The Far East'	/
music mix to 'eastern' theme	From China films of the
#65 GV crowd	national government delegates leaving for peace negotiat /

One essential factor in melding newsreel and radio, the move from studio to film and back, was thus in place but the tendency was still to leave the film in blocks. Each time the difficulty of cutting between the two was eased by use of a fade, rather than a cut, from Edwards to the telecine. The advantage gained by this was however offset by the need for Edwards to voice-over live considerable stretches of film. The degree to which he 'hit his marks', as it were, is impressive, although it must be said that he was aided by very loose writing, his own according to contemporary accounts, and/or ad libbing (Walker 1949b: 50). (Received opinion, which has Edwards and his NBC rival Swayze 'as relatively humble figures who *read* the news', must be rejected (Matusow 1983: 1; my emphasis). It seems possible that in these early days the newscasters had a personal power over the broadcasts which would never be theirs again.)

It might be thought that Edwards's language owed more to the newsreel than the radio and thus represented a real level of integration which I am ignoring. It is certainly true that he is very casual. Apparently, late stories aside, he wrote the scripts, memorized them and then used 'giant key-word charts' or cue cards to get through transmission (Walker 1949b: 50). Even allowing for this, the newsreel tradition seems to inform such language as the comic reference in the Army Day parade film to the canine corps over a shot of a single dog mascot; or, to camera, this: 'Russian delegate Malik said people should not stick their noses into other peoples' vegetable gardens. Objection overruled!' It is true that some of the reporting begins to border on newsreel crassness. However, the casualness of his language reflects a long-standing American radio news tradition.

Even the most solemn news was presented unpretentiously by the radio. KGU, Honolulu for instance reported Pearl Harbour thus: 'This battle has been going on for nearly three hours. One of the bombers dropped within fifty feet of Tanti Towers. It's no joke – it's a real war. The public of Honolulu have been advised' (Rose 1961: 286).

This style had been much reinforced by the informality of the news commentators, whose rise, as has been noted above, had been encouraged by newspaper restrictions on pure news programming in the 1930s (R. Smith 1957: 121). For example, Lowell Thomas commenting on Hitler in his first broadcast in 1930 said, 'A cardinal policy of his [Hitler's] now-powerful German Party is the conquest of Russia. That's a tall assignment, Adolf. You just ask Napoleon' (Henderson 1988: 96). Walter Winchell began every broadcast with: 'Good evening, Mr and Mrs America and all ships at sea' (ibid.: 98). Edwards was thus being true to his radio forebears and there was little in his language to suggests a specific newsreel influence.

This is not to deny the obvious newsreel influence elsewhere, though. An homage to the newsreel can be seen in the opening titles of the broadcast. In what was essentially a commercial message from Oldsmobile, one with appropriate automotive advertising music rather than a 'newsy' theme, the second shot was a newsreel-style four-way diagonal split screen, with image changes within the segments occurring on a clockwise wipe.

In the main body of the bulletin, the newsreel mode was further enhanced by the use of the historic present and other script techniques to disguise the actual date-lines on the filmed stories, for example, 'From

China films of the national government delegates leaving'. Or: 'From Japan meantime a progress report.' Or: 'Here's an outdoor angle on banking in New York; a Bay Side bank makes a pitch for the baby-buggy business.' Or: 'The day before the army at West Point' which relates to the time marker on the previous story: 'It was a very big day in Washington yesterday.' Attentive viewers could calculate from this that the West Point visit had occurred on 5 April.

To return to the visuals: there are only two other stories which combined visual material with to-camera presentation, but even this overstates the integration case. The Prince Charles item, one of these two, is not an example of modern practice; rather it represents a road not taken, at least in news presentation.

	Edwards to camera
Fade	/(F 22) And now right
#108 Edward wide M/S, picks up photo; b/g 'CBS-TV NEWS' above map	in the same mood we have some new pictures just received of Bonnie Prince Charlie, the future King of England.
	Edwards v/o
	/He's quite a growing
#109 CU hand holding photo of Charles; photo is turned down	boy now, today he's 19 months . . . er . . . 19 weeks old, I should have said; looking very fine here
	/playing with his
2nd photo, turn down	little bunny rabbit and / I would say that this
3rd photo, turn down	perhaps is my favorite of Bonnie King Charlie to be of the United Kingdom.
	Edwards to camera
	/Well here in New York the
#110 (as #108)	leaders in the taxi cab strike have issued an ultimatum to the mayor.

Edwards was in a wide mid-shot showing the whole desk and the 'CBS TV NEWS' sign above the map behind him for the first time in this transmission. He picked up the stills and held them at right angles to himself so a second camera could get a clear shot of them across the desk. Nevertheless, his hand repeatedly intruded into the close-ups of the baby photos. Newscasters holding photographs up to the camera were not to become a staple of the news presentational repertoire. Instead it was reserved for the talk show where, for instance, Johnny Carson was often pleased to become this physically involved with stills. There was no obvious technical reason for handling the story in this way. There were only eight other captions in the programme; five in the farm subsidy story, one (the New York skyline) in the second newsreel block and two at the close. There was ample time for these royal photos to have been placed on the caption stands and voiced-over in what was already the conventional way.

Leaving this aside, then, only one of the twenty-two stories covered in this broadcast approximates to the modern norm. This was A(1), the 1 minute 35 second farm subsidy item.

	Edwards to camera continued
#17 Edwards CU (tie Knot) continued	(A 3) Again today the president stuck by his original demand for additional taxes but [A 1] perhaps the biggest one [*sic*] Washington development came in the Agriculture Department which announced this new and very broad farm program we mentioned. Here's how it works. The wheat
	Edwards v/o
Fast fade	/belt out in the mid-West
#18 Farmer with f/g plant, WIDE CU	is sowing [*sic*] signs to [*sic*] another billion / bushel
#19 WS tractor f/g, combine b/g	crop, the sixth such / harvest in a row.
#20 f/g CU wheat, combine into lens	The farmers appear to be winning their gamble against weather, rust and insects, and they're making the most of the government guarantee to
Fade	keep the price up at / $2
#21 CAPTION: 'PRESENT LAW' farmer on top rung of gate marked 'Parity'; other rungs marked '90%'; '80%'; '70%'	bushel. Here's how that programme works: The Agriculture Department under the present law sets an arbitrary figure called parity which is the amount needed to keep the farmer's income up to what it was over a certain period of years.
	/If there were no
#22 CAPTION as #21 add box, white on black 'WHEAT PRICE'	government controls the price of wheat and other farm commodities might fall below parity with a bumper crop, cutting the farmers'

	income and reducing his standard of living. / To prevent this
#23 CAPTION, same gate but closer 'PRESENT LAW'; box (white on black) 'PRICE RAISED' with arrow beneath marked 'BY GOVERNMENT PURCHASE'	the government steps in. It buys enough of the commodity to keep the price up to 90 per cent of parity level. Farmers are then protected and big crop is encouraged. /
#24 CAPTION as #21; box: 'REMAINS AT MARKET LEVEL'	Today Secretary of Agriculture Brannan proposed a new law. If the market price of wheat drops below parity let it remain there at market price, he says. Let prices move freely according to support and demand and give the consumer
Fade	a break if the price is low. /
#25 CAPTION as #21 without 'PARITY', '90%' plus arrow over black box 'GOV'T PAYS FARMER A SUBSIDY'	But let the government pay the farmer a cash subsidy of the difference between the market price and parity so that his living standard is still protected. *Edwards to camera*
Fade	/Secretary Brannan told the joint
#26 EDWARDS (as #17)	meeting of the Congressional Agriculture Department today that the plan would cost less as a matter of fact than the present program.
	With other Washington news: Republican senators are still. . . .

While Edwards explained the new farm support system we saw three library shots of the harvesting on film (#18–#19–#20) and then a comparatively extended caption sequence (#21–#22–#23–#24–#25) involving five different cards. (CBS also had the capacity to do real-time animation. There were graphics which used 'some unique gadgets to animate them. A Rube Goldberg-like contraption, with wheels, interlocking disks, and long handles makes it easy for Edwards to talk about' complex topics (Walker 1949b: 50).) Edwards talked over both film and graphics, and fades were used to ease the transitions from him, to film, to captions and back to him.

This then is the one modern, integrated 'embedded' story to be broadcast by the 'prize-winning pace setter video news' of 1949. That it is the only one really illustrates the degree to which radio and newsreel norms were still apart and how real were the difficulties, conceptual rather than technical, of melding them together.

'IS IT TELEVISION? . . . IS IT NEWS?'

That radio and newsreel norms would have to be blended to produce such 'embedded' presentational modes – where film and graphics were 'embedded' into the newscaster's to-camera flow – was understood early, at least in some quarters. For instance, Friedrich Gladenbeck, head of the Nazi Reichspost Research Institute, in November 1938, laid out exactly the pattern of Edwards's farm subsidy coverage:

> Imagine, for example, that just before the beginning of the news, the German troops occupying the Sudetenland had conquered another important city. An announcer on the *Tagesschau* could first point out the line of advancement on a map, and then mix in some pictures of the city from our archives, and then show the most current footage we have of marching troops.
>
> (Hempel 1990: 139)

Apart from not leading with the most current footage, this is exactly how the news is done on television today, and how CBS was beginning to do it in 1949. But this is not how the problem of 'doing the news' on television was presented either at that time or in subsequent accounts.

Instead, received United States media history insists that the network news programmes of this period 'inevitably adopted newsreel patterns' (Barnouw 1990: 102). This erroneous belief seems to arise from contemporary professional discussion. Much was being made in the trade of the difficulties of melding radio and newsreel. As late as 1952 a college radio and television production manual lists seven methods for doing the news, four of which involve pointing the camera at print in various ways, and one recalls *The Esso Television Reporter* of 1940 (Ewbank and Lawton 1952: 321). Henry Cassirer, Edwards's programme editor, wrote in the *Journalism Quarterly* for September 1949:

> There are all kinds of 'news' programs on television today. One station presents a news summary sponsored by a newspaper. This report is read by an announcer and backed up visually only by such general titles as 'News of the World', 'News of the Nation', etc. It is news all right; it brings you the latest reports off the wires. However, you don't have to look in order to grasp it. Is it television?
>
> Many television stations use . . . a newsreel package of 8 minutes' duration that is flown from New York to every part of the country. Films are shown one or two days after the event when taken in the United States and many days later when they come from abroad. . . . A good proportion of the reel is strictly 'feature' material, anything from a

fashion show to a carnival abroad. This is television all right. You have to see it to get the gist of it. But is it news?

(Cassirer 1949: 277)

This rhetorical stance, which at one level can be dismissed as nothing more than disguised special pleading for network news as against local production, nevertheless appears to raise a real issue: to what extent was there by the late 1940s still an 'either-newsreel-or-radio' quality to the research agenda, if you will, on TV news practice? I believe that, despite the potency of this dichotomy as a network/local issue, as regards presentation it was already moot. The *CBS Evening News* and other surviving early broadcasts demonstrate that the formation of practice had advanced sufficiently for it to be obvious that a blend, as in the farm subsidy story or in the movements to and from film, was going to be the only option.

This is not to downgrade the technical difficulties of constantly moving to, from and between newscaster, graphics, outside broadcasts, film and other reporters and correspondents, but simply to stress that this was the real challenge and other more publicly acknowledged difficulties were not so serious. For instance, the slowness of film as a news medium.

As I have shown above, I do not believe that film topicality was a particular difficulty. To believe this elevates the 'visual imperative', which looms very large in professional attitudes, into a determining factor in this history. But, as we have elsewhere demonstrated, the visual imperative takes a back seat to the quality news agenda (Glasgow University Media Group 1976: 112ff.). The day's most important political and economic events will be reported, today as they were in 1949, without illustrative material if need be. The early broadcasters, as in this case, had already worked out how to deal with stories which lacked film and how to contextualize the delayed film they had. Cassirer's description of Telenews as newsreel is tendentious.

All this is not to say, however, that once 'embedding' had been adopted and refined, there were no more problems. The range of open issues persisting into the 1950s is surprising. For instance, how could broadcasters deal with a story which is not, in the time-honoured way, timely? How and should archive footage be used and marked? The release of the Yalta papers in 1955 occasioned questions along these lines (Aliski 1957: 131ff.). As late as 1957 it could still be said that:

An effective news format, which has long eluded television, may be developing along lines that emphasize inherent advantages. . . . Television news seems to be emerging as a unique medium and not as an imitation of the newspapers and of radio, a characteristic that during the years of trial and error made for a whole less than the sum of its parts.

(Lyle 1963: 165)

Current attention to this formative period of television news, for instance Brunovska Karnick's (1988) valuable research on the late 1940s at NBC, has not sufficiently examined the complex 'accidents, experiments and necessities' (as she calls them) required to complete the melding process. I believe the telerecordings must be examined and that primacy should be given to recovering the stages whereby 'embedding' became the dominant mode.

'Embedding' was the clue to melding the radio and newsreel but it required abandoning the tradition of the faceless newsreel voice and establishing new norms limiting the duration of the to-camera newsreader shot. All told, from the earliest experiments in the early 1940s, it would take more than fifteen years to accomplish these twin objectives.

However, a key, critical advantage accrued because of these difficulties. Within the naturalistic and transparent domain of television production, the slow discovery of answers to all these questions about the news had a major overall contributing effect to the 'naturalizing' of its presentational modes.

Solutions were found which carefully utilized previously established newspaper, radio and newsreel modes, but resulted in a 'natural' form. This outcome is, to say the least, curious; for, after all, whence these programmes? The setting is a mixture of office and classroom with a magic ever-changing blackboard; the performers' body language is as stilted and limited as that of an actor in a Noh drama; the continuities of time and space, especially now that we have instantaneity on a virtually worldwide basis but even back in 1949, are those of the conjurer; the narrative hegemony of the medium in general is nearly abandoned in favour of associative structures. All in all, the news is the most highly encoded television genre. Yet it is perceived as 'natural'. Paradoxically, the news, arguably then the least realistic of all presentational forms, is the site of the most realistic, indexical output.

This is the achievement of the late 1940s; the almost imperceptible accretion of solutions to the problems of presentation eventually produced a form that is perceived as 'ineffable'.

'TELEVISION NEWSREELS WILL, OF COURSE, CONTINUE TO DEVELOP'

I also believe that this slow development requires that the received history of British television news be somewhat re-examined. This account has been, of necessity, a chapter in United States television history. In the UK, the distinctions between the radio tradition (trailing clouds of wartime glory) and the newsreel model (tainted with the opprobrium of 1930s trivialization) were instantaneously enshrined in a major turf war within the BBC. After the restart of television in June 1946, Alexandra Palace, the home of television on the outskirts of London, struggled to find ways to accommodate the demands of the newsroom in Broadcasting House, but without much success.

From 1948, the television service revived in-house the prewar tradition of a newsreel. In 1951 its producers visited the United States and returned primed to make it more news-like, but this elicited further hostility from Broadcasting House. Nevertheless, slowly the frequency, and the serious content, of the newsreels increased. Attitudes, however, did not change. As late as 1953 the chairman of the BBC's board of governors was still of the opinion that: 'Television newsreels will, of course, continue to develop and be of the greatest interest and attention, but there is surely not the least possibility that they will ever replace the news on sound' (Paulu 1981: 197).

The huge success of the coronation coverage of that year and the passing of the Independent Television Act forced some rethinking. The result was British television's first live, that is radio-style, news which came, voice only over caption, at the end of each day's transmission, starting in March 1953. In July 1954 this joined the newsreel early in the evening on a daily basis. The *BBC Television News And Newsreel* thus took the form that Dumont had used in 1948 – a news with a film reel after, except that, in the BBC's case, the news was still at a 1940 *Esso Television Reporter* level.

In September 1955 ITN began broadcasting an up-to-the-minute integrated bulletin in the contemporary American fashion and the BBC had to follow suit, thus bringing to an end this less than glorious episode in the corporation's development.

Received history, as for instance in the BBC's own thirtieth anniversary TV documentary on the news, suggests that it took eight years (from the restart of television service) to reach this point simply and solely because of the prototypical turf war between Alexandra Palace and Broadcasting House (BBC 2 1984). My point is that the American experience suggests that this is somewhat to overstate the case. It was not until the early 1950s that the United States networks had made serious inroads on the problem of presentational integration. There were, therefore, in the late 1940s no readily available models for the BBC even if people of goodwill had sought them. However, the years of experiments – of invisible newsreaders, of inept correspondents uneasy in front of camera, of facile newsreels – prepared the ground well. When ITN introduced the American-style news it looked a lot more 'natural' than did the BBC's uneasy efforts.

Indeed, it looked ineffable.

NOTES

1. There has been no recent theoretical discussion about 'liveness' as the ontological mark of television:

'Liveness' may be defined by the congruence of discourse-time and reception-time, that is, no time gap exists between the narrative's production and its consumption. This quality of 'liveness' is rare in our contemporary experience of narratives. . . . In a sense this 'liveness' is a throwback to traditional oral story-telling.

(Kozloff 1987: 65)

Heath and Skirrow in the UK and Feuer in the USA have suggested that: 'television as an institution identifies all messages emanating from the apparatus as "live" ', (Fevur 1983: 14).

However, most of the output is not now nor has ever been live. Pioneers saw the medium as a delivery system for film (Winston 1986: 48). Instantaneity was not seen as the purpose of the technology; rather it was a problem which needed to be overcome – with multi-camera studios, telerecordings and, eventually, tape. Further it was during the early 1950s that film was indeed established as a major programming source – just as the pioneers intended.

Therefore, it might be as well, in grounding an argument for this 'ideology of liveness' (Morse 1986: 63) or 'meta-liveness' (as it might be termed) to look back to the radio. Radio was established as a mass medium before effective electrical recording technology was to hand. Radio was, indeed, live – whence the sense of 'disillusionment' about 'canned' programming in the radio audience.

Television, perhaps because it was not entirely the case, adopted this element of radio rhetoric with enthusiasm. For instance, in 1951 Douglas Edwards, denying his day-old films and his reliance on the wire news services, was nevertheless claiming that: 'With TV today the children get a sense of participation, of belonging to history, rather than relying totally on print' (Edwards 1951: 160). Obviously the discovery that there were audiences for congressional hearings, sports events and many moments of ceremonial contributed to the understanding that the essence of television was a 'live' essence. But given the relative amount of such output as against the dominance (after, say, 1953) of first film and then tape, it is difficult to argue that 'liveness' is in fact critical. It does not describe the output, even in the Edenic period before tape.

The question arises as to why television's essence should be located in an aspect of the medium which is not, in a temporal way, a dominant characteristic – which is, in effect, a production exception rather than the rule?

2 *The March of Time* was not a newsreel for all that it was awarded a special 1937 Oscar for 'having revolutionized' the newsreel. As Fielding points out, it had done no such thing. It was twice as long as the average newsreel, it embraced rather than eschewed controversy and it dealt with few topics per issue (and after May 1938 reduced itself further to covering only one story per issue). None of these factors was copied, not least because, unlike the newsreels which were issued bi-weekly, it came out once a month. Fielding makes it clear that it is *The March of Time*'s editorial toughness and savvy and its documentary film sensibilities that make it an example of a missed opportunity (Fielding 1972: 231f., 1978: *passim*).

3 For the 1945 season, CBS, changing the days it programmed, offered news shows Tuesdays, Wednesdays and Fridays. In 1946 it produced bulletins on Thursdays and Sundays as well as a *Week In Review* broadcast on Saturday. The network tried 8.15 p.m. as the time slot. In 1947 CBS switched the Sunday bulletin with the Saturday round-up and all three broadcasts fell back to 8 p.m.

For 1946, NBC celebrated its three-station East Coast hook-up with *Your Esso Reporter* (*sic*), Mondays and Thursdays at 7.50 p.m. Then NBC tried Monday 9 to 9.10 p.m. while leaving the Thursday show at 7.50 p.m. For two months in 1947 there was an additional Wednesday night programme for 15 minutes at

8.45 p.m. (Washkevitch 1958: *passim*).
4 In its last year, however, Swayze was replaced by Huntley and Brinkley. In 1957 the broadcast moved back an hour to 6.45 p.m. In 1963, expanded to half an hour, it went to 7 p.m. where it still is. (Large sections of the country, though, actually see this broadcast at 6.30 rather than at 7 p.m.)
5 Barnouw suggests that film subcontracts might have been occasioned by worries about union intervention; however NBC appeared to have little difficulty (Barnouw 1990: 101; cf. Walker 1949a: 44).
6 The 15 minutes were initially scheduled at 7.30 but went to 7.15 in 1955. The introduction of the half hour in 1963 occasioned another period of uncertainty before the show settled down opposite Huntley/Brinkley.

REFERENCES

Aldgate, Anthony (1979) *Cinema and History: British Newsreels and the Spanish Civil War*, London: Scolar.
Aliski, Marvin (1957) 'What is past may be prologue after all', *Journal of Broadcasting* 1 (2): 13ff.
Barnouw, Erik (1968) *The Golden Web; A History of Broadcasting in the United States*, vol. II, New York: Oxford University Press.
—— (1990) *Tube of Plenty: The Evolution of American Television*, New York: Oxford University Press.
Barthes, Roland (1973) *Mythologies*, trans. Annette Lavers, London: Paladin.
BBC (1930) *BBC Year-Book 1930*, London: BBC.
—— (1941) *BBC Handbook 1941*, London: BBC.
BBC 2 (1984) *BBC TV NEWS: The First 30 years*, writer/producer, Gordon Carr, chief picture editor, John Hinkly, presenter, Richard Baker (5 July).
Bohn, Thomas (1968) 'Broadcasting national election returns: 1916–1948', *Journal of Broadcasting* XII (3) (summer): 267ff.
Briggs, Asa (1979) *The History of Broadcasting in the United Kingdom volume iv: Sound and Vision*, Oxford: Oxford University Press.
—— (1985) *The BBC: The First Fifty Years*, Oxford: Oxford University Press.
Broadcasting (1948) 'Telenews plans news service', Washington DC, (5 January).
—— (1982) *The First Fifty Years of Broadcasting*, Washington DC: Broadcasting Publications.
Broadcasting 1944 Yearbook Number, Washington DC.
Brunovska Karnick, Kristine (1988) 'NBC and the innovation of television news, 1945–1953', *Journalism History* 15 (1) (spring): 26ff.
Cassirer, Henry (1949) 'Television news: a challenge to imaginative journalists', *Journalism Quarterly* 26 (3) (September), Iowa City: 131ff.
Edwards, Douglas (1951) 'One world of TV', *Parents Magazine* 26 (March).
Ewbank, Henry and Lawton, Sherman (1952) *Broadcasting: Radio and Television*, New York: Harper and Brothers.
Feuer, Jane (1983) 'The concept of live television', in E. Ann Kaplan (ed.) *Regarding Television*, Frederick, MD: University Publications of America/ AFI.
Fielding, Raymond (1972) *The American Newsreel, 1911–1967*, Norman, OK: University of Oklahoma Press.
—— (1978) *The March of Time: 1935–1951*, New York: Oxford University Press.
Glasgow University Media Group (1976) *Bad News*, London: Routledge & Kegan Paul.
—— (1980) *More Bad News*, London: Routledge & Kegan Paul.

Gorokhov, P. K. (1977) 'History of modern television', *Radiotekhnika*, translated and reprinted in G. Shiers (ed.) *Technical Developments of Television*, New York: Arno Press.

Greb, Gordon (1958–9) 'The golden anniversary of broadcasting', *Journal of Broadcasting* III(1) (winter).

Hempel, Manfried (1990) 'German television pioneers and the conflict between public programming and wonder weapons', *Historical Journal of Film Radio and Television* 10 (2).

Henderson, Amy (1988) *On the Air: Pioneers of American Broadcasting*, Washington DC: Smithsonian Institute.

Kozloff, Sarah (1987) 'Narrative theory and television', in Robert Allen (ed.) *Channels of Discourse*, Chapel Hill, North Carolina: University of North Carolina Press.

Lewis, Jonathon (1977), 'Before hindsight', *Sight and Sound*, 46(2) (spring).

Lott, George (1970) 'The press radio war of the 1930s', *Journal of Broadcasting* XIV(3) (summer): 275.

Lyle, Jack (1963) 'Television news – an interim report', *Journal of Broadcasting* 7(2).

Marvin, Carolyn (1988) *When Old Technologies Were New*, New York: Oxford University Press.

Matusow, Barbara (1983) *The Evening Stars*, Boston, Mass.: Houghton Mifflin.

Morse, Margaret (1986) 'The television news personality and credibility: reflections on the news in transition', in Tania Modleski (ed.) *Studies in Entertainment: Critical Approaches to Mass Culture*, Bloomington, Ind.: Indiana University Press.

Newsweek (1949) 'News via TV' (7 March), New York.

Norman, Bruce (1984) *Here's Looking at You: The Story of British Television 1908–1939*, London: BBC and Royal Television Society.

Paulu, Burton (1981) *Television and Radio in the United Kingdom*, Minneapolis, Minn.: University of Minnesota Press.

Rose, Ernest (1961), 'How the U.S. heard about Pearl Habor', *Journal of Broadcasting* 5(3) (autumn): 285A.

Scannell, Paddy (1986) ' "The stuff of radio": developments in radio features before the war', in John Corner (ed.) *Documentary and the Mass Media*, London: Edward Arnold.

Slide, Anthony (ed.) (1987) *Selected Radio and Television Criticism*, Metuchen, N J: Scarecrow Press.

Smith, Anthony (1974) *British Broadcasting*, Newton Abbot: David & Charles.

Smith, Robert (1957) 'The origins of radio network news commentary', *Journal of Broadcasting* 113ff.

Sperber, A. M. (1986) *Murrow: His Life and Times*, New York: Freundlich Books.

Uricchio, William (1989) 'Nazi television and its postwar representation', *Wide Angle* 11(1): 49.

Waldrop, F. C. and Borkin, J. (1938) *Television: A Struggle for Power*, New York: William Morrow.

Walker, Jerry (1949a) 'Daily news show set for NBC–TV network', *Editor and Publisher* (5 February): 49.

—— (1949b) '148 Man-hours Produce 15 Minutes of TV News', *Editor and Publisher* (12 March): 50.

Washkevitch, Victor (1958) 'An interpretive history of network news on television', unpublished MA thesis, Boston University.

Winston, Brian (1986): *Misunderstanding Media*, London: Routledge & Kegan Paul.

Woods, David (1967): 'Semantics v. the "first" broadcasting station', *Journal of Broadcasting* XI(3) (summer): 199.

Chapter 9

AIDS and the British press

Peter Beharrell

INTRODUCTION

It is widely assumed that the mass media have played an important role in communicating ideas about AIDS. Many analyses have focused upon the negative character of media representations which have demonized AIDS and stigmatized those with the virus. Not surprisingly, initial concern concentrated on the sensationalism of much of the media coverage and the problem of widespread misinformation about the transmission of HIV. There has been no shortage of such coverage and its specific characteristics are now well documented (Albert 1986; Altman 1986; Grover 1989; Watney 1987, Wellings 1988). These issues continue to be of major importance in the analysis of the media.

However, there have been fewer attempts to examine the range of responses to AIDS by 'the media' or to take account of the diversity which has emerged within media institutions or between different newspapers on this issue. Many otherwise valuable investigations typically take selections of press articles as their sample without systematically distinguishing between publications in the analysis (see, for example, Currie 1985; Herzlich and Pierret 1989; Stroman and Seltzer 1989; Wellings 1988). This chapter will look at some of the differences which have emerged within the British press over AIDS. In particular it examines the way in which newspapers have reported a key aspect of the government education strategy in the UK, the risk of heterosexual transmission of HIV.[1]

PERSPECTIVES ON AIDS

The mainstream media reporting of AIDS is not uniform. It draws upon a number of competing perspectives which are rooted in institutional arrangements, social movements and struggles. These involve not simply differences of strategy or policy but ways of understanding, with specific languages and terminology. They are in a wider sense ways of thinking about AIDS, frames of reference with their codes and conventions, priorities and assumptions.

It is possible to identify a number of broadly defined approaches to AIDS and HIV. The dominant perspective is that associated with the 'AIDS policy community' which emerged after 1986 and which was closely identified with the developing government strategy on AIDS, particularly the health education campaign and the growing institutionalization of the informal networks of activists in the fields of health care, education and welfare (Berridge and Strong 1991). In its development, there were political divisions and differences of experience between administrative, scientific and medical groups, gay activists and people with HIV. Differences persist, although a general strategy did emerge. Although it originally emerged as a belated response to a growing sense of crisis – a perception which has now diminished – the emphasis of this approach is on limited social intervention (based upon the assumption of a basic social and political consensus), public information and persuasion. Embracing a biomedical model, the approach assumed the scientific orthodoxy of research into the newly isolated and identified virus HIV, investigating its action on the immune system in the search for vaccines and therapies. The characteristic social strategy is a health education campaign aimed at the 'general population' focused on preventing the transmission of HIV. In this, the promotion of the general notion of 'safer sex' figures prominently if not very graphically or specifically. Notably, the strategy does not envisage segregation of people with the virus, compulsory testing or mass screening. This general approach has become the current orthodoxy.

A second, 'alternative', perspective can be identified which defines itself mainly in opposition to the orthodox strategy which it perceives as aiming AIDS health education 'propaganda' at heterosexuals. Instead it speaks of specific 'targeting' of 'risk groups', usually identified as gay men and intravenous drug injectors.[2] Often implied here is the need for more testing and screening to identify people with HIV, and in more extreme variants, a call for various repressive measures involving the segregation or restraint of people with the virus or AIDS illnesses.

A third, or 'radical', perspective might be identified which sees AIDS as presenting a challenge to a wide range of current social orthodoxies. In pragmatic terms this emerges as qualified support for the official health education campaign, with varying degrees of criticism aimed at the appropriateness or clarity of the 'safe sex' messages. Some would criticize the influence of moralistic messages imposed on the education campaign.[3] Others have called for a greater degree of sexual explicitness and the 'eroticizing' of safer sex. On the other hand, there is a feminist critique which has warned that 'by adopting representational practices which seek to eroticise safer sex, discourses of HIV/AIDS health promotion are inevitably allied with discourses of pornography' (Wilton 1991). These approaches are also generally critical of the lack of funding for drug research and health care for people with AIDS, and the absence of a clear strategy in defence of the rights and liberties of people with HIV against discrimination and prejudice. The perspective which encompasses these more radical ideas overlaps to some extent that inhabited by the official campaign. But there are differences in the degree to which they recognize the importance of social and economic reforms and changes, for example, in the laws which criminalize drug users and gay men. These differences become manifest in relation to some specific areas of policy. For example, in relation to the problem of HIV transmission in prison, the 'radical' policy preference would be for the distribution of free condoms and the availability of needle-cleaning materials and cleaning instructions.

These broadly defined fields of knowledge and belief constitute the basic resources for the media in reporting AIDS. In their professional activity, journalists – in common with anyone trying to form a judgement or reach an understanding – will draw upon these perspectives. They also consult sources who occupy strategic positions within key institutions and other actors engaged in political struggles over how the issues around AIDS and HIV infection are to be understood (see Chapter 6). The media are not generally the 'primary definers' of events or of their meaning or significance. At the same time, the sources' attempts to organize access to the media for their views are not always successful. Journalists will often need to report the 'definitions of the situation' of the powerful political or institutional actors (Hall *et al.* 1978: ch. 3), but such access for these 'official' views is not always guaranteed.[4] However, research in a number of areas of media has pointed to the way that the 'dominant' perspectives come to be more in evidence in the key areas of news, competing unevenly with those 'alternative' perspectives. In the 'softer' areas of news such as features or named columns it is more likely that less 'authoritative' perspectives will gain an easier access (Bruck 1989; Schlesinger, Murdock and Elliot 1983). This difference between formats of news reporting or between different sections of newspapers each with their own conventions will be examined below (pp. 230–7). In addition we will examine the degree to which 'political' differences emerge between newspapers on issues of government policy. First we need to recognize the degree to which the terms and concepts central to arguments about AIDS are rooted in social and political conflicts.

The history of AIDS includes a history of struggle over meanings and representations. Of crucial importance here are the issues of sex and sexuality. Simon Watney has made the point, 'Aids is not only a medical crisis on an unparalleled scale, it involves a crisis of representation itself, a crisis over the entire framing of knowledge about the human body and its capacities for sexual pleasure' (Watney 1987: 9). The story of the development of the concept of 'safe sex' – so central now to campaigns against the spread of HIV – is very instructive. The idea of 'safe sex' had already been suggested in the feminist critique of dominant heterosexual practices. The development of the idea and its application to HIV prevention emerged from the experience of gay activists who first organized around AIDS in America. Neale (1992) argues that it represented a victory, not just for the more radical sections of organizations such as Gay Men's Health Crisis, but for the wider gay liberation movement at a time when it faced uncertainty, repression and reaction. The biological reality was a virus which was transmitted sexually via blood and semen. The political response by some gay activists was to refuse celibacy, monogamy or the denial of sex and to propose instead the affirmation of sex in practices which avoided the danger of transmitting the virus by the exchange of these body fluids. Put into the common languages of communities and localities, this was a health education message which was attuned to the realities of people's lives, and a defence of the gains of gay liberation, a positive and practical strategy which saved lives (Kramer 1990; Shilts 1987).

This experience of struggle and practical activity also heightened awareness of the power of language to help or hinder our understanding of AIDS. The earliest representations of AIDS as a 'plague' or as a 'gay plague' suggested that AIDS was being made to carry a heavy burden of meanings and connotations quite extraneous to the virus itself and more to do with unresolved fears about sexuality and social order (Alcorn 1988; Porter 1986; Sontag 1989; Watney 1987; Weeks 1989). The mistaken belief that AIDS was contagious or that the virus itself could be 'caught' by normal social contact persisted for many years. And the failure to routinely distinguish between AIDS, the Aquired Immune Deficiency Syndrome, and HIV, the Human Immuno-deficiency Virus, leads still to the misleading notions of the 'AIDS virus', the 'AIDS carrier' and the possibility of 'catching AIDS' (Watney 1987). It is still common for media reports to speak of the 'AIDS test', carrying the implication that a simple solution might be the identification and isolation of 'carriers' (Patton 1990).

Meanwhile, the 'health education' message was predicated on a number of basic facts: first, AIDS is a condition in which many different infections may seriously threaten the health of the body because the immune system has become weakened by a virus, HIV. Second, the impairment of the immune system may take a number of years to become apparent. Third, the presence of HIV in the blood is not detected by 'the test', only the presence of antibodies which may have developed in response to the virus (it may be several months before these antibodies can be detected).

The concept of 'high risk groups' has also been criticized as misguided. The term was, however, used in earlier phases of the government campaign. What is known about the virus suggests that certain practices are 'risky' for anyone, not just certain groups of people who might thus be excluded from the rest of society either metaphorically or literally. There is evidently a punitive impulse to distinguish between the 'innocent' and the 'guilty victim' which has been widely expressed in the media (Wellings 1988). This spurious classification depicts certain groups as responsible for their self-inflicted condition and visibly marked out as morally reprehensible, a danger to themselves and others. Recent research into attitudes and beliefs suggests that this view is widely held within society (see Chapter 11).

Finally, there have also been divisions over the terminology used to describe people with HIV. On one side of the debate they are still described as 'AIDS victims' who are 'doomed' or 'human time-bombs', who are 'sentenced to death' or 'cursed' (see pp. 233,235). On the other, they are 'people living with AIDS', 'people with the virus' or 'HIV antibody positive' in recognition of the fact that many people live active lives for long periods of time without AIDS-related illnesses. These issues are an important part of the debate about the role of the media in our understanding of AIDS. As Watney argues, 'Fighting Aids is not just a medical struggle, it involves our understanding of the words and images which load the virus down with such a cargo of appalling connotations' (1987: 3).

HETEROSEXUAL RISK: PUBLIC INFORMATION OR MYTH?

In the urbanized societies of the west, HIV initially manifested itself among two groups: gay men and intravenous drug injectors. The fact that these two groups were already routinely portrayed as 'deviant' minorities encouraged in many the impulse to invest AIDS with the supernatural power to 'seek out' stigmatized and marginalized groups. But elsewhere, epidemics of AIDS illnesses were showing themselves in other groups. For example, in Uganda and Kenya epidemics developed first among young heterosexuals in the urban centres. But such knowledge had little impact on deep-seated anti-gay and racist prejudice, which preferred to see the disease as the evidence of inherent corruption, immorality and guilt. AIDS came to be seen as a problem of, and for, gays, junkies and foreigners. Thus in addition to 'gay plagues' we read of 'Aids-riddled Haiti' with its 'dirt-poor native boys', Uganda's children lived in the 'AIDS cradle of the world' and Africa was the 'Land of the living dead' (see pp. 231,235). This early history established an agenda of prejudice and ignorance which the education and information campaigns have had to confront. When the government's publicity campaign in 1986 used the slogan 'AIDS isn't prejudiced', it was a belated attempt to challenge the common perception that it was precisely that, and hence unlikely to concern the 'rest of society' or 'the wider population'.[5]

However, the Department of Health's AIDS education campaign from

1986 onwards was criticized by some as wasteful and dishonest for addressing 'everyone' and focusing on 'normal' heterosexual sex. These criticisms grew at the close of the decade as previous estimates of the expected totals of AIDS cases and HIV infections among heterosexuals failed to materialize and were subsequently revised downwards. In an increasingly politicized health education climate, the question was asked: was there a threat to heterosexuals? If so, where was the evidence? A high peak of controversy came in November 1989 when Lord Kilbracken, a minority voice on the All Party Parliamentary Group on AIDS, made his claim that only one proven case of AIDS attributable to heterosexual transmission could be found in the official figures. Several newspapers gave this claim prominent coverage. The *Daily Mail* front page declared it 'THE TRUTH ABOUT AIDS' (17 November 1989). The *Sun* headlined its inside-page report, 'STRAIGHT SEX CANNOT GIVE YOU AIDS – OFFICIAL' (17 November 1989). In making this claim it could be argued that Lord Kilbracken was repeating a well-established media practice of failing to distinguish between the syndrome AIDS and the virus HIV. Kilbracken quoted the Department of Health total of developed cases of AIDS illnesses, 2,372, and then claimed that the official figures could demonstrate only one case, a male, who was not a member of a 'high risk group'. His critics argued that the real danger should be measured by totals of known HIV infections, or by estimates of likely or probable levels of HIV infection. These latter figures would be much greater, indicating future AIDS cases resulting from current levels of risk activity.

In this way the epidemiological argument underpinning the official health education campaign has been conducted in a highly politicized context. The manner in which this wider political dimension has been reported by the press is the subject of this chapter, based on an examination of each of the national newspapers over a thirty-four-month period from November 1988 to August 1991 (Figure 9.1).[6] Figure 9.1 indicates the variation in total monthly coverage (reports, features and editorials) given to AIDS/HIV by the press as a whole in the sample period. The high peak shown in November 1989 includes the large number of press reports generated by the Kilbracken controversy that month.

There is variation, too, in the amount of coverage in different newspapers. There is a difference between the total coverage available in the tabloid press and the broadsheets. The only exception to this general picture is the *Sun* which had a relatively high total. Figures 9.2 and 9.3 focus on the first eighteen months of the sample period and indicate the number of items of coverage devoted to AIDS/HIV by each of the newspapers. Among the Sunday newspapers, the *Sunday Times* stands out with a wide variety of reports and features on AIDS/HIV in addition to its long-running coverage of the campaign by haemophiliacs for compensation for HIV infection from National Health Service (NHS) blood products (see

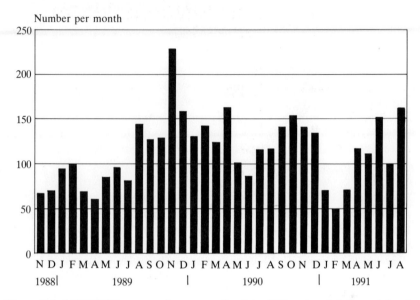

Figure 9.1 AIDS/HIV reports, features, editorials: UK national daily and Sunday press

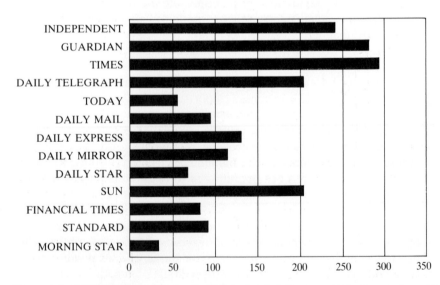

Figure 9.2 AIDS/HIV coverage in the UK national daily press 1988–90: number of items

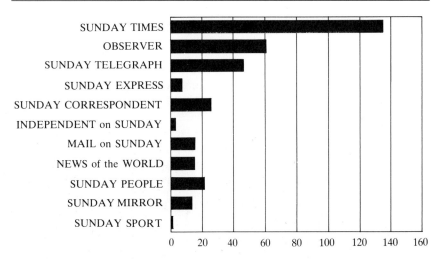

Nov. 1988 – April 1990

Figure 9.3 AIDS/HIV coverage in the UK national Sunday press 1988–90: number of items

Figure 9.3). (The totals for the *Sunday Correspondent* and the *Independent on Sunday* are misleading for comparative purposes as they were not published for the whole of the sample period.)

There are also clear differences between newspapers in the choice of story, news angle and style of presentation. Some of the ways in which these differences manifest themselves in AIDS/HIV reporting are discussed below (pp. 221,230). (In addition, the 'AIDS story profile' for selected newspapers is included in the appendix for reference.)

EPIDEMIOLOGY, POLITICS AND THE KILBRACKEN CONTROVERSY

There are differences among the press in reporting the Kilbracken controversy. Three daily newspapers, the *Sun*, *Daily Mail* and *Daily Express*, stand out clearly in endorsing Lord Kilbracken's claim that official figures showed the government's health education message to be unjustified. All three newspapers accepted 'the figures' (cases of AIDS, presumably resulting from HIV infection perhaps eight or more years previously) without doubt or qualification. The language of the reports, however, focused on AIDS as a disease (rather than HIV) which is 'caught' or 'given'. The concern is to exclude 'normal' sex from risk status, and a key argument is that any other claim is 'homosexual propaganda'.

The *Daily Mail*'s front page carried the by-line of the medical correspondent and described how 'a major row broke out last night' and 'controversy flared' but the headline imposed on it was clearly partisan: 'THE TRUTH ABOUT AIDS – Of 2,372 confirmed cases only one person caught disease in a normal relationship.' Editorial comment was unequivocal: 'as this newspaper has repeatedly pointed out, the Government's advertising campaign – mainly beamed at heterosexuals indulging in normal sex – is focussed on the wrong group. Now Lord Kilbracken has reinforced our argument by obtaining the relevant figures' (*Daily Mail*, 17 November 1989).

At the *Daily Express*, too these claims were given prominent coverage on front-page and leader columns: 'NORMAL SEX IS SAFE ROW – Ads warning over AIDS misrepresent risk says peer' (*Daily Express*, 17 November 1989). This story was covered by news staff, not the medical reporter.[7] The editorial, headed 'Facing facts', declared 'It will not do for the Department of Health to decry Lord Kilbracken's claim. . . . For the Department's own figures bear him out.'

The *Sun* did not give Kilbracken the front page but it went further in claiming that this was support for that newspaper's own argument: 'STRAIGHT SEX CANNOT GIVE YOU AIDS – OFFICIAL' (*Sun*, 17 November 1989). This assertion was underlined by an editorial:

AIDS – THE FACTS NOT THE FICTION. At last the truth can be told. The killer disease AIDS can only be caught by homosexuals, bisexuals, junkies or anyone who has received a tainted blood transfusion. FORGET the television adverts, FORGET the poster campaigns, FORGET the endless boring TV documentaries and FORGET the idea that ordinary heterosexual people can contract AIDS. They can't . . . the risk of catching AIDS if you are a heterosexual is 'statistically invisible'. In other words impossible. So now we know – anything else is just homosexual propaganda. And should be treated accordingly.

(*Sun*, 17 November 1989)

The following day, the *Sun*'s resident doctor, Vernon Coleman, alleged a wider conspiracy: 'AIDS – THE HOAX OF THE CENTURY. . . . Why it paid prudes, gays and Business to scare us all' (*Sun*, 18 November 1989). Coleman argued that drug and medical companies and the doctors who are linked to them had vested interests in the policy, and that moral campaigners were interested in frightening young people into celibacy,[8] while gay activists were 'worried that once it was widely known that AIDS was NOT a major threat to heterosexuals, then funds for AIDS research would fall'.

In the *Daily Mail* the columnist Ann Leslie voiced a similar view:

Shameful conspiracy of deceit – this newspaper is growing weary of pointing out the facts. . . . 'Everyone' is NOT at risk from AIDS: only those who belong to high-risk groups. . . . So why have we, the taxpayers, been forced to waste money on this costly and farcical campaign? First of all, because our government, like many others, fell for militant gay propaganda. . . .

(*Daily Mail*, 18 November 1989)

Lord Kilbracken later distinguished his views from those of the *Sun*. He was granted a prominent space to restate his argument:

DOUBLE DISASTER OF AIDS AD CAMPAIGN – I welcome this chance to put the record straight. I have never said, nor is it true, that it is impossible for a heterosexual to catch AIDS, as stated in a *Sun* leader last Friday. It isn't as simple as that. I have always held that the risk of AIDS to heteros in Britain has been widely exaggerated by the government and the media – except the *Sun*. The figures I have at last extracted from the DHSS have at last proved this. . . . We still have to ask why the government is taking the line it does. . . . Their slogan – AIDS is not prejudiced – was a disaster. Its clear implication was that gays are no more at risk than heterosexuals. This message was totally false. . . . It is widely believed that the government adopted this phrase to avoid offending gays.

(*Sun*, 25 November 1989)

The following year, a Press Council adjudication upheld a complaint against the *Sun*'s reporting of the Kilbracken controversy:

The report in the *Sun* was misleading in it's interpretation . . . and the headline . . . was a gross distortion of the statistical information supplied by the minister. That distortion was compounded by an editorial the same day. . . . The *Sun* should forthwith publish an appropriate correction and apologise to it's readers.

The *Sun* duly reported the adjudication and declared simply, at the foot of the column, 'The *Sun* says: The *Sun* was wrong to state that it was impossible to catch AIDS from heterosexual sex. We apologise' (*Sun*, 12 July 1990). The reporting of Kilbracken by the *Sun*, *Daily Mail* and *Daily Express* was forcefully expressed in terms which challenged the orthodox perspective on AIDS. For these papers it was a major news story. However, two other tabloid newspapers, the *Daily Star* and *Today*, did not report Lord Kilbracken's claims at all. The other main UK tabloid, the *Daily Mirror* gave only a small news report: 'The risk of catching AIDS from normal sex is "statistically invisible" it was claimed yesterday' (17 November 1989). Kilbracken's criticism of the campaign and his call for it to be abandoned were reported. The counter-argument was covered the following day as Kilbracken's critics responded. The report began: 'Straight sex AIDS warning – Thousands of men and women are at risk of catching AIDS from straight sex, researchers warned yesterday. "Normal sexual intercourse is certainly a form of transmission", said Professor Roy

Anderson of Imperial College, London' (*Daily Mirror*, 18 November 1989). There was no editorial on the issue. The pro-heterosexual risk theme was highlighted by a feature a week later: 'AIDS – THE REAL RISK: Straight sex IS threat' (*Daily Mirror*, 29 November 1989). The feature was billed as 'SHOCK REPORT' and was based on the quoted views of Chief Medical Officer Sir Donald Acheson, Roy Anderson, Professor Michael Adler and Dr Brian Gazzard. This was very much the orthodox view and included no critical or contrary positions. However, the language of 'catching AIDS' and 'normal sex' is mixed with 'transmission' and 'spread' of 'the virus'.

Among the broadsheets, the *Guardian*, *The Times* and *The Independent* took a low-key, sceptical approach to the Kilbracken story. These papers carry regular reports from specialist correspondents on the health and AIDS 'beats'. Only in the *Daily Telegraph* did a news angle suggest any credibility for his views. The *Daily Telegraph* did not report Lord Kilbracken on 17 November, but carried 4 column inches the next day headed, '£2m Aids alert goes ahead under protest', which linked his claim to the new phase of the publicity campaign 'to be implemented by the government in spite of charges that the disease only affects certain high risk groups such as drug users and homosexuals. . . . A spokesman said this view by someone who was not an expert on Aids, would not affect government policy. Lord Kilbracken, a Labour Peer, said the proposed targetting of the whole population was "alarmist, wasteful and insane" ' (*Daily Telegraph*, 18 November 1989).

However, very little credence appeared to be given to Kilbracken's claims by *The Times*, *The Independent* and the *Guardian*. His views are noted, but they do not provide the basis for serious critical analysis in either editorial or news columns. In fact such views were more likely to be dealt with in terms of the problem they posed for the health education strategy. On the day that the *Sun*, *Daily Mail* and *Daily Express* reported Lord Kilbracken's claim, the *Guardian* carried only a tiny item noting the release of the official figures in parliament: 'Aids case breakdown' (*Guardian*, 17 November 1989). The *Guardian*'s agenda was different, indicated two weeks later by the science correspondent's article on World AIDS Day: 'New waves of Aids predicted – scientists paint a bleak picture as public education is cut and voluntary campaigners strive to combat false sense of security.' The article noted 'a recent claim by Lord Kilbracken that Aids was almost completely confined to the homosexual population suggests that an air of complacency has set in' (*Guardian*, 1 December 1989).

In *The Times*, Kilbracken became a news story only the day after his claims had been aired in the *Sun*, *Daily Mail* and *Daily Express*, and then only in terms of the unfavourable reaction: 'Peer's claim on Aids condemned – anger at "misleading" remarks.' The item quotes a host of official authorities: 'misleading' – Department of Health; 'dangerous and unsubstantiated and people heed it at their peril' – National AIDS Trust; 'grossly foolish' – members of Parliamentary AIDS Group; 'enormously damaging to health education' – British Medical Association (BMA); 'Heterosexual contact is the most common form of HIV transmission in the world. Britain is not an island in that respect' – Susan Perl, Health Education Authority (HEA) (*The Times*, 18 November 1989). *The Independent* did much the same: 'Aids claim by peer attacked as "foolish".' Most significantly this item drew attention to the distinction between HIV and AIDS:

> Underlying the dispute is the difficulty in obtaining reliable information on the number of people with HIV, the Aids virus, who remain well. . . . the Health Education Authority estimates that about 2,000 heterosexuals are infected. This conclusion is based on the estimate that for every known HIV case there are another two unknown cases. It believes 5 per cent to 10 per cent of all HIV cases are heterosexuals infected by other heterosexuals.
>
> (*The Independent*, 18 November 1989)

This information provides a perspective not available in the other press reports.

HIV RISK AND THE POLITICS OF THE PRESS

The *Sun* consistently put forward the editorial view that the government's message was a lie, arguing that AIDS was not a problem for 'straight' society. It was now less likely to speak of AIDS as a 'gay plague' but it definitely regarded it as a 'homosexual disease'. Its response to the 1988 advertising campaign was characteristic: 'Why do these ads show only boy and girl couples? Showing love's young dream makes pretty pictures. The truth is uglier. There have been 44 cases in Britain involving heterosexuals. But a massive 1079 homosexuals have been affected' (*Sun*, 3 March 1988). An editorial denounced the following year's campaign in similar terms:

> Wrong Sex – The feminists are complaining about the use of a beautiful girl in advertisements warning about AIDS. They point out that in the past six months there have been only eight cases involving women. That is a fair argument. AIDS is overwhelmingly a homosexual disease. Maybe pictures of gay men would be less appealing. But they would serve more purpose.
>
> (*Sun*, 13 February 1989)

The '*Sun* doctor', Vernon Coleman, elaborated these themes and was a persistent critic of the Department of Health. Dr Coleman argued, for example, that evidence suggested that the rate of infection between HIV positive male haemophiliacs and their female sexual partners was very low. The conclusions he drew from them were very forcefully expressed: 'Those who still claim that AIDS is a major threat to those who enjoy straight sex are either illiterate or irresponsible'(*Sun*, 3 November 1988). His column vigorously campaigned against the advertising campaign:

> STOP THESE POINTLESS AIDS LIES NOW . . . two years ago I was probably the only doctor in Britain to believe that the government's advisers had got it wrong. Now more and more people working in the National Health Service are fed up with our longest running fake scare. . . . AIDS is basically a disease which affect homosexuals.
>
> (*Sun*, 23 February 1989)

He quoted research:

> AIDS STORM IS ALL HYPE – It is almost impossible to catch AIDS from straight sex, according to a new European Survey. Their figures prove that if you are a heterosexual and practice safe sex, you are as likely to be killed by lightning as AIDS. I'm now waiting for the government to spend £3 million on a campaign telling us all to have lightning conductors fitted to our heads.
>
> (*Sun*, 9 March 1989)

Coleman's 'Health Matters' column demanded that the campaign be abandoned: 'Kill off the AIDS epidemic' (*Sun*, 10 August 1989):

> End costly AIDS lie! . . . as everyone now knows, it's homosexuals and drug addicts who are mainly at risk – NOT ordinary, healthy heterosexuals. . . . Either the Health Education Authority is being run by sexual prudes who dislike the idea of young people making love. Or they are so incompetent that they just don't know that it is homosexuals, not heterosexuals, who need to be warned about AIDS.
>
> (*Sun*, 19 October 1989)

The *Sun*'s endorsement of Lord Kilbracken's claims can be seen as consistent with its longer-term commitment to the view that AIDS should be seen as 'a homosexual disease'. In the autumn of 1990, almost a year after the Kilbracken controversy, the government released figures indicating a rise in heterosexual HIV infection. Again an editorial challenged the health message:

> Bending Truth – Sir Donald Acheson, the government's chief medical officer, rings the alarm bells because AIDS cases among heterosexuals have increased by 95% in a year. We agree that this is a cause for concern. But heterosexuals with AIDS number only 1,361 in a total of 18,521 known cases. The mass of victims are homosexuals. AIDS remains overwhelmingly a disease of the gay community. Instead of

concentrating on helping these sad victims, officialdom seems more concerned to conceal the truth. Out of fear of the gay lobby, they could be condemning more homosexuals to death.

(*Sun*, 17 October 1990)

Despite the unfavourable Press Council ruling, the *Sun* continued unabashed with its main line of argument. The *Sun*'s concern was the promotion of the idea that homosexuals were responsible for AIDS and that the government were somehow protecting them. 'Bushell on the Soap Box' the following day underlined this theory:

Anyone reading the 'heavy' papers this week would be forgiven for thinking Britain was in the grip of an AIDS epidemic. . . . So why don't the AIDS campaigners target the high risk groups? Why the lie? Firstly to pump up dosh for AIDS research. And secondly to stop people coming to awkward conclusions about the dangers posed to society by promiscuous homosexuals. They are terrified that voters will demand radical solutions, like outlawing homosexuality. Or quarantining AIDS sufferers and chemically castrating anyone who is HIV positive. I've even heard some people advocate tattooing a massive A on the foreheads of carriers, although one on the base of their spine would be sufficient. What about a luminous tattoo; 'Abandon hope all ye who enter here?' The truth is there is NO heterosexual AIDS explosion. There never will be.

('Straight talking will nail the great AIDS lie', *Sun*, 18 October 1990)

Two weeks later, Professor Michael Adler of Middlesex Hospital was granted space to respond to Bushell's views. Under the headline 'WHY ANYONE CAN CATCH AIDS', he argued, 'AIDS is not a gay plague. In case you don't believe me', he quoted the cases of two of his own patients, women who had contracted the virus through sex with their male partners, concluding:

The only way to stop this disease is for the government to spend large amounts of money educating the public. Everyone must reduce the number of their sexual partners and practise safer sex using a condom. Everyone must realise they are at risk – before it is too late.

(*Sun*, 3 October 1990)

The *Sun* used its editorial column to attack Michael Adler's argument:

AIDS is not a gay plague, Professor Michael Adler writes . . . but he chooses a strange example to support his case. He says a woman patient became infected with AIDS from her husband, who was bisexual. The implication is that he had relations with other men. It was not a normal marriage . . . people accept that heterosexuals are crazy if they do not take precautions. Yet why do some medical authorities deny that AIDS is predominantly a homosexual disease?

('Truth tells', *Sun* 2 November 1990)

The editorials of the *Daily Express* voiced the same allegation that the government's susceptibility to lobbies and pressure groups was distorting the message:

> Time to tell the truth about AIDS . . . yet the government and the health education authorities still refuse to focus attention on those whose way of life makes them more vulnerable to the AIDS virus: homosexuals and drug addicts. Still we are subjected to a campaign of mis-information and dis-information to convince us that we are all at risk. Saying that anyone can get AIDS is theoretically true but thoroughly misleading. . . . At first the public was panicked, now it is apathetic. . . . If the government has been running scared of any group or lobby it must now stand and tell the truth for all our sakes.
>
> (*Daily Express*, 28 August 1989)

The *Express* was consistent in this editorial view, even though its medical correspondent's coverage differed. The next phase of the government's campaign in the new year of 1990 was criticized in similar terms:

> Ministers must not spread this AIDS hysteria – Here we go again. . . . The government's persistence with such campaigns can now be explained only by ministerial sensitivity towards not just the homosexual lobby but also wantonly alarmist doctors. . . . What the British public needs is frankness about the AIDS threat, not deception and cowardice.
>
> (*Daily Express*, 14 February 1990)

This editorial also repeated the allegation that publishers were conspiring to prevent the publication of a British edition of Michael Fumento's contoversial book *The Myth of Heterosexual AIDS* (1990).

The *Daily Mail* had a medical reporter on the regular 'AIDS beat' but the paper displayed a distinctively oppositional stance in editorials towards the government's AIDS policy. Editorials criticized anonymized testing because it did not reveal the identity of individual 'carriers', welcomed the prime minister's veto on the national sexual behaviour survey and rejected the education campaigns because they were not targeted at the homosexual and drug injecting 'risk groups'. The *Daily Mail* also had a number of well-known columnists who aggressively attacked the HEA AIDS campaign. The columnist George Gale was prominent in his criticism of gay men:

> In this irresponsible behaviour, it [the Department of Health] has the support of the homosexual community. Outfits like the Terence Higgins Trust . . . have fought against the disease as a homosexual plague. Yet that is what it is. . . . The message to be learned – that the Department

of Health should now be propagating – is that active homosexuals are potentially murderers and that the act of buggery kills.

('Straight talk is the way to save lives', *Daily Mail*, 21 July 1989)

A major guest article by Sir Reginald Murley, former president of the Royal College of Surgeons, put a similar case: 'Phoney face of the war on AIDS.' His prime target was the HEA advertisement in the press featuring two identical photographs of a young woman ('If this woman had the virus which leads to AIDS, in a few years time she could look like the person over the page. WORRYING ISN'T IT. . . . A person can be infected with HIV for several years before it shows any signs or symptoms.') He argued: 'a single picture would be more appropriate with the caption: Fortunately this young woman is unlikely to develop Aids unless she becomes a drug addict or allows herself to be buggered' (*Daily Mail*, 7 November 1989).

In the summer of 1991 a controversy arose over data on HIV infection from sexually transmitted disease clinics. The medical correspondent of the *Daily Mail* reported the exchange of letters in the *Lancet* about the proportion of heterosexuals registered at clinics who were actually infected in this country: 'The spread of the Aids virus among heterosexuals in Britain involves people from Africa or those who have had sexual partners from that continent, doctors say' (*Daily Mail*, 9 August 1991). The editorial page saw implications here within the broader framework of immigration policy: 'The hidden menace. . . . The case for medically screening immigrants from such high-risk areas of the globe grows even stronger' (*Daily Mail*, 9 August 1991). The columnist Ann Leslie seized upon the controversy as vindication of her own position: 'In other words, the so-called explosion of heterosexually transmitted HIV infection is largely accounted for by foreign drug-abusers or has been imported by people coming here from "high-risk" areas abroad' ('Lies, damned lies, and AIDS statistics', *Daily Mail*, 14 August 1991).

Editorials in the *Sun*, *Daily Mail* and *Daily Express* were consistent in attacking the government education campaign. In addition, as we have seen, the *Daily Mail* and *Sun* had several columnists who vociferously backed the editorial view that the campaign should be aimed at male homosexuals and drug injectors as 'high-risk groups'. They were at their most insistent, however, in alleging that pressure from gay men prevented this.

It is clear that this is a distinctly political stance which is not reducible to 'tabloid journalism'. The very different approach of the *Daily Mirror* illustrates this clearly. Such a popular tabloid might well make a front-page sensation out of AIDS. The *Daily Mirror* did this on a number of occasions: 'KEEP THOSE CONDOMS HANDY!' (23 March 1989), 'AIDS HELL OF STARSKY'S FAMILY' (26 August 1989), 'DI'S LEVEL 42 POP HERO ALAN DIES OF AIDS' (21 October 1989), 'LET ME KEEP MY BABY – AIDS mum's plea to judge'

(19 February 1990). But the *Daily Mirror* differed from the *Sun*, *Daily Mail* and *Daily Express* in that it raised no major argument with the health education campaign. The proprietor, Robert Maxwell had become very publicly associated with the AIDS campaign as co-founder of the National AIDS Trust. This may have accelerated the divergence between the *Mirror* and Rupert Murdoch's *Sun* on the question of the government's health education campaign.

The *Mirror* did argue strenuously in favour of compensation for infected haemophiliacs, and editorial comment on AIDS was reserved for their case. In common with the rest of the press, the *Daily Mirror* was critical of the government's unwillingness to grant financial aid. And like much of the press it focused on this particular group as 'innocent victims': 'The men, women and children . . . are victims. Innocent victims. Victims of a terrible error. Of a tragic accident . . . . Yet the mean-spirited government denies decency and the truth in refusing compensation' (*Daily Mirror* 15 November 1989). Other leader headlines snarled, 'Beneath contempt' (21 September 1990) and 'Cheap tricks' (17 October 1990). Significantly, the Kilbracken affair, which was reported with such enthusiasm in the *Sun*, received only a small news report. The *Daily Mirror*'s routine news coverage and features expressed broad sympathy with an orthodox health education view concerning HIV transmission risks. Typically, the feature marking World AIDS Day 1988 summed up:

> And what we must never forget is that there is still no cure or vaccine for AIDS. So the way to stop its spread is through information, education and changes in human behaviour. Only then will there be any hope of controlling this deadly scourge.
>
> (*Daily Mirror*, 1 December 1988)

The tabloid *Today*, although under the same ownership as the *Sun*, adopted a stance on the AIDS campaign which was close to that of the *Daily Mirror*. While government advertising was coming under renewed attack in summer 1991, *Today* still appeared at this late stage to accept without reservation the health education orthodoxy upon which the Department of Health strategy was built. Its editorial column drew attention to the results of its own commissioned research showing 'evidence that millions of people are continuing to ignore the safe sex message':

> the unpalatable truth is that everyone, irrespective of their sexuality, who is sexually active but not in a monogamous relationship, runs the risk of contracting the HIV virus. Radio and television adverts using real people have made this point powerfully and it is impossible to believe that those at risk do not understand their message. Yet, as their responses to our survey show, the campaign must continue. . . .
>
> ('Aids peril we still ignore', *Today*, 5 August 1991)

Today gave extensive coverage to the Princess of Wales's involvement with patients, focusing particularly on her effect on the campaign against stigma and prejudice. A page-long feature at the year end recording the short history of AIDS summed up:

> 1991 – Whether it is because of ignorance, prudery or fear, ten years on in the figures show that in Britain we have done too little too late to prevent the spread of AIDS. It is now spreading faster through the heterosexual population than through any other group.
>
> (*Today*, 1 December 1990)

A different set of editorial preoccupations was displayed by the tabloid *Daily Star*. Although equally vociferous, the *Daily Star*'s approach to AIDS differed significantly from that of other tabloids. The *Daily Star* ignored the Kilbracken argument and the attack on the Department of Health's educational message to heterosexuals. But editorial statements chose other targets, proposing unfashionably repressive measures and scapegoating of the 'guilty victims'. For example, International AIDS Day 1988 was marked by an editorial proposing 'Leper-type colonies':

> Surely, if the human race is under threat, it is entirely REASONABLE to segregate AIDS victims – otherwise the whole of mankind could be engulfed. Some experts have even suggested that offshore islands should be used for the colonies. Pro-homosexual groups like the Terence Higgins Trust will scream that it is unfair. But they would. The truth is that promiscuous homosexuals are by far the biggest spawning ground for AIDS. They COULD curb the spread of the disease if they curbed their sexual appetites, but that does not seem to be happening, despite all the warnings and all the condom campaigns.[9] Right now, ideas like AIDS colonies have got to be worth serious consideration.
>
> (*Daily Star*, 2 December 1988)

This attack on 'promiscuous homosexuals' was not unique. But the segregation or internment proposal was quite exceptional as an editorial stance at this time. The imagery is that of plague and pestilence, from which the 'human race is under threat', 'the whole of mankind could be engulfed' unless we seek out the 'spawning grounds' and isolate the polluted in 'colonies'. The attempt to distinguish between 'innocent' and 'guilty' victims – not exclusive to the *Daily Star* – was a major issue in this newspaper. But the 'guilty' are not just responsible for their own predicament, they are to blame for the deaths of others. A columnist's comment on the widely publicized case of the family of *Starsky and Hutch* actor Paul Michael Glaser was typical:

> Just how many innocents like the Glasers are there in Britain? How many families have been sentenced to death by faceless blood donors

who were drug addicts or permissive homosexuals? And how long are we going to support spurious charities for those who brought this awful curse upon themselves? Sympathy is fine. But would not our support be better directed towards the innocents who received tainted blood through no fault of their own?

(*Daily Star*, 29 August 1989)

The imagery again is medieval: 'innocents' are 'sentenced to death' by 'faceless' ones who bring the 'awful curse'.

In December 1990 a report alleged that singer Cliff Richard had 'refused an appeal from a sanctuary for AIDS victims. He replied on a postcard, saying: "I do not feel it is the sort of thing my name should be associated with" '. The story was accompanied by editorial comment:

Cliff is quite right. Why should anyone feel obliged to help people who, mostly, have only themselves to blame for their predicament? Despite all the homosexual propaganda, AIDS is still almost entirely a disease passed on by poofters and junkies. Only their promiscuity and stupidity has spread it like wildfire. Thank goodness someone of Cliff's stature has stood out against the AIDS industry. Let's hope that other showbiz stars follow his example.

(*Daily Star*, 18 December 1990)

The call to marginalize social groups by association with the disease is here expressed in language that even the *Sun* was by now thinking more carefully about using.

In comparison with the tabloids, the broadsheets each carried a wider coverage of AIDS and related issues. The coverage provides an in-depth focus on the institutions of the state, the professions and the voluntary organizations, with regular reports from conferences and journals. This is closely related to the prominent role of the specialist journalist in these newspapers. The subject of AIDS is covered by medical correspondents, science correspondents, home affairs correspondents, health services correspondents, social services correspondents and even specialists in technology and in environment. With these influences, editorial comment on AIDS thus typically demonstrates a greater sensitivity to the viewpoints dominant among the health professionals and departmental officials. For example, *The Times* welcomed the government plans for anonymous testing, arguing the need for more information and that 'if reliable figures are to be found, the anonymity of the survey must be protected'. *The Times* warned against complacency: 'Aids will be here for a long time – longer than the reach of any public relations campaign. The more that is understood about its transmission the better. Too little is known about the epidemiology of Aids' (*The Times*, 24 November 1988). This is the direct opposite in all respects to the editorial view of the *Daily Express* on this policy. It also differs very sharply from the approach of the *Sun*, which is interesting since both the *Sun* and *The Times* are owned by Rupert Murdoch.

The proximity of the broadsheets to the world of the 'Aids policy community' is extremely well illustrated by the *Guardian*'s editorial on the same issue of anonymous testing. The *Guardian* here deals with a technical distinction which it feels is not properly understood elsewhere in the debate: 'Is it ethical to test someone for Aids and then not disclose the result? . . . The argument is likely to become confused unless two different types of medical tests – clinical and epidemiological – are kept separate.' The editorial argues that the former should always be available with suitable expert advice and counselling for individuals and are private and voluntary. The latter it argues are essential to enable epidemiologists to monitor the progress of the virus through populations and should not be confused with the individual clinical situation (*Guardian*, 24 November 1988). However, in the course of this technical and terminological discussion, the editorial perpetuates the myth of the 'AIDS test'.

The features sections of *The Independent* and *Guardian*, in particular, reflect their familiarity with the worlds of social welfare, health, community organizations, sexuality and gender. *The Independent* also had an article by freelance writer Angus Finney on press sensationalism and misinformation ('Reports that foster ignorance about Aids', *The Independent*, 2 August 1989). This provoked a letter from the *Sun*'s Vernon Coleman protesting, 'your article has simply helped to perpetuate a long-standing myth – that Aids is a threat to heterosexuals' (*The Independent*, 3 August 1989).

The science correspondent of *The Times* wrote from a perspective firmly located in the orthodox medical and educational perspective. In a major feature on the eve of World AIDS Day 1989, he described the problem as he saw it:

> Aids is still seen as a sordid disease largely restricted to promiscuous homosexual men and intravenous drug abusers. The belief that 'normal' people are somehow immune to it is almost as entrenched now as it was at the beginning of the epidemic. The evidence, human and scientific, tells a different story. . . . Against this background, the insistence that Aids is a 'gay plague' would be laughable were it not so tragically short-sighted. In the Western world, Aids merely showed up among homosexual men first.
>
> (*The Times*, 30 November 1989)

These correspondents are not, however, uncritical of the Department of Health and Health Education Authority information campaigns. But their criticisms are typically ones about the style, timing or language of the message to heterosexuals – not about the need for such a message. *The*

Times's science correspondent believed that the fact of the increase in HIV infection was due in part to previous 'muddled messages' – 'the public was led to believe that a catastrophe was at hand; when it did not materialise, they became complacent'. A more realistic message should now be:

> Aids is a sexually transmitted disease that so far in Britain has affected a great many more homosexuals than heterosexuals. The first phase of an epidemic that will last for decades is over. A second phase has begun. The risk of infection through heterosexual intercourse is very small. Only individual responsibility will keep it that way. Carelessness kills.
> ('Aids; this time send the right message', *The Times*, 17 October 1990)

An earlier editorial in *The Independent* had pointed to the possibility of complacency and disbelief:

> A conventional way to fight complacency is for the government to run an alarming series of advertisements. The trouble with this approach is that it has already been tried, and since, in the present state of knowledge, it seems to have been based on an exaggerated estimate of the risk posed to heterosexuals, the force of official pronouncements has diminished.
> ('Danger of alarmist warnings', *The Independent*, 5 September 1989)

NEWS FORMATS AND ACCESS TO THE PRESS

The *Sun*'s identification of AIDS as a distinctly 'gay' issue received regular reinforcement in several different sections of the newspaper. *Sun* columnists in particular took the themes of editorial and '*Sun* doctor' pages even further, making explicit the idea that the disease 'belonged to' or was 'caused by' particular groups. Fiona McDonald Hull provided classic examples:

> Give it a rest all you gays – Hands up everyone who is a little bit sick and tired of homosexuals telling us how NORMAL it is to be one, and how the rest of us really SHOULD try it. The latest in the long line of hetero-bashers is Blackadder star Stephen Fry. . . . Stephen also curses heterosexuals who curse homosexuals for the AIDS plague. Bit unfair that, since homosexuals – whether they like to admit it or not (and they don't) – DID start it.
> (*Sun*, 6 October 1989)

Ms Hull chose the occasion of Ian Charleson's death to urge:

> Gays must learn from actor Ian's death. . . . Ian died because he caught AIDS. And it is almost certain that he caught AIDS because he was a homosexual. If his death has done nothing else, surely it must make our

gay community face up to the fact that AIDS is a homosexual, drug-related disease. It is not a heterosexual disease. It becomes a heterosexual disease ONLY when gays or drug addicts become either blood donors or switch sides. It is time the homosexuals and drug addicts cleaned up their act. They, and they alone, are responsible for people dying from AIDS.

(*Sun*, 12 January 1990)

Other prominent columnists have taken up this theme. The *Mail on Sunday*, a newspaper which provided very little basic news reporting on AIDS or HIV, had Julie Burchill to put forward the 'gays caused it' theory:

simply because a large number of rich, white homosexuals went on holiday to AIDS-riddled Haiti in the seventies and eighties and indulged themselves with the dirt-poor native boys for the price of a Pina Colada, we are now in a second Dark Age of sexual misery. It ill behoves them now to wag their fingers at us, as we attempt to clean up the mess they've made.

(*Mail on Sunday*, 21 October 1990)

In the *Sun*, the TV criticism column 'Bushell on the Box' was a regular source of such comment:

The poof's party line, regurgitated in the bitty HYSTERIA 2, is to exaggerate grossly the AIDS threat to straights and play down its causes. They do this to boost funds for AIDS research and keep us from discussing radical solutions, like outlawing homosexuality and hanging heroin pushers.

(*Sun*, 6 December 1989)

Yet the *Sun* is a popular tabloid newspaper which features the dominant sexual culture, with all its contradictions. This involves more than just a frantic form of heterosexuality once known as bonking, for the *Sun* also contains regular Woman pages and features. Within these, there are stories which implicitly challenge the editorial line by reporting the problems of safe sex and foolish heterosexuals who take risks. 'Has AIDS really killed the one night stand?' asked the Woman page with a survey of young people which apparently gave cause for concern: 'their attitudes are those of totally irresponsible people who refuse to face the facts about the virus', fooling themselves with excuses like, 'Risk is not high – Leanne, 21. I take a chance – Amanda, 19. Only gays get it – Michele, 17' (*Sun*, 27 April 1989). Given the relentless homophobia of the editorials and columnists in the *Sun*, a most poignant example of differences between formats was perhaps the small item in the 'Allan Hall's America' column, on problems experienced by gay groups in America:

Gays get it tough – The tide has turned against gay groups in America.

> Councils are scrapping the laws which gave equal or preferred treatment to homosexuals. . . . The National Gay and Lesbian Alliance said, 'There is a new menace in the air'.
>
> (*Sun*, 10 October 1989)

These apparent contradictions are partly a function of the different rules and requirements which may operate in different parts of a newspaper. We must recognize that there are potentially different forms of writing or formats. News reports, editorials, features, columns, cartoons and letters to the editor, for instance, can represent what Bruck has called 'various types of narratives and formats which follow different rules and conventions of composition and subject treatment' (1989: 114). Bruck suggests that these formats can affect the way in which competing or alternative discourses may be taken up.[10] The news report, with its conventional requirements of 'fact', 'hard news' and authoritative sources, will tend to favour the 'official' agenda and viewpoint. Features or lengthy specialist reports, with 'softer' news angles, longer production time-scales and more contextualization, may allow greater access to conflicting views and a wider spectrum of opinion. They are, however, often written by specialist journalists close to the official sources of power and other institutional interests. There are a variety of reasons why the range of opinion in these areas of a newspaper may increase. For example, a marketing strategy might involve introducing a greater diversity of political opinion in the attempt to pick up readers.

The 'column' format would appear to offer the greatest extremes of 'openness' or 'closedness' to alternative discourses, written by individual authors with few formal constraints or requirements placed upon them. The columnists in the *Sun*, or those in the *Daily Mail*, might thus be regarded as extreme examples of (right-wing) oppositional or alternative perspectives. The *Sunday Telegraph*'s columnists, too, were not sympathetic to the HEA: 'From the beginning, the advertising campaigns have been close to mendacity' (*Sunday Telegraph*, 23 July 1989); 'Aids does not discriminate, the experts say. But the experts, it seems, do. They discriminate against heterosexuals' (*Sunday Telegraph*, 10 December 1989). The paper's regular medical expert, Dr James Le Fanu, accused the BMA of 'sensationalism and distortion' on AIDS ('Myths of epidemic proportions', *Sunday Telegraph*, 21 July 1991).

There are examples where columnists espouse views different to the editorial and where columnists contradict each other. In the *Sunday Times*, for example, there were columnists scathingly critical of the educational message (Susan Crosland) and columnists passionate in its defence (Julia Neuberger). Features argued the case for the national sex survey and reported the emergence of positive images of gays and people with AIDS in Hollywood; writers attacked the advertising campaign (Digby

Anderson) and others defended it (Michael Adler); the medical correspondent's reports showed an orthodox sympathy. In the midst of allegations of a publisher's boycott, the *Sunday Times* published two lengthy extracts of Michael Fumento's controversial book *The Myth of Heterosexual AIDS* (1990), but also carried articles by epidemiologists presenting the orthodox case. The following year, the 'New Grubb Street' column accused the Department of Health of 'official disinformation' on the heterosexual HIV statistics (*Sunday Times*, 11 August 1991) and an article on 'high-risk' groups accused the HEA of 'trying to conceal information out of some misplaced notion of political correctness' (*Sunday Times*, 18 August 1981). The *Sunday Times* also regularly reported the campaign for compensation for haemophiliacs infected with HIV from NHS blood products, under the banner 'The forgotten victims'.[11]

The tabloid *Sunday People* provides a further example of where the editorial expressed the heterosexual risk view while the paper's columnist 'The Man of the People' questioned the relevance of the advertising campaign from within the 'gay sex/gay disease' perspective: 'the propaganda funds would be better spent in targetting the gay community. For the ugly truth is that, with few exceptions, AIDS can be blamed on buggery' (*Sunday People*, 19 November 1989). Meanwhile, the paper ran editorials on the scandal of teenage prostitutes: 'human time-bombs riddled with the AIDS virus . . . with the AIDS threat we ignore them at our peril' (*Sunday People*, 19 February 1991), and on the threat of AIDS to young couples: 'even the most innocent are at risk unless they take every precaution' ('Grim reminder', *Sunday People*, 18 August 1991).

Fragmentary and often inchoate political and popular cultures fill the pages of any mass circulation newspaper. Some of the formats of popular journalism necessarily draw freely and casually from elements of these cultures. Many of the stories in the *Sun*, for example, could be regarded as typical, formulaic, 'tabloid stories'. The interesting point about this 'format' is the extent to which it can draw upon alternative or oppositional discourses, however piecemeal or contradictory. In the half-mythical world of heterosexual promiscuity and endless casual sex, the question of AIDS inevitably intrudes, albeit not in the formulations of health education. What could be more typical for a popular tabloid than a feature on sunshine, sea and sex?:

> SEX-SPREE HOLIDAY BRITS IN AIDS PERIL – British girls are ignoring the terrifying risk of AIDS to go on sex orgies in the sun. . . . And many admit they do not make holiday lovers wear a condom. *Sun* reporter Antonella Lazzeri went to the Greek holiday island of Rhodes to investigate. . . .
>
> (*Sun*, 20 July 1991)

The *Sun* editorials, doctor and columnists had, of course, explicitly argued against these ideas on numerous occasions. The *Daily Star* too ran the story that: 'Holiday sex can costa [*sic*] your life – Hordes of young Britons are still risking their lives through holiday sexual flings, a top doctor warned yesterday. They are casually leaping into bed with each other despite the risk of catching AIDS.' The doctor is quoted, 'There's no doubt that heterosexuals can catch AIDS off other heterosexuals' and 'In Africa AIDS has become a standard heterosexual disease' (*Daily Star*, 3 May 1989). The *Star*'s coverage never seriously doubted or contradicted these ideas. It was not a central issue and, as we have seen, editorial energy was devoted to other targets.

Such features and stories are common in the tabloids, particularly so in the *Sun* and *Daily Star*. They often appear as surveys of sex or dating behaviour, as medical advice or health features. The *Daily Star* reported:

> YOUNG LOVE IS BLIND TO AIDS SCARE – The threat of AIDS holds no fears for most young people in Britain. Three out of four are ignoring warnings about the deadly virus, according to a survey published on the same day as the World Health Organisation predicted that 10 million children will have AIDS by the year 2000.
>
> (*Daily Star*, 26 September 1990)

These findings were highlighted in the editorial columns: 'Careless love – The youth of Britain are ignoring the AIDS threat . . . perhaps they don't care. . . . The government has spent millions worrying about AIDS. But it is not getting the message across.' 'GIRLS IN THE NAUGHTY 90's' featured a survey from *Cosmopolitan* magazine: 'Survey lifts lid off saucy habits. . . . They'll even risk pregnancy or AIDS' (*Daily Star*, 19 November 1990); and *Woman* magazine was plundered to provide 'TOO SHY TO PLAY SAFE? – Girls ignore AIDS threat, survey reveals. One in three would never use a condom' (*Daily Star*, 12 December 1990). As Christmas approached the *Daily Star* offered:

> SURVIVOR'S GUIDE TO OFFICE RAVE-UPS – Take care behind the filing cabinets. . . . Here's what you could be catching . . . AIDS: This is still rarer than the experts predicted. But a new report says that in one London district (Riverside) at least one in every hundred younger men has the virus. So there's definitely some risk from casual sex this Christmas.
>
> (*Daily Star*, 13 December 1990)

Whatever the editorial line on AIDS, Joan Collins is news:

> JOAN AGONY AT PAL HIT BY AIDS – Star bans sex cheats. Joan Collins is demanding her lovers sleep with no one else after learning that a friend is dying of AIDS. Now four-times wed Joan, 57, is terrified that she too could fall a victim to AIDS. She said, 'I know a girl, quite well known,

who got AIDS from her boyfriend. She's dying. It's a horror story'. Joan told Marie Claire magazine, 'Just imagine, the thought of somebody doing something to bring that disease to me is abhorrent. I couldn't forgive it. Fidelity is terribly important. How can you be sure what they've picked up?'

(*Sun*, 16 August 1990)

Around this time the HEA was running television advertisements based on 'personal testimony' accounts of heterosexuals who had become infected with HIV. Personalized and dramatic life-stories are a staple of popular journalism, and the *Daily Star* carried some examples:

Alison is 24, rich and got AIDS from the man of her dreams . . . in a one-night stand several years ago – and now she's dying of AIDS. Alison, 24, is far removed from the high-risk, homosexual, drug-taking world usually associated with the disease . . . she could not know he was a bisexual with the AIDS virus. The statistics say it shouldn't have happened. But it did – and now Alison lives with a ticking time-bomb of despair. . . . She says, 'I want to help other people, to warn kids that AIDS is a real danger, that it took only one night eight years ago for me'.

(*Daily Star*, 23 August 1990)

In this version the person 'got AIDS' from someone with the 'AIDS virus', becomes a 'ticking time-bomb' destined to 'die of AIDS'. In the *Daily Star*'s version of heterosexual transmission the subjects 'Catch AIDS off other heterosexuals.' The *Daily Star* also ran a centre page spread on two consecutive days highlighting the plight of thousands of orphaned children in Uganda – Africa becomes 'THE LAND OF THE LIVING DEAD', 'pitiful', an alien place of 'ignorance':

Husbands and wives, homosexuals and heterosexuals, are being buried each day as the death toll escalates. But now children are the latest victims of a curse fuelled by their parents' sexual ignorance. And pitiful Uganda is the AIDS cradle of the world.

(*Daily Star*, 30 January 1990)

The *Daily Star* also reported on sex-tourism in Thailand, which was portrayed as 'the Far East sex paradise that can be a fatal attraction for Brits'. The bar girls are depicted as 'Angels of Death', 'SO SWEET, SO CHEAP, SO DEADLY'. 'While the British government is tackling the AIDS war at home, it faces a frightening new threat from pleasure seekers bringing the virus back from Thailand' (*Daily Star*, 7 September 1990). The *Sun*'s version was written from the standpoint of the 'tourists': 'Scandal of vice-spree Brits – lads get high on young Thai girls'. The lads are quoted 'I try not to think about AIDS . . . I don't care about AIDS' and anyway, 'Most don't even know how it is caught' (*Sun*, 14 July 1989).

International coverage in the *Daily Star* included a report on the AIDS situation in Cuba. Without any reference to its own position on this issue, the *Daily Star* reported:

> Tyrant's Evil AIDS lock-up – AIDS victims in Cuba are being locked up for life by cruel dictator Fidel Castro. . . . Anyone found with the killer syndrome is put into quarantine until a cure is found – or until they die. . . . Sufferers are still allowed to work but rulers say they must be locked away for the sake of the rest of the population.
>
> (*Daily Star*, 28 April 1990)

The *Daily Express* provides further examples of the possible effect of journalistic formats on content. The issue of AIDS appears as a story in a number of different ways. 'The medical reporter' was responsible for the regular reports of government, medical and scientific matters on AIDS. This ranged from the Cox Committee report, 'Straight sex thousands are infected with AIDS' (*Daily Express*, 1 November 1988), 'AIDS warning to women over high-risk sex', based on a study of HIV transmission rates in the *British Medical Journal* (17 February 1989), to 'AIDS threat on increase for non-gays', on the Institute of Actuaries' predictions (2 *Daily Express*, March 1989). But most of the AIDS stories are not by specialist staff. Splash headlines such as 'SYRINGE PERIL ON BEACHES – Exclusive; mother hits out as Sarah, 2, steps on a junkie's needle' (*Daily Express*, 27 June 1989) or 'AIDS RAPE DEATH FEAR – victim's nightmare as attacker with killer virus gets 11 years' (*Daily Express*, 11 July 1989) are more tailored to the newspaper's major news priorities.

The distinctive editorial view of the *Daily Express* on AIDS was that the government's health education message was wrong. But the editorial column, the news pages, features and pieces by the medical reporter are not a uniform production. Within a relatively short period the following items appeared in different sections of the newspaper, implying other priorities and perspectives than those established by the editorials: first, a feature several pages long based on the orthodox WHO model of heterosexual transmission headlined, 'AIDS – THE KILLER TAKING US INTO A GLOBAL CRISIS WITHIN THE NEXT TEN YEARS', and 'FACT – It is the main killer of young women in Europe's big cities', quoting the WHO surveillance team that by the year 2000 'heterosexual transmission will predominate in most industrial countries' (*Daily Express*, 1 August 1990). Second, there was the inevitable holiday feature on 'The sizzling combination of sun, sea, sand and sangria', an investigation of heterosexual risk and the realities of unsafe sexual behaviour on the Club 18–30 holiday where, 'The beer is cheap, the sex is as casual as the day-glo t-shirts and AIDS is about the only four-letter word that goes unspoken' (*Daily Express*, 23 August 1990).

Third, other stories reported on: 'AIDS fear for women' (*Daily Express*, 13 November 1990), 'Shock rise in AIDS cases' (*Daily Express*, 20 November 1990), 'Killer disease timebomb is revealed by secret checks' (18 *Daily Express*, 18 May 1991), 'AIDS despair that knows no barriers' (*Daily Express*, 25 April 1991).

A similar variation in content can be seen in the *Daily Mail*, the *Daily Express*'s main rival. The *Daily Mail* had established an editorial stance firmly against the campaign aimed at heterosexuals. But, throughout this period, the medical correspondent provided reports from 'official' sources around the campaign. For example: 'Drug addicts bridge to AIDS epidemic . . . the danger was spelled out yesterday by Health Minister David Mellor, deeply worried by apathy over the disease' (*Daily Mail*, 20 May 1989); 'New AIDS campaign with global warning . . . chief medical officer Sir Donald Acheson, said: "AIDS may not seem very serious now – like the greenhouse effect – but if we do not act it could have a disastrous effect on the future of our children and grandchildren" ' (*Daily Mail*, 15 February 1990); and 'Rise in "normal sex" AIDS cases. . . . The number of AIDS cases transmitted by heterosexual intercourse is "increasing rapidly" according to new figures from the Department of Health' (*Daily Mail*, 12 April 1990).

Occasionally the views of sources and authorities quoted in such reports will be directly challenged by editorials in the same newspaper. For example, the reports, 'AIDS in pregnant women soaring' (*Daily Mail*, 17 May 1991) and 'Aids toll warning for city couples' (18 May 1991), were followed by the editorial:

> Fatuous Figures . . . these findings are held to justify the Department of Health's campaign. . . . They do nothing of the kind. What they show is that the disease is highly localised, mainly in the mobile, cosmopolitan and exceptionally promiscuous population of Central London. . . . They certainly do not support the huge sums spent on advertising the AIDS danger directed indiscriminately at everyone in the land.
>
> (*Daily Mail*, 18 May 1991)

THE PRINCESS, THE PRESS AND AIDS

The Princess of Wales excites contradictory impulses in the popular press. She is at once praised, mythologized, and patronized. The *Sun* columnist Richard Littlejohn revealed some of the discomfort caused by her involvement with AIDS:

> The royal clothes horse seems to have a fascination with terminal illness. One day she is shaking hands with lepers, the next snuggling up to AIDS

victims. Maybe Prince Charles should buy her a stethoscope for Christmas, he might get to play doctors and nurses.

His message was used to make the point that:

> The government has been conned into devoting a disproportionate amount of money to AIDS research and publicity. After all, it is hardly a disease which threatens the vast majority of the population despite the misleading propaganda being peddled by the gay lobby. If you stay clear of sleeping with woofters and drug users you should be safe.
>
> ('Don't fall for AIDS hype Dr. Di', *Sun*, 4 December 1989)

The attitudes declared by the *Daily Star* were bound to be a potential problem when Princess Diana was so publicly visiting AIDS hospices and hospitals. Brian Hitchen's 'Straight talking from the *Star*' column had stated:

> isn't it about time her husband put down his royal foot and told Princess Diana 'No more visits to adult AIDS centres'. . . . Whoever plans her schedules should cut out the endless hand-shaking with unstable drug addicts and the time spent listening to endless tales of woe from homo-sexuals whose promiscuity has made them HIV positive. There's nothing exotic about sticking needles in yourself and there is no romance in buggery.
>
> (*Daily Star*, 1 August 1990)

However, the newspaper was able to present images it found more acceptable:

> Di to help the tots hit by killer virus – The Princess, who has led the fight for a better deal for AIDS sufferers, is fully aware of the growing crisis and next week she will give a hard-hitting speech aiming to shock the nation out of its complacency over the disease. . . .
>
> (*Daily Star*, 15 April 1991)

Princess Diana working with 'innocent' children and families was some-thing the *Daily Star* felt more comfortable with and it produced features on the issues on three consecutive days.[12] The *Daily Star* began with an editorial declaring:

> We must help the AIDS kids . . . because of saloon bar stigmas attached to this odious disease, they find themselves shunned. It is right that we should seek to improve the lot of these pathetic mites. They have done NO wrong. The problem is growing all the time as AIDS bites deeper into the heterosexual community. We cannot hide ostrich-like from the awful truth. That's why it's so good to see Princess Diana ready to stand up and broach the unpleasant subject of AIDS and the family.
>
> (*Daily Star*, 15 April 1991)

However, when Diana made her speech as new patron of the National AIDS Trust, she made demands the *Daily Star* found hard to meet. In the words of their own front-page report, taken from her speech, 'she warned people who shunned the victims: "Don't be so smug – it could be you next". . . . "HIV does not make people dangerous to know. So you can shake their hands and give them a hug – heaven knows they need it" ' (*Daily Star*, 23 April 1991). The same day's editorial column took up the challenge:

> Princess is wrong – Princess Diana is a lovely caring person. But she is sadly misguided about AIDS victims. . . . If Diana had been talking about the innocent children who have AIDS or who are orphaned by it, that would have been fine. But clearly she was talking about ALL AIDS victims . . . in appealing for love for EVERY AIDS sufferer she is endorsing the anti-social behaviour of those who have turned the problem into a plague that threatens mankind . . . she and her advisers should think very carefully about the causes she supports.
>
> (*Daily Star*, 23 April 1991)

Despite the front-page splash, 'HUG AIDS VICTIMS SAYS DI – "Open your hearts and don't be afraid" ', the *Daily Star* had printed an editorial attacking the Princess's judgement. But this editorial was then pulled from later editions. In the place of 'Princess is wrong', the editorial was now headlined 'The caring Princess'. It began: 'Princess Diana is a wonderful, caring person. . . . Diana wrote every word of the speech herself. It was a cry from her very soul on behalf of the tragic children who have been infected or orphaned by this tragic disease.' The suggestion of criticism of Diana was removed, but the *Daily Star* did not withdraw its condemnation of the 'guilty' people with AIDS. It reversed its claim that Diana was 'endorsing the anti-social behaviour' of the 'guilty victims' to read that she 'was NOT condoning' such people. The editorial simply asserted that the *Daily Star* and Diana were speaking the same language:

> When she asked us to hug AIDS victims and shake their hands, to share their homes and toys, she was NOT condoning the activities of those who are spreading AIDS promiscuously. She was NOT endorsing rampant homosexuals and junkies who are just indulging their appetite for drugs or sex without a thought for the dangers to mankind.
>
> (*Daily Star*, late editions, 23 April 1991)

The problem which the newspaper was trying to resolve derives from the contradictions of maintaining its ruthless 'innocent/guilty' discrimination without alienating the public support for Princess Diana in her work on AIDS and without coming into conflict with 'The Palace'. The following day, the *Daily Star* printed a small eight line item on page five, headed 'You back Di on AIDS plea', stating 'Princess Diana's "Hug an AIDS

victim" plea gained overwhelming support from *Daily Star* readers yesterday. Callers voted 3–1 in favour of her appeal for the tragic sufferers.'
Research into attitudes and beliefs suggests that a significant proportion of
readers do in fact make 'innocent/guilty' distinctions in thinking about
AIDS (see Chapter 11). This, however, would not necessarily guarantee
approval of attacks on Princess Diana.

But Princess Diana had become a problem for sections of the popular
press. As they constantly reminded their readers, she was the first royal to
shake the hand of someone with AIDS. She then became patron of the
National AIDS Trust. When in the summer of 1991 she made another visit
to the AIDS Unit at Middlesex Hospital, this time accompanied by United
States first lady, Barbara Bush, the *Daily Star* gave it full picture coverage:
'Caring Princess Diana held the hand of an AIDS patient with just two days
to live and whispered words of comfort yesterday.' The headline was her
own widely quoted remark, 'Anywhere I see suffering that is where I want
to be' (*Daily Star*, 18 July 1991). Then a month later, along with every
other national newspaper, the *Daily Star* covered the visits of the princess
to the bedside of her friend and well-known arts figure Adrian Ward-
Jackson who was dying of AIDS-related illness. 'DIANA IN AIDS VIGIL'
reported that she had visited him several times at the hospital and had been
secretly visiting him at his home before that, and had cut short her family
holiday at Balmoral to be at his bedside (*Daily Star*, 23 August 1991). The
newspaper reported, as did all the national press, her last visit the following day, 'DI's GRIEF AS HER AIDS FRIEND DIES'. The funeral the following
week was covered as 'Di keeps pledge to AIDS pal' (*Daily Star*, 30 August
1991).

This apparent change of heart with regard to Diana's work was no less
marked at the *Sun*, which joined the rest of the national press in sympathetic reports of her visits to Adrian Ward-Jackson: 'Heartbroken Princess
Diana wept last night after visiting a friend dying of AIDS in hospital'
('Vigil at hospital', *Sun*, 23 August 1991). His death the following morning
was reported as 'DI's FAREWELL KISS'. Most striking, however, was the
editorial celebrating her as a 'wonderfully warm-hearted, compassionate
girl', with its headline 'Wonder Girl' (*Sun*, 24 August 1991). Her attendance at the funeral was given extended coverage: 'Di's funeral grief for
AIDS victim Adrian', 'THE HAND OF LOVE – Di gives comfort' (*Sun*, 30
August 1991).[13]

Among all the coverage given to Diana's hospital visits, with her friend's
eventual death and funeral, only two articles (by columnists in the *Evening
Standard* and the *Mail on Sunday*) voiced criticisms. The *Sun* and the *Daily
Star* were silent by this stage, but Peter McKay in the *Evening Standard*
echoed the arguments used earlier by their columnists:

it seems to me that Diana has become caught up in the mythology of

Aids. Plenty of men and women die early, friendless and virtu<i>al</i>
from a variety of diseases over which they had no control. Ho
die of Aids because medicine has not yet found a way of protec<i>ung</i>
from one possible consequence of their sex lives. . . . After all, you are
unlikely in this country to contract Aids outside of homosexuality and
intravenous drug use.

('Aids and the princess', *Evening Standard*, 30 August 1991)

John Junor questioned Princess Diana's

apparent obsession with the victims of AIDS. And in particular the
strangeness of her conduct in relation to the late Mr. Adrian Ward-
Jackson. . . . Just what then do you suppose can explain her preoccupation with the disease? Could she really want to go down in history as the
patron saint of sodomy?

('A lovely lady's odd obsession', *Mail on Sunday*, 1 September 1991)

CONCLUSION: PRESS DIVERSITY AND FACTORS INFLUENCING CONTENT

The press reporting of AIDS shows both similarity and diversity. The
coverage has not all been negative or simply sensational. The differences
between newspapers demonstrates the analytical weakness of the notion of
'the press' and of the term 'the media'. The range of approaches to AIDS
goes beyond a simple division between 'tabloids' and 'broadsheets'. The
differences within newspapers indicate the various demands and opportu-
nities of format and journalistic specialism. The apparent contradictions
and changes over time suggest the various pressures and priorities of the
commercial market as well as of politics and professionalism.

The way in which we have examined the reporting of 'heterosexual risk'
has attempted to recognize the importance of the context within which
journalism and the commercial press operate. This analysis suggests that
there are three areas in which we can understand the key influences on
content. We can call these proprietorial, editorial/journalist and marketing
strategies. In the first area, we noted that the proprietor of the *Daily
Mirror* had a public stance on the issue of AIDS and took an interest in its
coverage in the newspaper. In the case of the Murdoch press (*Sun*, *Today*,
The Times and *Sunday Times*) there have been areas of coverage where the
views and interests of the proprietor are clearly reflected. For instance,
both *The Times* and the *Sun* endorse conservative political views on the
economy although they sell to very different readerships. Both have been
extremely critical of the BBC and advocate more open competition in
broadcasting. Yet in the case of AIDS coverage there was no consensus
among the Murdoch press. The respective editorial approaches of the *Sun*

and *The Times*, for example, placed them on opposite sides in terms of the current political and medical orthodoxy.

Where there is this latitude, the 'line' of the paper is more likely to be determined by its editorial staff. There are a number of variables which will influence decisions made here. First, the sense of the paper's 'natural' audience and where the paper will take a particular stance in relation to the supposed preferences of that audience. The *Daily Mail* and the *Daily Express*, for example, are both widely recognized as 'middle class' and conservative papers which have endorsed much of the 'Thatcherite' political agenda on declining moral standards, law and order, local government and trades union power. The *Sun* adds other populist elements of anti-foreign and anti-gay attitudes. It treads an uneasy line between its political agenda and the actual composition of its audience which is substantially working-class and labour voting. There were also special problems for some of the newspapers in stories about Princess Diana and her well-known sympathy and support for people with AIDS. To attack the Princess of Wales, the most popular member of the royal family, might create problems with their own readership.

There is a second dimension within the editorial/journalist area which may influence content. There may be divisions among staff between types of journalistic practice. Some staff have a specialist brief, for example, as medical correspondents. Their specialist knowledge and professional commitments may run counter to the editorial line. Thus we saw contradictions in coverage such as those in the *Daily Express*, where the medical correspondent's work on AIDS differed from the sensational reporting by news staff and the political stance taken by editorials.

Another source of potential contradictions in the tabloid press is the need to follow 'good' story angles.[14] 'Sun, sand, sea and sex at Club 18–30' appeals to their most basic news values, despite the fact that the message about AIDS dangers runs counter to the editorial line of 'no risk to heterosexuals'. Some news stories create specific problems for the tabloid press, since they generate contradictory impulses within their populist rhetoric. We have seen the contradiction involved in the *Daily Star* reporting on the 'dictator' Fidel Castro locking up people with HIV, when this policy had previously been advanced for the UK by the *Daily Star* itself.

There is a further constraint on editorial decisions which we might consider here. This is to avoid problems with the law, libel suits and the strictures of various commissions. The *Sun* and columnist Garry Bushell were censured by the Press Council in May 1990 for using offensive language about gays. Following this, previously unfamiliar terms such as 'gay community' appeared in the *Sun* ('Bending truth', *Sun*, 17 October 1990) (see p. 222). It may be that falling sales, expensive libel defeats, growing public disapproval of editorial excesses, the Calcutt Commission into press behaviour and the decline and fall of Mrs Thatcher have all contributed to some change of direction at the *Sun* (see Chippendale and Horrie 1990). On the subject of AIDS, however, their TV critic could still attack the serial *Eastenders* as 'propaganda' for the 'belief that the disease plagues Cockneys ahead of shirtlifters, junkies and sub-Saharan Africans' (*Sun*, 11 September 1991).

Some of the above points relate to the limits imposed on journalism by general editorial concerns with marketing and assumptions about the typical audience for the paper. But there are also moments when stories are chosen or news angles shaped very specifically to target new sections of the audience. This becomes most obvious when a newspaper is under pressure from falling sales or is attempting to break into a different market section. The *Sun* is well known for its conservative political stance, but has recently featured columns by the MP Ken Livingstone, who as 'Red Ken' was a major bogey man of the right in the early 1980s. This is a further example of how the formats of different sections of a paper (in this case the 'signed' column) can be used to diversify the potential readership. We noted above that the *Sunday Times* included a range of signed columns by different writers in the AIDS debate.

The tabloids the *Daily Sport* and *Sunday Sport* illustrate another variant in this process. In most areas they offer a similar populism to that of the *Sun* with its mix of 'sex, sensation, scandal and sport'. We can see, for example, that their attitudes to foreigners are very similar. The *Sunday Sport* had nothing to learn from the *Sun* when it suggested in an editorial that the channel tunnel should be used as a dump for the nuclear industry because 'no one wants to be that close to the ponging Frogs anyway' (*Sunday Sport*, 24 July 1991). Yet its attitudes to gays are very different. It expressed these as follows:

> Your broadminded *Sport* believes in sexual equality. That is why we launched a gay section in our lonely hearts column. For whether you are black or white, heterosexual or a homosexual, all need friends. And thanks to your *Sport*, thousands of gay guys and lesbians are no longer lonesome.
>
> (*Sunday Sport*, 26 June 1991)[15]

And, of course, the revenue which 'classified' and other gay advertising attracts must also be a welcome addition to the paper's funding.

Many of these pressures on content are contradictory and can mean that the message of the press, especially of the tabloids, is very confused. The contradictions we have examined are part of the reason why audiences may discount views and opinions in their newspapers. Studies of audience groups indicate that while some *Sun* readers were aware of the prominent 'no heterosexual risk' view, it was discounted because of its context in that particular newspaper (Kitzinger and Miller 1991). The key actor in the supply of information to the mass audience is therefore likely to be television, with its high degree of credibility as a source. Since the BBC and ITN substantially endorsed the government strategy on AIDS and HIV it is to be expected that the views of the tabloids on issues such as heterosexual risk would be regarded sceptically by much of the audience. This is confirmed by audience research, even where many audience groups actually share the attitudes and preferences (towards those with HIV) which have been expressed in the tabloids.

APPENDIX: AIDS PRESS ITEM CATEGORIES AND PROFILES

The AIDS press items over the eighteen-month period from November 1988 to April 1990 can be divided into a number of broad categories to compare and contrast the coverage provided by different newspapers.

In the *Sun*, for example, 'AIDS campaign' includes all reports of ministerial announcements, press conferences and Department of Health launches. 'Latest figures' are reports of official statistics of AIDS cases and HIV infections, predictions, etc. 'Criticism' denotes news stories of attacks on and criticism of the official campaign and health education strategy. Of the other categories, two stand out: 'PWA', which are 'human interest' (not all of them sympathetic) items about individuals with AIDS illnesses, and 'celebrity AIDS', almost a tabloid speciality, often of dubious origin or

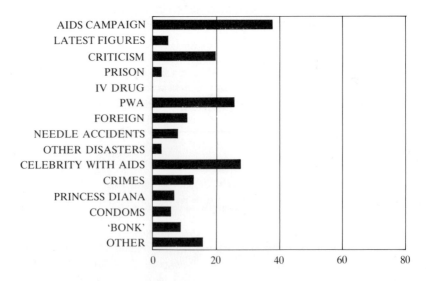

18 months, Nov. 1988 – April 1990

Figure 9.4 Sun – HIV/AIDS coverage: category of items

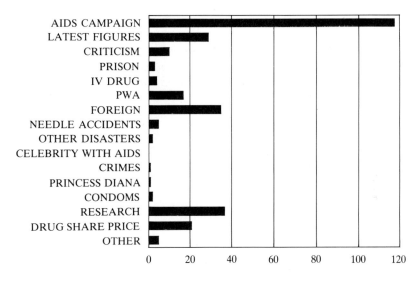

18 months, Nov. 1988 – April 1990

Figure 9.5 The Times – HIV/AIDS coverage: category of items

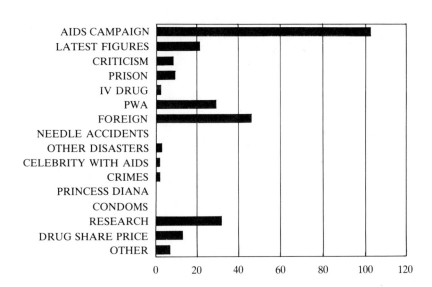

18 months, Nov. 1988 – April 1990

Figure 9.6 Guardian – HIV/AIDS coverage: category of items

factual content. The 'bonk' category includes sex exploitation stories with an AIDS 'angle'.

Comparison with *The Times* and *Guardian* shows all aspects of the official 'AIDS campaign' are of greater news value and prevalence. Many types of story common in the tabloids dwindle into relative insignificance or disappear, such as 'Needle accident' and 'Other disaster' horror stories, or 'Crime', mainly assaults or threats with 'infected' instruments. 'Princess Diana' needs no explanation. These are displaced by regular reporting of scientific and medical research developments ('Research'), reports of the situation in other countries ('Foreign') and reports of market fluctuations in drug company shares.

NOTES

1 The research for this chapter was done as part of an ESRC-funded project based at Glasgow University; the AIDS Media Research Project. I would like to acknowledge the help of the ESRC, my colleagues Jenny Kitzinger, David Miller, Kevin Williams and the grant holders John Eldridge, Greg Philo, Sally Macintyre and Mick Bloor. Thanks also to Middlesex University students Linda Steel, Michael Foley and Lesley Parker for assistance in coding data.

2 There is a 'liberal' view which, from a standpoint firmly within the orthodox perspective and accepting the seriousness of heterosexual transmission, might neverthelesss recommend the targeting of specific groups of heterosexuals such as, for example, the sexual partners of intravenous drug injectors and bisexual men.

3 In attempting to combine 'realistic', practical information on safer sex, with a deterrent 'moral' message, the government campaign resulted in confused and muddled advice. For example, Chief Medical Officer Sir Donald Acheson on television:

> The advice is, don't undertake casual sexual liaisons. Know your partner. If you don't, or have any doubt, wear a condom or insist that one is worn. And the other rule is, avoid intravenous drug abuse, and in particular, sharing needles and syringes.
>
> (*Channel 4 News*, 30 November 1988)

4 Schlesinger rejects the notion of 'primary definer' because 'the sociological question of how sources organise media strategies and compete with one another is completely neglected. "Primary definition", which ought to be an empirically ascertainable outcome is held to be an a priori effect of priveleged access' ('From production to propaganda?', review essay, *Media, Culture and Society* 11 (1989): 283). See also Schlesinger (1990).

5 The text of the poster continued: 'It's true more men than women have AIDS. But this does not mean it is a homosexual disease. It isn't.' Watney (1988) has argued that, whatever the intention, the message does not challenge prejudice ('it's not "only" killing queers') as it seems to imply that there *are* viruses that consciously select victims, that some diseases *are* the intrinsic property of gay men.

6 The sample was composed of all press items on AIDS/HIV appearing in the UK national daily and Sunday newspapers for the whole of the thirty-four-month period from November 1988 to August 1991, a total of over 4,000 items of which 3,924 were news reports, articles, features or editorials, and 223 were letters to editors.

7 Whereas the front-page story on Kilbracken in the *Daily Mail* carried the by-line of the medical correspondent, that in the *Daily Express* appeared under the names of reporters Paul Crosbie and Peter Hooley.

8 Others, quite unsympathetic to Vernon Coleman, also believed that the government health education campaign was wastefully directed at everyone largely because it was motivated by a moral attack on 'promiscuity'. Some argued that this was part of a wider commitment to 'defending the traditional family' against sexual diversity and homosexuality in particular. See, for example, Michael Fitzpatrick and Don Milligan (1987), *The Truth about the AIDS Panic* and (1990), interview in *Living Marxism*.

9 In fact the evidence available at this time was understood and reported elsewhere as indicating the opposite. For example, the government commissioned report on heterosexual risk: 'Today's report shows the spread of AIDS has slowed this year but the reason is that homosexuals have heeded the safe sex message. Figures from clinics treating sexually transmitted diseases show heterosexuals have not – and that's worrying the experts' (*Channel 4 News*, 30 November 1988).

10 A similar point is made by Schlesinger, Murdock and Elliott (1983), distinguishing between 'open' and 'closed' types of television programmes in terms of the range of perspectives and approaches to the subject which might be made accessible to the viewer.

11 In contrast, the *Observer*'s occasional articles on the AIDS campaign were firmly within the orthodox 'heterosexual risk' perspective. Other 'liberal' items dealt with AIDS activists' demonstrations against unsympathetic journalists, arguments against Mrs Thatcher's cancellation of the national sex survey and the dangers of press denials of heterosexual transmission, 'a campaign to deny the scientific evidence' (*Observer*, 21 October 1990).

12 Two weeks after the feature coverage of AIDS and families to which they obviously referred, two letters to the editor were printed. The first was from Sir Donald Acheson, Chief Medical Officer: 'It is most encouraging that such a popular newspaper as the *Star* is making it clear that this tragic infection is NOT limited to gay people, drug abusers and foreigners. Please keep up the good work.' The second was from Margaret Jay, director of the National AIDS Trust:

> Well done to the *Star* . . . . Everyone at the National AIDS Trust has been very encouraged by the detailed research you have obviously put into your stories and the editorial comment. It is often difficult to get the popular press to take AIDS seriously and treat them sensitively, but your pieces have been really helpful.

(*Daily Star*, 30 April 1991)

The author of the AIDS reporting being praised was not a member of the *Daily Star*'s news staff but was freelance journalist Peter Miller. His articles appeared in the *Daily Star* on 15, 16 and 17 April 1991.

13 Princess Diana's attendance at the funeral was recognized as breaking with protocol, and one newspaper had already published an article noting her dedication and commitment to work on AIDS since 1987. See 'How Diana defeated the palace – "No-one else will help. I must do something" ' (*Sunday Express*, 25 August 1991).

14 Derek Jameson, experienced Fleet Street tabloid editor, now broadcaster, has claimed that the 'four essential ingredients' or the 'four S's' of a successful tabloid newspaper are 'Sex, sensation, scandal and sport' (BBC Radio 4 news programme interview, 1991).

15 Only one item on AIDS could be found in the *Sunday Sport* in the sample period. This was on the alleged problems posed for vampires in ensuring uninfected blood supplies ('Vampires wing it to beat AIDS', *Sunday Sport*, 27 August 1989).

REFERENCES

Albert, E. (1986) 'Aquired Immune Deficiency Syndrome: the victim and the press', *Studies in Communication* 3: 135–58.
Alcorn, K. (1988) 'Illness, metaphor and AIDS', in P. Aggleton and H. Homans (eds) *Social Aspects of AIDS*, London: Falmer Press.
Altman, D. (1986) *AIDS and the new puritanism*, London: Pluto Press.
Berridge, V. and Strong, P. (1991) 'AIDS in the UK – contemporary history and the study of policy', *Twentieth Century British History* 2(2).
Bruck, P. A. (1989) 'Strategies for peace, strategies for news research', *Journal of Communication* 39(1) (winter): 108–29.
Chippendale, P. and Horrie, C. (1990) *Stick it up your punter! The rise and fall of the Sun*, London: Heinemann.
Currie, C. (1985) 'Press coverage of health-related topics with special reference to AIDS', *Working Paper no.12*, Edinburgh: Research Unit in Health and Behavioural Change, University of Edinburgh.
Fitzpatrick, M. and Milligan, D. (1987) *The Truth about the AIDS Panic*, London: Junius Publications.
—— (1990) interview with Linda Ryan, *Living Marxism* (January): 14–19.
Fumento, M. (1990) *The Myth of Heterosexual AIDS*, New York: Basic Books.
Grover, J. Z. (1989) 'Reading AIDS', in P. Aggleton, G. Hart and P. Davies (eds) *AIDS: Social Representations and Social Practices*, London: Falmer Press.
Hall, S., Critcher, C., Jefferson, T., Clarke, J. and Roberts, B. (1978). *Policing the Crisis*, London: Macmillan.
Herzlich, C. and Pierret, J. (1989) 'The construction of a social phenomenon: AIDS in the French press', *Social Science and Medicine* 29(11): 1235–42.
Kitzinger, J. and Miller, D. (1991) 'In black and white: a preliminary report on the role of the media in audience understandings of "African AIDS" ', *MRC Working Paper no. 27*, Glasgow: MRC Medical Sociology Unit, University of Glasgow.
Kramer, L. (1990) *Reports from the Holocaust – The making of an AIDS activist*, Harmondsworth: Penguin.
Neale, J. (1992) 'The politics of AIDS', *International Socialism* 5 (January).
Patton, C. (1990) *Inventing AIDS*, London: Routledge.
Porter R (1986) 'Plague and panic', *New Society* (12 December): 11–13.
Research Unit in Health and Behavioural Change, University of Edinburgh (1989) *Changing the Public Health*, London: Wiley.
Schlesinger, P. (1990) 'Rethinking the sociology of journalism: source strategies and the limits of media centrism', in M. Ferguson (ed.) *Public Communication: the new imperatives*, London: Sage.
Schlesinger, P., Murdock, G. and Elliot, P. (1983) *Televising Terrorism: political violence in popular culture*, London: Comedia.
Shilts, R. (1987) *And the Band Played On – politics, people and the AIDS epidemic*, New York: St Martin's Press.
Sontag, S. (1989) *AIDS and its Metaphors*, Harmondsworth: Allen Lane.
Stroman, E. and Seltzer, A. (1989) 'Media use and knowledge of AIDS', *Journalism Quarterly*

Strong, P. and Berridge, V. (1989) 'No one knew anything: Some issues in British AIDS policy', in P. Aggleton, P. Davies and G. Hart (eds) *AIDS: Individual, Cultural and Policy Dimensions*, Brighton, Sx: Falmer Press.

Watney, S. (1987) *Policing Desire: Pornography, AIDS and the Media*, London: Comedia.

—— (1988) 'Visual AIDS: advertising ignorance', in P. Aggleton and H. Homans (eds) *Social Aspects of AIDS*, London: Falmer Press.

—— (1989) 'The subject of AIDS', in P. Aggleton, G. Hart and P. Davies (eds) *AIDS: Social Representations and Social Practices*, London: Falmer Press.

Weeks, J. (1989) 'AIDS: the intellectual agenda', in P. Aggleton, G. Hart and P. Davies (eds) *AIDS: Social Representations and Social Practices*, London: Falmer Press.

Wellings, K. (1988) 'Perceptions of risk – media treatments of AIDS', in P. Aggleton and H. Homans (eds) *Social Aspects of AIDS*, London: Falmer Press.

Wilton, T. (1991) 'Feminism and the erotics of health promotion', Bristol Polytechnic, Paper presented at the 5th Conference of Social Aspects of AIDS at Southbank Polytechnic (March).

Part IV

Message reception: opinion and understanding

Chapter 10

Getting the message

Audience research in the Glasgow University Media Group

Greg Philo

The Glasgow University Media Group began its research with the analysis of television news content. We were interested in how differences in the use of language and definitions might relate to conflict and divisions within the society as a whole. We sought to show how individual meanings might relate to competing ways of understanding the nature and movement of the social world. In our case study method, we saw the first task as to lay out these 'ways of understanding' and to relate them to the specific conflicts through which they were generated. In *Bad News* (1976) and *More Bad News* (1980), we showed how divisions between right and left on the political spectrum corresponded to quite different explanations of the reasons for economic crisis. The language and definitions used were one level of the battleground for competing groups. It seemed clear that these different ways of explaining the world emerged from social divisions such as those between classes and between subgroups within these. Our interest was in examining how the key themes of social ideologies were represented in news accounts.

In the event, we found in our research that the social relations which structure the wider society were referred to implicitly and explicitly in news reporting. A knowledge of these relations and what 'ought' to happen within them was assumed by the broadcasters and by those who supplied them with news. Such a world-view involved assumptions of cause and responsibility which shaped the descriptions which were given. Obviously, not all information on the news was the subject of clearly competing viewpoints. Statements on the cause of an industrial dispute were more likely to be the subject of competing interpretations than a statement about what time the dispute started or which unions were involved. Our main interest was in the treatment of themes on which there were manifestly different interpretations and in analysing how some of these dominated and gave direction to news accounts. In practice our method revealed the 'preferred' meanings of the news. We showed how the repetition of certain views and explanations together with the embracing and underlining of them by journalists were part of a process by which the news was structured. This was reflected in the choice of material, the themes that were emphasized, the links that were made between these and the final conclusions that were drawn. The next logical stage of our research was to examine how the structuring of news messages related to processes of understanding and belief within television audiences.

We began this work at a time of very extended debate over what the influence of the media actually was. The earliest theorists of mass communications, such as Le Bon and Lippmann, had believed the media to be tremendously powerful in influencing mass publics. The First World War was taken as an archetypal example of patriotic fervour being worked on by newspapers. Later, there were other extraordinary instances of 'media power', such as the Orson Wells radio version of *War of the Worlds* which panicked New Yorkers in 1938. Another was the effect of Kate Smith's appeals for American war bonds when she raised $39 million in a single day (Merton 1946).

Later research began to cast doubt on such a direct impact of media. Instead, it suggested that any 'effect' was confined simply to the reinforcement of pre-existing beliefs (Klapper 1960). This was a very different perspective from seeing the media as an all-powerful force on the individual. The new focus was on how messages were received and used by people in the audience either as individuals or in the context of small social groups. The 'uses and gratifications' approach assumed that the individual's values and interests led to a selective perception and shaping of what was seen and heard. What was taken from the media might depend upon individual preferences and psychology. For example, a programme might be attractive to one person for its dramatic or exciting qualities, while someone else might be interested in it for the information which it contains. Some early research in the USA used survey techniques to ask people about the 'gratifications' which they took from programmes such as quiz shows.

The attempts which had been made to assess media effects had largely focused on possible changes in attitude following exposure to campaigns on the issues such as health, voting or buying goods. The general conclusion was that they had no or very little effect. But, as McQuail (1977) has argued, these results were in part conditioned by the limited nature of the studies, which were designed to measure short-term variations in individual attitudes. But messages and their meanings to audiences must be examined in a much wider social context. The media are part of a process of cultural reproduction and their content consists of much more than isolated pieces of information or opinion. Thus a campaign message during an election does not simply tell us how to vote. It also implicitly assumes the legitimacy of a certain type of political system. Similarly, an advertisement for a product may contain implicit assumptions about 'acceptable' or desirable lifestyles. Messages are situated within political and cultural assumptions about what is normal and acceptable within the society. In news production, these include beliefs about hierarchies of access, about who has the right to speak, what are the key political institutions and what is 'acceptable' behaviour. On an everyday level, the television, press and radio also provide information about specific events, which tacitly relate to these unspoken assumptions. For example, news journalists might assume a consensus among their audience that violence should not be used in resolving industrial disputes. News programmes might then give reports of violent behaviour in a specific dispute and allocate blame to one 'side' in the conflict. Such information might then affect public beliefs and become part of the store of social knowledge about the past history of 'trades union strife'. News reports are thus situated within, and contribute to, political and social cultures which are constantly developing.

The problem with many traditional attempts at 'effects' studies has been that they utilized a crude stimulus/response model and did not analyse either the specific content of the message or how it related to wider systems of values and beliefs. The complexities of cultural meanings and ideologies cannot be reduced to a simple set of yes/no answers on what programmes people have seen and which way they vote. But because we reject such methods it does not follow that the source of ideologies and the impact of media is of no interest to us. Indeed we have recently seen more 'spectacular' examples of the apparent influence of media, notably the Band Aid phenomenon and the shaping of public opinion in relation to the 1991 Gulf War. Band Aid began with the news report on the Ethiopian famine of 1984, narrated by Michael Buerk and filmed by Mohamed Amin of Visnews. The worldwide media coverage of this, followed by the Band Aid record and fund-raising concerts in Britain and the USA were extraordinary phenomena in their own right. They raised the political profile of Third World issues as well as generating over £100 million for famine relief. Later developments included the Comic Relief television events and the extraordinary Sport Aid which in 1986 involved athletes from 274 cities in seventy-eight countries staging simultaneous events. But interestingly, none of this was predicted by media professionals. Indeed the initial judgement of most of the key news organizations was that the Buerk/Amin report was a minor news story or need not be covered at all. Michael Buerk himself commented on this that:

> Everything [believed] about the British and other publics proved to be wrong. I remember talking to NBC, who also ran the piece and had this amazing reaction. They told me: 'It'll only last a week; the American public will soon get bored with that sort of stuff'. I almost agreed with them at the time, but they proved to be terribly wrong.
>
> (Cited in Harrison and Palmer 1986: 130)

The news coverage of the famine and the fund-raising events which followed tapped into a level of public concern which surprised both media professionals and politicians.

The Gulf War in January 1991 was a different case since it signalled a major attempt by politicians in the USA, France and Britain to shape opinion in an area where there had previously been very little public knowledge or interest. Both the decision to fight a war and its actual conduct once begun were crucial terrain for these attempts at opinion forming. They became so overt that some journalists began openly to question the methods that were being used. In rare moments these criticisms actually surfaced on television. For example, in an early morning discussion between three senior BBC journalists, David Dimbleby asks the Paris correspondent about changes in public opinion in France. He replies:

> We have that last minute peace initiative, which I am told President Mitterand knew perfectly well didn't stand a chance. But he did it for internal opinion, to persuade the French public that he really had done everything and there was no alternative. And he's coaxed them slowly in press conference after press conference into believing that war was the only option and I think he has been remarkably successful.
>
> (BBC 1 10.00 a.m. News, 23 January 1991)

David Dimbleby also asks Mark Mardell, the BBC's political correspondent about the situation in Britain and comments himself that:

> [Dimbleby] I'm getting a bit uneasy about the way that this war seems to be being presented politically. There seems to be, creeping in, a feeling that Washington and No. 10 ought to be able to raise and lower expectations at will about this war. They start off with everybody terrified there will be casualties, and so they say it has been a very successful first day. They then see newspaper headlines and public opinion thinking, or they think it thinks that the war is going to be over very quickly, so they then induce a mood of pessimism. Now you are reporting this morning that No. 10 is very keen to make sure that people don't feel pessimistic. I'm not sure that I like the idea of my opinion and yours and the public as a whole being subjected to this kind of psychological pressure about the war. . . . Don't you get the feeling that there is slightly too much pulling of the levers of public psychology on this?

To which Mark Mardell replies: 'I always get that feeling to be perfectly honest' (BBC 1 10.00 a.m., News 23 January 1991).

But media coverage of the Gulf War was not always conducted at the behest of western politicians. At the end of the war, at least, the effect was rather the contrary. On 3 April 1991 the *Guardian* gave its whole front page to a story headlined 'THE VALLEYS OF DEATH' which dealt with the plight of the Kurds in northern Iraq. The story was then taken up by other papers, notably the *Daily Mirror*, and on television news. There were bitter criticisms made in press editorials and on television news of western politicians for encouraging the people of Iraq to revolt against Saddam Hussein and then abandoning them to their fate. This media campaign forced the issue on to the political agenda and resulted in the policy of setting up 'enclaves' for the Kurds in northern Iraq with western guarantees of their safety.

This is an exceptional case and did follow a period where the media had been used and controlled very tightly by the military and political authorities. This led to considerable professional resentment among many journalists. A similar professional response was seen after the Falkland War of 1982 when virtually the whole of the British press and television had criticized the government's information policy (Glasgow University Media Group 1985). None the less, as John Berger has argued, the Gulf War did show that the relation between political priorities and media content can be contradictory:

> On one hand, the Gulf War showed how politicians have reason to fear the media; or, rather, have reason to fear public reaction to what the media may show. . . . On the other hand, the Gulf War showed . . . that a scenario of lies can be written for the media which will then transmit it, with excitement, commentary, analysis, etc., as if it was the truth.
>
> (*Guardian*, 4 September 1991)

Few would doubt that under some circumstances the media can have an impact on public opinion. But what are these circumstances? The crucial question for audience research is to explain how exactly these different and sometimes contradictory messages are received and interpreted.

NEW METHODOLOGIES

There were two issues which we saw as crucial when we began to develop audience studies. The first was how exactly messages work to convince those who receive them (or not as the case may be). The second question which follows from this is how might a message 'work' for some groups but not others? If messages are 'differentially' or 'aberrantly' decoded by various social groups, then what are the factors which condition this? If we look again at the issue of the reporting of industrial disputes, we might see that there is a consensus among most of the population that violence is 'wrong' as a way of resolving such conflict. But this is not likely to be matched by a common agreement on who should be blamed for violence when it does occur. For example, attitudes on whether the police and pickets are more likely to start trouble may vary between different groups in the society (as between groups of working-class trades unionists and middle-class professionals). Such differences within the audience may affect the way in which information from the media is received. This acceptance or rejection of the television message is conditioned partly by differences in political cultures. These are not static and cannot be seen as simply determining how individuals respond. The cultures themselves are clearly subject to changes from a variety of influences, one of which could be new information which is received from the media.

There were other crucial variables which might affect how new information was interpreted. These could include gender and regional differences as well as class experiences. These 'pre-existing' structures of consciousness within the audience had all to be investigated as well as the use by audience members of common-sense knowledges of logic and ways of evaluating what was seen and heard.

We were unhappy with earlier approaches to effects studies which had depended on showing specific programmes to groups of people followed by attempts at measuring changes in attitudes or behaviour. It seemed clear that much of the process of attitude and belief formation would have taken place before such an experiment could be conducted. In a sense we needed to establish what people already 'knew' and to show the processes by which they had arrived at their beliefs. We devised a new method which involved asking audience groups to write their own news programmes. This would show what they thought the content of the news to be on a given issue. It would then be possible to compare this with what group members actually believed to be true and to examine why they either accepted or rejected the media account. The initial study applying this method used the miners' strike of 1984–5 as a focus for work with audience groups (Philo 1990). Others developed since include Jenny Kitzinger's analysis of beliefs about AIDS (see Chapter 11) and a study by David Miller on beliefs about the conflict in Northern Ireland. This approach has enabled us to look at long-term processes of belief, understanding and memory. We can illustrate some of these now by looking at the results of the miners' strike study.

For this study a main sample of 169 people were interviewed, some in their places of work, others in the areas in which they lived. Some groups were selected because they had specific knowledge of the strike, such as police officers and miners. Others were chosen so that they might highlight possible differences in the understanding of news events, caused by factors such as class or cultural background or their location in different parts of the country. For example, there were two groups of people selected who worked in solicitors' offices, one in Glasgow and another in the south-east of England. Everyone in the study answered questions on their own beliefs and memories and also took part in small group exercises. For these, a group of three or four people would be given a set of photographs which were taken from television news programmes. They were then invited to imagine that they were journalists and to write their own news stories about the strike. Their 'news reports' which were written one year after the strike had ended, were then compared with actual news programmes from BBC and ITN. There were extraordinary similarities. For example, a group of residents from a housing estate in Shenfield, Essex, produced this phrase in their 'news': 'As the *drift back to work* in the mines began to gather momentum, *violence erupted*.' A group of workers from different trades unions in Scotland also highlighted the link between the 'drift back' and violence: 'On a day that saw in *increased drift back to work . . . further violence* was taking place.' We can compare these with an actual headline from ITN: '*Worst picket violence* yet but miners continue *their drift back*' (ITN 17.45 News, 12 November 1984). During the strike, television news had offered a persistent commentary on the increasing number of people going back to work and the apparently increasing level of 'new violence'. The focus of the news became what the current 'record' was for both of these, as in this BBC bulletin:

> The battle between the miners and the Coal Board created *two new records today*. More miners returned to work than on any day since the strike began and their return brought with it the worst violence seen on the picket lines. . . .

The theme of escalating violence is then taken up by the news reporter on the spot: 'A dozen Yorkshire pits were the targets for the worst concentrated violence of this dispute so far. . . . *Another escalation* in the bitter struggle inside Britain's mining industry' (BBC 1 *Six O'clock News*, 12 November 1984). Compare the above BBC news with these phrases written by groups of people in the Glasgow solicitors' office, one year after the strike had ended: '*Increasing violent clashes* between pickets and police'; 'There were ugly scenes . . . and what was said to be an *alarming escalation of violence*.' The theme of 'escalation' runs through the stories of several groups, who wrote 'violence is escalating' (a group of women in Bromley, Kent), 'escalating the violence' (a group of retired people in Glasgow) and 'as the picketing escalated' (supervisors working for London Transport).

One of the main arguments between the miners' union and the Coal Board had been over the 'return to work' and the number of miners who had given up the strike. One of the groups wrote, for example, that 'today the NCB [National Coal Board] announced figures on the operational pits . . . Arthur Scargill, the President of the Union at a meeting in Congress House *disputed the figures put out by the NCB*' (group of electronic workers). On the actual news we heard that: 'The Coal Board say a record number of miners ended their strike today. Arthur Scargill says *the figures are being mixed like cocktails*' (headline, BBC 1 *Six O'clock News*, 18.00, 4 February 1985). These arguments had been a recurring theme on the news. Three months earlier ITN had reported that: '350 more miners returned to work today, last Tuesday 936 went back – *the miners union disagrees with the figures*' (ITN 17.45 News, 27 November 1984). There were many direct parallels between the language of the group news and that of television. In the Glasgow solicitors' office, for example, a phrase was used on 'miners returning to work at *increasing rates every day*' while on the actual news, we could hear: 'With the return to work of the drivers and the *ever increasing numbers of miners going back*' (ITN *News at Ten*, 12 November 1984).

Another of the major arguments between the union and Coal Board concerned the tactics which were allegedly being used by the strikers. The following extract was written by a group from Glasgow, two years after the strike had ended. In it they construct an imaginary quote from Ian MacGregor, the Coal Board Chairman:

> He also said that this incident was typical of the disruptions that we have seen throughout the strike, employed to reverse the flow of strikers back to work. And he was sure that the police in their role as peacemakers will continue to do their utmost to protect the innocent workers from these kinds of *'bullyboy' tactics*.

Compare this with an actual statement made by Ian MacGregor during a televised debate with Arthur Scargill, the miners' leader, which had been shown on *Channel 4 News* during the strike. In this, he commented that: 'I have every indication that the bulk of [miners] want to go back to work – the only reason they are not there is because *his bully-boys continue to intimidate* them and their families' (*Channel 4 News*, 22 August 1988).

The arguments between Scargill and MacGregor and their long pro-tracted negotiations were featured in the stories of several of the groups. For example, 'discussions broke down between Scargill and MacGregor' (electronics workers), 'meetings with MacGregor were held at TUC head-quarters, talks broke down' (London Transport supervisors), 'meanwhile against a background of no movement between the parties to break the deadlock' (Glasgow solicitors) and 'another meeting . . . finished abruptly with more arguments and no decisions reached' (group of women in south London). Compare these examples with the tone of this BBC news report which summarized some of the events in the dispute: 'Agreement remained as far away as ever – the TUC insisted on talks, once again they went badly. The TUC tried to negotiate a better deal but the miners rejected the new proposals from the Coal Board' (BBC 1 21.10 News, 3 March 1985).

It was remarkable how closely some of the group stories reflected not only the thematic content of the news but also the structure of actual headlines. One of the surprises in this research was the clarity with which the groups were able to reproduce themes from the news. It also surprised the group members. One of these, a woman from Bromley in Kent, had told us that she never watched the news because 'it was so boring'. But after completing the exercise she commented that: 'When you first asked me, I said I never watched it – then when you asked the questions I found it was amazing how much I remembered – how much you take in.' Our research showed that people could recall key themes from the news. But the crucial issue was whether they actually believed what they had seen.

SEEING AND BELIEVING

After the news exercises, each group member was asked a series of questions on issues such as picketing and violence in the strike. We distinguished between what they had seen on the news and what they believed had actually taken place. There was a remarkable unanimity of belief among the groups about what had actually been shown. For example, 98 per cent believed that most picketing which they had seen on television news was violent. The remaining 2 per cent either were unsure or believed the picketing shown was 'intimidatory' rather than physically violent. But perhaps what is most remarkable is the number of people who believed that these television images represented the everyday reality of picketing. There was occasionally a fear expressed of even going near a picket-line, because of the high levels of physical fighting which were believed to be going on. In all, 54 per cent of the general sample believed that picketing was mostly violent.

The source for these beliefs was overwhelmingly given as television and the press with the emphasis on TV, because of its immediate and more dramatic quality. With some people in the sample, it could be seen how this new information on violence had been absorbed into a system of beliefs with the consequence that elements of that system had changed. For example, an office worker from Croydon stated that she believed the BBC and ITN news to be 'fair' (in the sense of being impartial) and that most picketing in the strike had been violent, and that most of what was shown of picketing on television was violent. The sources for her beliefs about picketing were television and the press, by which she meant television news and the *Sun* newspaper. Her opinion of the police had altered as a result of what she had seen of the strike because, as she said, 'you do not realize what they have to put up with'.

It was clear that some key elements of beliefs about violence were being provided by the media. But it would be wrong to see people as being totally dependent on such messages, as if they are simply empty vessels which are being filled up by *News at Ten*. To accept and believe what is seen on television is as much a cultural act as the rejection of it. Both acceptance and rejection are conditioned by our beliefs, history and experience. A high degree of trust in the BBC, for example, might result from a knowledge of its history and its peculiar role in British society as an authoritative 'national' voice. Television news itself works very hard at strategies to win our trust. It scorns the crude editorializing of newspapers and uses presentational techniques which suggest neutrality and balance. Whether the audience actually accepts this television presentation depends very much on what beliefs, experience and information they bring to what they are shown.

Beliefs about violence were very different among those in our sample who had a specialist knowledge of the strike, such as miners and police officers. None of these believed that picketing was mostly violent. As it turned out, everyone who had any direct contact at all with picket-lines rejected the notion that the television images were typical. This was so even when the contact had been very fleeting, such as driving past a picket-line on the way to work. A trades unionist who was picketing in Scotland gave us this description of what it had been like:

> People would sit around doing very little, police and pickets. Often, police would just sit in their vans until it was nearly time for the shifts to change. Then people would take up their positions and as the working miners went in and out, there was a bit of a shove and a bit of a shout and then they would all sit down again for another six hours.

We had the same description from miners in Yorkshire and police officers from all over the country. This does not mean that the miners' strike was entirely 'peaceful'. Some events in the dispute were clearly violent and people actually lost their lives. Pickets were run over and crushed and a Welsh taxi-driver died when a concrete block was pushed on to a motor-way. But the focus on such incidents by television and the press clearly creates a gap between the beliefs of those who rely on the media for information and those who have direct experience of the strike. It is important to grasp the magnitude of the events in the dispute in order to see how such a process of selective reporting can work. At the time of the strike there were a total of 190,000 mine-workers. There were also tens of thousands of police and workers from other unions and support groups who were involved in actions at different times during the strike. There were 174 pits, plus other sites for picketing such as power stations, ports and steelworks. In such a huge number of people over such a large period, we might expect to find many varieties of behaviour. There would be miners trained in first aid who would pause to help policemen who had fallen (which did happen), and we would find people who would throw metal bolts and bricks. When tens of thousands of police, miners and their supporters confronted each other in such a stressful period, there was a very real possibility that there would be violent incidents. But it is the relentless focus on these by television and the press, accompanied by the comments on 'escalation' and 'new records', which established for many of the audience the belief that violence was a persistent feature of most picketing.

By contrast, the police officers whom we interviewed were openly scornful of such a view of 'violent picketing'. They were asked 'do you think that picketing during the strike was mostly violent . . .?' In reply, there was literally a chorus of 'No!'. They stated that 'a lot of it was good natured banter'. When the pickets and police did confront each other they described it as being rather like a rugby scrum: 'Come on lads it's time for a good heave', said one officer. Their most profound memories were of endless frustration as nothing happened at all. They commented on how 'boring' it was 'sitting around in vans'. Interestingly, one of the main categories of people in our audience groups as a whole who rejected the television images of the strike, were those who had police officers as friends or neighbours and who had been told not to believe what they saw. Another main category of 'doubters' were those who knew miners' wives or pickets. A woman from Scotland described the experiences which changed her mind:

> When I first saw the TV pictures I thought it was terrible because I thought it was really violent. Every time it came on I would just walk away and not watch it. Then most of my friends at work, their husbands are miners at Polkemmit pit – they stood at the picket lines and there was never any violence, never any. The cameramen must have deliberately filmed a violent bit for television.

But for most of the people in our sample, violence was associated very strongly with the dispute. This raises the crucial question of who was seen as being to blame for such violence. Other research by Alastair Hetherington (1985) has suggested that, on the news, violence outside collieries was attributed over ten times to miners/pickets as to the police.

We examined audience beliefs on this issue by including in the news-writing exercise a picture of a shotgun lying on a table. We then asked all of the group members individually: 'Who did they believe the gun had belonged to, when they first saw it?' The gun had actually belonged to a *non-striking* miner who was reported briefly on the news saying that he would shoot anyone who tried to intimidate him. But in our results, over half of the people in the main sample associated the gun with *striking* miners or pickets. Some people gave improvised explanations on its owner-ship such as 'renta mob pickets', 'a picket out of bravado' (residents of Beckenham, Kent) or 'a striking miner shot someone' (London print-worker). But the interpretation of the gun picture could be very different where the groups were sympathetic to the miners' cause. As well as a group of Yorkshire miners, we also interviewed women's support group members and a large group of Scottish trades unionists. Here, only 16 per cent of these associated the gun with striking pickets or miners. But 46 per cent of them believed that the gun belonged to the police, either as a weapon or as 'planted' evidence.

There is no necessary reason why the gun should be associated with any 'side' in the dispute. No shotguns were ever reported to have been found on the picket-lines and none were fired in anger. In this study, 10 per cent of the people reflected this view and did not link the gun to anyone in the strike. The associations that the groups made with the weapon varied and to some extent illustrated the differences in cultural assumptions and experience which existed between them. It was clear that a strong sympathy with the miners could lead to a rejection of any link between them and the gun. But this was not always the case. It is important to note that the link *was* sometimes made by people who were overtly sympathetic to the miners. The news had affected them, in a sense in spite of their personal views. For example, we interviewed a solicitor in Glasgow who read the *Guardian* and watched 'alternative Channel 4 documentaries'. She was sympathetic to the miners and did not believe that most picketing had been violent. Yet she did associate the gun with them and said that the connection probably came in spite of her beliefs from what she had seen on the news: 'I thought it was the type of thing they would have shown and that it had been taken from a picket.' Television, of course, had not actually portrayed the strikers as having a gun, but it had linked them very firmly to violence.

NEGOTIATING THE MESSAGE

In this study, some people clearly accepted the television images of picketing as being typical of what had actually occurred. But others adapted parts of the message and changed key elements of its meaning. For example, some believed that the strike was mostly violent because of what they had seen on television, but blamed the police for provoking the trouble. These group members could be quite aware that television news had not explained the origins of violence in this way. The disjunction between what they had seen and what they believed was explained by saying that television 'only showed violence from miners, not police' (woman in Glasgow). In such an example, what is finally believed results from news images being interpreted through beliefs about both the police and television. Most of the black people in this study associated the gun with the police rather than with pickets and cited experiences from their own lives of contact with the police to back up their views.

We saw a different negotiation among a group of elderly people interviewed in Glasgow. They had a very high degree of trust in television news and were largely dependent on it as a source of information. Most accepted its account of the violent nature of picketing, but there was also a high degree of sympathy with the miners. There was also strong support for the police, which is not surprising given the vulnerability of the group. These contradictions were partly resolved by a focus on 'outsiders, infiltrators, and militants' as the cause of the trouble. This negotiation was not completely successful in rehabilitating the miners, as there was also deep unhappiness expressed about the violence and how it had reflected on the miners' cause.

The process by which people understand a television message depends in part on the beliefs which they bring to it and, crucially, on how these beliefs are utilized. There were cases in this study where people had a critique of television latent in their beliefs. In one example, some group members stated at first that they thought picketing was mostly violent and then moved away from this position as they began to comment on the nature of television as a medium, with its tendency to select and to focus on the sensational. In these cases, the exercise itself seems to have provided the stimulus for the emergence of this view. But it is important that the beliefs about picketing had in a sense rested with them until they were pressed to explain them. These again seemed to be examples of the messages being absorbed in spite of other beliefs which were held. Where no critical view of television exists, the likelihood of accepting its account may be very great. One person from the group of elderly people in Glasgow commented that television was the most important source of information and took her opinion of picketing from it because as she said: 'Seeing is believing.'

If we look at the reasons given for rejecting the television account, it is clear that the most powerful factor is the effect of direct or indirect experience. This was most obvious in the case of people who had been at picket-lines. In the general sample, 43 per cent of the people believed that picketing was mostly peaceful. When giving reasons, about a third of these based their belief on the experience of knowing or having met policemen or miners. The effect of such experience could traverse class and political culture. For example, we interviewed two residents of Bromley in Kent whose views were generally on the right of the political spectrum and whose key memories of the strike had been of 'Arthur Scargill talking rubbish' and 'lies'. Yet they rejected the view that picketing was mostly violent because of their very favourable contacts with miners and their families while on holiday. A second major reason for doubting television news was the comparison of it with other sources of information, such as the 'quality' and local press or 'alternative' current affairs programmes and radio. About 16 per cent of the general sample made such comparisons. These comments were sometimes linked to remarks on the tendency of television to exaggerate and focus on violence to the exclusion of other events. In the general sample, 14 per cent of the people made this criticism and gave it as a reason for rejecting the news presentation. This is a relatively low proportion given that it is sometimes thought that beliefs about the tendency of media to exaggerate are generally held in the population. It might in fact be that they are. But what is significant about this result is that even where such beliefs existed they were not always used to discount what was seen in the news. It was also noteworthy that where people relied only on this criticism to reject the news account, there was a tendency to estimate the level of violence as being very high. Some of the group in the Glasgow solicitors' office made such estimates, although their conclusion was that for the majority of the time picketing was probably peaceful. These criticisms of television as a medium and the comparison of it with other accounts were made by people with varied political views. But there was another strand of criticism which saw the focus on violence as a conscious attempt to denigrate the miners' case.

This view was most prominent among the Scottish trades unionists. A supervisor with London Transport had also commented that the media 'picked out the violence so as to get the majority of people against the miners'. The trades unionists had criticized several aspects of news presentation, such as the focus on 'violence instead of support groups'. There was a strong belief among them that picketing was mostly peaceful. In arguing this, some also commented on the scale of the strike and the numbers involved, saying that people could not have been fighting most of the time. This is an important issue since this deduction could apparently be made irrespective of sympathies with the strike. One woman in a group from Penge in south London said that she would have shot striking miners (had she been a working miner), but also argued that, 'because of the amount who were actually on strike . . . it can't all have been violent'. A print-worker also commented that 'if they had been really violent, the police couldn't have coped, it would have been the army'. Within such opinions, there are attempts being made to relate news accounts to assessments of 'reality' using everyday systems of logic.

The interpretation of the news by audience members is obviously very complex. Many of the above elements of culture, logic and experience could be combined in the evaluation of news coverage made by a single person. For example, we interviewed a Salvation Army officer in Beckenham, Kent, who had a strong personal conviction that most people were not violent. She was unhappy with the news because of this but also used her personal history as well as the religious material that she had read to inform her critique. As a child she had grown up in Durham and she believed that those in mining communities were decent people who would not be involved in violence. She stated: 'With a TV camera you can take one shot and made it look like 100 shots. You can take it from one angle and make it look like there are hundreds fighting – in short, cheat shots and manipulation.' She had read of this in a religious book, which had used the analogy of the manipulation of film images to comment on personal morality. As she said: 'If you didn't live your life correctly, you were doing cheat shots.' The example which the book had used was of stunt photography in Hollywood. But the woman had applied the analysis to television coverage of picketing and had decided that it too was a 'cheat shot'.

In another example, a woman working in the solicitors' office in south

London used her own work experience and her personal history to inform the 'news story' which she wrote about the strike. She wrote this by herself and it is noteworthy because it is the police who are associated with 'arms' and 'threatening behaviour': 'Serious disruption and fear was caused by the police today at the coal mines, as a result of them using arms and threatening behaviour towards the pickets and the coal miners.' At first sight, we might understand this as a straightforward critique of police behaviour. But, in fact, the writer gave a very complex explanation of how she had arrived at her story. From her professional experience in seeing court cases reported, she thought that the media concentrated on the sensational. The reporting of a strike would therefore focus on violence but she did not herself believe that most picketing had been like this. She had also written in her replies to questions that her attitude to the police was, on the whole, positive and that she actually believed that the gun belonged to a striking miner. She was asked how she could reconcile these beliefs with what she had written in her news story. She replied:

> I understand that the police do things which are not 'by the book'. It wouldn't surprise me if an officer had picked up the gun and used it. Things which I have done to people taken in for questioning might surprise some people, but in certain circumstances it would be understandable. I can see why they do it.

She was then asked why, if she saw the police in this way, she described them as causing 'serious disruption' in her news story? She replied:

> In the miners' strike, I did see the police as a disruptive force. I didn't feel that all those police officers should be sent in. The miners and pickets may have sorted it out between themselves. When I see the police I associate them with criminals and the miners are not criminals. I do have very mixed feelings, I do sympathise with the miners but I tend to see things from both sides. All my life I have had dealings with the police in my work and socially. My father was a police constable and my boyfriend was a CID officer.

The final comment about being a policeman's daughter comes almost like a punch-line at the end to explain the complexity of her attitudes. Because she was so close to the police, she could both sympathize with them and know they might sometimes break the rules. At the same time she had a clear and professionally defined view of what police responsibilities are. Through this extraordinary set of filters she was able to envisage a situation in which the police might fire unlawfully at pickets, while retaining sympathy both for them and the miners. At the same time she used her professional background both to assess what the proper role for the police should be and to reject the media account of what had occurred in the events.

This study has illustrated some of the processes by which messages were negotiated or rejected. It has also shown some of the complex cultural reasons behind the acceptance of the message by many in the audience. But we must not forget the social context within which these messages are constructed and their relation to competing political views.

SUPPLYING THE MESSAGE

The media and especially television were a crucial arena for arguments about the strike and the manner in which it was being conducted. The reporting of violence was important since it became part of the Coal Board's case against the mine-workers. As the BBC journalist, Nicholas Jones, has written:

> The NCB thought that public opinion was largely on their side – because of the prominence that the news reports had given to picket line violence, which in turn had helped create a favourable climate for the NCB's policy of keeping the pits open for work.
>
> (Jones 1986: 103)

At the same time the Coal Board and the government stressed their own view of the economics of the industry. Our own research shows that it is this view which dominates the stories given by the audience groups, when they attempt to explain the issues behind the strike. A group of women from Glasgow wrote of the effort to 'streamline' the industry: 'a government effort to streamline and make the coal industry economically productive.' The supervisors from London Transport had spoken of 'reshaping': 'Today Coal Board management and union meet at Congress House over pit closures and the reshaping of the industry.' A second group of supervisors attributed the following statement to Sir Ian MacGregor, the Coal Board Chairman: 'MacGregor says closures to come to uneconomic pits'. There were echoes of this in a story by a group of Bromley residents who included the phrase: 'Mr MacGregor and his threat to close uneconomic pits'. A group of retired people in Glasgow had also spoken of many pits being 'uneconomical to run' and 'millions of pounds of tax payers money being wasted'. This was very much the Coal Board's point of view. The miners' union did not accept this economic analysis and argued that Britain already produced deep-mined coal very efficiently. The apparent cheapness of foreign coal, they argued, came from artificial subsidies. It was also suggested that a key issue behind government policy at the time was the political and economic pressure for nuclear power. If this was to expand, then coal had to contract. None of this is mentioned in any of the groups' news stories. In these stories economic logic and rationality are seen as being the prerogative of the Coal Board.

There were many factors which might explain the dominance of the Coal

Board's view. An effective public relations campaign was not the main priority of the miners' leadership. By contrast the Coal Board and government had very extensive resources which could be devoted to this area. They could mount extensive advertising and publicity campaigns and the media would routinely relate to them as key suppliers of information. Michael Crick, a journalist with *Channel 4 News*, wrote at the time of the strike of how the Coal Board's view came to predominate in news accounts. He notes how the 'return to work' and phrases such as 'the drift back' became a routine part of news coverage:

> The National Coal Board's skilful propaganda claims that men are returning daily in hundreds, even thousands, and detailed figures are supplied first thing to news desks everyday. Some journalists don't bother to attribute the figures to the Board . . . and most have generally adopted the Board's phrase 'the drift back' despite its suggestion of a continuous and inevitable process.

(Crick 1985: 248)

The miners and other trades unionists interviewed in this study saw the treatment of the return to work as crucial. For them, the images of the return symbolized the breaking of the strike and were a central feature of what they saw as a biased media presentation. As one miner commented, television had shown 'returning miners, the more the better'. Another had stated that: 'The thing that most of all comes to mind about what was shown on TV was that they were trying to drive us back to work.'

This raises the crucial issue of the effect of news reporting on the morale of people involved in such conflicts. The issue of how a struggle is presented in the sense of who is said to be 'winning' or the strength of support for different sides, etc., can be crucial factors which influence both public support and the commitment of those involved. In some of our earliest research, we had looked at television coverage of industrial disputes at British Leyland. Some of the thoughts of the miners were echoed by a Leyland worker after the defeat of a strike in 1981:

> Most meetings are at 7.30 as we start work. Being on strike, the unions fixed them all for two hours later, which gave us time to read the papers and listen to the radio and in the end the morale went.

(*Guardian*, 4 November 1981)

In understanding the impact of mass media there is a second crucial area which we have begun to explore here. This is that media accounts may influence how we understand the relationships which constitute our world – what is seen as legitimate, necessary or possible. This could be in the sense of which political or economic policies are seen as 'rational' or 'inevitable'. The media are a crucial site of struggle for such contested meanings and for the attempt to gain legitimacy and to win the consent of the various groups and classes which make up our society. We must understand that such meanings are purposefully constructed – phrases such as 'one-sided disarmament', 'the winter of discontent', 'inflationary wage demands' and 'popular capitalism' do not simply evolve independently of human action. They are thought up and *used* in response to specific situations and conflicts. A crucial question for us is which interests have the most power to influence and direct the flow of information and whether such control actually makes any difference to the way in which the relationships of our world are explained and understood.

REFERENCES

Crick, M. (1985) 'Reporting the strike', *Granta* 15.
Glasgow University Media Group (1976) *Bad News*, London: Routledge & Kegan Paul.
—— (1980) *More Bad News*, London: Routledge & Kegan Paul.
—— (1985) *War and Peace News*, Milton Keynes: Open University Press.
Harrison, P. and Palmer, R. (1986) *News Out of Africa*, London: Hilary Shipman.
Hetherington, A. (1985) *News, Newspapers and Television*, London: Macmillan.
Jones, N. (1986) *Strikes and the Media*, Oxford: Basil Blackwell.
Klapper, J. (1960) *The Effects of Mass Communications*, New York: Free Press.
McQuail, D. (1977) 'The influence and effects of mass media', in J. Curran, M. Gurevitch and J. Woollacott (eds) *Mass Communication and Society*, London: Edward Arnold.
Merton, R. (1946) *Mass Persuasion*, New York: Free Press.
Philo, G. (1990) *Seeing and Believing*, London: Routledge.

Chapter 11

Understanding AIDS

Researching audience perceptions of Acquired Immune Deficiency Syndrome

Jenny Kitzinger

INTRODUCTION

> Representation is a very different notion from that of reflection. It implies the active work of selecting and presenting, of structuring and shaping: not merely the transmitting of already-existing meaning, but the more active labour of making things mean.
>
> (Hall cited in Watney 1987: 124)

Audiences' understandings take many forms; what we 'know' is expressed through 'facts' and theories, images and words, jokes and stories. Our knowledge consists of unspoken assumptions, 'common sense', carefully constructed accounts and hotly defended beliefs. Whether we are acting as members of different audience groups or as journalists on different newspapers we are not passive reproducers of information. We recall some ideas and forget others, we accept some and reject some, we highlight, oppose, censure and reinforce different messages at different times for different audiences of our own (whether these are newspaper readers or our friends, families and colleagues).

This chapter unpacks the many levels of audience understandings of one particular topic which has received massive media attention – Acquired Immune Deficiency Syndrome (AIDS). The chapter aims to achieve three things. First, it introduces a particular methodology – the news game. Second, empirical data about audience understandings are presented. The ways in which media messages enter into public consciousness are explored and the language, images and conceptual structures that inform audience understandings of AIDS are examined. In particular, I focus on audience ideas about 'innocent victims', their images of people with AIDS, their knowledge about transmission via saliva and their understandings of tales about AIDS and revenge. Third, the implications of this research for theories about audience reception processes are addressed. This study challenges the 'uses and gratifications approach' and the 'hypodermic model'. It seeks, instead, both to locate the sources of alternative or oppositional accounts and to identify the cutting edge of media power as it operates in a given cultural context.

METHOD

Working with groups

How we conceptualize (and investigate) audience understandings of media messages is, itself, a political issue. As Seiter *et al.* point out: 'much is at stake in talking about television and its assumed effects: political and economic agendas are always served by conceiving of the audience as controlling or controlled, as duped or resistant, as making meanings or receiving them' (1991: 2). This research was designed to extend our understanding of 'the audience' beyond traditional investigations of the 'active' or 'passive' viewer. We started from the assumption that there was no single unified audience and that the ways in which people relate to the media 'is much more complicated than the poles of activity and passivity can accommodate' (ibid.: 2). Our methodology was designed to explore the ways in which social interaction mediates audience understandings. Therefore, instead of working with isolated individuals, or collections of individuals drawn together simply for the purposes of the research, we elected to work with pre-existing groups – people who already lived, worked or socialized together.

A range of 'types' of people were included in the study so as to tap into a wide variety of understandings about AIDS and the media. As well as reflecting different demographic characteristics (for example, an age range of between 14 and 81 years old) research participants were selected to reflect a wide range of potential interest in the issues. Some people were chosen because they might be expected to have particular knowledge of, or perspectives on, AIDS: for example, research participants included a group of doctors working in the same infectious diseases unit and a group of young male prostitutes working from the same street site. Other groups were chosen precisely because, as a group, they were not necessarily expected to have any special interest in this issue. For example, the sample included a group of people, all over 65 attending the same retirement club, a group of women residents living on the same housing estate and a team of civil engineers who worked in the same office. Sessions were conducted with fifty-two different groups comprising a total of 351 individuals. Figure 11.1 shows the range of people involved in the study. Research sessions lasted approximately 2 hours and each discussion was audio-taped and transcribed. Research participants were asked to complete three short questionnaires and 'the news game' exercise; where possible they also played 'the card game' and did 'the advert exercise'. This chapter focuses on 'the news game'; for an overview of all the methods see Kitzinger (1990).

Figure 11.1 Chart showing the range of people who participated in the study

Group	No. of groups of this type	Total no. of participants in these groups
I People with some occupational interest, involvement or responsibility		
Doctors	1	4
Nurses/health visitors	1	6
Social workers	1	4
Drug workers	1	5
SACRO* workers	1	3
Police staff	2	16
Prison staff	5	32
Teachers	1	5
African journalists (Nigeria, Zaire, Zimbabwe, Uganda)	1	4
Community council workers	1	3
II People targeted as 'high risk groups' by the media or with some special knowledge of, or political involvement in, the issue.		
Male prostitution	2	6
Gay men	2	9
Lesbians	2	6
Family of a gay man	1	4
Prisoners	5	28
Clients of NACRO and SACRO*	4	27
Clients in drug rehabilitation centre	1	7
Young people in intermediate treatment	1	5
III People who, as a group, have no obvious special interest or involvement in the issue.		
Retired people	3	25
Women living on the same Glasgow estate	1	4
School students	3	26
Women with children attending playgroup	2	14
Engineers	2	18
Round table group	1	14
American students	1	25
Janitors	1	7
Market researchers	1	3
Cleaners	1	4
British college students (England, Scotland and Wales)	3	37
Total number of all groups	52	
Total number of participants in all groups		351

Note: * These acronyms stand for the National and the Scottish Associations for the Care and Resettlement of Offenders.

The news game

The news game originally was used as a teaching method. It was designed to encourage students to explore the ways in which the media construct reality. The exercise was developed as a research technique by Greg Philo who used it in his study of audience understanding of the 1984–5 miners' strike (see Chapter 10). Each audience group is given a set of pictures taken from the media coverage of a particular topic and asked to play the role of journalist in producing a related text. For our purposes a set of thirteen still photographs were taken from television news and documentary reports on AIDS. These included, for example, a photograph of a woman holding a child, a scene showing a crowd of people in the street and a picture of a man in bed.

Each audience group was divided into two or more teams consisting of, on average, three people each. The teams selected pictures from the set of photographs and used them to write a news report about AIDS. The scripts were then presented and discussed in the group as a whole.

RESULTS AND DISCUSSION

The practice and structuring of reports

In spite of initial reservations about their ability to produce a script most research participants, once they started the task, entered into the spirit of the presentation with enthusiasm.[1] They debated what would (and would not) appear on the news (for example, would the reporters display an unwrapped condom?) and drew distinctions between different strands of the media (for example, 'Channel 4, it doesn't matter what you write, you can put in as many swear words as you like' (police staff, group 2)).

The tightly structured and often repeated news format provides a convenient framework for this exercise. Most people find it relatively easy to reproduce news presentation techniques and style. The groups' news bulletins often started with phrases such as 'Good evening, today . . .' and one team (members of the Round Table) used their ceremonial gong to replicate the chimes of Big Ben that intersperse the headlines on the *News at Ten*:

> [As one member of the group beats on a gong] 'more bonging. Can we have a bong please. Good evening and welcome to the News at Ten . . .'.
> (Round Table group)

> Good evening. Today the Health Secretary, Mr Norman Fowler, has been releasing new public information on the increasing problem of AIDS . . .
> (school students, group 1)

Paul McLeod, News at [name of place]. Welcome. Here we have the latest news on HIV.

(prison staff, group 4)

Good evening, this is the 6 O'Clock News and I'm Trevor Macdonald.

(drug workers)

Research participants displayed familiarity with the way TV news may refer to televised events of the preceding day, for example 'Health Secretary, Norman Fowler, stated on *Panorama* last night that AIDS is becoming rife in this country' (janitors). And reports were often concluded with remarks such as 'and that's all from us. See you at 10' (drug workers). The one session that we videotaped even shows the 'news presenter' (in this case an ex-prisoner) looking up at the end of his report, smiling and shuffling his papers (identical gestures to the routine followed on TV).

Patterns of interpretation

In addition to reproducing news structures, format and even gestures, people were able to reproduce specific media and health education messages about AIDS using the concepts, language and rhetorical techniques employed in news reports, documentaries and advertisements. Particular photographs generated very definite associations and even phrases for some people. Often these associations were very similar between groups; clear patterns of interpretation are evident in the final collection of news bulletins. This can be illustrated by looking at how diverse audience groups worked with the three different images already mentioned: the picture of a woman holding a child; the crowd scene; and the photograph of a man in bed.

The woman holding a child

The image reproduced below generated comments about two, often inter-twined, themes. First the picture was used to illustrate statements about 'society at large'. For example, the picture was held up to accompany statements such as 'everyone is at risk and nobody is safe' (lesbians, group 2), 'AIDS can affect anyone' (police staff, group 2) and that HIV is increasingly a problem for 'the general population' (market researchers). This image of woman and child was used to represent 'normal people'. In straightforward reproductions of news texts, and in self-conscious paro-dies, several groups in fact produced statements which explicitly assumed that all women and children were, by definition, heterosexual: 'Dr Black felt the public should be informed about the growing rate of known AIDS cases within the heterosexual community as is shown by an increasing number of cases among women and children' (lesbians, group 1).

Second, the photograph acted as a cue for discussions about the

Figure 11.2 One of the news game photographs: a woman holding a child

'innocent victims' of the AIDS epidemic. The 'innocent victim' category
was often synonymous with 'the general population' and both categories
were routinely used in ways which excluded gay men, drug users or
prostitutes. The reports were framed in terms of the 'tragedy' and 'misfor-
tune' of someone becoming infected in spite of having done nothing wrong.
The woman's innocence was emphasized by explaining that she had been
infected by her unfaithful husband or via a blood transfusion.

> This unfortunate woman's baby was infected with the AIDS virus when
> the virus was passed to her from her husband who caught it while away
> on a business trip abroad.
>
> (retired people, group 1)

> This is the wife and kid who both contracted AIDS through the husband
> and now tragically both have AIDS.
>
> (school students, group 3)

> A tragic story to start this evening's news, Mrs. Thomas and her son
> Ivor John have just discovered that whilst pregnant and receiving a
> blood transfusion, she contracted the HIV virus quite innocently.
>
> (Round Table group)

Both mother and child were routinely referred to as 'innocent parties' (prison staff, group 2) or 'innocent bystanders' in contrast to 'promiscuous, irresponsible, drug-users or gay people' (clients in drug rehabilitation centre). However, the woman was not always exempt from blame, it was sometimes only the child who was presumed to be truly innocent. One group of prison staff used this picture to represent all those victims, 'subjected to the virus in the womb due to promiscuity and drug-using mothers' (prison staff, group 2).[2]

Such statements parallel media accounts. The innocent victims referred to in the headlines shown below are men and women infected through blood transfusions, children at risk of mother-to-child transmission, and people who might accidentally step on discarded needles (see Figure 11.3).

Figure 11.3 Examples of some newspaper headlines about 'innocent' victims of AIDS

These are the human beings who are deemed to become infected 'through no fault of their own' and are to be distinguished from 'rampant, promiscuous homosexuals and junkies' (*Daily Star*, 23 April 1991). Similarly consistent patterns of interpretation which closely echo aspects of the media coverage were evident in the use of the other two pictures to be discussed here. The crowd picture was either, like the mother and child image, used to represent the 'general' (i.e. heterosexual) population or used to illustrate the very specific point that you can not tell who is infected with HIV just by looking. The image of a man in bed was used to illustrate gloomy, doom-laden warnings about people with AIDS wasting away and suffering a slow and painful death.

These pictures are reproduced below, accompanied by some of the statements made about each photograph by the audience groups.

The crowd scene

Figure 11.4 One of the news game photographs: the crowd scene

How can you tell if he or she has AIDS, whether they are walking along a crowded street or dancing in a disco? . . . the simple truth is that you can't tell if they're carrying the deadly disease. AIDS doesn't manifest itself.

(school students, group 3)

Anyone in that photo could be an AIDS victim and you wouldnae know.

(prisoners, group 4)

One of these people might have AIDS but they all look perfectly healthy.

(young people in intermediate treatment)

Can you spot the AIDS victim in this group of people? No.

(school students, group 2)

A lot of people walking around have AIDS. But you cannae see it.

(male prostitutes)

The man in bed

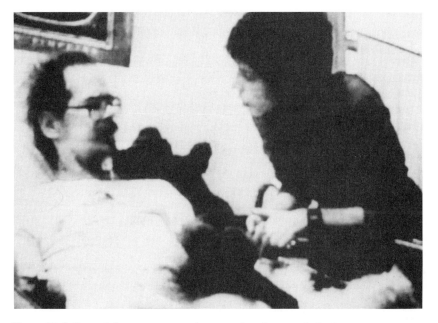

Figure 11.5 One of the news game photographs: the man in bed

Victims can suffer long, slow, agonising deaths.

(prison staff, group 3)

He is dying and medical staff are helpless to save him.

(family group)

The devastating result is a long, slow illness leading to certain death.

(prison staff, group 2)

The effects of AIDS can waste away your body so much, so watch out you don't end up like him.

(school students, group 2)

The final ending obviously is hospitalisation and leading to dementia etc. and death.[3]

(prison staff, group 1)

What can we tell from these patterns of interpretation?

The way in which people reproduce such 'facts' and sentiments in their news bulletins begins to tell us something about the relationship between AIDS media messages and people's theories, language, images and associations with HIV/AIDS. First, it reveals audience knowledge of the 'facts' and 'theories' propounded through the media. For example, the use of the crowd picture demonstrates the apparently successful communication of a specific health education message (which was central to the health education campaign running around the time of our fieldwork) – 'You can't tell who is infected with HIV just by looking.'

Second, the news game exercise allows us to examine the extent to which people are able to reproduce the *language* of media accounts. The exercise initiates discussion about AIDS in people's own words, and the words they attribute to the media, without the researchers introducing their own terminology. This is a particular advantage where the language used is, itself, an object of study. In this case our data show that many people are closely echoing language peculiar to the AIDS media coverage (for example, employing terms such as 'the heterosexual community'). But the data also reveal a definite gap in audience awareness of specific health education terms. This is evident in the use of the photograph of the crowd scene. In using this picture people recall the notion that infection is invisible but still talk about AIDS or 'the AIDS virus' rather than using the correct term HIV which is the form of expression now commonly used in such health education messages.

Third, because the news game involves constructing a narrative, the exercise allows us to explore the extent to which people are able not just to recall 'facts' or individual words but to reproduce *assumptions, images* and *associations* typical of some aspects of the media. It is this kind of structuring of thought which was evident when audience groups reproduced concepts of 'risk groups' versus 'the general population', or used HIV positive women to 'prove' that HIV was 'not just a gay disease' or identified a subcategory of people with AIDS as 'innocent victims'.

Such conceptualizations of the problem have been widely noted (and criticized) by media analysts and AIDS activists (Carter and Watney 1989; Watney 1987). Using images of women with HIV to illustrate that 'the disease is not just confined to the gay community' erases the existence of lesbians. Portraying certain victims as innocent implies that others are somehow guilty. And statements such as that quoted below provoke fear without providing hope when referring to people with AIDS enduring: 'a slow and painful end, filled with suffering, almost constant agony and illness . . . a twilight world from which death, when it came, would be a welcome relief' (*Woman's Own*, 12 July 1986; cited in Watney 1987).

Recalling the message: cultural context and cues

Given the demonstrable parallels between media- and audience-produced statements as discussed above, it was no surprise that most research participants claimed that their primary source of information about AIDS was the TV or press. Nor were we surprised to find that most of them readily 'recognized' the images presented to them in the news game. In fact the research participants often experienced the pictures as very 'closed'. Some people felt that the pictures determined what they could write: 'Some of the photographs really wrote the script by themselves. I mean that one – the baby and mother – would write its own script by launching itself at the microphone really' (gay men, group 1). However, as Greg Philo points out, the photographs stimulate a flow of memories and news language but they do not determine the text and 'even the pictures which may seem most evocative of the events . . . only appear as such to us because of the cultural knowledge which we have already imbued' (Philo 1990: 134). He tested this out in his work on the 'miners' strike' by presenting the set of relevant pictures to a group of American students who had *not* been exposed to the extensive British media coverage of this event:

> Only one of twenty-eight people could identify a picture of Arthur Scargill and in general they had very little prior knowledge of the issues involved. In the news accounts which they produced, one group effectively gave up and wrote a story on the '*minors*' strike, using the pictures for a spoof story about children who refused to grow up.
>
> (ibid: 134).

The fact that many groups completing the news game in a variety of research areas experience some of the photographs as *determining* the script is tribute to the power of media/cultural messages to control, define and confine audience understandings and associations. This point is also illustrated in our work on AIDS by the way in which groups used two particular photographs not mentioned so far. One photograph showed a group of black men, women and children, the other showed a white man in a white coat looking down a microscope. The former photograph was routinely used to illustrate comments about HIV having come from, or being widespread in, Africa. Some people said this was the only way of interpreting this image. However nobody suggested that the second picture – showing the man looking down a microscope – had only one possible interpretation or used it to illustrate an alternative origin theory – that HIV was invented in a laboratory. This reflects the media focus on the African origin theory at the expense of other theories (such as the idea that the virus was 'man-made'). It also echoes the homogeneity of reports about AIDS and Africa in contrast to the diversity of stories about AIDS and laboratories.

However, correlation does not in itself prove causation. An image may generate very specific ideas for people even though they are unaware of the particular media coverage under discussion. No image is 'read' in isolation and people's associations with certain pictures are not necessarily due to recall of the media coverage exclusive to the topic under debate.

This point is clearly illustrated by looking at how people work with images of women. Sexism (both in terms of structural factors and the politics of representation) powerfully frames how women are perceived. David Miller, in his work on audience understandings of Northern Ireland, used a selection of photographs including one of Carmen Proetta – a key witness to the shooting of three IRA members in Gibraltar. Her credibility as a witness had been eroded in the British media by the (false) accusation that she was a prostitute. Miller found that many of his British audience groups did indeed associate her with prostitution. However, the *same* link was made by a few members of a group of Americans who, in fact, had not seen any of this type of media coverage. They assumed that she was a prostitute because of her physical appearance combined with the fact that she was featured in a news bulletin: women wearing lots of make-up, they reasoned, only make it on to the news as someone's mistress or whore. They could *not* reconstruct the type of allegations made about her in the British press but they thought that her sexual behaviour must be at issue in some way. This was because they were familiar with a certain genre of reporting about women. In particular, they referred to 'sex scandals' which were current at that time in their own country, such as the widely publicized sexual indiscretions of the evangelical Christian, Jimmy Swaggart (Miller forthcoming).

Similar processes may be in operation when the photograph of a white woman and child used in the AIDS news game calls forth statements about 'innocence' or when another of our photographs – showing two women in short skirts standing on a street at night – triggers statements about prostitutes posing a threat to family life. The presentation of women as either innocent victims or threatening predators is not restricted to the media coverage of AIDS. Woman (and child) imagery carries particular associations in western culture – ideas reflected in phrases such as 'women and children first', in conceptual divisions such as virgin/mother/whore and in common understandings of women either as guardians of the moral order or as the source of all evil.[4]

The news game, then, can locate parallels between audience statements and parts of the media but the scripts on their own do not tell us the exact source of the messages that people are reproducing. Nor do they tell us why people are reproducing certain messages and not others. The phrases used in the scripts may be traceable to specific news coverage but the overall associations may also be embedded in (and therefore reinforced by) the wider cultural and broader media context.

It is also important to note that the scripts do not, in themselves, tell us what people actually believe. Some of the research participants *did* express allegiance to the ideas reiterated in their bulletin. For example, a group of retired people, commenting on their use of the picture of the woman and child, declared:

Resp. 1: We are agreed that it was really started by irresponsible people, as far as we know, and it's been carried on, in most cases, by irresponsible people. But in some cases, [such as the] one lady there with her baby in her arms, we assumed that this was a lady who had contracted the AIDS virus through a blood transfusion in the hospital and it has been passed on to her child, which is rather unfortunate . . . but the majority of cases we find that it is irresponsible people that's carrying it on.

JK: What kind of irresponsible people?

Resp. 1: Gays, lesbians.

Resp. 2: Oh and of course prisoners.[5]

(retired people, group 1)

However, other people produced reports which they took to be a fair rendering of what actually appeared on the news but with which they themselves begged to disagree.

A close examination of the production and presentation of the news text, combined with the subsequent discussion, is therefore necessary to be able to interpret the data generated by the news game. Through examining the debate that *leads up* to constructing the news text, and exploring issues in the discussion *after* the presention of the text, we can begin to explore questions such as: what is the interrelationship between the wider cultural associations and the immediate media sources of information? What are the diverse sources of public understandings and what credibility is given to different sources? To what extent are people consciously reproducing or even parodying media statements? What factors influence audience recall of, and belief in, certain ideas? Why do different audiences find some aspects of the media coverage so easy either to accept or reject, to recall or 'forget'?

The next part of this chapter addresses precisely these questions. The issues are explored through a closer analysis of audience use of particular words, images, theories and stories. These four levels of 'knowing' are illustrated with reference to: first, people's knowledge about the term 'HIV', second, the images which they associate with AIDS; third, their understandings of the theories about a particular route of (non) transmission – saliva; fourth, audience recall and repetition of a particular type of story – revenge stories.

'HIV' or 'the AIDS virus' – audience selection of terminology

The use of the term HIV has been a specific site of struggle in the production process of AIDS media messages. The use of terms such as 'AIDS virus' or 'AIDS' as a synonym for HIV has been criticized for, among other things, confusing people about the time-lag between becoming infected and becoming ill, and writing off anyone with HIV as someone who is already 'as good as dead' (see Watney 1987). Until 1988 most of the health education material and the bulk of media accounts fell into this trap. Following challenges on this point the Health Education Authority (HEA) adapted its material and in the 1988–9 campaign deliberately set out to familiarize people with the term 'HIV'. Some journalists have followed this lead. However, parts of the mass media still avoid using the term 'HIV' and even some of the specific health education communications on this issue are vague or confusing. It is partly this history of struggle and ongoing confusion that is reflected in audience use of this term. Some people were unclear about the distinction between HIV and AIDS and others, although aquainted with the term 'HIV', were unaware of its significance as distinct from 'AIDS' and were not prepared to use it in conversation with each other. Even when, during the course of another exercise, audience groups were shown a slogan reading 'How to recognize someone with HIV' they often repeated the sentence replacing 'HIV' with 'AIDS'. 'HIV' was dismissed as a 'fancy' word for AIDS: 'doctors just like using posh terms'. People's alienation from this term may also reflect the reality that 'HIV' is currently far more likely to appear in the context of explicit health education and the speech of experts than in popular journalism. This shows that people do not indiscriminately absorb all media messages but make conscious or unconscious decisions about which of the many diverse forms of language about a topic they will adopt and use in their day-to-day interaction.

'Shadows of their former selves' – the death's head image of 'AIDS victims'

Just as many research participants had access to the term 'HIV' but did not incorporate it into their everyday talk about 'AIDS' so many research participants could draw on more positive images of people with AIDS, but this was not the image that sprang to mind when thinking about the topic. Prior to, or during the course of, our fieldwork, there were several programmes which represented people with AIDS as active personalities, living with courage and fighting against their diseases and the discrimination they faced. These sorts of portraits (for example the documentary *Remember Terry*) were recalled and identified as significant by many of the research participants. However, the association that came most readily to mind was one of doom and gloom. When asked what images they associated with AIDS people replied with statements such as:

Resp. 1: A person lying in a bed that's obviously got the AIDS virus. Someone white and skeletal.

(school student, group 1)

Resp. 1: Disease-ridden emaciated body sat in a bed.

(prisoners, group 5)

Resp. 1: Images like Ethiopia.

Resp. 2: Just fading away.

Resp. 3: Dying.

(male prostitutes, group 2)

Even though we had deliberately avoided the most extreme 'death's-head' images of AIDS, and chosen a photograph for the news game which showed someone looking ill but not 'at death's-door', most people still used it to illustrate statements about suffering and despair. Some research participants also replicated the common media assumption that they were addressing an exclusively HIV-negative audience (the message produced by one group – 'watch out you don't end up like him' – is presumably not supposed to be relevant to someone who is already infected).

In discussion it became clear that dramatic images of people with AIDS as walking skeletons has a powerful and immediate impact on audiences. Such images had impressed themselves on many people's minds early on in the AIDS crisis. This had been effected particularly through the coverage of Rock Hudson's death, scenes from San Francisco and media portraits of people 'before' and 'after' AIDS.

JK: When did you first hear about AIDS?

Resp. 1: It was in 1984, in the *News of the World*. It had like this bloated face of some San Francisco person dying of it . . . it was like before and after the AIDS effect.

(gay men, group 1)

Resp. 1: These pictures of Rock Hudson at the end . . . they were really horrific . . . he looked really, really terrible . . . and when you remember how he was in the films and that and saw . . . it was horrific.

(women with children at playgroup, group 1)

Resp. 1: I seen a programme once with a lassie in Australia, she had AIDS and they followed her every couple of months, how she was dying and all that . . . it showed you in the last one what she's looked like *before* . . . she had totally wasted away.

(school students, group 2)

These type of before/after portrayals were remembered even when referring to more detailed and complex media representations of people with AIDS. The ability to reproduce such portrayals is not a simple measure of the consistency with which they have been promoted in the media, but also reflects the ways in which such images are processed by many of the audience. These representations are recalled because they are 'shocking' or 'frightening' or, in the words of one research participant, 'they just looked so disgusting, they looked really horrible'. In addition such images can incite a voyeuristic fascination and they receive an exposure over and above that actually given to them in the media because they are recalled and reproduced in discussion, 'joking' and 'games'. Research participants referred to the day-to-day use of AIDS in the course of 'teasing'. A schoolgirl with severe facial eczema is taunted with the name 'Aidsey', colleagues make jokes about cold sores and friends pretend to recoil from anyone who might be infected. During the research sessions themselves there was a great deal of 'horseplay' along these lines. One young man took evident delight in drawing a monster-type picture of 'the look' of someone with AIDS while, in another group, participants enthusiastically sought to reproduce 'the face of AIDS' through acting it out – contorting their faces, starting to squint, shake and drool.

Such behaviour draws on a well-established (pre-AIDS) western tradition of deriding and fearing people with disabilities, a tradition illustrated by the legion of TV and cinema film villains with 'deformities' such as limps or half-paralysed faces (Campling 1981). There also seems to be a sort of 'Fungus the Bogeyman factor' – some people revel in transgressing taboos about body fluids and delight in tales of the disgusting or horrific. (*Fungus the Bogeyman* is a popular children's book about a revolting-looking green monster who adores anything slimy, dank and disgusting and spends his time wallowing in excrescences of one sort of another (Briggs 1977).)

The 'Fungus the Bogeyman factor' can clearly work against people with

AIDS and undermine progressive health education. However, in other circumstances, it can also apparently help people to recall certain health education messages. This is demonstrated, for example, by the ways in which people made sense of the risks attached to 'body fluids' in general and saliva in particular.

'Six pints bottled just for you' – the dangers of saliva

'Body fluids' is a phrase which has appeared in some of the AIDS media and health education material. We are told that body fluids contain HIV and that 'mixing body fluids' or 'the exchange of body fluids' may result in the transmission of infection. Such terms have been picked up by the audience and were spontaneously, even enthusiastically, used in many of the discussion groups (complete in one case with a mime of 'mixing body fluids' as if pouring different substances into a witches' cauldron).

Sometimes journalists use the phrase 'body fluids' as a convenient euphemism for 'rude' words like semen which might be judged too 'unpalatable' to present to readers over the breakfast table (Diamond and Bellitto 1986; Edgar, Hammond and Freimuth 1989). Often reference is made to 'body fluids' or a list of a variety of bodily secretions is provided without any explicit indication that saliva is probably *not* a realistic route of transmission. Such vague use of the generic concept of 'body fluids' encourages some people to believe that saliva must be infectious. An office janitor, a member of a retirement club and a market researcher all argued that saliva must be infectious because: 'It's a body fluid is it not?' (janitors); 'It's body fluid' (retired people, group 2); 'I guess if it's possible to be transferred by body fluids and saliva is a body fluid, you know, it must be possible in some way to catch it by that mode of transmission' (market researchers).[6] The fear that saliva is a route of transmission may also be encouraged by headlines such as: 'Spitting AIDS woman bailed' (*Daily Record*, 20 January 1989), 'AIDS virus "could be spread by a passionate kiss" ' (*Sunday Telegraph*, 22 January 1989); 'Anguish of kiss of life barman – Kenny awaits AIDS test' (*Glasgow Evening Times*, 3 March 1989) and 'AIDS fear of bitten policeman' (*Sun*, 6 February 1990). These type of stories were certainly recalled and reiterated in several groups when the subject of saliva came up: 'About six months ago I remember there was something in the paper. . . .He spat in a policeman's face' (janitors); 'You see the prisoners are doing this to the warders, they're spitting and they could get AIDS' (retired people, group 1). However, the source of such information was not necessarily directly attributed to the media. 'A policeman died not very long ago because somebody spat on him, and you always get AIDS. . . .I heard this from a . . . a nurse who lived beside him' (retired people, group 2). Some people volunteered that they had even more direct experience of this issue. In this group of retired people one woman told a story about an incident that had happened to someone she knew:

> My friend was walking along the street and this old drunk came out and spat on her and she immediately walloped him with her umbrella and the police were called and she was charged with assault and she told the policemen, she said 'I'm worried in case I have AIDS . . . I'm not moving from here until we go to the hospital to check it out'.
>
> (retired people, group 2)

Another research participant volunteered information from a period of jury service:

> I even heard it when I was on Jury Duty. It was a boy that had been lifted, spitting on them, told them he had AIDS, . . . the police were making a big issue of it, him spitting and threatening that he had AIDS. . . . I don't think he should have got away with it . . . you've got the AIDS thing, I think it's bloody dangerous, it's frightening.
>
> (women with children attending playgroup, group 2)

Such stories explicitly establish a link between saliva and HIV transmission. Given factors such as those discussed above perhaps it is not surprising that a high proportion of people are unclear about the risks posed by saliva. For example, surveys suggest that about a third of the population may believe that HIV can be transmitted through kissing (Ford 1991; McQueen, Robertson and Nisbet 1991).

However, some people accept the current medical orthodoxy on saliva and it is equally, if not *more*, important to look at why some people *accepted* that saliva poses no risk as to look at why others rejected this idea. Debate within the groups suggested that there was one particularly important factor influencing audience belief in the fact that saliva was unlikely to be a route of HIV-transmission. When some members of the group talked about saliva being a 'body fluid' or described occasions when saliva was used as a weapon, other research participants countered their arguments using another commonly recalled fact – the fact that one would need intimate contact with a great deal of saliva before transmission could occur. Someone would need to 'bathe in it, while covered in open sores' or 'inject massive quantities' (market researchers). Alternatively they would need to drink: 'one pint', 'two pints', 'five pints', 'six and a half pints', 'a litre', 'nineteen buckets', 'a gallon', 'ten gallons' or 'a thousand gallons' (prisoners, group 5; women with children attending playgroup, group 1; family; school students, group 3; intermediate treatment group; market researchers). One would be unlikely to encounter such quantities even, as one young woman put it, if you spent 'all night snogging' (school students, group 3). Similar statements are evident in some press and health education material, according to one newspaper article, for example, 'you'd have to drink saliva by the gallon to run any significant risk of acquiring the HIV virus' (*Scotsman*, 29 December 1989). Such discussions in the groups caused a great deal of laughter and were accompanied with jokes about pints of saliva being 'bottled just for your use' (women with children attending playgroup, group 1) or remarks such as: 'You've got to have a mouth big enough to take one and a half litres in one go – they'd probably drown first anyway!' (prison officer in charge of prisoners, group 5). In this case it would appear that the half-fascinating, half-repellant images conjured up by the thought of vast quantities of saliva generates humour and interest and encourages recall and repetition. The 'Fungus the Bogeyman factor' seems to be ensuring that this particular message enters everyday currency – it is recalled and repeated between members of the audience thus reinforcing and increasing exposure to the original media version.[7] Other factors lead to similar popularity for another theme – the revenge story. It is to this theme that I now turn.

'Welcome to the AIDS club': the spectre of the vengeful 'AIDS carrier'

The use of HIV as a weapon of intimidation or revenge is a recurring theme in the media coverage of HIV/AIDS. As already discussed, some stories feature people with HIV spitting on prison warders, policemen or passers-by. Other stories are about people who deliberately donate HIV-infected blood or who threatened their enemies with 'dirty' needles. The *Sun* carried headlines such as: 'AIDS robber squirts blood at victim' (*Sun*, 21 November 1988); 'Nut tries to give kids AIDS blood – I wanted revenge says dying junkie' (*Sun*, 12 October 1989); 'Jab gang sparks AIDS fear' (*Sun*, 30 October 1919); and 'AIDS death plot' (*Sun*, 5 February 1990). The *Daily Record* reported another story with the headline: 'Bogeyman jailed – AIDS threat of a monster'. This told the story of a man, calling himself 'The bogeyman', who threatened to inject 'HIV-contaminated' blood into shampoo (*Daily Record*, 29 September 1989).

Sometimes these stories report acts of revenge (or wilful carelessness) carried out through seduction (or rape). There are some explicit references in TV news bulletins to people who 'may have been infected knowingly by sufferers seeking revenge' and newspapers quote warnings about 'the avowed intention of some AIDS victims to deliberately infect as many other people as possible' (ITN 17.45 News and BBC 1 *Six O'clock News*, 26 January 1988; *Glasgow Herald*, 17 February 1989).

The press have focused on specific cases (trawled from all over the world). There was the woman in Belgrade who 'owned up to bedding FIFTEEN of her colleagues. The pretty victim kept quiet about her illness as she moved from man to man' (*Sun*, 9 March 1989; emphasis in original). There was the man in the Soviet Union who, 'deciding he has only four or five years to live, announced he has left his wife and is going to sleep with every woman he can' (*Observer*, October 1989; reprinted from a letter in Soviet newspaper). There was the prostitute who has the 'killer disease' but 'still regularly plies her trade on the streets' (*Daily Star*, 21 April 1990) and the gay man – 'Clive' – who, knowing he was infected, 'seemed to be developing a grudge' and had sex with half a dozen men in one night 'and had definitely not used a condom' (*The Independent*, 21 March 1989). Extensive media coverage was given to the lawsuit brought against Rock Hudson's estate alleging that Hudson had continued to have unsafe sex with his boyfriend after knowing that he had the virus but without inform- ing his lover of this fact. Some parts of the media also reported a story that originally appeared in *And The Band Played On* – a chronology of events written by an investigative journalist. This book recorded the activities of a handsome airline steward called Gaetan Dugas: 'He would have sex with you, turn up the lights in the cubicle, and point out his Kaposi sarcoma lesions. "I've got gay cancer," he'd say. "I'm going to die and so are you" ' (Shilts 1987: 165). This sort of theme was even made into a drama plot in one episode of NBC's *Midnight Caller* which featured a man who delibera- tely spread HIV by having prolific, unprotected intercourse with many different women.[8]

Variations on such themes were spontaneously raised in many of the audience group discussions. Research participants repeated a variety of stories featuring HIV positive people who deliberately infected others:

> there was a guy who was sleeping with other men and saying 'Ha, ha. I've got gay skin cancer and you're going to die too'.
>
> (gay men, group 2)

> there was a girl, and she actually went out and pulled about half a dozen blokes in a day and just went to bed with them and afterwards said 'Guess what, you've got it'.
>
> (prison staff, group 5)

> There was the incident in the Sunday papers a few months back about the girls . . . on holiday in Spain, and they had Spanish boyfriends and they got the present to take home in the aeroplane and when the girl opened it up it was a small replica of a coffin saying 'Welcome to the AIDS club'.
>
> (nurses)

> It's like those birds going off and meeting those guys on holiday and waking up and seeing on the ceiling or on the mirror or something – 'Welcome to the AIDS club'.
>
> (SACRO clients, group 1)

According to some of these research participants the world is populated with 'malicious people who themselves have caught it, and are deliberately passing it on' (retired people, group 1). 'They know they are going to die anyway so . . . they're going to take somebody else away with them' (women with children attending playgroup, group 2). Their attitude is: 'That bastard gave me it, so I should give some other cunt it' (SACRO clients, group 1). Such sentiments were particularly attributed to prostitutes, an attribution sometimes backed up by reference to identifiable media reports:

> an interview that took place with a prostitute in Edinburgh would indicate to me that now that some of the prostitutes have contracted AIDS, that their attitude is 'I don't give a damn who I pass it on to now' and they're carrying on their trade.
>
> (retired people, group 1)

> If a prostitute gets AIDS off a lad she picks up in the street, she wants revenge. She'll give her body for anything and give AIDS all the way round.
>
> (janitors)

In some cases the revenge theme seemed to have the status of an urban myth. It wasn't just a case they had read about but this had actually happened to 'a friend of a friend': 'I know of somebody who started having a little holiday affair and later got a card saying "Welcome to the AIDS club" ' 'my friend's daughter at university in Edinburgh had a relationship with somebody, and when she woke up there was a note on her door which said – exactly the same idea' (nurses); 'That happened to my pal by the way. He fucking ran right down to the doctors' (SACRO client, group 1).

The frequent discussion of revenge tales in a variety of audience groups partly reflects the ubiquity of such tales in a wide range of media. But it should be noted that neither the stories in the media, nor those repeated from 'personal contact' carry any guarantee of veracity. Indeed, the newspaper account about 'Clive' – who had unsafe sex with half a dozen men in one night – was later exposed as a 'fiction' based on a 'composite character' (*Sunday Telegraph*, 21 May 1989), and even face-to-face interviews are not necessarily accurate (let alone representative). Ruth Morgan Thomas, who has worked extensively with Edinburgh prostitutes since 1987, comments that she knows of no 'working girl' deliberately seeking to infect clients (although there are some women who will accept sex without a condom if *the client* insists). She says that prostitutes have been offered 'considerable sums of money' to make particular statements to journalists who have 'very clear ideas about what they want from an interview'. She also points out that there is no evidence that clients of prostitutes in the UK are at any more risk than other men (see Delacoste and Alexander 1988).

The fact that revenge tales are pursued by journalists, used as fictional

themes by film script-writers and seem to capture the imagination of media
workers and the general public alike suggests a more complex process than
simple 'generation', 'reception' and 'reproduction' of messages in any
straightforward, mechanical sense. These stories are sought after, elaborated and incorporated into people's ways of thinking about AIDS. In the
repetition such tales serve as warnings, as cautionary tales which carry the
attractive frisson of the thriller plot. They can be used to articulate and
express different moral positions (such as the dangers of anonymous sex)
and they articulate anxieties – not just about AIDS but about sexual threats
more generally. For heterosexual men, this 'urban myth' expresses male
fears of the seductive vamp – as epitomized in the film *Fatal Attraction*. For
women, it reflects vulnerability to sexual trickery, danger and attack:
'Another thing that frightens me about this AIDS virus is I don't like going
out at night by myself in case of rape . . . I think most women have got a
fear about being raped' (women with children at playgroup, group 1).

In addition, these stories fit into, and perhaps epitomize, the logic of a
primary theme in one of the dominant AIDS discourses – the theme of
individual responsibility combined with the presumed collective guilt of
deviant groups. The notion of deliberate infection is latent in the way
AIDS is often discussed, even when 'revenge' is not explicitly alluded to.
Health education advertisements which use *double entendre* slogans such
as 'It only takes one prick to give you AIDS' certainly suggest that 'AIDS'
is something given to you by someone else (and a not very nice 'someone
else' at that). The idea that HIV transmission could occur due to 'chance'
or 'bad luck' is absent, or only very selectively adopted, in this discourse.
This is true even, or perhaps *especially*, where 'innocent victims' are
concerned. In such cases HIV is sometimes personified as a vengeful virus
– which, like the wicked fairy at the christening party, 'reached out and
touched that defenceless new-born child with death' (*Woman's Own*, cited
in Watney 1987: 92).

Such attributions of intentionality in the transmission process are not
about some free-floating psychological tendency to blame others – the
blame is not indiscriminately applied. The scapegoats are carefully
selected. It is 'deviants' who are denounced for the spread of the virus:
'They, and they alone are responsible for people dying of AIDS' (*Sun*, 12
January 1990). Even when reports concern the failure of the National
Health Service to screen blood supplies blame is sometimes laid squarely at
the door of anti-social individuals. As the *Daily Star* demands: 'How many
families have been sentenced to death by faceless blood donors who were
drug addicts or permissive homosexuals' (29 August 1989).

'Junkies', 'whores' and 'queers' are already perceived as a menace to
society. AIDS and the revenge story reassert this image and reinforce ideas
about our immorality and irresponsibility. But, above all, revenge tales
serve to justify the 'need' for coercive measures to identify, control and, if

'necessary', destroy people with HIV. As one ex-prisoner concluded after a lengthy exchange of various HIV revenge tales in his group: 'What they should do, man, is take everybody that's got AIDS and put them into one corner and just blow their heads off' (SACRO clients, group 1).[9]

Contradictions, oppositions and alternative presentations

The above discussion has emphasized the coherence within groups and the interlocking, mutually reinforcing nature of many of the ideas. However, with regard to all of the themes discussed above, there was always at least one research participant who exhibited contradictory elements in their thinking around these issues, expressed outright opposition to the general perspective or constructed alternative accounts. It is to these contradictions, oppositions and alternatives that I now turn.

Contradictions

People can 'know' something on one level but reject it on another, or they may know what they 'ought' to think but find it hard to act on this. For example, most research participants agreed that 'you can't tell by looking' who is infected with HIV. However, in practice, many of them reported employing visual criteria to discriminate between potential partners. They still had expectations about the likely appearance of someone who might be infected. This 'mental image' seemed to be partly due to long-standing links between disease and dirt/poverty, but it was also reinforced by contradictions within the media campaigns themselves. The emphasis on 'risk groups' and the stereotypes surrounding gay men and drug users meant that people thought they could at least tell by looking whether someone was *likely* to be infected (for further discussion of this see Kitzinger 1991).

Some people also drew a distinction between 'knowing' and 'really believing' something and being prepared to act accordingly. During the group discussions acknowledgement of such distinctions were usually heralded by one particular phrase, 'better safe than sorry', and concluded with some reference to the uncertainty of scientific knowledge about AIDS. For example, one woman told me how she had warned her daughter not to share a can of drink with a particular girl at school whose parents were known to be drug users. This was in spite of her own professed knowledge that HIV is *not* spread via saliva:

> *Resp. 1*: I had warned her [my daughter] – 'no, don't take any thing off of her' [the 'suspect' child]. But again that is ignorance . . .
> *Resp. 2*: Aye.
> *Resp. 3*: Of course it is!

JK: And yet you've also said to your daughter that she shouldn't take any thing off this girl?

Resp. 1: Aye, don't drink. . . .Aye, because I just . . . I don't know . . . I don't know what . . . I mean, I'm not saying . . . they've not got AIDS, but . . . I mean, they are junkies.

Resp. 2: It's just to be on the safe side. It's just that you don't know. You're just making sure till they find out what they can get it from.

Resp. 1: Aye, this is it!

(Women living on the same Glasgow estate)

This final point was greeted with assent by other members of the group who added comments such as: 'a lot of them [AIDS experts] don't know what they are talking about'; 'There's too many mistakes'; 'Too many ifs and buts'. Another member of the group then confided that she always pulls her sleeve down over her hand before pressing the button at a Pelican crossing – in case she cuts her finger and the button is already contaminated with infected blood from someone else – 'and if [my son] says "can I press it?" I make him put his gloves on before I let him'.

Earlier in this chapter I drew attention to a tendency to find someone to blame for AIDS but pointed out that blame was selectively targeted at 'marginalized' groups. The 'better safe than sorry' rationale discussed above is similarly selectively applied. For example, none of the women suggested that it was 'better to be safe than sorry', and therefore always use a condom during sexual intercourse with their husbands. This was in spite of making remarks about never knowing if your partner is faithful and professing to believe in the heterosexual transmission of the virus. Clearly the 'better safe than sorry' dictum only operates in *some* situations. People's ability or willingness to avoid actual or supposed risk depends on their power to change (for example, whether or not they can insist on condom use, see Holland *et. al.* 1990) and on the perceived social/moral/personal acceptability of the evasive actions concerned.

When debating the advisability of warning her child not to share a can of drink with the drug users' daughter not one of the women commented on the possible consequences for the girl who was the victim of such injunctions. Indeed, some research participants seemed to accept that evasive action which might stigmatize a 'suspect' child was an acceptable (although regrettable) option when it came to protecting 'your own flesh and blood'. This was clearly spelt out during a different discussion session with some women whose children attended a playgroup in another area of Scotland. One woman declared that she thought they ought to know if any child in the group was infected. But, she added, 'I don't like the persecution though, I just totally hate it.' However, another woman retorted:

But how would you feel if . . . at the playgroup, two kids fell and the two of them cut themselves at the same time and your kid, God forbid, got AIDS through that? You wouldn't be worrying about persecuting them then – *you think of your own first.*

(women with children attending playgroup, group 1, my emphasis)

The ideology of the family and a passionate commitment to their children were used by several participants to justify protecting their own offspring *at all cost* from even the most hypothetical risk. This commitment could include, if necessary, riding roughshod over wider social responsibilities.

The *reluctance* of some of these women to try using condoms with their husbands and their relative *willingness* to discourage their children from relating 'too closely' to any child who might be infected clearly indicates the ways in which power imbalances, structural position and different ideologies intervene between simple acceptance of a fact and putting that belief into practice. (The approach of some of these women is in direct contrast to the sense of wider *community* responsibility and the adaptation to safer sex displayed by many gay men in the AIDS crisis.)[10]

Oppositions

It was not only that some people live with contradictions or compromises or that they are uncertain about how much to believe of what they hear and see. Some people quite simply rejected ideas which were dominant within the media or even within their own group. Some people dissented from the categorization of people as 'innocent' or 'guilty victims', some people refused to contrast 'risk' groups with some mythical 'clean', 'general population' and a few rejected the 'death's head' image of people with AIDS. Similarly, in spite of all the arguments advanced by other members of the group, there were people who persisted in believing that HIV *could* be transmitted via saliva. Although they were well aware of the information that vast quantities of saliva are necessary to pose any risk, some participants continued to believe that saliva was dangerous. This was partly, as already discussed, because of media language about dangerous 'body fluids' and media stories about spit being used as a weapon. However, these research participants also explained or justified their beliefs with reference to the behaviour of professionals (such as policemen or food retailers), their own 'logic', their images of the body, their knowledge about the nature of viral infection and their distrust of government sources. One woman argued that saliva must be dangerous as this would explain the popularity of throw-away utensils: 'I think that's why Macdonalds and people like that give us cardboard cups. Its not so much the economics of a dishwasher, it's the fact that they're absolving themselves' (retired people, group 2). Another research participant in the same group declared:

If a policeman is spat on and he reports this he is actually watched for the AIDS virus . . . if they don't think this can be transmitted through saliva they wouldn't watch that policeman [*JK*: And how do you know this?] Because I know this police sergeant.

(retired people, group 2,)

One young man argued that saliva easily enters the blood stream through kissing because: 'your mouth is an open wound' and went on to reject the idea that you would need to be exposed to vast quantities of saliva before infection could occur: 'If you're HIV positive right, even a wee bit of your saliva is going to have it' (SACRO clients, group 1). This point of view was shared by a participant in one of the other groups of ex-prisoners: 'One spot and you could catch it, because if you've got it in your system, it is in your system so whatever you are spitting out, that probably has a bit of that virus in it' (SACRO clients, group 2). In any case the fact that 'the experts' keep changing their minds about HIV/AIDS made some people lack confidence in the official view: 'You begin to think, "well, where does it end?" I mean is it ignorance and only just now, the fact that nobody has caught it through exchange of saliva' (market researchers). Even if the 'experts' knew that saliva was infectious, some research participants believed that this fact would be suppressed as otherwise 'there would be mass hysteria' (janitors).

Alternative presentations

People did not only reject media messages, some groups created alternative, or even oppositional, accounts. In spite of the consistency with which a wide variety of groups produced similar language, stories and images about AIDS, some teams or individuals within groups produced very different interpretations. The photograph of the woman and child, although routinely used to illustrate themes about 'the general public' and 'innocent victims', was used by one team to discuss British government inertia over the problems facing Romanian orphans with AIDS: 'Our government is just turning our back on them' (school students, group 1). Similarly, the photograph of the crowd, although routinely used to represent 'the heterosexual community' or to make the point that you 'can't tell by looking', was used by one team of ex-drug users in a metaphorical way to illustrate 'The world walking by and ignoring what's going on.' The same photograph was used by a group of community council workers to represent a crowd of demonstrators converging on city hall to protest about local authority policy. Similarly, the picture of the man in bed, while frequently used to illustrate themes about death and despair, was used by a few groups in ways which allowed people with AIDS an active voice or addressed the issue of care and resources, for example, 'Michael Stuart, 35, commented that drugs are unavailable to those who need them' (social workers). These 'deviant' research participants are just as important in developing our understanding of media processes as those who conformed to a more general pattern of response (and it must be remembered, this was a 'structured' rather than a 'representative sample'). Their 'deviance' demonstrates that there are other ways of 'reading' these images, that other associations are possible.

In most cases, such as those cited above, the 'alternative' captions given to certain pictures expressed those individuals' or groups' *own* opinions. They were not claiming that such statements were typical of media coverage, instead they were explicitly using the news game as a vehicle to express their own point of view. The school student who came up with the attack on the government for inertia about Romanian babies had been greatly moved by the recent media coverage of this issue. She was angry on behalf of the orphans and had a particular political perspective on this issue. She explicitly stated that her team's version of a news bulletin would never appear on television: 'They wouldn't be slagging off the government in any way because they'd be taken off the air' (school students, group 1). Similarly, the ex-drug users who talked about 'The world walking by and ignoring what's going on' were very aware of the risk to themselves and their friends and were angry about the lack of attention paid to their plight. When shown a picture of Norman Fowler and asked what he might have to say on the subject of AIDS one man succinctly replied: 'Gas the junkies' (clients in drug rehabilitation centre). The community council workers who used the photograph of the crowd to represent a demonstration were, in the same way, cynical about government actions and were using the news game to articulate their own point of view, as were the social workers who used the photographs to express their occupational-related concern about the resources available for people with HIV and AIDS.

Even those who produced more 'typical' news game statements sometimes made it clear that they personally had a different point of view. Indeed recall, repetition and reproduction could take the form of parody and rejection. The gay men who produced a bulletin which talked about 'compulsory testing for AIDS' were aware that the correct term should have been HIV: 'We knew that was wrong but that was how the BBC would say it.' They also employed terms in their bulletin that they were critical of and would not normally use themselves – terms such as 'homosexual acts' ('It's a clinical way of looking at what is basically gay sex') and 'heterosexual community ('I don't think you would like to say that – "heterosexual community" if it were up to ourselves, because we are all one community, but they would like to see the heterosexual community . . . like a minority or something') (gay men, group 1).

These men had closely followed the AIDS issue since it first appeared in the mass media and had many other sources of information – they read the gay press, one man in the group had a lover who worked on an AIDS helpline and some of them had friends who were HIV antibody positive.

One man described how AIDS meant 'you've got to change your whole life – how you talk, how you discuss and what you actually say':

> *JK*: In what way?
> *Resp.*: There was a time when AIDS always happened to someone else, it can't actually happen to you and you may have a cavalier attitude and to start with you actually knew it was getting nearer and nearer to people you knew. . . . Your views on AIDS became more toned and more sensitive and now you have to face the fact that people you know may actually be carrying HIV, you know people who have HIV or people who actually are dying . . .
>
> (gay men, group 1)

'Phrases automatically come to mind . . .'

The gay men quoted above had the strong foundations of a political gay identity. They were part of an 'alternative' community and, by virtue of their distinct location *vis-à-vis* the AIDS issue, related to media messages about AIDS from a perspective different to that of their heterosexual counterparts. As Watney points out, for lesbians and gay men media power and prejudice is: 'baldly exposed in the space between our lived experience, and the representations made of us in the media' (1987: 125). However, even the gay men in our study identified limits to their ability to consciously pick and choose among media messages. These research participants, like many other participants in the study, found that they were producing statements, assumptions and images that, at least on reflection, did not accord with their preferred political position or, indeed, their own personal experiences of reality.

During the course of completing the news game participants were often surprised by the ease with which words and whole phrases came to mind: 'you don't realise how much you know until you try this!', 'it's uncanny how much I've absorbed'. Sometimes they were disturbed by the assumptions that they made or comments that they included: 'Where did that come from?' exclaimed a client in a drug rehabilitation centre on reading out a negative reference to prostitutes. 'I'm not happy with that' commented a market researcher as he read out part of his news text which referred to 'the Afro/Caribbean community' as a high-risk group. Later he explained that they'd made this assumption because of all the media reports associating AIDS with Africa, but having thought about it decided that 'we probably made a boob there' (market researchers). Similarly, the gay men, while consciously parodying some aspects of the coverage found themselves producing phrases about 'society at large' with which they themselves disagreed, at least in retrospect. It was this sort of experience that led one man to conclude:

You find that you look at pictures and automatically you are conditioned by the news media. Phrases automatically come to mind . . .
that is the thing about the media – no matter what they report on you
are conditioned by it to a certain extent.

(gay men, group 1)

In this way the research itself was a form of intervention – encouraging
people to explore their assumptions and examine inconsistencies, provoking them to reflect on and express a critique of the media coverage and to
produce alternative versions of reality. It is not surprising that the news
game should operate in this way given its roots as a teaching exercise
designed to alert people to the values informing media constructions. It is
ironic that, for the very same reason, research participants sometimes
resented the exercise for 'tricking' them into saying certain things. It is this
very tension between the experience of the pictures 'writing the script by
themselves' and the ability of the creators of that script to reflect on and
criticize their own bulletins that is the strength of the method. It is in these
contradictions that the news game captures the processes of audience
understandings and the ambivalence of the relationship between audiences
and texts. It is in these contradictions that we can begin to identify the
cutting edge of media power where the media succeeds in enforcing
acceptance of dominant assumption which are at odds with people's own
perspectives or interests.

CONCLUSION

The news game demonstrates the aptitude with which people can reproduce media accounts – including the formats, the 'facts', the theories, the
language and the concepts common in media reports about AIDS. Most of
the audience groups showed a high degree of familiarity with basic information about HIV/AIDS, many of them also accepted some of the more
problematic ways in which the issue has been conceptualized within the
mass media. Through the language, images, 'facts' and stories drawn from
the media they 'knew' that AIDS was a certain kind of problem, affecting
certain kinds of people in a certain kind of way. In the group discussions
AIDS was often framed in terms of individual behaviour rather than
government policy, passive suffering rather than active resistance, risk
groups rather than risk activities and as a minority concern rather than an
important social issue. Mass media sources are crucial 'signifying agents' in
this process of understanding AIDS. The media have the power to set the
agenda and, in some cases, to structure people's thinking in spite of their
own 'better judgement'.

However, audiences do not indiscriminately absorb all new information,
nor do media messages about AIDS exist in a vacuum. Both media and

audiences are part of wider cultural and political contexts that may either facilitate or obstruct the acceptance of certain kinds of representations. Our research located systematic 'misreadings' of particular media messages and highlighted the fact that neither the media nor 'the audience' are single, homogeneous entities, although both may operate within a broadly defined consensus about 'reality'.

Audiences are active (although not equal) participants in the construction of meaning. They interpret what they hear and see in the context of what they already know or think. They select between (and also simultaneously retain) competing versions of reality. They sift and shift between different words (such as 'HIV' versus 'the AIDS virus'), different images (such as the helpless 'AIDS victim' or active person with AIDS) and different frameworks of thinking (for example, about 'innocent' and 'guilty victims'). Audiences selectively highlight, oppose or reconstruct statements and they are able to deconstruct dominant themes and to construct alternative accounts drawing on personal experience, political belief or a general critique of media or government sources.

If we are to understand the impact of media messages and to develop any form of constructive intervention in the communication process then we need to explore what happens to media messages as they enter into the social worlds of audiences. We need to know how people 'make sense' of new information and how they, like journalists, are actively engaged in the process of re-presentation – 'the active labour of making things mean' (Hall 1982: 64). Through this kind of detailed, empirical investigation we can explore the reasons for the success or failure of particular health education messages, we can identify the precise ways in which media power operates to construct and sustain meaning and we can locate the sites and forms of audience resistance to dominant constructions of reality.

ACKNOWLEDGEMENTS

This study was part of the AIDS Media Research Project – a three-year study set up to examine the process of production of media messages about AIDS, the content of those messages and the impact on the audience. The support of the Economic and Social Research Council is gratefully acknowledged (award no. XA44250006). I would like to thank my colleagues on the project – Peter Beharrell, David Miller and Kevin Williams – and the grant-holders – Mick Bloor, John Eldridge, Sally Macintyre and Greg Philo – for their contributions to this chapter.

NOTES

1 The ease with which people can complete the news game depends partly on the cultural relevance of that particular issue. One of our audience groups for the

AIDS project had, a few months earlier, participated in a research project on Northern Ireland involving a similar news game exercise. These young men from the west of Scotland commented that they had found it far easier to write a bulletin about Northern Ireland – 'because we know all about Ireland, we don't know about AIDS'. Northern Ireland was an issue that the religious and cultural divides in their own part of the world made particularly pertinent.

However, some issues can be so 'close to home' that people actively avoid being exposed to media coverage. For example, one woman, who was awaiting the results of an HIV antibody test said 'Every time it came on I'd switch it off or turn it over because I'm so frightened of having it myself. The reaction is to turn off' (lesbians, group 1).

2 I suspect that, had this picture shown a *black* woman and child, there might have been more statements assuming that the mother was a drug user or sexually irresponsible and blaming her for the child's infection. As Juhasz points out: 'There are two kinds of mothers depicted in [AIDS documentaries]: the minority, poor and guilty, single mothers of sick babies and the white, middle-class married mothers of innocent victims' (Juhasz, 1990:53). Juhasz describes an American programme in which the camera showed a close-up shot of two baby black girls and the image of a young Latino boy alone in a hospital bed. The voice-over stated: 'Almost all of the hundreds of children born with AIDS are *victims* of drug users: either drug-addicted mothers or mothers who got the virus from an IV-infected [*sic*] husband or lover' [emphasis original].

Such statements parallel the one statement from prison staff which presented the child as a victim of its own mother's irresponsible behaviour.

3 In choosing a picture to represent the recurring media image of a person with AIDS, we deliberately avoided using a graphic of someone who was very ill, and chose instead a picture which showed a man sitting up in bed with a woman holding his hand (she is not in nurse's uniform, her relationship to him is ambiguous). However, this did not prevent people producing statements about imminent death, nor did it prevent many from assuming that the man was gay:

> *Resp. 1*: I don't think its his wife. I think he is gay . . . I take that as an image of the West Coast of the United States. To me he's gay.
> *Resp. 2*: That's right.
> *Resp. 1*: That's right, he's gay . . . I just immediately saw that and thought 'gay guy with AIDS'.
>
> (family group)

4 Racism is a similarly powerful (and compounding) influence on audience 'readings' and encourages a particular range of associations with images of black people. In one of the few groups which did not at first associate the photograph of black women, men and children with the theory that AIDS came from Africa they still produced very definite associations none the less. They identified the picture as showing 'a Third World country' and associated it with 'a South Africa story' or news reports of famine. We have argued elsewhere that such pre-existing associations may provide fertile ground for accepting media statements about Africa being the source and hotbed of HIV infection (see Kitzinger and Miller 1992).

5 This woman's casual inclusion of lesbians as one of the 'types' of people who irresponsibly 'spread AIDS' is merely one illustration of the widespread popular belief that lesbians are a 'high-risk group' (Brook 1988). The source of this belief seems partly due to the fact that the media sometimes talk about lesbians and gay men in the same breath in relation to AIDS. It may also be linked to the media's

use of the term 'homosexual' both in its accurate generic sense and in a male-specific way (Hamilton 1988). However, it also indicates how audiences are able to 'read between the lines' of media coverage and deduce 'facts' which are never explicitly stated but are implied in the structure of the debate. The media often talk in terms of 'risk group' and link AIDS to perversity. It therefore 'made sense' to many research participants that lesbians must have a high rate of HIV infection: 'They're leading the same life as what two men are' (women living on the same Glasgow estate); 'Apart from anything else the point is this, biologically your body is not made for either homosexuality or eh, or eh, lesbianism' (retired people, group 2); 'God made two kinds of sex, male and female. They go together. He didn't mean males to go with males and females to go with females. And that's how they got it [AIDS]' (SACRO clients, group 2).

6 If the generic use of the term 'body fluids' were alone responsible for the confusion about the dangers of saliva one would expect similar confusion to be expressed about another body fluid – tears. However, this was not the case. No one suggested that tears were dangerous. This may be partly because tears are not perceived as a potential weapon that may be ejected from one person's body on to another's. Tears also carry particular affective associations (joy/sorrow/regret). It may also be that tears, unlike saliva, are not seen as contaminating and polluting in and of themselves. Tears are a relatively 'clean' and 'pure' body fluid.

7 Other reasons for arguing that you can not 'catch AIDS' from saliva included: first, deduction: 'You can't get AIDS easily from a drinking glass . . . Saturday night, last order has just been called, they're running out of glasses – wham – they don't wash them – if it's that easy to catch . . . we'd all be dead' (prisoners, group 5). Second, taking their cue from the behaviour of AIDS buddies they've seen on the media: 'These volunteers are on the spot, you see them kissing AIDS patients . . . and they don't seem frightened. So I don't think it could be passed on that way' (women with children attending playgroup, group 2). Third, distrust of alternative sources which argue that saliva is dangerous. One prison officer, for example, had come across the theories of Masters and Johnson which received extensive media coverage during the early part of 1989. He referred to the 'world sex expert' who wrote a book saying you could get it from saliva. However, he dismissed their point of view – 'they don't tell you always the whole truth, they tell you a bit of it because it sells books or it gets attention'. He prefers to trust 'medical books' because 'they don't scare people they just tell them the facts' (prison officer in charge of prisoners, group 5). Fourth, other sources of information over and above the mass media. Some research participants had also been exposed to very specific education material stressing that saliva was unlikely to be dangerous, for example, the prison video shown to staff and inmates.

8 Subsequent to writing this chapter massive attention was given to a 'home-grown' case of a 'vengeful AIDS carrier'. Under headlines such as 'Sex bomb: AIDS man infects 4 women in revenge rampage' (*Daily Mirror*, 23 June 1992) and 'AIDS maniac on Killer sex spree' (*Sun*, 23 June 1992) the media reported the case of a Birmingham man who allegedly infected several women knowing that he had HIV.

9 The interplay between stigma, social control and the revenge theme is also evident in discourses surrounding other illnesses, including VD (Brandt 1985) and typhoid (for example as personified in 'Typhoid Mary'). During the Great Plague in 1665 Defoe reported that 'there was a seeming propensity or a wicked inclination in those that were infected to infect others'. Defoe goes on to discuss the various contemporary theories about why this should be so. But he, himself concludes, that this presumed propensity was not really true: 'I say that the thing

is not really so, but that it was a general complaint raised by the people inhabiting the outlying villages against the citizens to justify or at least excuse, those hardships and severities' (Defoe 1988: 167–8). (I am indebted to Mick Bloor for drawing my attention to this passage.)

10 Parental obligations do not *have* to be interpreted in this way. Not all the women acquiesced to the perspective discussed here and the ideology of maternal love can be used to articulate and justify commitments to broader social reforms. See, for example, the struggles over definitions of 'good mothering' in relation to women's campaigns for nuclear disarmament (for example, at the Greenham Common peace camp). However, the ways in which the rhetoric of maternal love ('you put your own flesh and blood first') can be used to excuse oneself from fulfilling wider social obligations vividly exposes the dangers of sentiments, such as those expressed by Margaret Thatcher, that there is no such thing as society, only individuals and families. It is also particularly ironic in view of widespread accusation that those without children are somehow inherently less moral and more selfish. This idea has often been implicit in media coverage of AIDS, but was most outrageously articulated in an article in the *Guardian* by Rupert Haselden. He wrote that because gay people are 'unable to reproduce' (*sic*) we are inherently irresponsible and lack any ability to see beyond our own individual existence:

> There is an inbuilt fatalism to being gay. Biologically maladaptive, unable to reproduce, our futures are limited to individual existence and what the individual makes of it. Without the continuity of children we are self-destructive, living for today because we have no tomorrow.
>
> (*Guardian*, 7 September 1991)

REFERENCES

Brandt, A. (1985) *No Magic Bullet: A social history of Venereal Disease in the United States since 1880*, Oxford: Oxford University Press.

Briggs, R. (1977) *Fungus the Bogeyman*, Harmondsworth: Puffin/Penguin.

Brook, L. (1988) 'The public's response to AIDS', in R. Jowell, S. Witherspoon and L. Brook (eds) *British Social Attitudes, the 5th report*, Aldershot: Gower.

Campling, J. (1981) *Images of Ourselves: women with disabilities talking*, London: Routledge.

Carter, E. and Watney, S. (eds) (1989) *Taking Liberties: AIDS and cultural politics*, London: Serpents Tail.

Defoe, D. (1988) *A Journey of the Plague Years*, Harmondsworth: Penguin.

Delacoste, F. and Alexander, P. (eds) (1988) *Sex Work*, London: Virago.

Diamond, E. and Bellitto, C. (1986) 'The great verbal coverup: prudish editing blurs the facts of AIDS', *Washington Journalism Review* 8 March: 38–42.

Edgar, T., Hammond, S. and Freimuth, V. (1989) 'The role of the mass media and interpersonal communication in promoting AIDS-related behavioral change', *AIDS and Public Policy Journal* 4(1): 3–9.

Ford, N. (1991) *The Socio-sexual Lifestyles of Young People in the South West of England*, Exeter: South Western Regional Health Authority/Institute of Population Studies, University of Exeter.

Hall, S. (1982) 'The rediscovery of ideology: return of the repressed in media studies', in M. Gurevitch (ed.) *Culture, Society and the Media*, London: Routledge: 56–89.

Hamilton, M. (1988) 'Masculine generic terms and misperception of AIDS risk', *Journal of Applied Social Psychology* 18(14) 1222–40.

Holland, J., Ramazanoglu, C., Scott, S., Sharpe, S. and Thomson, R. (1990) 'Sex, gender and power: young women's sexuality in the showdown of AIDS', *Sociology of Health and Illness* 12(3): 36–50.

Juhasz, A. (1990) 'The contained threat: women in mainstream AIDS documentary', *Journal of Sex Research* 27(1): 25–46.

Kitzinger, J. (1990) 'Audience understandings of AIDS media messages: a discussion of methods', *Sociology of Health and Illness* 12(3): 319–35.

—— (1991) 'Judging by appearances: audience understandings of the look of someone with HIV', *Journal of Community and Applied Social Psychology* 1(2): 155–63.

Kitzinger, J. and Miller, D. (1992) 'African AIDS', in P. Aggleton, P. Davies and C. Hart (eds) *AIDS: Rights, Risk and Reason*, London: Falmer Press.

McQueen, D., Robertson, B. and Nisbet, L. (1991) *AIDS-Related Behaviours. Provisional Data from the RUHBC CATI Survey. No 26. Nov/Dec 1990*, Edinburgh: Research Unit in Health and Behavioural Change, University of Edinburgh.

Miller, D. (forthcoming) *The Struggle over and the Impact of Media Portrayals of Northern Ireland*, Glasgow: University of Glasgow.

Philo, G. (1990) *Seeing and Believing*, London: Routledge.

Seiter, E., Borchers, H., Kreutzner, C. and Warth, E. W. (1991) *Remote Control: Television, Audiences and Cultural Power*, London: Routledge.

Shilts, R. (1987) *And The Band Played On: Politics, people and the AIDS epidemic*, New York: St Martin's Press.

Watney, S. (1987) *Policing Desire: Pornography, AIDS and the media*, London: Methuen.

Chapter 12

The light at the end of the tunnel
The mass media, public opinion and th Vietnam War*

Kevin Williams

The Vietnam War is often used to demonstrate the power of the mass media to mobilize public opinion. The MacBride Report, for example, refers to the war as one of 'the most recent examples of the press's ability to unearth facts, to forge opinion and to encourage the people to act' (MacBride 1981: 197). Many Americans blame the media for 'losing' the war. Hawks and doves, despite their different perspectives, subscribe to this view. For hawks the media turned the people against the war by misrepresenting what was going on in Vietnam. Some argue that misrepresentation was the product of the media's bias against the military effort. Robert Elegant advances this position: 'Never before Vietnam had the collective policy of the media – and no less stringent a term will serve – sought by graphic and unremitting distortion to bring about the victory of the enemies of the correspondent's own side' (1979: 26). Others argue that misrepresentation was not so much a product of political bias but the result of a lack of professionalism among the correspondents. Inaccuracy and distortion reflected 'inexperience' and 'immaturity'. Reporters were described as 'young men in a hurry, not willing or not having the time to check the facts' (cited in Mercer, Mungham and Williams 1987: 240).

For opponents of the war the media were decisive not because they misrepresented the war but because they reported war as it was. The advent of television and the lack of formal censorship allowed the media to present a vivid and unfettered picture of the carnage and destruction. A vice president of ABC Television is reported as saying at the time: 'By showing war in its stinking reality, we have taken away the glory and shown negotiation is the only way to solve international problems' (cited in Epstein 1975: 211). The conventional wisdom is that the mass media, by representing or misrepresenting the war, had a profound impact on public opinion, turning it against the war and thereby clearing the way for the eventual communist victory.

This view is firmly etched in the popular memory. It has become the dominant paradigm for understanding media–military–government relations in the postwar period. The handling of information during the

Falklands conflict was motivated by such a perception (see Harris 1983: 65–6; House of Commons, Select Defence Committee Report 1982). Israeli policy towards the foreign media during the invasion of the Lebanon in 1982 was also haunted by the spectre of Vietnam (see Mercer, Mungham and Williams 1987: 261–91) and, nearly ten years after the last American soldier left Saigon, the Reagan administration, with the experience of the war firmly in mind, excluded the media from the initial period of the United States invasion of the tiny island of Grenada (see Block and Mungham 1989).

The Gulf War was a deliberate attempt to wash away the stain of Vietnam. George Bush and his military commanders had learned the 'lessons' of Vietnam and were determined that the conduct of the war would not be affected by adverse public opinion. By careful management and control of the news media (see Fisk 1991) the Bush administration sought to prevent horrific pictures of death and carnage reaching the American public. For observers such as Phillip Knightley these efforts marked a new and sinister development in the history of censorship. Not only did the administration seek to manipulate information to ensure support for the war but it also attempted 'to alter public perceptions of the nature of war itself, particularly the fact that civilians die in war' (Knightley 1991: 5).

If the Vietnam experience is seen in terms of the media's power to influence public perceptions, it is also seen as confirming the media as the 'fourth estate'. The conventional wisdom places emphasis on an adversarial relationship between the media and the government. The picture of the war painted is that of the media's reporting running counter to the statements of those in positions of authority. Journalism is represented as an effective interrogator and investigator of official policy. The media were in this sense never 'on team'.

This chapter argues that the actual impact of the media coverage of the war was not as clear-cut as this simple view implies. There are questions to be raised about the kind of pictures the media presented of the fighting. Television, in particular, operated under considerable technical and practical constraints and doubts can be raised about whether the resulting film gave any sense of the horrors and brutality of the war. Most importantly, there is the explanation the media gave for what was happening in Vietnam. For most of the war the media, it will be argued, shared the same framework for understanding events in South-East Asia as the government. Only after public opinion had moved decisively against the war did the media begin to regularly challenge the official explanation.

The change in the reporting, however, was not a response to developments in public opinion but rather a reflection of the increasing fragmentation of the official perspective on the war. In Vietnam there was a lack of political leadership and confused and uncertain objectives. Differences that existed inside the political establishment were exposed as the war progressed and the White House found it increasingly difficult to set the agenda for the media. The failure to provide a dominant story-line led journalists to look elsewhere to make sense of what was happening. The Tet crisis in March 1968 was a critical point in this process. For the American armed forces it was a triumph. For the Johnson administration it was a major set-back. Tet shattered the already faltering credibility of the government's explanation of events. From Tet until the final withdrawal of United States troops in 1973 the media were more sceptical of the official view. Even in this period it is possible to exaggerate the critical stance of the media. Media coverage was perhaps a significant factor in determining the fate of Lyndon Johnson's presidency (see Braestrup 1977; Hallin 1986), but the reporting – or rather lack of reporting – of the invasion of Cambodia in 1970 could be described as the low point in the media's performance in Vietnam. Up until 1968 the media – with a few notable exceptions – did report the war largely as the government wanted it reported. From 1968 it increasingly challenged the official perspective. However, this challenge was limited and determined by the debate which took place within Washington rather than throughout America.

THE LIVING-ROOM WAR

In reporting the war the media took 'many forms, many outlets and many viewpoints' (Braestrup 1977) and any assessment of the coverage must take into account that the media do not form a monolithic entity. However, Vietnam was significant in media terms because it was the 'first television war'. Those who argue that the media played a crucial role in America's first military reversal focus on the role of television. This is understandable. In the 1960s television established itself as the main source of information for the American public. It also became the most believed medium by the majority of Americans. These statistics had an impact on those looking to account for the erosion of public support for the war. They saw a correlation between the outcome of the war and the way in which the public learned about it; that they were learning about war in a different way was regarded as significant. Two particular aspects of television's reporting were highlighted. First, television as a visual medium could show the brutality and horror of war in a way in which magazines and newspapers could not. It brought war to people in a more vivid and direct manner. That most people's recollections of the war are dominated by images from our television screens – the execution of a Vietcong suspect in a Saigon street, the little girl, burned by napalm, running down a country road or the United States marine using his cigarette lighter to set fire to some peasant huts – is seen as attesting to the impact of television. Second, television by its nature depends on sensation, spectacle and drama to hold its audience. Such requirements are found in stories which dwell on conflict and scandal – a 'bad news syndrome'. Television, in the words of one knighted for his services to broadcasting, is more concerned with 'emotion rather than intellect' and 'exposure rather than elucidation' (Day 1985). The constant outpouring of negative stories concerning American involvement in Vietnam and the failure to provide any background to this involvement is seen as a major cause of the public's alienation. Thus it is argued the war was not lost in the fields of Vietnam but in the living-rooms of America.

The data gathered to test this hypothesis is far from conclusive. Setting aside the problem of measuring public responses through opinion polls (see Entman and Paletz 1982; Mueller 1973), poll data on the impact of TV tends to point to an opposite conclusion. For example, in 1967 a nationwide poll conducted by Harris for *Newsweek* found 64 per cent of the sample saying that TV coverage had made them more supportive of the United States effort in Vietnam; only 26 per cent said it had intensified their opposition to the war. *Newsweek* concluded, 'TV has encouraged a decisive majority of viewers to support the war' (cited in Epstein 1975: 217). It is possible to accept that the nightly presentation of young American boys fighting and dying for their country could have stirred patriotic sentiment and caused the public to react more sympathetically to the military effort. In 1972 another *Newsweek* poll found the American public had developed a tolerance of the brutality and horror of war (Knightley 1975: 411). The findings of this poll point to TV deadening public sensitivity to war. Michael Arlen, who is credited with coining the term 'living-room war', supports the notion that television could have made the war 'less real' to its audience:

> It seems to me that by the same process they are made less real – diminished in part by the physical size of the television screen, which for all the industry's advances still shows one a picture of men, three inches tall shooting other men three inches tall and trivialised, or at least tamed, by the cosy alarums of the household.
>
> (Arlen 1968: 8)

Charles Mohr points out that a more direct experience of war does not necessarily produce a decline in the will to prosecute a war. He gives the example of the London Blitz which did not make the people of London less willing to fight. Similarly, the bombing of North Vietnam did not lead to a collapse of the will to fight. Mohr notes Americans appear unaware that 'most wars literally, not merely photographically, go through people's living rooms' (cited in Mercer, Mungham and Williams 1987: 225).

The conventional wisdom assumes that television has a simple and direct impact on the viewer's beliefs and behaviour. It holds to a 'hypodermic model' of media effects. The message is injected into the public's veins with a corresponding change in attitude and action. While such a model exerts a hold over common-sense views of the media, it is not certain that the audience responds in the manner depicted by the hypodermic model. Audience responses are complex and often contradictory. Viewers often perceive what they want to perceive in the images pouring out of their TV screens. They select what fits in with their own opinions and reject or reinterpret views which are at variance with their own. There is certainly evidence to point to audiences picking out what they wanted from the Vietnam coverage to reinforce their position on the war. A 1968 survey, for example, found 75 per cent of respondents who considered themselves 'hawks' believed that Walter Cronkite, the CBS news anchorman, was also a hawk. A similiar number of 'doves' saw Cronkite as a dove (Hallin 1986: 101). Another study in the same year concluded that TV coverage tended to reinforce previously held beliefs: 'few people say that their attitudes toward the war have been changed by the nightly fare of violence on TV' (*US News and World Report* 1968). People with differing stances and opinions on the war could thus find material in the TV coverage to support their own views. This meant that even if TV was 'always seeking and getting pictures that hurt the military' (Robinson 1977) or if there was an 'anti defense bias in network programs' (Lefever 1974) it did not mean the audience was influenced to be less supportive of the war.

There is also evidence to suggest the audience pays less attention to the content of television than any other media. In the 1970s a study found 50 per cent of those tested could not recall any of the stories from a broadcast they had just watched (cited by Hallin 1986: 107). There is data to show that Vietnam stories were of more interest to the viewer, but still a large number of them did not recollect the content of these stories. At a conscious level it appears people do not pay close attention to television content. Newspapers and other forms of the print media, it can be argued, have more influence on their audience as readers have to pay more attention and spend more time and effort reading them. With television becoming the main source of information during the Vietnam War it is possible to say Americans learned less about this war than they had about previous wars.

It is not only the manner in which the audience interpreted the images of the Vietnam War that is open to doubt. There is doubt about the kind of images television served up. Combat or 'bang-bang' footage did dominate TV screens but this did not, in Michael Arlen's words, present Americans with 'goyaesque images in their living rooms' (Arlen 1982). Rather there was 'a near total absence on nightly network news broadcasts of any explicit reality of war – certainly of any blood and gore or even the pain of combat' (ibid.). The image television presented for most of the war – at least up until Tet in 1968 – is described as:

a nightly stylised, generally distracted, overview of a disjointed conflict which was composed mainly of scenes of helicopters landing, tall grass blowing in the helicopter wind, American soldiers fanning out over a hillside on foot, rifles at the ready, with now and then (on the sound-track) a far off ping or two, and now and then (as a visual grand finale) a column of dark, billowing smoke, a half a mile away, invariably des-cribed as a burning Vietcong ammo dump.

(ibid.)

In the early years of the war there was 'little shooting, little killing or little death' on the TV screens of America. TV presented a sanitized picture of combat (Esptein 1975; Hallin 1986; Knightley 1975). The lack of blood and gore was due in part to self-censorship inside network newsrooms. There was a policy not to show graphic pictures of American casualties unless the families of those concerned had been notified by the Pentagon. Editors were instructed to delete excessively bloody bits and they were obliged to give warnings before pieces of film likely to cause offence. The result was to introduce caution in handling film and, according to Fred Friendly, a former head of CBS news, to 'shield the audience from the true horror of war' (Friendly 1970).

The primary reason, however, for the lack of bloody images in the early years was the nature of the war itself. Much of the war was fought at night when TV cameras could not operate. The typical military operation had little direct contact with the enemy. There were few set battles before the Tet offensive in 1968. This is not to say Vietnam was not, at this stage, a 'nasty little war' but that its nature mitigated against capturing it on film. Reporters had to go out and look for the war. In the case of television this posed particular problems. TV camera crews at this time were limited in their mobility. They had to carry around more than 30 pounds of equip-ment. Technical advances in the late 1960s, in particular, the introduction of new lightweight equipment, meant television was better able to film on-the-spot reports. However, the most significant technical development was the introduction of satellite stations in 1968. This made it possible to screen film the same day it was shot in the field. Prior to 1968 film had to be flown back to the west coast for transmission. This resulted in it ending up on the network news two or more days after the event. The lapse caused the production of 'timeless pieces'; film reports that would not date. Hence the vast amount of footage of helicopters taking off and landing and artillery barrages. Technological advances made it possible to produce more vivid pictures of the war.

The images of the war were not as bloody as the conventional wisdom holds. Major-General Winant Sidle, former chief of information in Saigon, said, after reviewing the coverage, that it was not as bad as he had believed it to be at the time (Mercer, Mungham and Williams 1987: 232). This could mean that we have become more used to violence on our TV screens or that a few dramatic images dominate our recollections. However, images should not be separated from the context within which they are shown. For Hallin it is the context not the pictures that is significant. He points out that the newsreels of the Second World War were sometimes graphic in their descriptions of the violence of war. However, these descriptions occurred in a context highly supportive of the overall war effort (Hallin 1986: 130). In Vietnam the images of violence and suffering, the conventional wisdom tells us, were presented within a framework highly critical of United States involvement. Yet analysis of the content of television during the war years indicates the stance taken by the medium was not consistent or constant. In the early period of the war – the 'years of commitment' from 1962 to 1967 – television, apart from a few reports of indiscriminate brutality, such as Morley Safer's report of the burning of the village of Cam Ne by United States troops, was positive and supportive of American involvement. One television producer notes: 'Until the fall of 1966 and really into 1967 the vast majority of the reporting of Vietnam was positive . . . the proponents, the hawks, very much outnumbered those on television who were criticising the war' (Lichty 1983). In 1963 television did express criticism of the South Vietnamese regime. Like the press, the networks were hostile to what they saw as the corruption and ineffiency of the government of Ngo Dinh Diem (see Browne 1964). Opposition to Diem was not, however, the same as opposition to the war. Much of the criticism emanated from the desire to see the war prosecuted more effectively. Following Diem's ousting by the Americans one network newscaster expressed the hope that 'we can now get on with the war' (cited in Epstein 1975: 220). Positive reporting of the war can be found in TV's coverage of the key event in the escalation of United States involvement in the war in 1964 – the Gulf of Tonkin incident (see Hallin 1986: 70–5; Stillman 1970–1). Overall, the tone of the TV coverage up to 1967 was optimistic and supportive; it appeared as 'an appendage to the war effort or a channel of official reassurance in the face of growing frustration' (Entman and Paletz 1982: 185).

It was the Tet crisis that brought about change in the context within which the war was reported. The Tet offensive in March 1968 saw the Vietcong launch a wave of attacks against the cities of the south. For the first time they felt strong enough to come out of the shadows and take the fighting into the streets. This meant the war came to the reporters. Previously journalists had to go and look for the war; for camera crews this meant being taken by military information officers to preselected sites. But with Tet, 'merely by stepping out of their hotels correspondents found themselves willy nilly in the midst of bloody fighting' (Epstein 1975: 220). Tet occurred in front of the reporters' own eyes. The picture initially was one of confusion with American forces on the defensive throughout South Vietnam. The images thrown up in the confusion were some of the most vivid and powerful of the whole war. Despite the eventual military victory of the United States forces, Tet proved a psychological shock for those inside the newsrooms of America. The impression of progress established in the years prior to Tet was shattered. Walter Cronkite expressed the shock of many editors when on hearing about the offensive he said: 'What the hell's going on. I thought we were winning the war' (cited in Entman and Paletz 1982: 186). The result was a change in the overall tone of the coverage. Military activities still dominated the output of TV, but now they were accompanied by 'the rhetoric of stalemate not victory' (Epstein 1975: 225). As the stalemate wore on television started to look at other aspects of the war, in the process discovering the Vietnamese people. Up until Tet television had focused on the American presence – 'our boys over there' type coverage. From Tet onwards the suffering of people caught up in a situation over which they had no control became part of the television news agenda and arguably produced some of the most compassionate reporting of the war. Ultimately peace negotiations began to replace combat footage. Fewer action pieces were shown between 1969 and 1973 even though there were as many casualties in this period as there were in the years prior to Tet. From 1969 onwards the TV networks showed less interest in Vietnam. The number of stories declined (Entman and Paletz 1982). However, the theme, as one senior producer told his Saigon bureau at the time, was 'We're on our way out' (Westin 1982: 14).

A comparison between the development of public opinion on the war and the changing nature of the coverage seems to suggest that the most critical reporting took place after public opposition to the war had become a 'majority opinion'. John Mueller (1973) has collated the evidence of all the polls taken throughout the war. Until 1965 few Americans were aware of the existence of the war. In 1965 the large-scale commitment of United States ground forces increased public awareness. Initial approval was high. In August 1965 approval for the war effort stood at 61 per cent in favour with opposition at 24 per cent. In 1966 support began a 'slow and somewhat ambiguous decline' while opposition rose at 'a slightly faster rate'. In May 1967 50 per cent declared for the war while 37 per cent were opposed. From July 1967 support for the war began to crumble and by October more people were against the war than for it – 44 per cent for, 46 per cent against. These figures remained at around this level until mid-1968 despite a number of so-called momentous events – the Tet crisis, the replacement of Westmoreland as commander of the United States forces in Vietnam, President Johnson's decision to stand down and the opening of peace talks. The majority of the American people were opposed to the war long before Tet. The Tet offensive actually produced a small surge of support – a 'rallying around the flag in time of crisis' factor. From mid-1968 a rapid decline in support set in and by mid-1971 the same number of people opposed the war as had supported it in August 1965.

Polls, however, hide almost as much as they reveal. They do not show the intensity with which people hold opinions. In particular, they mask the variety and shades of opinion that exist within the 'public'. Polls treat the public as a homogeneous entity, simply the sum of all the individuals who compose it. This is the 'public' addressed by politicians and promoted by the mass media. Public opinion in this sense is the total of all individual opinions, each carrying the same weight. However, as the MacBride Report points out, 'Public opinion is not simply the sum of individual opinion, but rather a continuing process of comparing and contrasting opinions based on a variety of knowledge and experience' (MacBride 1981: 195). Thus it is more appropriate to talk about 'publics'. Dissatisfaction with the Vietnam War developed at different rates and in different ways within American society, among young and old, black and white, republican and democrat, conservative and liberal, college educated and high school educated, Congress and the presidency, general and soldier and so forth. In this world of overlapping publics certain opinion holders can be seen as being more influential than others. For the mass media those in position of authority are more 'newsworthy' and are thus guaranteed more access to the channels of communication than ordinary men and women. The change in the nature of television coverage can be explained more satisfactorily in terms of the medium's relationship with 'establishment' opinion than 'popular' opinion. Television became more critical when serious disagreement on the war entered the living-rooms of the American political establishment and the corridors of government.

FOLLOWING THE STORY

It is a fundamental tenet of modern journalism that the media and the state are separate. Vietnam is regarded as an example of the media's independence. This claim is accompanied by a recitation of the 'tensions' that existed between between news organizations and government during the war. Kennedy's attempt to persuade the *New York Times* to recall its correspondent, David Halberstam, from Saigon, Morley Safer's report for CBS about the burning down by United States marines of the village of Cam Ne, Walter Cronkite's declaration against the war after Tet and the publication of the Pentagon Papers are all used as illustrations of the 'adversarial relationship'. The regular daily briefings for reporters in Saigon, the so-called 'Five O'Clock Follies', are seen as encapsulating media-state relations. These briefings are often characterized as cut and thrust affairs between military briefers who failed to convey the realities of battle, played up enemy losses and minimized United States set-backs and probing journalists who fought to report the truth in the face of official deception.

Tensions between officials and reporters in Saigon did indeed exist;

however, they can be seen as being relatively superficial. While journalists might have grumbled about news management at the 'Follies', most of them wrote up as straight news what came out of these briefings. It is for this reason David Halberstam can describe the 'Follies' as a 'success' in terms of news management. For most of the war the media shared the perspective of the state. As Hallin states:

> From 1961 to 1967, for all the tensions between the media and the government, for all the mythology of the press as an adversary or watchdog of the state, the independence of the American news media . . . was very limited. Even on an issue as explosive as Vietnam, an undeclared war in a distant and often hostile land, without censorship or extensive restrictions on access, the media was remarkably docile.
>
> (Hallin 1986: 162)

Tet did initiate greater scepticism towards the official version of events. The confusion and disarray within the political establishment allowed the media to become more independent from their élite informants; however, Tet did not result in a fundamental break between the media and the state. What Dorman (1985) has described as the media's 'statist inclinations' were apparent in the reporting of dissent. Coverage of the political debate over the war widened after Tet but there were still opinions – in particular, those associated with the anti-war movement – which were regarded as unworthy of consideration. The media in this period played a role in laying down the parameters of dissent.

In explaining how the media act as an instrument of those in power we cannot simply focus on conspiracies or editors taking their orders from those in positions of authority. News management is a product of the process of accommodation that occurs between the media and the environment within which they have to operate. Media institutions in America are formally independent of government. This independence has, however, been obtained at a price. In return the media have had to guarantee privileged access to those in positions of authority. This is reflected in the professional practices of journalism. Today's news-gathering routines tie journalism to the 'powers that be'. News-gathering is organized around official sources of information and the activities of those in positions of authority make up much of the news.

Other informal constraints tie the media more closely to the corridors of power. The media in America are big business. Television has, for example, been one of the country's most profitable industries over the last few decades. Fear of losing commercial sponsorship and pressures from local TV stations who purchase network programmes lead to caution in handling controversial issues. Editors cited the pressure from local affiliates as being greater than from any other source during the war (Epstein 1975: 211). Corporate profit-making has implications for reporting. As

Dorman says of the behaviour of journalists, there is 'an intuitive assumption that for corporate journalism to reach a mass audience it must rule out taking a strong adversarial stance against the state' (Dorman 1985: 121). Media institutions are part of the established power structure of society through their ideological orientation. This is apparent in the way in which America perceives the outside world. Perceptions have been shaped by the ideology of the Cold War. Hence the language of the Cold War permeated the reports from Vietnam. The North Vietnamese were labelled as the 'Reds'.[1] There were, as Hallin notes, repeated references by journalists to the 'battle for democracy' or the fight against 'communist aggression'. Seeing the events in South-East Asia through the prism of the Cold War meant seeing them in 'a framework of understanding that made fundamental questioning of American policy essentially unthinkable' (Hallin 1986: 110).

The media thus operate within a web of informal constraints that tie them to established political authority. Corporate profits, Cold War ideology as well as direct pressure from government were all factors that influenced the reporting of the Vietnam War. However, it was the news-gathering routines that most clearly attracted the media to the activities of the powerful.

The modern media adhere to the conventions of 'objective journalism'. The role of the journalist is perceived as that of a 'neutral observer'. He or she is expected to be detached from events. Personal judgement should not influence reporting. She or he is required – usually by law in the case of broadcasters – to be impartial; free from partisan interests, including political parties, and commercial concerns as well as the news organization worked for. In practice this means that in reporting events the journalist should report views and opinions in a 'balanced' manner. The conventions of objective journalism can be summed up by the terms – balance, neutrality and impartiality.

These conventions are closely bound up with the way in which news is gathered, and, in particular, the sources of that news. Journalists rarely observe many of the events they report on; not that all news is observable, in any case. They usually obtain information from others; in this sense news is 'not what happened but what someone says has happened or will happen' (Sigal 1973: 69). The vital component in the news-gathering process is thus the source of information; in fact it is often the source who does the reporting. Sources need to be reliable, regular and credible suppliers of information. The main pressure on the reporter is to produce stories for the news desk on a daily basis, so a regular flow of information is vital. Organizations which can devote considerable money and resources to the production of information are likely to be good sources. Regularity of the provision of information has to be accompanied by reliability. Working under the tyranny of the deadline limits the time the reporter has to check the reliability of information. Sources which let reporters down in the quality of the information they supply are less likely to be used again. To mitigate against the lack of reliability sources are selected who have a high degree of credibility. The more authoritative the source, the higher the credibility. Authoritativeness is often associated with those who hold high positions in leading institutions. As Walter Lippmann puts it:

> The established leaders of any organisation have great natural advantages. They are believed to have better sources of information. The books and papers are in their offices. They took part in the important conference. They met the important people. They have responsibility.
>
> (cited in Sigal 1973: 69)

News is primarily about the activities and views of important people. Human interest stories do focus on ordinary people but the 'hard news' is dominated by those in positions of authority.

The institution best able to meet these requirements is government. News-gathering is as a result centred on the institutions of government. The relationship between the public official and the reporter has in a sense been institutionalized with the establishment of news 'beats' at every major department of state. There are press corps at the White House, the Pentagon, the State Department as well as at other branches of government, the Congress and Supreme Court. Public officials are the main source of news. Leon Sigal found that of 2,850 stories that appeared on the front pages of the *New York Times* and the *Washington Post* in a period between 1949 and 1973 public officials were the source for 78 per cent of them (Sigal 1973: 124–5). American government officials accounted for over half of them. Besides contributing the bulk of information for stories from Washington, they served as the source for many stories from around the world. They, for example, accounted for 54 per cent of the stories from Saigon. Breaking down government into its various branches Sigal found that officials from the executive branch predominated. This reflects the expansion of the news-making capacities of the presidency in the postwar period. As a source the president is now without rival; whatever he says, significant or not, true or not, comprehensible or not, is reported. Sigal also found that most of the information gathered by reporters came through routine channels – that is from press releases, news conferences, daily briefings, such as the 'Follies', and official proceedings. Of the 2,850 stories, 58 per cent came through these channels. Formal interviews made up 24 per cent while informal channels, such as leaks and disclosures, constituted almost 15 per cent. The credibility of the public official in the eyes of the media was underlined by the fact that of the 405 stories in the sample with only a single source, 57 per cent were from United States government officials. In contrast, stories emanating from leaks usually had public officials as secondary sources. The news-gathering process strengthens the ties between the media and the corridors of power. It is in this sense that Tom Wicker can say that objective journalism 'always favours establishment positions and exists not least to avoid offence to them' (Wicker 1979: 39). The confidence of the White House at being able to 'use' the media was indicated in the Vietnam War by the decision of the Johnson administration to waive the last legitimate control the democratic state can impose on the media, namely the imposition of military censorship in times of national emergency.[2]

Public officials as primary providers of information exert a considerable influence over the shape of news. Dependence on routine channels means that much of the task of selecting news is left to sources. However, the official does not necessarily determine the shape of news. Commitment to balance, 'getting the other side of the story', is not simply part of the rhetoric of journalism. Journalists do search for 'balance' and this can limit the influence the official can bring to bear. However, the application of 'balance' is restricted; by and large it is only regularly exercised between 'responsible sources'. As most sources are found within the political establishment then the conventions of objective journalism are applied within these confines.

In the early years of the Vietnam War the mass media depended on two kinds of sources – public officials and the military. Hallin, from his analysis of the output of TV and the press in this period, found that most of the officials were from the executive branch. They were primarily Washington-based (Hallin 1986: 10). The ability of the White House to dominate the flow of information on the war in these early days was vital. Halberstam states that doubters on the war in the State Department made up nearly two-thirds of the high-ranking officials (Halberstam 1979: 688). These doubts were kept private, many arguing they were in a better position to change policy from within. Initially Congress had supported the decision to commit United States ground forces to Vietnam following the Gulf of Tonkin incident in 1964. The resolution which effectively committed the USA to war passed the House and Senate with only two votes against. But unease started to grow as the United States troop build-up began to increase. Few members of Congress were willing, however, to openly criticize the president. Johnson exerted considerable influence over the democratic majority in the Congress. Despite the uncertainties of some inside the corridors of power, the consensus built around the White House's perspective on the war held. The media's reporting of the war, by and large, took its cue from the waves of optimism and patriotic fervour pouring out of the White House. However, when the uncertainty began to be made more public the reporting reflected the differences within the political establishment.

Differences within the military over the prosecution of the war were apparent from the outset. The upper echelons of the United States armed forces were unhappy about the restrictions placed on the way in which the war should be fought. Some of this feeling did emerge through supporters in Congress and made it into print. Perhaps more significant in terms of the final outcome of the war was criticism to be found among the ranks of the officers in the field. These officers shared the same frustration about the restrictions placed on the use of force but were more pessimistic about the progress of the war. Some were prepared to share their frustrations with reporters. They were the source for much of the 'critical' reporting that existed at this time.

The media's reporting of the war could almost be described as a battle between two press corps – Saigon and Washington. Reporting from Saigon was generally more downbeat and pessimistic than the message coming out of Washington. This, in particular, angered the Kennedy administration which in 1962 launched an attack on the small group of reporters who made up the Saigon press corps, thereby creating one of the first myths about media–state tensions. The distinct coolness between the Saigon corps and the White House has to be put into context. Objective journalism requires balance and government officials were always given space to comment on reports from Saigon. Editors at home also relied more on their Washington press corps whose reports, based on official sources in the nation's capital, tended to be more upbeat and optimistic. Some reporters in Saigon complained of the difficulty in getting their version of events accepted by editors. Others told of reports from Washington being used to offset reports from the front (Mercer, Mungham and Williams 1987: 243). One Saigon based reporter in this period concluded: 'For years the Press corps in Vietnam was undermined by the White House and the Pentagon. Many editors ignored what their correspondents were telling them in favour of the Washington version' (cited in Knightley 1975: 376).

The reticence of editors to use material from their people in the field was not necessarily an indication of their view on the war. Most were journalists who had been weaned on the Washington beat. They had learned their journalism in the era of close co-operation between the government and media and ultimately felt more comfortable with official sources in Washington than unnamed sources in the field. A clear hierarchy existed – the president was more credible and authoritative as a source than a middle-ranking army officer. Reporters in Saigon had to go to greater lengths to substantiate their 'facts'; editors would not defend Saigon stories unless they were convincingly supported by evidence. This was far from easy. There were regular army and CIA investigations of reporters' sources and, according to Halberstam, 'resident reporters found a great deal of time and effort went into protecting sources' (1979: 628). The military as an hierarchical institution had the power to dissuade its members from talking to reporters. For the bulk of the war the media found it difficult to interview enlisted men. Such factors resulted in most of these sources remaining anonymous; they could not appear on television or be directly quoted in print. Following stories which carried criticism of the official version of events therefore required a great deal of commitment on behalf of the journalist. And even when the story did appear it was more often than not tucked away on the inside pages of the newspaper or as an item in the middle of a bulletin.

Much of the reporting from Saigon in these years was not critical of the war itself but of the way in which it was being fought (Knightley 1975: 380). The stories reflected the concerns of their sources that the war 'wasn't working'. There were stories about lack of equipment, mismanagement, wrong tactics and the poor quality of the South Vietnamese forces. Despite the outcry from the White House such stories could be seen as being part of a legitimate debate – in Hallin's words, they were part of a 'sphere of legitimate controversy'. Voices more hostile to the war fell outside this sphere and were not reported. Editors saw them as not 'newsworthy'; they had no official standing. For example, there were the 'teach ins' on college campuses against the war. Hallin found only three occasions on which such events appeared on the front page of the *New York Times* before 1966 (Hallin 1986: 88). On each occasion the news angle was the appearance of a member of the Johnson administration. A story on McGeorge Bundy's appearance is typical. The first several paragraphs are devoted to his defence of the administration's policy and the headline read 'Bundy says US must block reds'. Hallin's study of the content of the United States media between 1961 and 1966 indicates that the vast majority of the coverage of the war was favourable to the administration. What criticism there was reflected a debate within the corridors of power over the best way to prosecute the war. Away from this debate little attention was paid to popular dissent.

Public expression of dissent began to emerge from within the ranks of the establishment in February 1966 with the hearings of the Senate Foreign Relations Committee under the chair of Senator William Fulbright. Halberstam remarks that this was the first time in nearly fifteen years of national television that the new medium had given a platform to a major congressional figure to challenge the foreign policy of the United States (Halberstam 1979: 688). Halberstam may overstate the nature of Fulbright's challenge, but it did represent a major development in the escalation of opposition to the war inside the political establishment. Fulbright's decision to hold public hearings was in part a response to his frustration at the way in which the White House was able to use the media, especially television, to sell the Vietnam policy. He found it difficult, despite holding a senior position in the Senate, to gain access to television. This was in contrast to the president, the Secretary of State, the Secretary of Defense and even presidential advisers with no formal constitutional position who appeared regularly. The hearings were an attempt to gain publicity, geared as they were to the spectacle and drama of television. It represented the first direct challenge to the president's domination of the new medium of mass communication.

For the networks the hearings became a *cause célèbre*. They illustrated the 'timidity' of television in handling dissent, even when it came from 'responsible sources'. CBS initially decided to broadcast the hearings live. After running testimony from a critic and a supporter of United States policy, CBS management chose on the day an outspoken critic, George Kennan, was due to appear, to cancel the broadcasts. A rerun of *I Love Lucy* went out instead. Fred Friendly, the head of CBS News, resigned in protest. In public, the CBS management cited the cost of such broadcasts as being the major determining factor; in private they expressed worry about 'rocking the boat', 'embarrassing' the president and the 'divisive nature of the hearings' (Friendly 1967: 248). CBS also stated that Kennan's testimony was not newsworthy as 'he holds no official position'. Friendly in his letter of resignation said:

> I believed, for my part, healthy debate by responsible leaders could build national understanding of the President's position and that the spectacle of congressional leaders debating the war was far better than the epidemic of one sided teach ins and hostile demonstrations that had filled the void in the absence of national debate. In my opinion responsible debates and the subsequent Senate hearings actually deescalated the demonstrations and draft card burning that so embarrassed the Administration.
>
> (ibid: 217)

Both Friendly and CBS indicate the kind of debate television and perhaps the media in general prefer – a debate between responsible leaders; even though on this occasion they disagreed over whether Kennan fitted this category.

The Fulbright hearings proved not to be decisive in breaking up the official consensus in support of the war. However, from late 1966 to early 1967 public opinion on the war was slowly beginning to change. In response the administration stepped up its efforts to convince the public all was going well. Johnson resorted to 'Madison Avenue' techniques to sell the war to the people. Upbeat rhetoric dominated the output of what Fulbright had come to call the 'Pentagon propaganda machine'. The claims of victory and progress pumped out by the White House and the Pentagon were reported at face value. Hallin found that for all the battles and operations reported by television in the pre-Tet period 62 per cent were presented as 'US victories' and 28 per cent as successes for the other side (Hallin 1986: 162). Bailey found that despite the problems in checking the accuracy of casualty reports the TV networks labelled them as estimates for only 2 per cent of the time in their reporting between 1965 and 1970 (cited in Entman and Paletz 1982). The whole tone of the TV coverage was optimistic, depending as it did on officials whose job it was to stress optimism. According to Hallin, in terms of overall assessments of how the war was going, 79 per cent of the reports put the situation as favourable to America. From 1965 to the end of 1967 the war – as it appeared on TV – was going well for America. Hallin concludes: 'It must have been very hard in this period for the average television viewer to imagine the possibility that American arms might not ultimately be successful in Vietnam' (1986: 146).

The dependence of the United States news media on the executive branch – as well as the faith placed in the authority of the White House – enabled the Johnson administration to manage the news agenda[3] on the war up until 1968. Tet saw Johnson lose this ability; it destroyed his credibility as a source of information.

For the public at large Tet was not the 'crossover' point many believe – public opinion poll support for the war, as has been noted, had steadily declined from mid-1966. Johnson's PR campaign had succeeded in slowing down the rate of decline of public support for the war, but by Tet the majority of the American public was firmly against the war (Hallin 1986; Mueller 1973). Tet had a decisive impact not on the woman or man in the street but inside the corridors of power. There was an upheaval in the White House; many saw the events as indicating that the United States could not win the war no matter what the level of United States troop commitment in Vietnam (Herman and Chomsky 1989: 215–17). A furious debate over the future of United States policy ensued.

The administration ceased to speak with one voice – in fact for much of the Tet period it ceased to speak at all. During February and March 1968 no official line came out of the White House. President Johnson did not address the nation for two months after the start of the crisis; when he finally did it was to announce his retirement from the 1968 presidential race. He made no attempt to rally support around the White House as previous presidents had done in times of a foreign policy crisis. This was in spite of the fact that in the wake of the Vietcong's offensive opinion immediately became more supportive of the administration. Johnson let the situation drift; no coherent scenario was provided for the media. This left the stage clear for more critical voices. As Entman and Paletz state:

> Tet also destroyed the accord that normally pervades foreign policy leadership circles. Important senators – some of whom had already been expressing doubts – were emboldened to dissent by the news out of Saigon; criticism was increasingly and regularly voiced in official Washington. Even members of the Johnson administration (Defense Secretary Clark Clifford for example) conducted agonising reappraisals. With elite sources forcefully expressing dissenting views, reports could no longer convey so unified a picture.
>
> (1982: 186)

Some argue as a result that Tet was a failure of 'political leadership', a 'self inflicted wound' (Braestrup 1977). However even if Johnson had 'seized the initiative' it is not certain whether his administration would have had enough credibility left to get its message across.

For editors and news executives at home, if not most of the reporters in the field, Tet was a 'shock piled on a surprise'. Tet came in the middle of an outpouring of official optimism. Operation Success had been launched in May 1967 in response to the slipping support for the war in the polls. Johnson, as well as his commander-in-chief in Vietnam, General William Westmoreland, were high profile in this campaign. Westmoreland returned from Saigon to make a tour of the United States – as one information officer said, 'over the dead bodies of his Public Affairs advisors' who realized he was putting his credibility on the line. It was the president, however, who led from the front. His press conference of 17 November 1967 is typical of the tone of the official view prior to Tet. He summed up his views thus: 'We are making progress. We are pleased with the results . we are getting. We are inflicting greater losses than we are taking . . . overall we are going forward' (Braestrup 1977: 49). Westmoreland on his tour announced, 'I am absolutely certain that whereas in 1965 the enemy was winning, today he is certainly losing.' The administration stressed that South Vietnam was invulnerable to enemy penetration (Entman and Paletz 1982). These statements were reported as 'straight news'. Doubts did start to creep into the media reporting as the end of the year round-ups in the news magazines and the press indicated (see Braestrup 1977: 58–69). The news columns were nevertheless still full of progress and optimism as the press listened to the president's account of events. Braestrup sees the Tet experience as making 'clear the requirement for maximum candour on the part of the President and his spokes[persons] *before* crisis and for Presidential coherence *during* crisis' (ibid.: my insertion 526).

The Tet offensive thus dented the natural ties the media had with its élite informants. Many reporters felt they had been deceived. Cronkite went to Vietnam to see for himself. He came back and went on air to call for swift negotiations with North Vietnam and the end to United States escalation. It is recalled that Johnson, watching Cronkite's special documentary said, 'If I have lost Walter, then I have lost America' (cited in Jessel 1982). For some, Cronkite, like William Howard Russell in the Crimean War, had brought down the government. What was rather more pertinent was that Johnson had lost the support of official Washington, including key figures inside his own administration. He had also lost his pre-eminence as a source of information for the media, thereby reducing his administration's credibility over United States policy in Vietnam. This was reflected in the reporting of Tet and what came afterwards.

The crisis reporting of Tet, when picture and words streamed into news rooms over the satellites and wires, soon gave way to the 'normal routines' of journalism. There were now differences in the coverage of the war. First, disagreement was apparent within the government and the political élite. As the media saw disputes between the powerful as newsworthy, more criticism of the war figured in the coverage. Second, the administration's account was treated with more scepticism. The government's assessment of Tet was to be the first casualty. The United States military's success in the Tet campaign was downplayed or underestimated by the reporting (see Braestrup 1977). Third, the image of the war changed. There was still 'guts and glory' coverage, but the overwhelming theme was one of stalemate and frustration. Reporters no longer referred to it as 'our' war; it was 'the' war. After Tet, 44 per cent of reports on battles and operations were described as United States victories', 32 per cent as 'defeats' and 24 per cent 'inconclusive' (Hallin 1986: 162).

More attention was paid to those caught up in the war – the people of Vietnam. Their suffering was now recorded in some detail. However the 'discovery' of the Vietnamese people has to be put in the context of the policy of Vietnamization – handing the prosecution of the war over to the South Vietnamese – which was pursued by the newly-elected Nixon administration. The reporting of the Vietnamese was accompanied by coverage of atrocities by American soldiers. Atrocity stories did not 'fit the frame' for the reporting of Vietnam prior to Tet. Home editors wanted 'good news' about a war they thought the USA was winning. By 1969 – post-Tet – a new mood prevailed and a different story-line began to emerge. In the new climate of guilt, frustration and cynicism stories such as the My Lai massacre now fitted the frame. Even so, when My Lai was first reported the media was resistant to the story. It was not until nearly two years after the event that it was reported in any significant detail in the United States press – and only then after diligent investigations by a single reporter to gain prominence for the story (Herman and Chomsky 1989: 196–7; Knightley 1975: 391–3). Throughout the war television was far more comfortable with attributing civilian casualties to the other side (Hallin 1986: 154). Television accounted for civilian casualties committed by the North Vietnamese as part of a deliberate strategy, whereas casualties inflicted by the United States were either the result of accidents or error (ibid.: 156). But, as Knightley points out, such practices as My Lai were not an aberration but commonplace (Knightley 1975: 393–7).

From Tet onwards the United States media was more critical of the war. But it is mistaken to exaggerate the media's opposition to the war. It never became 'anti-war'. The coverage of the anti-war movement reveals the media's unease in dealing with 'popular opinion'. The media began to treat dissent in a more consistent and serious manner following the Fulbright hearings. Criticism that came from Congress and other established political institutions was treated 'with respect'. But the media were always circumspect in their reporting of the anti-war movement, even after Tet. Clear themes were identified by Hallin in his study of the TV networks coverage of the anti-war movement prior to Tet. Two themes in particular stood out: 'giving comfort to the enemy' and 'creating law and order problems' (Hallin 1986: 193–4). For example, ABC News began a report on an anti-war group in October 1965 with the sentence 'while Americans fight and die in Vietnam, there are those in this country who sympathise with the Vietcong' (ibid.: 193). The law and order theme was illustrated by a CBS report in 1967 which began: 'Anti war demonstrators in New York provoked a series of clashes today with counter demonstrators and the police' (ibid.: 194). Such reports were accompanied by film of the demonstrations, which anybody involved in CND protest in Britain now would recognize – long hair, colourful scenes and deviant behaviour. Coverage of this kind simply marginalized protest by the anti-war movement.

From 1968 onwards, when the movement became more central to mainstream political debate, more sympathetic treatment occurred. The New Hampshire presidential primary in March was crucial in bringing anti-war activists into the political mainstream through their support of the peace candidate Eugene McCarthy. McCarthy's electoral success perhaps did more to influence the media's portrayal of the anti-war movement than the Tet crisis (see Gitlin 1980). Greater respect was given to what were now described as 'earnest, clean shaven college students, full of facts not rhetoric' (Hallin 1986: 197). However, much of this coverage focused on the activities of the movement rather than its views on the war. Hallin found 64 per cent of TV film reports of the anti-war movement after the invasion of Cambodia in 1970 contained no discussion of the war. In only 16 per cent of reports of marches were extracts from speeches used (ibid.: 200). As it has been pointed out, the media, in particular television, were far more comfortable with dissent from within the establishment. Despite mounting political protests and growing public opposition to the war the debate in the media remained primarily centred on official Washington. After the New Hampshire primary 49 per cent of the criticism of the war on television came from public officials or former officials, 16 per cent from reporters in commentaries and 35 per cent from all other sources including soldiers and anti-war protesters (Hallin 1986: 201). This reflects the day-to-day power of establishment opinion to gain access to the mass media.

The election of Richard Nixon enabled the presidency to re-establish some of its credibility in the years after Tet. The reporting of the war during these years never recaptured the patriotic fervour of the Kennedy and Johnson period, but the new administration did build a new official consensus around the policy of 'peace with honor'. The reporting of the secret bombing by America of Vietnam's neutral neighbour, Cambodia, shows how far this was successful. Denials by the president and the

Secretary of State of the bombing were not challenged by the media. Only later, in the wake of Watergate when it was fashionable, was the duplicity of the Nixon White House in this matter exposed (Entman and Paletz 1982). Nixon's success was in part due to a campaign against the media, spearheaded by Vice-President Agnew. Previous administrations had brought pressure to bear on the media but always behind closed doors. Agnew went public in his media bashing (Gitlin 1980: 278). The result was a downturn in coverage of the war and increased caution in its reporting. Despite the expansion of the war into Laos and Cambodia there was less war coverage. This was also a result of a switch of tactics from a ground war to an air war, but the media's fear of losing their direct access to their primary source of information was uppermost in the minds of news executives. As Entman and Paletz (1982: 190) say of TV news: 'It is conceivable that business orientated, profit conscious network executives espoused aggressive news reporting less enthusiastically in the fearsome atmosphere Nixon and his men promoted.'

The final indication of the media's close ties with official sources came with the reporting of the conclusion of the war. This coverage clearly represented the return to the consensus between élite sources and the media over the war. There was little attempt by American TV news to examine the reasons why officials had embroiled the United States in Vietnam; no critical questioning of the basic assumptions of United States foreign policy; and no assessment of guilt and blame. Walter Cronkite's words on the fall of Saigon typify the reporting of that time:

> In Vietnam we have finally reached the end of the tunnel and there is no light. What is there, perhaps, was best said by President Ford: a war that is finished. And ahead, again to quote the President, the time has come to look forward to an agenda for the future, to unify, to bind up up the nation's wounds and to restore its health and its optimistic self confidence.
>
> (cited in Entman and Paletz 1982: 195)

Turning to the president to make sense of the war's end only emphasized the media's reliance on élite sources throughout the conflict.

CONCLUSION

The Vietnam War has perhaps provided one of the most persistent myths about the role of the media at times of armed conflict: that television coverage of war leads to a loss of public support. There is little evidence to support this view. Television did not provide a regular flow of graphic representations of the horrors of the Vietnam War. There were limits on what could be shown – mainly imposed by the networks themselves. It was not military censorship or restriction that curtailed what the public saw or heard but self-censorship inside the broadcasting media. This was, by and large, a product of the working practices of journalism, in particular the daily dependence on élite sources or informants. This dependence, as Hallin's analysis indicates, led for the most part to an acceptance of the 'the language, agenda and perspective of the political "establishment" ' (Hallin 1986: 8). However, it is important to differentiate between media – the press was able to achieve more critical distance from its sources than television. Even within television, certain formats such as news were more dependent on élite sources.

Elite sources are not always successful in their attempts to dictate the agenda. The political élite is not homogeneous and the divisions are reflected in the media's reporting. For example, in the early days of Vietnam the disagreement over how the war should be fought was a part of the media's agenda. However, such disagreement was within the boundaries of appropriate and responsible debate, in other words a debate between élite sources. The reporting of the Vietnam War did not reflect the growing opposition to the war among the public. As this opposition grew the media coverage, by and large, followed the White House's view of a war being waged successfully and effectively by the United States armed forces. It was only when divisions inside the élite concerning the very nature of the war itself emerged that the media took the cue from their informants and became more critical in their reporting. For a while in the wake of Tet the media did turn to the public to try to make sense of the war as the Johnson White House shut down its information machine. This flirtation was, however, brief. The re-establishment of a consensus among élite opinion with the election of Richard Nixon led to the reporting being redefined within the new parameters set down by official sources. In the early years of the Nixon administration the White House did have to resort to direct pressure to bring the media back into line, but by the early 1970s it was clear that normal service had been resumed.

NOTES

* This chapter is a revised version of a paper presented at the British Association for the Advancement of Science Conference, Belfast, August 1987.
1 The networks were sensitive to the use of such labels. After 1966 CBS and NBC dropped the term. ABC followed a couple of years later (Hallin 1986: 141).
2 There were also practical and technical reasons for the decision not to impose censorship in Vietnam. For a discussion of these see Mercer, Mungham and Williams (1987: 250–4).
3 Distinction in this period should be made between different media forms and outlets. Within TV there was a distinction between nightly news and the documentaries produced by the networks. Some of the documentaries were more critical of the war. Fear of alienating the White House led to the introduction at CBS, for example, of the careful scrutiny of documentaries. The effect of this

was 'to curb extreme attitudes' (Entman and Paletz 1982). Although the front pages of the prestige press and the news magazines were dominated by the official view of the war, inside questions were beginning to be asked in late 1966 and 1967. In opinion pieces and news analysis round-ups critical reporting occurred. News analysis columns which are a feature of the United States press today were not as prevalent in the 1960s.

REFERENCES

Arlen, Michael (1968) *The Living Room War*, New York: Viking Books.
—— (1982) 'The war: the Falklands, Vietnam and our collective memory', *New Yorker* 16 August.
Block, Marcia and Mungham, Geoff, (1989) 'The military, the media and the invasion of Grenada', *Contemporary Crises* 13: 91–127.
Braestrup, Peter (1977) *Big Story: How the American Press and Television Reported and Interpreted the Crisis of Tet, 1968, in Vietnam and Washington*, New Haven, Conn.: Yale University Press.
Browne, Malcolm (1964) 'Vietnam reporting: three years of crisis', *Columbia Journalism Review*, autumn.
Day, Robin (1985) cited in *Television: A History*, Central TV documentary series.
Dorman, William (1985) 'The media: playing the government's game', *Bulletin of Atomic Scientists* August, 118–24.
Elegant, Robert (1979) *How to Lose a War: The Press and Vietnam*, Washington DC: Ethics and Public Policy Center Reprint.
Entman, Robert and Paletz, David (1982) 'The war in Southeast Asia: tunnel vision on television', in William Adams (ed.) *Television Coverage of International Affairs*, Ablex, Norwood, NJ: Ablex.
Epstein, Edward (1973) *News From Nowhere*, New York: Vintage Books.
—— (1975) *Between Fact and Fiction*, New York: Vintage Books.
Fisk, Robert (1991) 'Free to report what we're told', *The Independent* 6 February.
Friendly, Fred (1967) *Due To Circumstances Beyond Our Control*, New York: Vintage Books.
—— (1970) 'TV at the turning point', *Columbia Journalism Review*, winter: 70–1.
Gitlin, Todd (1980) *The World Is Watching*, Berkeley, CA: University of California Press.
Halberstam, David (1979) *The Powers That Be*, New York: Dell.
Hallin, Daniel (1986) *The Uncensored War: The Media and Vietnam*, Oxford: Oxford University Press.
Harris, Robert (1983) *Gotcha! The Media, the Government and the Falklands Conflict*, London: Faber & Faber.
Herman, Edward and Chomsky, Noam (1989) *The Political Economy of the Mass Media*, New York: Pantheon.
House of Commons, Select Defence Committee (1982) *The Handling of Information During the Falklands Conflict*, vols 1 and 2, London: HMSO.
Jessel, David (1982) *Trumpets and Typewriters*, BBC TV documentary, July.
Knightley, Philip (1975) *The First Casualty*, New York: Harcourt, Brace, Jovanovich.
—— (1991) 'Here is the patriotically censored news', *Index on Censorship* 20 (April–May).
Lefever, Ernest (1974) *TV and National Defense*, Boston, VA: Institute for American Strategy Press.
Lichty, Lawrence (1983) *Vietnam: Ten Years On*, transcript of a seminar held at Fort Benjamin Harrison, Indiana: United States Army Publications.

MacBride, Sean (1981) *Many Voices, One World: Communication and Society, Today and Tomorrow*, London: Kogan Page and UNESCO.

Mercer, Derick, Mungham, Geoff, and Williams, Kevin (1987) *The Fog of War*, London: Heinemann.

Mueller, John (1973) *War, Presidents and Public Opinion*, New York: John Wiley.

Robinson, Michael (1977) 'Television and American politics 1956–76', *Public Interest* 48 (summer).

Sigal, Leon (1973) *Reporters and Officials: The Organisation and Politics of Newsmaking*, Lexington, Mass.: D. C. Heath.

Stillman, David (1970–1) 'The Gulf of Tonkin incident: what we should have said', *Columbia Journalism Review*, winter.

US News and World Report (1968), 4 March.

Westin, Av. (1982) *Newswatch: How TV Decides the News*, New York: Simon & Schuster.

Wicker, Tom (1979) *On Press*, New York: Berkley Publications.

Part V

Conclusion

Chapter 13

Whose illusion? whose reality?
Some problems of theory and method in mass media research

John Eldridge

If people define a situation as real it will be real in its consequences. When W. I. Thomas coined the aphorism he was pointing to the power that beliefs could exercise over the actions of individuals and groups. Sociological and anthropological research contains many illustrations of the dictum, from the protestant ethic to cargo cults. We can recall the events at Jonesville (named after the religious leader Jim Jones) in Guyana, when a whole community defined a situation in a way that led them to participate in a mass suicide. Yet to define a situation as real is to say nothing of the truth or falsity of what is being stated, believed in or acted upon.

It happens that in the history of the mass media a notable instance exists of a situation being defined as real by large numbers of people and which indeed had real consequences for them and yet it was not true but fictional. This was in October 1938 when CBS broadcast a version of H. G. Wells's *War of the Worlds* in its radio play slot, Mercury Theatre of the Air. The effect on many listeners, particularly those who tuned in after the Orson Welles programme had begun, was to create panic and distress. According to Hadley Cantril and his colleagues (1940) at least 1 million out of the 6 million listeners were severely frightened or panicked, believing that the United States really had been invaded by the Martians. In this drama, delivered in the format of an actuality news programme, many of the audience came to accept the reality of a large number of events, which would have taken much longer than the short time span of the programme to have occurred in fact.

We may say that this section of the radio audience was suffering under an illusion. Yet the episode intervened in their everyday lives and was real in its consequences. For them fiction became fact and the illusion shaped their experience and so they proceeded to define their reality. In trying to account for this we might want to refer to the skill of the producer and the actors, the news format, which as a source of public information people had come to trust, and so on. But it remains that the people who panicked based their action on a mistaken belief.

As social scientists we are not too surprised that such a thing could happen, although we do well to note that 5 of the 6 million were not so persuaded. Things are not always as they seem. In *The Rules of Sociological Method*, Durkheim (1982) has some interesting comments on the distinction between illusion and reality. In the exposition of his basic rule that we must consider social facts as things he comments:

> Several centuries ago Copernicus dispelled the illusions our senses experience concerning the movements of the heavenly bodies, and yet it is still according to these illusions that we can only regulate the distribution of our time. For an idea to stimulate the reaction that the nature of a thing demands, it need not faithfully express that nature. It is sufficient for it to make us perceive what is useful or disadvantageous about the thing, and in what ways it can render us service or disservice.
>
> (1982: 61)

Durkheim argued that while notions formed in this way can sometimes be practical, they may also be dangerous and inadequate. He continues:

> It is not therefore by elaborating upon them, however one treats them, that we will ever succeed in discovering the laws of reality. On the contrary, they are as a veil interposed between the things and ourselves, concealing them from us even more effectively because we believe [them] to be more transparent.
>
> (ibid.: 61)

Durkheim here is pointing out that perceived reality can be based on an illusion, even though that perception can have real consequences. Yet these notions, Durkheim adds, resemble:

> ghost-like creatures, distort the true appearance of things, but which we nevertheless mistake for the things themselves. It is because this imagined world offers no resistance that the mind, feeling completely unchecked, gives rein to limitless ambitions, believing it possible to construct – or rather reconstruct – the world through its own power and according to its wishes.
>
> (ibid.: 62)

Durkheim, in his trenchant way, is attacking both subjectivism and idealism as adequate ways of analysing social reality. He also suggests why it is that we (including social scientists) succumb to such illusions. If the details of social life swamp our consciousness from all sides, as it were, we do not think in terms of a structured reality which conditions that consciousness, though we may carry with us some summary representations of our collective existence – the things that we take for granted in our everday life. But for Durkheim this is a problem and not a solution for sociological method. The difficulty for analysis is compounded precisely because of the role

which common sense plays in our everyday lives. These illus
short, part of our experience. As Durkheim puts it:

> Not only are they within us, but since they are the product of repeateu
> experiences, they are invested with a kind of ascendancy and authority,
> by dint of repetition and the habit that results from it. We feel their
> resistance when we seek to free ourselves from them, and we cannot fail
> to regard as real something which pits itself against us. Thus everything
> conspires to make us see in them the true social reality.
>
> (1982: 63)

Durkheim's refusal to treat social phenomena at face value is at the root
of his distinction between social science and ideology and also between
social science and 'common sense'. Indeed it is the relationship between
ideology and common sense that makes the task so difficult. What is more
generally at issue here is whether the human mind can exhibit a form of
consciousness about the social world that can enable one to distinguish
between illusion and reality. The task of the human sciences is to explore
the possibility that it can. The inherent difficulty is that both illusion and
reality proceed from the same source – the human mind. We can recall how
Marx commented on this:

> Consciousness can never be anything else than conscious existence, and
> the existence of men is their actual life process. If in all ideology men
> and their circumstances appear upside down, as in a *camera obscura*,
> this phenomenon arises just as much from their historical life process as
> the inversion of objects on the retina does from their physical life
> process.
>
> (Marx and Engels 1965: 37)

For him, as for Durkheim, it was necessary to distinguish between conventional thought and science. That is why he criticized bourgeois economists.
He maintained that they were analysing surface manifestations of the
political economy of industrial societies and hence were promulgating
ideology in the name of science. What was needed was an analysis of
society grounded in real life social processes, the 'ensemble of social
relations'.

The differences between Marx and Durkheim have been well explored.
In drawing attention to the emphasis they both give to the importance of
the analysis of structures I am making a point which has been stated
forcefully by Robert Merton among others. In his essay 'Structural analysis
in sociology' (1976b) he claims that the basic ideas found in their work are
complementary rather than contradictory and references work on social-
structural sources of deviant behaviour, the formation of bureaucratic
personality and the growth and institutionalization of science. Actually
these examples are all drawn from his own much-cited volume *Social*

Theory and Social Structure (1957). He takes pleasure in pointing out Gouldner had emphasized the way that the affinities between Marx and Durkheim are worked through in that volume. In the well-known essay on 'Social structure and anomie' in that volume he had, according to Gouldner, 'used Marx to pry open Durkheim'. All this, of course, predates the more amorphous, interdisciplinary body of thought labelled 'structuralism'.

Merton has been a notable contributor to the study of the mass media and this substantive area is the stimulus for this present chapter. But before turning to that more explicitly I think it worthwhile teasing out his theoretical orientation since it leads us into a consideration of the relationship between agency and structure. How, after all, do we situate human experience and action within the analysis of social structures? Where does purpose and intention come in?

Merton's response to the Thomas dictum, with which I began, is not to deny the importance of considering what people believe, perceive, feel or want but to point out that if people do not define real situations as real, they are nevertheless real in their consequences. As he writes in 'Social knowledge and social policy':

> Total subjectivism leads us astray by failing to provide a theoretical place for *systematic* concern with objective constraints upon human action. Those social, demographic, economic, technological, ecological and other constraints are not always caught up in social definitions. To ignore these constraints is mistakenly to imply that they do not significantly affect both the choices people make and the personal and social consequences of those choices.
>
> (Merton 1976a: 176)

There is then an interplay between the subjective and the objective aspects of social reality and the task of social science is to offer explanations that go beyond perceived experience or common sense. This means that we have to allow not only for the situations people define as real but ask under what conditions those definitions come to be present. We also have to allow for the possibility that some socially induced situations are not generally defined as real and to understand the circumstances in which that comes to be the case. Such knowledge, once obtained, can then help us to redefine situations as real, but on the basis of improved knowledge rather than ignorance.

The position here being outlined is one which rejects both subjectivism and cognitive relativism as an adequate stance in social theory. This finds further support in the writings of social philosophers such as Steven Lukes and Ernest Gellner. Lukes (1977) has pointed out, for example, that unless we have some way of discovering whether the beliefs people hold about their own or other societies are false or distorted and what the consequences of this might be, we cannot claim to make any contribution to the study of ideology:

> It is only by assuming that one has a reliable, non-relative means of identifying a disjunction between social consciousness or collective representations on the one hand and social realities on the other than one can raise certain questions about the ways in which belief-systems prevent or promote social change.

(Lukes 1977: 149)

This, incidentally, could apply to the very concept of the individual in society, as Durkheim sought to show. For him the concept of the individual is irredeemably social, so that ideas of the noble savage, who preceded the formation of society and whose individuality and freedom were later taken away by society, are the inverse of the case. For Durkheim it is the social individual, who is the masterpiece of civilization, who is made by but also contributes to the making of society. What this means is that individual action is social and contributes to the social construction of reality – with its language, its beliefs, ideologies and symbols, its collective representations. The task of social science is both to understand that social construction of reality and allow space for critique by drawing attention, for example, to the existence of logical contradictions, demonstrable ignorance, inconsistencies, fantasies, lies and deception, the social basis of competing definitions of reality and so on.

Gellner's views are also relevant and take us a little further. When, as individuals, we define reality, we will communicate it through the appropriation of concepts. But it would be a misguided methodological charity to assume that the concepts are intrinsically not open to critique. We must at least allow for the possibility that beliefs are absurd or illusory.

So where does this leave language and concepts, which are familiar illustrations of Durkheimian social facts, so far as social theory is concerned? Gellner's answer is instructive:

> The truth of the matter seems to me to be this: concepts do indeed constrain us. But they are not the only things which constrain us. Our life is lived in an environment whose constraints are at least in part physical, in the sense of being independent of the conventions, ideas, and expectations of the society which harbours us. Concepts do not kill or nourish; but killing and nourishing are socially important. The two kinds of constraint, conceptual and extraneous, pervade each other and are fused with each other in a complex and bewildering manner. For instance, a physical imperative may leave open a number of ways of executing its demands, not all of which however are socially permissible, 'conceivable'. Or a conceptual imperative may be disguised as a physical one, to give it an extraneous authority. And so on. The complications

are endless. It is no doubt one of the tasks of sociology to disentangle this.

(Gellner 1979: 57–8).

The intellectual position we take on matters such as these is crucial. It conditions what we would take to be an adequate explanation and what we would regard as suitable methodology in the analysis of society. The Gellner position rests on the actual reality of a distinction between culture and non-culture, even though they can be mutually interrelated in many and complicated ways. How instructive, therefore, to recall that within Marxist argument the matter has been the occasion for keen theoretical debate. This after all was a major issue in Edward Thompson's *The Poverty of Theory* (1978). Not only was this an attack on the idealism of Althusserian structuralism but it resulted in continuing arguments about the relation between agency and structure and discussions about culturalism (which in Marxist writings Thompson sees as subjectivist and idealist). For Thompson the category of 'experience' is a way of approaching the culture/non-culture issue. Elsewhere (1981) he unpacks this by distinguishing between experience I – lived experience – and experience II – perceived experience. What is this lived experience?

Experience walks in without knocking at the door, and announces deaths, crises of subsistence, trench warfare, unemployment, inflation, genocide. People starve: their survivors think in new ways about the market. People are imprisoned: in prison they meditate in new ways about the law.

(Thompson 1981: 406)

Thompson suggests (and the parallel with the non-Marxist Gellner is very striking) that many contemporary epistemologists and sociologists treat experience solely in terms of perceived experience. Thus ideology is located and we are invited to recognize that different persons experience the same thing differently. But Thompson's point is that the theoretical task is to discover, in an historically informed way, the substance of the interplay between experience I and II. Experience I will not be directly reflected into experience II – which is a similar point to the one Durkheim made about social facts and the individual's perception of them. Yet the pressures of this lived experience cannot be denied and can be expected to have some effect on social consciousness, notwithstanding all the illusions and ideological baggage that may be located there:

How else, at a time like our own, are we to suppose that there can ever by any human remedy to the hegemonic domination of the mind, the false descriptions of reality reproduced daily by the media? Experience I is in eternal friction with imposed consciousness, and, as it breaks through, we, who fight in all the intricate vocabularies and disciplines of experience II, are given moments of openness and opportunity before the mould of ideology is imposed once more.

(Thompson 1981: 406)

Thompson, as was Marx, is preoccupied with the question of power in society. How do particular individuals come to occupy particular social roles? How do particular organizations with their property rights and structure of authority get to be there? Patterns of relationship can be discovered embedded in institutions and structures. The struggles that take place and the conflicts of interest that are manifested can tell us something about the contours of power. When he tells us, for example, that the English working class made itself as much as it was made he is drawing attention to the interaction of agency and structure (Thompson 1963). There was the changing production system of the industrial revolution and the productive relations and working conditions to which these gave rise. Yet these were not any people. They had been surrounded by different influences and traditions – Paine, Bunyan, village rights and craft traditions, the politics of Jacobinism and so on. On the one hand, this was a class that was subject to tremendous pressure, on the other, they were able to construct organized political and trades union responses, with varying degrees of success and failure. But in this way we learn something about the dialectic of power and resistance.

Still drawing upon the Durkheim/Marx parallels in structural analysis it is relevant to observe Merton's attention to the importance of macro-level studies of changing structures of control which, for him, entail looking at the social distributions of authority, power, influence and prestige. Notwithstanding his functionalist orientation, his interest in power leads him to state: 'Social structures generate social conflict by being differentiated in historically differing extent and kind, into interlocking arrays of social statuses, strata, organisations, and communities that have their own and therefore potentially conflicting as well as common interests and values' (Merton 1976b: 124–5). Moreover, according to Merton, normative structures do not have unified norm-sets: 'Sociological ambivalence is built into normative structures in the form of incompatible patterned expectations and a "dynamic alternation of norms and counter-norms" in social roles' (ibid.: 125).

Merton's own work stands as a testimony to the need to relate theory and method in sociology. His two complementary essays – 'The bearing of sociological theory on empirical research' and 'The bearing of empirical research on sociological theory' – clearly reflect his own experience, not least in mass media research (Merton 1957). For example, in the second of the essays there occurs his celebrated comments on the serendipity pattern – 'observing an *unanticipated, anomalous and strategic datum* which becomes the occasion for developing a new theory or for extending an existing theory' (Merton 1957: 104; emphasis in original). He describes the discovery of a 'social illusion' in the course of a community study which leads him to reflect on the limitations of conspiracy theories in sociology:

> What first made this illusion a peculiarly intriguing instance of a general theoretic problem was the difficulty of explaining it as merely the calculated handiwork of vested interests engaged in contrary-to-fact belief. Generally, when the sociologist with a conceptual scheme stem-ming from utilitarian theory observes a patently untrue social belief, he will look for special groups in whose interests it is to invent and spread this belief. The cry of 'propaganda!' is often mistaken for a theoretically sound analysis. . . . To be sure, vested interests often do spread untrue propaganda and this may reinforce mass illusions. But the vested-interest or priestly-lie theories of fallacious folk beliefs do not always constitute the most productive point of departure nor do they go far toward explaining the bases of acceptance or rejection of the beliefs.
>
> (ibid.: 106)

Merton's own theoretical move was in the direction of reference group theory, but what I also think is important is that space is provided in this kind of social analysis for recognizing that people may be mistaken in their beliefs and opinions in ways which are demonstrable. This is not the same as treating 'false consciousness' as an explanation of what otherwise you cannot explain or perhaps do not wish to explain, but it does put a marker down in relation to the problem of relativism in social theory.

In his discussion of the way in which new data can exert pressure for the elaboration of a conceptual scheme Merton again draws upon his mass media research. The reference is to the marathon radio broadcasting appeal of Kate Smith for people to pledge war bonds. This was a very successful appeal and Merton and his colleagues undertook an extensive interview programme among New Yorkers who pledged their support as a result of the broadcast. They found that despite a good deal of disenchant-ment with advertising and the feeling that they were objects of manipu-lation, people nevertheless were persuaded in this instance. They were impressed by the sincerity of Smith. Her readiness to take on broadcasts over an 18-hour period was regarded as proof enough. Interviewees reported that feelings of scepticism and distrust gave way to acceptance of her integrity. The question then becomes, under what conditions are people persuaded to respond to propaganda? The question remains with us today. In the wake of sophisticated media campaigns for the relief of famine in Ethiopia, with again examples of marathon appearances by front men such as Lenny Henry, it is clear that very definite effects follow in terms of money collected. Interviewing programmes could no doubt help to clarify exactly why the responses are as they are. But, of course, they do testify to the power of the media to achieve certain clear aims in these particular instances.

Merton was, I think, very aware of the dilemmas he faced as a researcher in this area. He was worried about the possibilities that people might be manipulated by the mass media. This was why he emphasized that not all propaganda was based on lying and deceit – there was also a propaganda of facts:

> It is by indirection, not prescription, that the propaganda of facts operates. It has *guidance-value*. The cumulative force of facts carries its own momentum, so to speak. It is virtually a syllogism with an implicit conclusion – a conclusion to be drawn by the audience, not the propagandist.
>
> (Merton 1957: 526)

There was a normative concern with the preservation of individual autonomy which he held to be grounded in empirical evidence that suggested that the propaganda of facts was more effective than emotional appeals to patriotism and the like. Yet he also recognized that what he termed pseudo-facts could supplant facts – so that without counter-evidence the audience would not be in a position to discriminate between them, at least in the short run.

I think Merton was also sensitive to the social origins of the research in which he was engaged. As a theorist he wondered whether the immediate tasks of applied social research which were shaped by market or military demands obscured the long-distance tasks of basic research. And he raises a number of questions which are still with us:

> have the researches oriented toward the needs of government and industry been too closely harnessed to the immediate pressing problem, providing too little occasion for dealing with more nearly fundamental questions of social science? Do we find that social science is neither sufficiently advanced, nor industry and government sufficiently mature to lead to the large-scale support of basic research in social science as in physical science? These are questions growing directly out of the social history of research in mass communications, and they are questions of immediate concern for the sociologist of knowledge.
>
> (ibid.: 453)

But there is also a domain assumption in Merton's work. It has to do with the need for propaganda in the process of postwar reconstruction. The propaganda of facts, the logic of which he likens to the logic of progressive education, can, he maintains, be used to supplant cynicism with common understandings. In other words, the propaganda which promotes consensus in a democracy is one mechanism for defending against social anomie. The ghost of Durkheim is not far away.

Questions of agency and structure, subject and object and the associated issue of how power is to be understood and theorized are at the heart of much social theory. The way these questions are responded to has consequences for theory construction and will come to constitute the ground-rules by which empirical studies of society proceed, or research programmes envisaged. In this respect studies of the mass media represent only a specific illustration of what is entailed. To those with knowledge of the ways in which these issues are addressed and nuanced in social theory, terms like functionalism, positivism, hermeneutics and structuralism carry their own connotations. It is the contention of Anthony Giddens that these positions do not resolve the dualisms of subject and object, structure and agency. His own theory of structuration sets out to do just that.

In *The Constitution of Society* (1984) there is a developed statement of his theoretical position. For Giddens, to analyse the structuration of social systems is to study the modes in which systems, that are themselves grounded in the knowledgeable activities of situated actors who draw upon rules and resources in a diversity of action contexts, are produced and reproduced in interaction. From this perspective we are invited to recognize the importance of the duality of structure: the proposition that structures are both constraining and enabling. We may suppose that in many situations structures are more enabling for some individuals and groups and more constraining for others and this may also help to account for the fact that some intentions of actors are not realized and some consequences of actions are not anticipated. What does Giddens have to say about this question, which yet again is the question of power?

> Resources (focused via signification and legitimation) are structured properties of social systems, drawn upon and reproduced by knowledgeable agents in the course of interaction. Power is not intrinsically connected to the achievement of sectional interests. In this conception the use of power characterises not specific types of social conduct but all action, and power is not itself a resource. Resources are media through which power is exercised, as a routine element of the instantiation of conduct in social reproduction. We should not conceive of the structures of domination built into social institutions as in some way grinding out 'docile bodies' who behave like the automata suggested by objectivist social science. Power within social systems which enjoy some continuity over time and space presumes regularised relations of autonomy and dependence between actors or collectivities in contexts of social interaction. But all forms of dependence offer some resources whereby those who are subordinate can influence the activities of their superiors. This is what I call the *dialectic of control* in social systems.
>
> (Giddens 1984: 15–16)

There are two elements of this position, as elaborated by Giddens, which

I wish to emphasize for present purposes. Taken together they offer an approach to the relationship between the macro and micro aspects of social structure. First, in his discussion of the properties of social systems Giddens identifies three dimensions – signification, domination and legitimation. Each of these is referred to a theoretical domain and an institutional order. For signification it is the theory of coding associated with symbolic orders and modes of discourse. For domination there is both a theory of resource authorization linked with political institutions and a theory of resource allocation linked with economic institutions. For legitimation there is a theory of normative regulation linked with legal institutions. There is an important implication here which is that, so far as a theory of coding is concerned, signs must not be regarded simply as given properties but have to be understood as the medium and outcome of communicative processes in interaction. That is why Giddens claims: 'Structures of signification have always to be grasped in connection with domination and legitimation. Once more this bears upon the pervasive influence of power in social life.' And, in a sharp reference to Habermas, Giddens continues:

> 'Domination' is not the same as 'systematically distorted' structures of signification because domination – as I conceive it – is the very existence of codes of signification. 'Domination' and 'power' cannot be thought of only in terms of asymmetrics of distribution but have to be recognised as inherent in social association (or, I would say, in human action as such).
>
> (1984: 31–2)

This is why a society without power is literally unthinkable. Although differently elaborated and taking account of recent developments in philosophical discussions on intention and a wide range of social theory, the approach here has clear affinities with Weber's social action perspective. In *Economy and Society* (1978), it will be recalled, Weber begins his conceptual work with an analysis of social action and social relationships, which he then seeks to incorporate in discussion (and subsequently by empirical application) of forms of legitimation and types of domination.

The second point has to do with the relevance of Goffman's work for Giddens with its focus on examining the routines of everyday life. Goffman's own characterization of his work is as the study of interaction order (1959, 1974, 1981). To do this he uses a multitude of illustrations – from gambling casinos to hospital theatres – a range of metaphors to show how individuals in their social relationships negotiate reality, such as dramatic performance, games, framing and keying. In the working through of this he deals with the nature of talk, gesture, role, face work, impression management and the ways in which meaning is sustained in the process of social interaction. Some of this action is habitual and taken for granted by the participants; some of it demands thought, attention and an element of

risk. These situated activities take place in what Giddens terms circumstances of co-presence. Goffman shows that much of this activity serves to
facilitate routines that generate order and encourage trust. But order may
not always be accomplished, hence the need for remedies and repair work
when order is threatened or breaks down. Trust, when obtained may not
always be justified, of course, as readers of John Le Carré know well.
There are deadly games as well as friendly ones. There is deception as
well as shared knowledge. Now Giddens sees this as an important exem-
plification of his theory of structuration. It represents not only a micro-
sociology – in which the detailed accounts of interaction show us how
communication is linked with issues of power, norms and sanctions, all of
which may be contested in actual relationships – but also points to the
reciprocity of action and structure since institutional forms are implicated
even in transient encounters. The actors themselves, while variously described by Giddens as knowledgeable agents and capable of monitoring
their activities reflectively, may be limited in their awareness of such
linkages.

It is here that we come back to our central theme of the relationship
between illusion and reality. So in general terms, as Giddens points out,
the social location a person occupies will affect the means of access he or
she has to knowledge and also the nature of his or her direct experiences of
social life. Again, everyday claims to knowledge may be formulated in
fragmentary, dislocated and unexamined ways. One of the tasks of social
science is to make more visible the nature and significance of different
forms of discourse in their social settings. Giddens is clear, as Durkheim
and Marx were before him, that 'individuals may operate with false
theories, descriptions or accounts both of the contexts of their own action
and of the characteristics of more encompassing social systems' (Giddens
1984: 92). While allowing that there may be psychological considerations
which affect what people are able to say about their reasons for action, he
adds: 'But obviously there can be more systematic social pressures that can
influence how far false beliefs are held by the members of a society about
features of that society.' Among other things it encourages us to think
about the means of dissemination of available knowledge. Here Giddens
draws particular attention to 'the relations, historically and spatially, between oral culture and the media of writing, printing and electronic
communication. All of the latter have made a difference not only to stocks
of available knowledge but also to types of knowledge produced' (ibid.:
92).

We live today not only in a media saturated society but in a media
saturated world. It is difficult to analyse the significance of mass media which
have multiplied in forms (books, radio, television, press, records, cinema,
video), have developed in technologies to the most sophisticated kinds of
electronics, have increased the speed of production and distribution of

their products, and within each medium have diversified in the genres available. These products are commodities and as such become part of the everyday life of those who buy and consume them. The research agenda which is entailed in explaining and interpreting these developments is formidable and intimidating. And the activity of disseminating such work can scarcely be done today without employing the mass media, which become, in consequence, both a topic and a resource for the researcher. So, in their time Marcuse's *One Dimensional Man* (1964) and McLuhan's *Understanding Media* (1964) became paperback best sellers.

The difficulty and importance of the task is shown if we reflect on Lucien Febvre and Henri-Jean Martin's brilliant study, *The Coming of the Book* (1984). This is an account of the impact of printing between 1450 and 1800. It is enough for present purposes to mention that the study encompasses material factors relating to the growth of paper-making in Europe; technical considerations concerning the nature of the printing process; economic and commercial questions affecting costs, finance and distribution (the book as a commodity); the social organization of book production and the geographical locations; and a discussion of the book as a force for change, with notable reference to the Reformation, and its impact on the use of national languages at the expense of Latin. As the authors point out, this was a fateful development with incalculable and certainly not wholly intended consequences. They also make clear that whatever the advantages of mass circulation might be for propagandizing and social control from above, this was far from the whole story since this medium was also a vehicle for subversion – with challenges to existing political and religious authorities – and booksellers and printers could come under surveillance and harassment as a result of their pivotal activities. Yet this study relates to one medium only.

When we come to consider the multi-media world we now inhabit, with its multi-messages, multi-signifying systems and modes of discourse, the size, the scope and the velocity of it all, with its spiralling interconnections and its fragmentary discontinuities, the classical enlightenment task of understanding, explaining, interpreting and evaluating is difficult to accomplish. Let us acknowledge the difficulties but also suggest that the denial in principle of the enlightenment project (farewell to reason) may itself be a product of intellectual vertigo (all that is solid melts into air) and perhaps, if understandably, a failure of nerve. Let us take Jean Baudrillard (1980) as an instructive case in point. In particular, consider what he has to say about hyper-reality – a term which in his usage would displace and make superfluous the questions of this essay: whose illusion?; whose reality? This is most evident in his essay 'Simulacra and simulations': 'Of the same order as the impossibility of rediscovering an absolute level of the real, is the impossibility of staging an illusion. Illusion is no longer possible, because the real is no longer possible' (Baudrillard 1988: 77). What can this mean? Baudrillard starts with a discussion on the possible relationships between representations (signs) and reality and goes on to distinguish three of these modes from simulation, where there is no relationship to reality. The first three define a position on the distinction between appearance and reality. Thus appearances in the form of representations may be regarded as reflecting a basic reality so there is no illusion: they are therefore reliable *good* appearances. Or they may be seen as masking and perverting a basic reality and are unreliable *evil* appearances. Or representations mask the absence of a basic reality and have the character of manipulation and sorcery. The theological and metaphysical resonances of this are commented upon by Baudrillard. Having pointed out that in western theology there is the assumption that a sign could refer to a depth of meaning, and that something could guarantee this meaning, namely God, he asks:

> But what if God himself can be simulated, that is to say, reduced to the signs which attest his existence? Then the whole system becomes weightless; it is no longer anything but a gigantic simulacrum: not unreal, but a simulacrum, never again exchanging for what is real, but exchanging in itself, in an uninterrupted circuit without reference or circumstance.
>
> (ibid.: 170)

This indeed is the fourth category. This death of God is the death of all metaphysics so that the notion of a mirror – whether true, distorting or inverted – linking appearances with reality, is also dead. By extension this is the death of the critical project of Marxism because the age of simulation results in the liquidation of all referentials, so it is pointless to suppose that enlightened thought can seek to control capital by imposing rules on it. For the left, therefore, to hold out 'the mirror of equivalence, hoping that capital will fall for this phantasmagoria of the social contract and fulfill its obligations to the whole of society' is useless because 'capital is a monstrous, unprincipled undertaking, nothing more' (ibid.: 173). But in saying this Baudrillard actually reverts to the third category since he defines capital as a sorcery of the social relations – a challenge to society which should be responded to as such. How can this be if, in his own terms, the category of the social itself is, like God before it, reduced to the signs which attests to its existence? Carried to its conclusion this is to abandon the possibility of critique since such activity only multiplies the signs and accelerates the play of simulation. So categories like production and power can no longer be subject to critical appraisal – it is always, in his view, a false problem to want to restore the truth beneath the simulacrum. And yet, in its place, we have mysticism and melancholy reflection. Societies without power are societies without the social, and according to Baudrillard we do not know how to handle the mourning process. In my view he resorts to paradox and metaphysics in the name of anti-metaphysics, which I think is well enough illustrated in the following quotation:

> Power . . . for some time now produces nothing but signs of its own resemblance. And at the same time, another figure of power comes into play: that of a collective demand for *signs* of power – a holy union which forms around the disappearance of power. Everybody belongs to it more or less in fear of the collapse of the political. And in the end the game of power comes down to nothing more than the *critical* obsession with power: an obsession with its death; an obsession with its survival which becomes the greater the more it disappears. When it has totally disappeared, logically we will be under the total spell of power – a haunting memory already foreshadowed everywhere, manifesting at one and the same time the satisfaction of having got rid of it . . . and grieving its loss.
>
> (Baudrillard 1988: 180)

We can note the rhetorical devices here: the use of terms like nothing but and nothing more than, the reference to logic and the metaphor of sorcery – the total spell of power. But it is one thing to recognize that sign systems can multiply and feed on each other and can indeed serve to 'hype' reality through public relations, collusion in the staging of media events and so on, but quite another to postulate that power is disappearing in its own simulations. However adequately or imperfectly the mass media may define, interpret or narrate the existence of torture, starvation and forms of oppression in the world, they are pointing to an experienced reality. It is because we have the capacity to protest this and claim that things could be other – a capacity that finds expression in the media events of Band Aid and the like, in Mandela concerts and music tours for Amnesty International and a response from millions of people across the world – that we do not find it logically or empirically necessary to follow Baudrillard in his cult of death – mourning for a post-modernist society that owes more to his own fevered imagination and obsessions than to an analysis that has any evidential weight or substance.

A more interesting and instructive case is that of Umberto Eco. I refer specifically to the collection of essays, *Travels in Hyper-Reality* (1987). As with Baudrillard the site for discussion is the USA. For Eco the reason for his journey into hyper-reality is to search for instances:

> where the American imagination demands the real thing and, to attain it, must fabricate the absolute fake; where the boundaries between game and illusion are blurred, the art museum is contaminated by the freak show, and falsehood is enjoyed in a situation of 'fullness', of *horror vacui*.
>
> (Eco 1987: 8)

So we visit, among other places, the Lyndon Johnson centre in Austin, Texas, with its full-scale reproduction of the Oval Office; the Museum of the City of New York, where a portrait of Peter Stuyvesant is 'reproduced' as a three-dimensional statue; and the Movieland Waxwork Museum in California. Of this we read:

> As a rule there are mirrors, so on your right you see Dracula raising the lid of a tomb, and on the left your own face reflected next to Dracula's, while at times there is the glimmering figure of Jack the Ripper or of Jesus, duplicated by an astute play of corners, curves, and perspective, until it is hard to decide which side is reality and which illusion.
>
> (ibid.: 13)

So:

> When you see Tom Sawyer immediately after Mozart or you enter the case of The Planet of the Apes after having witnessed the Sermon on the Mount with Jesus and the Apostles, the logical distinction between the Real World and Possible Worlds is definitively undermined.
>
> (ibid.: 14)

And there is Disneyland (which is also discussed by Baudrillard). For Eco it is at once absolutely realistic and absolutely fantastic. The Main Street reconstruction of the nineteenth-century frontier street calls to mind an imaginative past – yet in that street you can enter shops and buy obsessively within the play fantasy mode. 'What is falsified is our will to buy, which we take as real, and in this sense Disneyland is really the quintessence of consumer ideology' (ibid.: 14). Yet this mixture of fake and truth, fantasy and reality, fact and fiction is used by Eco not to say, as Baudrillard does, that Disneyland is America, but to offer it as an allegory of the consumer society, where choice is regulated and truth reconstructed and the individual controlled and made passive by the system. However, the real world of the multinationals, the conglomerates, the world of advertising – with its fact and fiction intermingled – remains open for critique. Whereas Baudrillard becomes a participant in the cultural pessimism he identifies, Eco retains an ironic, critical detachment, while being sceptical with existing critical positions within Marxism. Why is this?

Here we must recall that Eco is the author of the highly formal, systematically presented *A Theory of Semiotics* (1977). This is based on models that indicate senders and receivers of messages and the channels through which messages come. From this flows a discussion of codes – their varieties and contexts – which itself is necessarily associated with the ways in which sources encode their messages and receivers decode them. Hence we can learn about and identify the nature of communicative power. Yet in the real world Eco found difficulty in identifying power and intentions. In 'The multiplication of the media' (Eco 1987) he takes as an example the production and advertisement of polo shirts with a brand logo, which can then be found on a TV programme with young people wearing the shirt, which then becomes an encouragement for viewers to buy the shirt with 'the young look'. So the media act and interact – they are media of media. Who then is sending the message and producing the ideology? Eco does not deny the role of ideology but 'according to the channel under consideration, in a certain sense the meaning of the message changes, and perhaps also its ideological weight. There is no longer Authority, all on its own (and how consoling it was!)' (Eco 1987: 189). That is to say, from the shirt designer through to the manufacturer, the advertisers, the TV personnel all are in but also outside of authority: 'Power is elusive, and there is no longer any telling where the "plan" comes from. Because there is, of course, a plan, but it is no longer intentional, and therefore it cannot be criticised with the traditional criticism of intentions' (ibid.: 149). So the simple solutions are no longer credible. But this is a challenge: 'We shall have to start again from the beginning, asking one another what's going on?' (ibid.: 150).

I was reminded of the way in which the various media can interrelate, reinforcing or passing opinions on one another, during the miners' strike. The interrelationship becomes part of the reality we seek to comprehend. The Edinburgh Television Festival was itself a media event in 1984, when a debate took place on media coverage of the miners' strike with Arthur Scargill and Alastair Hetherington as the main protagonists and with other contributions from journalists, a miner and the wife of the general secretary of the National Union of Mineworkers. The debate itself made use of video which had either been shown on television or film, or was from amateur video material. So there were arguments, references back to material and evidence and differences of interpretation. The following day on BBC *Newsnight* the debate was covered as a journalistic item. If one had been present at the debate, as I had, it was possible to see what kind of selecting and editing had taken place between the original event and its treatment in this new context. It is possible for a researcher to indicate the differences by careful accounts. What also interested me, however, was that the debate about the 'fairness' of the coverage became an occasion to suggest that there was additional evidence to show that television coverage was fair. So we had reference to some British Film Institute (BFI) research which had received coverage in yet another medium – the *Sunday Times*. Upon comparison of the two accounts it was possible to indicate some crucial differences, namely the reference in the *Sunday Times* to the finding that 6 per cent of questions to Mr MacGregor, then Chairman of the National Coal Board (NCB), were recorded as hostile by the researchers as against 39 per cent of questions to Mr Scargill. And then, yet

medium, the opinion poll, was cited to show that the majority of ..ewers thought television coverage of the miners' strike was 'fair'. The opinion poll did not relate to either the experience or knowledge of the strike of the people sampled, but it was in any event used as evidence. Now I do not think it possible to give a final account of all these and subsequent interrelations, but I do think it possible to analyse the processes that were going on. But there is a reality – experienced reality – which the media both comment on and are part of. It is the reality of broken bones and bruised bodies, of lost jobs, of protracted court cases, of dying communities. The explanations and contextualizing of these things will remain in some measure matters of controversy, but there are recalcitrant facts which cannot be relativized out of existence.

If power is elusive that does not mean it is disappearing, but rather that it is difficult to locate precisely. I think this is why, in another essay, 'Towards a semiological guerilla warfare', Eco (1987) emphasizes the importance of developing strategies that will enable audiences to control the message and its interpretative possibilities. For him the battle for the survival of people as responsible beings in the communications era is to be won not where the communication originates but where it arrives. The concern here is to restore a critical dimension to passive reception. This educational task can sound formidable, even utopian, but for Eco it is an emancipatory project:

> The methods of this cultural guerilla have to be worked out. Probably in the inter-relation of the various communications media, one medium can be employed to communicate a series of opinions on another medium. To some extent this is what a newspaper does when it criticises a TV programme. But who can assure us that the newspaper article will be read in the way we wish? Will we have to have recourse to another medium to teach people how to read the newspaper in a critical fashion?
>
> (Eco 1987: 143)

But it is the educational task to seek for ways of doing this work – displaying to viewers and readers and listeners the possibilities for highlighting perspectives, checking codes and interpreting messages. This practice would be a response to the technological imperatives of the mass media and a form of resistance to the elusive, sometimes anonymous power which produces and suffuses the media.

I have considerable sympathy with this view with its emphasis on a coping strategy of resistance to the power of the mass media, which also serves as a stimulus for the development of reception theory. At the same time the strategies of control are not always so opaque and diffuse as to make scrutiny and critique possible. There is much that can be done in the area of news management and information control and the role of public relations. Agendas are not simply set within the media but as a product of on-going relationships with specific interest groups. Thus Karin Newman (1986) has shown how the British government's privatization policy was accompanied by policies of media manipulation and information management. There is no deep mystery about this. The marketing of British Telecom involved a campaign in which audiences were segmented and targeted to receive appropriate messages in different parts of the media. This kind of research calls for tenacity and staying power rather than deep analytical insight. It is still possible to identify interest groups even in a multi-media world. Some interests are more visibly evident than others – sometimes they are expressed directly, at other times there is deception. We can as researchers make more visible the nature and activities of multinational conglomerates in the field of communications and draw attention to matters of value-relevance. We can articulate the relationships between government and the media and the tactics and strategies of control and resistance in that sphere. Such work can be seen as complementary to that which Eco advocates. That is why I choose to conclude with a quotation from Raymond Williams which is found in *Towards 2000*:

> there are very strong reasons why we should challenge what now most controls and constrains us: the idea of such a world as an inevitable future. It is not some unavoidable real world, with its laws of economy and laws of war, that is now blocking us. It is a set of identifiable processes of *realpolitik* and *force majeure*, of nameable agencies of power and capital, distractions and disinformation, and all these interlocking with embedded short-term pressures and the interwoven subordinations of an adaptive common sense. It is not in staring at these blocks that there is any chance of movement past them. They have been named so often that they are not even, for most people, news. The dynamic moment is elsewhere, in the difficult business of gaining confidence in *our own* energies and capacities.
>
> (1985: 268)

REFERENCES

Baudrillard, Jean (1988) 'Simulacra and simulations', Mark Poster (ed.) *Selected Writings*, Cambridge: Polity Press/Blackwell: 166–84.
Cantril, Hadley (1940) *The Invasion from Mars: A Study in the Psychology of Panic*, Princeton, NJ: Princeton University Press.
Durkheim, Emile (1982) *The Rules of Sociological Method*, London: Macmillan.
Eco, Umberto (1977) *A Theory of Semiotics*, London: Macmillan.
—— (1987) *Travels in Hyper-Reality*, London: Pan Books.
Febvre, Lucien and Martin, Henri-Jean (1984) *The Coming of the Book*, London: Verso.
Gellner, Ernest (1979) *Spectacles and Predicaments*, Cambridge: Cambridge University Press.

Giddens, Anthony (1984) *The Constitution of Society*, Cambridge: Polity Press/ Blackwell.

Goffman, Erving (1959) *The Presentation of Self in Everyday Life*, New York: Doubleday.

—— (1974) *Frame Analysis*, New York: Harper.

—— (1981) *Forms of Talk*, Oxford: Basil Blackwell.

Lukes, Steven (1977) 'On the social determination of truth', in *idem. Essays in Social Theory*, London: Macmillan: 138–53.

McLuhan, Marshall (1964) *Understanding Media*, London: Routledge & Kegan Paul.

Marcuse, Herbert (1964) *One Dimensional Man*, London: Routledge & Kegan Paul.

Marx, Karl and Engels, Frederick (1965) *The German Ideology*, London: Lawrence & Wishart.

Merton, Robert (1957) *Social Theory and Social Structure*, Glencoe, Ill.: Free Press.

—— (1976a) 'Social knowledge and social policy', in *idem. Sociological Ambivalence*, New York: Free Press: 156–79.

—— (1976b) 'Structural analysis in sociology', in *idem. Sociological Ambivalence*, New York: Free Press: 109–44.

Newman, Karin (1986) *The Selling of British Telecom*, New York: St Martin's Press.

Thompson, E. P. (1963) *The Making of the English Working Class*, London: Gollancz.

—— (1978) *The Poverty of Theory*, London: Merlin Press.

—— (1981) 'The politics of theory', in Samuel Raphael (ed.) *People's History and Socialist Theory*, London: Routledge & Kegan Paul: 396–417.

Weber, Max (1978) *Economy and Society*, Los Angeles, Calif., and London: University of California Press.

Williams, Raymond (1985) *Towards 2000*, Harmondsworth: Penguin.

Index